THE FATE OF PROGRESSIVE LANGUAGE POLICIES AND PRACTICES

The Fate of Progressive Language Policies and Practices

Edited by

Curt Dudley-Marling
Boston College

Carole Edelsky
Arizona State University

National Council of Teachers of English
1111 W. Kenyon Road, Urbana, Illinois 61801-1096

Staff Editors: Rita D. Disroe and Bonny Graham
Interior Design: Jenny Jensen Greenleaf
Cover Design: Barbara Yale-Read

NCTE Stock Number: 16736-3050

It is the policy of NCTE in its journals and other publications to provide a forum for the open discussion of ideas concerning the content and the teaching of English and the language arts. Publicity accorded to any particular point of view does not imply endorsement by the Executive Committee, the Board of Directors, or the membership at large, except in announcements of policy, where such endorsement is clearly specified.

Library of Congress Cataloging-in-Publication Data

The fate of progressive language policies and practices/edited by Curt Dudley-Marling, Carole Edelsky.
    p. cm.
    Includes bibliographical references and index.
    "NCTE Stock number: 16736-3050"—T.p. verso.
    ISBN 0-8141-1673-6 (pbk.)
    1. Native language and education—United States. 2. English language—Study and teaching—United States. 3. Multicultural education—United States. 4. Language policy—United States. I. Dudley-Marling, Curt. II. Edelsky, Carole.
LC201.6 .F38 2001
306.44'973—dc21

                                                00-067894

CONTENTS

Contents

INTRODUCTION: NO ESCAPE FROM TIME AND PLACE

CURT DUDLEY-MARLING
Boston College

CAROLE EDELSKY
Arizona State University

Nazi policy was beyond racism, it was anti-matter, for Jews were not considered human. An old trick of language, often used in the course of history. Non-Aryans were never referred to as human, but as "figuren," "stücke"—"dolls," "wood," "merchandize," "rags." Humans were not being gassed, only "figuren," so ethics weren't being violated. No one could be faulted for burning debris, for burning rags and clutter in the dirty basement of society. In fact, they're a fire hazard!

ANNE MICHAELS, *Fugitive Pieces*

This book is about aftermaths—follow-ups, outcomes (sometimes multiple for single cases), continuing histories, projected trajectories—of a variety of language practices and policies that have attempted (or are still attempting) to change current wisdom, current practice, the status quo—all in the direction of greater equity for all students. In telling about what happened *after*, each contributor to this book has also necessarily told about the project itself and about the dream behind it. In this introduction, we offer our own thinking in pulling this collection of aftermaths together.

Language Practices and Policies as Actions

Words don't just *mean* things; words *do* things. Words mean by evoking common experiences or understandings; ultimately, however, the meaning of any utterance or text is a function of what it does: inform, threaten, demand, assert, warn, promise, question, and so on (Searle, 1969). The epigraph, from Anne Michaels's novel *Fugitive Pieces* (1996), informs, shocks, and outrages as it illustrates the power of language to construct a reality in which monstrous atrocities are transformed into "reasonable" actions. This quote raises the question: Who gets to define whose reality? As Norman Fairclough puts it: "language use . . . is not just a matter of performing tasks, it is also a matter of expressing and constituting and reproducing social identities and social relations, including crucial relations of power" (1989, p. 237).

Language practices in school—from policies about the language of instruction to the materials used to teach reading to assessment of writing to classroom interaction influenced by dialect-specific norms—also do things. Besides achieving (or not) their aims, they become additions to the stewpot bubbling on the back burner (and sometimes the front) of public opinion on language issues (e.g., bilingualism, reading instruction, nonstandard dialects, literacy test scores, and so on). Directly or indirectly, educational language practices and policies serve a variety of functions, from gatekeeping to strengthening or weakening ties between schools and local communities. They enter and affect long-standing conversations, not only about what education is for but also about who should be educated and how. School-based language practices also affect relationships within families and, through deeply felt memories (Coulter, 1999; Dudley-Marling, 2000), they affect relationships with one's self.

Educators with strong commitments to work for social justice and challenge systemic, institutionalized inequities see language practices in school as a means of enacting their commitments. At the level of classroom instruction, local school programs, state testing programs, and nationally and internationally organized efforts to improve educational quality, these educators have envisioned and enacted practices, programs, and policies that might well be considered progressive in that they are intended to promote equity for those who are denied equity based on race, class, and/or gender. Progressive, too, in that they are meant to transform the discourse about educational quality to include a focus on equity and, therefore, to change the meaning of "quality education." As with any plan, the intentions behind progressive language practices are not the entire story; nor is the practice as played out. The "players" are not only those directly involved in creating, revising, and participating in the innovative assessment project or the instructional program development or the policymaking activity. Parents, media, voters, local church groups, national movements, even disembodied current "commonsense" approaches participate in and affect the life histories of progressive educational language practices and policies.

Language Practices and Policies Have Histories

The practices themselves, of course—as they are envisioned and enacted—are interesting. By looking at innovative and hierarchy-unsettling, against-the-grain practices, we get a glimpse of broader possibilities in language education. To our minds, though, the life histories of these practices are equally intriguing. In looking at the way a practice was received and what happened to it, we gain a grounded understanding of the historical, sociopolitical nature of school language practices. We come to appreciate, almost viscerally, that the inherent quality of projects in language education is not necessarily the major determinant of their longevity, their approval ratings, or their success in terms of meeting their espoused intent.

What actually does determine the "outcome" for any given project is not at all clear. What is clear, however, is that each progressive language practice or policy is ultimately lived out locally. The life stories of the particular cases assembled in this volume, for example, provide details about the local workings, embedded in more global contexts, that were involved in the unequally successful lives of equally good ideas. The purpose of sharing these stories in this volume is twofold: (1) to promote ever-improved progressive language practice through presenting specific examples of fine projects; and (2), paradoxically, to direct attention away from the language projects themselves and onto the actors, agendas, and activities that "enacted" these projects. In the end, we believe educators will have to become as sophisticated, deliberate, and conscious of the contexts through which their projects live as they are about language practices themselves.

Progressive Language Practices: The Vision

Underpinning progressive language practices is an understanding that language creates social identities, reproduces relations of power, and constructs realities, as well as a recognition of the power of language to enable (and disable) people in their efforts to live rich, fulfilled lives. Such a view of language puts language users—their sense of themselves, their social positions, their realities, their struggles for meaning and purpose—on center stage.

Progressive language practices in education establish a central role for the students' language in classroom learning. Such a position is congruent with a history of theory and research in language arts education (Barnes, 1976; Cazden, 1988; Edwards & Furlong, 1978; Hynds & Rubin, 1990; Jones, 1988). From a constructivist perspective, oral language provides the means by which students make sense of classroom learning by drawing on their background knowledge and experience as social and cultural beings. Additionally, language-rich classrooms, which immerse students in language, extend students' language competence by expanding the range of purposes for which—and the physical, social, and cultural settings within which—students use language.

As a collection of social practices, language is a means of enacting "ways of being in the world, or forms of life which integrate words, acts, values, beliefs, [and] social identities" (Gee, 1990, p. 142). Public spaces that make room for people's "ways with words" (Heath, 1983), including elementary, secondary, and university classrooms, also accommodate people's various ways of being in the world; that is, their social and cultural identities.

For example, the progressive position in the "great Ebonics debate"—whether "Black English" should be valued as a marker of black identity or stigmatized as "slang" or "bad English" (Ogbu, 1999)—is based on the assumption, confirmed by linguistic research, that "Black English" is a legitimate, rule-governed, systematic language that "should be affirmed, maintained, and used to help African-American children acquire fluency in the standard code" (Perry, 1997). The Ebonics policy seeks to counter exclusive language policies in our schools that, by questioning the legitimacy of some students' "ways with words," deny the legitimacy of these students' social and cultural identities (Ogbu, 1999). The exclusion of Black, Hispanic, and American Indian identities, for example, from school curricula is, arguably, a major factor in poor academic achievement by many of these students. As McCarthy and Crichlow (1993) put it: "The intolerable level of minority failure in schooling has to do with the fact that minority . . . cultural heritage is suppressed in the curriculum. . . . Students fail because schools assault their identities and destabilize their sense of self and agency" (p. xv). Recognizing that language is a carrier of identity and culture, heritage language and English as a Second Language programs affirm the language of children's homes and thereby attempt to make space for children's social and cultural identities in our classrooms.

Advocates of progressive language practices are also interested in expanding the range of reading and writing practices in the schools as a means of helping students access the transformative power of literacy. Expanding definitions of literacy beyond narrow notions of school literacy (i.e., "basic skills") seeks to ensure that reading and writing will make a difference in the lives of children and adults outside the walls of school and the workplace. From a progressive perspective, literacy is not just a "skill," but rather, an important means by which people make sense of their lives.

Progressive literacy practices also challenge school literacy practices that contribute to the disproportionate degree of failure among minority students. School literacy practices—for example, storybook reading, the telling of fanciful stories, talking *about* language (e.g., explicitly stating phonics rules), and essay-text literacy (which assumes that speakers/writers should ignore what listeners/readers know and explicitly say it anyway) —mirror the literacy practices in many middle-class homes (Gee, 1990; Heath, 1983). Privileging the literacy practices of middle-class homes advantages students from those homes while it disadvantages students from non-middle-class backgrounds (Gee, 1990) by rendering invisible the literacy practices valued in their homes. It is not that non-middle-class students are illiterate or even less literate than their middle-class peers. Rather, they are differently literate (Gee, 1990; Taylor, 1997). Valuing a range of literacy practices in the classroom empowers students whose "ways with words" typically fall outside the scope of schooling.

Progressive language practices that affirm the diversity that exists in most of our schools are not solely for the benefit of racial, ethnic, and linguistic minorities. Just as the survival of a species depends on genetic diversity, the ability of a society to endure may also depend on a cultural diversity in which people remain open to the possibility that the voices of difference may change how they think about themselves. In the case of the United States, our ability to apprehend the social, political, ecological, and moral problems that confront us demands that we enrich our Eurocentric/Anglocentric traditions by cultivating the cultural and linguistic abundance that surrounds us.

Ultimately, advocating on behalf of progressive language practices is part of a larger political project: creating a more just and democratic society. For Maxine Greene, democracy means creating communities in which difference is viewed as an opportunity to enrich existing communities with the cultural and community values of others. As she puts it, "democracy . . . means a community that is always in the making. Marked by an emerging solidarity, a sharing of certain beliefs, a dialogue about others, it must remain open to newcomers, those too long thrust aside" (Greene, 1993, p. 227). Democratic communities do not attempt to assimilate others into existing cultural practices; rather, they remain open to the possibility of being changed themselves. From this perspective, the idea of a "cultural melting pot" in which the voices of difference, including linguistic differences, are effaced in the name of assimilation is profoundly undemocratic. We believe that a democratic community makes a place for the voices of all its citizens and finds ways to ensure that those voices are heard.

However, language policies and practices that make a place for the voices of difference are necessary, but insufficient, for achieving the goal of creating a more just and democratic society if extant language practices have the effect of marginalizing those voices, as we believe they do. Again, the meaning of any utterance or text is a function of what it does, and one of the things language does is to fashion and maintain relations of power by constructing subject positions and shaping worldviews for people as they participate in various language practices. Choices made by speakers and writers, for example, can be seen as efforts to establish or maintain particular kinds of power relationships. The reassurances of political leaders or administrators can position them as those who know what is best for their people. On the other hand, polite forms of request from subordinates can be interpreted as a willingness to accept their subservient status. From this perspective, what makes language sexist or racist, for example, is not merely that it is offensive or insulting, but that it seeks to locate groups of people in particular kinds of social roles, embedded in particular systems of privilege. A male who addresses female colleagues as "honey" or "sweetheart" not only demeans but also seeks to assert his dominance over women. Similarly, within a "male" discourse, appropriate language for a "lady" is language that signals acceptance of social roles and relationships men find useful. Such language serves a many-tentacled system of male privilege. An alternative discourse challenges these "traditional" roles, which may account for the chilling hatred for Hilary Clinton and other outspoken women (women Rush Limbaugh calls "feminazis") that dominates the airways of right-wing talk radio.

Language use also attempts to shape people by locating them within particular ideological spaces, each with its own worldview entailing certain norms, attitudes, values, and beliefs (Gee, 1990). As Fairclough puts it, "Texts do not typically spout ideology. They so position the interpreter through their cues that she brings ideologies to the interpretation of texts—and reproduces them in the process" (1989, p. 85). Talk about the "immigration problem," "dropouts," the "literacy crisis," or the "unemployment problem" invokes certain understandings by positioning listeners within a discourse of extreme individualism, which, in this case, focuses our gaze on the individual's role in being "an illegal immigrant," a "dropout," "illiterate," or "unemployed," while masking other interpretations that implicate, for example, structural defects in the economy—and not worker skill—as the cause of chronic unemployment. Similarly, situating "questions" about the relative abilities of racial groups within a "scientific" discourse makes such questions seem perfectly natural, worthy of objective debate in the pages of the *New Republic* and *Newsweek* or on *Larry King Live*. Embedded in a discourse of difference, what Cornel West (1993) calls the "new cultural politics of difference," the very question would be seen to be racist.

Just as particular language practices—sexist or racist language, for example—disadvantage groups of people, progressive language practices—from language use to instructional programs to language assessment to educational language policies—encourage a critical look at how language maintains relations of power and, ultimately, challenge those power arrangements.

The Life History of Progressive Language Practices

At the time of this writing, progressive language practices—and the commitment to an inclusive, participatory democracy underpinning these practices—are under unprecedented attack, as many of the chapters in this volume illustrate. Policies that promote linguistic diversity—dialect awareness, ESL, and heritage language programs, for example—are being savaged in some quarters for undermining "standards of correctness" or as a threat to common culture (e.g., Stotsky, 1999). Efforts to expand the range of (multicultural) literature in the schools and universities are assailed for promoting a kind of cultural relativism that elevates mediocre texts to canonical status by virtue of their source (e.g., black, women, or Hispanic authors) rather than their content and style. (There is great concern in the land that teaching Alice Walker in our high schools, for example, might reduce the amount of time available for reading Shakespeare, despite hard evidence to the contrary [Fish, 1994].) The assault on the progressive literacy practice known as "whole language," the popular villain in America's latest "literacy crisis," has reached the halls of state legislatures and, incredibly, the U.S. Congress, as well as the covers of several weekly newsmagazines. Those who discourage the use of racist and sexist language that demeans as it excludes are increasingly dismissed as pandering to the purveyors of "political correctness." Critical language practices in schools that portray governmental or corporate interests in a negative light face the prospect of censorship (for a recent example of school censorship, see Karp, 1997). Of course, progressive language practices and policies, since they necessarily threaten somebody's interests by challenging relations of power, have encountered and will always encounter fierce resistance. Nevertheless, for progressive language educators and policymakers, these are particularly hard times.

For this volume, we invited progressive language educators, theorists, and policymakers from across the United States and Canada to reflect on the fate of progressive language practices and policies with which they had firsthand knowledge. Alleen Pace Nilsen examines her involvement in NCTE's guidelines for nonsexist language. Caryl Crowell and Bob Wortman share their efforts to create quality bilingual education in an ethnically and linguistically segregated neighborhood. Sheridan Blau recalls his participation in the progressive California Learning Assessment System (CLAS), for which continued funding was eventually vetoed by Pete Wilson, then governor of California. Other chapters recount efforts to establish and/or maintain a range of progressive assessment, language, and literacy practices. We wanted insiders—organizers, planners, key participants—to write about responses to these against-the-grain projects. We expected that their involvement and intense interest would have caused them to remember, and indeed would prod them to want to retell, subtle twists and up-close details (who said or did what and why) en route to the end-thus-far of "their" projects, thus revealing the profoundly local character of these life histories.

We have also placed three framing chapters by Patrick Shannon , James Paul Gee, and John Willinsky at the beginning of this collection. We intend for these to provide a theoretical and historical backdrop for interpreting the stories of progressive language practice that follow and to encourage readers to view the local and the particular within larger contexts. The stories themselves are grouped according to their intended scope: those projects limited to practice in a single school; those pertaining to an entire school district, city, or region of a country; and those aimed at affecting practice nationally or internationally.

What counts as "progressive" is not always clear, a point made by John Willinsky in his contribution to this volume. No doubt some readers will disagree with the vision of particular progressive language practices and policies discussed in this volume; that is, they will question whether all these practices are indeed "progressive." But there is no one single meaning of *progressive*, although, as we have indicated, we believe that the "progress" in *progressive* must mean movement toward a more inclusive democracy that makes a place for the voices of all its citizens. We will, of course, discover from time to time that particular language practices heralded as progressive may not be so progressive after all. For example, professional organizations such as the National Council of Teachers of English (NCTE) offered a progressive alternative to narrow, behaviorally based standards. In the end, however, it appears that more regressive notions of standards have come to dominate the educational reform movement (for critical views of the standards movement and the participation of professional organizations in that movement, see Ohanian, 1999, and Shannon, 1996), although individual teachers may take some comfort in the broad-strokes approach to standards taken by NCTE and the International Reading Association (IRA).

Progress also depends on a willingness to examine critically our most cherished language practices and policies. The contributors to this volume share a commitment to progressive language practices and the democratic vision that underlies it even if they might not agree with each other, or even us, about the meaning of *progressive*. Each of the contributors also has something to teach us about the fate of progressive language practices. It is clear from the stories presented here, for example, that caring and commitment are rarely sufficient to sustain the democratic vision inherent in progressive language practices, although caring and commitment are always necessary. Often, the good intentions of a committed group of individuals are undone by a hostile political community, as in the case of the CLAS project. Sometimes, progressive policies or practices fail to take hold because of a structural or theoretical mismatch between the policy or practice and the culture of the institution within which the policy or practice is enacted. Petrosky and Delandshere's efforts (Chapter 16) to create more progressive assessment practices were thwarted, in part, by behaviorist assumptions underlying the culture of tests and measurements.

At the local level, progressive language practices are sometimes sustained by a committed patron. Bilingual programs at Dool School (see Carpenter and Castro, Chapter 7), for example, have the support of a dedicated principal. Of course, programs that depend on patrons can easily be undone when key people leave their positions (see Serafini and Rogers, Chapter 9). Other projects depend on invisibility to survive in political or hostile climates. Crowell and Worton (Chapter 5) suggest that their progressive bilingual program survives amid a policy of benign neglect. No one challenges what they are doing, in part because no one is really paying attention. Still, what is invisible today can easily become visible tomorrow.

Our purpose in putting this volume together, however, is not to proclaim the "moral" to be taken from each story. After all, what the cases teach will depend on who is learning and why (a practitioner's position, a project's contextual conditions, a policy's goals). We do, however, draw one lesson from them all: the enduring truth that context matters. The activity of particular persons—both "insiders" and "outsiders"—moving locally within larger political, historical, and cultural currents is what creates the fate of a project. The life stories of progressive language projects, then, are both biographical and historical. They are events of history—patterned, fitting into overriding themes of the times. Yet they are also creatures of biography (idiosyncratic and unpredictable in detail), occasionally overcoming the odds by countering, for a while at least, prevailing systems of privilege. Exactly which progressive, against-the-grain language project will beat the odds? From the cases assembled here, the substance of the project itself seems not to determine its reception. Nor does the degree of deviation from mainstream practice or even the extent of a project's potential for rocking the boat of established power arrangements. And seemingly friendly, tolerant, or hostile larger contexts do not always predict the course of a project either.

In assembling these stories, then, we wish to avoid attempting the impossible, that is, offering specific advice that others might use mechanically in order to enhance the prospects of new projects. Instead, we had two other purposes in mind. First, we wish to offer the stories themselves, told by someone who was or is there and who cares, because the stories are fascinating to us and, we hope, to others. They take us behind the scenes where previously we had only the "official" version. They also help us imagine future projects that might build on these, might come at problems addressed by these projects but from different directions. Second, we wanted to deepen others' (and our own) understanding of what happens to progressive language projects. The purpose of qualitative research is an analog here. That purpose is not to generalize the findings or apply the results to a new situation but to heighten one's sensitivity, complicate one's understandings, increase one's appreciation of nuances of a phenomenon. Similarly, our goal is to present multiple specific cases about how a variety of progressive language education projects turned out, against the backdrop of some broad discussions of overarching issues, in order to deepen understandings of the life-thus-far of a "good idea." We hope that such deeper understandings, while they may prevent an occasional misstep in future projects, will primarily help those language educators working against the grain to be less inclined to blame themselves, more inclined to keep heart, better prepared to act with awareness of competing agendas, and, most important, inspired to keep on working on progressive language practices.

Overall, the stories of the fate of progressive language practices shared by contributors to this volume are complicated stories. They illustrate the passion and vision of committed individuals trying to make a difference by drawing on the power of language to empower individuals and communities and by challenging language practices that limit the life chances of women; racial, linguistic, and ethnic minorities; people living in poverty; and so on. What we learn from these caring and committed people inspires all of us to continue in our struggle to create a more just and democratic society for all of our citizens. The stories here also illustrate just how hard the struggle can be. But we cannot give up. The goal is too important.

References

Barnes, D. (1976). *From communication to curriculum*. Harmondsworth, UK: Penguin.

Cazden, C. B. (1988). *Classroom discourse: The language of teaching and learning*. Portsmouth, NH: Heinemann.

Coulter, D. (1999). The epic and the novel: Dialogism and teacher research. *Educational Researcher, 28*(3), 4–13.

Dudley-Marling, C. (2000). *A family affair: When school troubles come home*. Portsmouth, NH: Heinemann.

Edwards, A. D., & Furlong, V. J. (1978). *The language of teaching: Meaning in classroom interaction*. London: Heinemann.

Fairclough, N. (1989). *Language and power*. London: Longman.

Fish, S. (1994). Speaking in code, or, how to turn bigotry and ignorance into moral principles. In S. Fish (Ed.), *There's no such thing as free speech, and it's a good thing, too* (pp. 89–119). New York: Oxford University Press.

Gee, J. P. (1990). *Social linguistics and literacies: Ideologies in discourses*. London: Falmer.

Greene, M. (1993). Imagination, community, and the school. *Review of Education, 15*, 223–231.

Heath, S. B. (1983). *Ways with words: Language, life, and work in communities and classrooms*. Cambridge: Cambridge University Press.

Hynds, S., & Rubin, D. L. (Eds.). (1990). *Perspectives on talk and learning*. Urbana, IL: National Council of Teachers of English.

Jones, P. (1988). *Lipservice: The story of talk in schools*. Philadelphia: Open University Press.

Karp, S. (1997). Banned in Jersey, welcomed on Broadway. *Rethinking Schools, 12* (2), 14–15.

McCarthy, C., & Crichlow, W. (1993). Theories of identity, theories of representation, theories of race. In C. McCarthy & W. Crichlow (Eds.), *Race, identity, and representation in education* (pp. xiii–xxiv). New York: Routledge.

Michaels, A. (1996). *Fugitive pieces*. Toronto: McClelland & Stewart.

Ogbu, J. U. (1999). Beyond language: Ebonics, proper English, and identity in a Black-American speech community. *American Educational Research Journal, 36,* 147–84.

Ohanian, S. (1999). *One size fits few: The folly of educational standards.* Portsmouth, NH: Heinemann.

Perry, T. (1997). "I 'on know why they be trippin'." *Rethinking Schools,* 12, 3–5.

Searle, J. R. (1969). *Speech acts: An essay in the philosophy of language.* London: Cambridge University Press.

Shannon, P. (1996). Mad as hell. *Language Arts, 73,* 14–19.

Stotsky, S. (1999). *Losing our language: How multicultural classroom instruction is undermining our children's ability to read, write, and reason.* New York: Free Press.

Taylor, D. (Ed.). (1997). *Many families, many literacies: An international declaration of principles.* Portsmouth, NH: Heinemann.

West, C. (1993). *Race matters.* New York: Vintage Books.

I

PROGRESSIVE LANGUAGE PROJECTS: SOME FRAMING ISSUES

Turn, Turn, Turn: Language Education, Politics, and Freedom at the Turn of Three Centuries

PATRICK SHANNON
Penn State University

If a nation expects to be ignorant and free, in a state of civilization, it expects what never was and will never be. . . . I propose schooling in reading and writing, arithmetic, and history at common expense to all.

THOMAS JEFFERSON

Since Thomas Jefferson made these remarks to the Virginia Congress in 1779, schooling in the United States has been associated with nationhood, and education, especially literacy education, has been considered protection against tyrannies of all sorts. Jefferson established a dialectic with which we are still struggling to this day—schooling as a key builder of state and national identities and, simultaneously, a primary tool for establishing and defending freedom. Working from assumptions of the Enlightenment, during which the state and freedom could be understood as pulling in the same direction, Jefferson and other founding fathers were able to make these linkages work, at least theoretically. As we face the limits of these assumptions, however, language educators often confront these links as hostile contradictions rather than working dialectics.

In this chapter, I sample ways in which the dialectic of state and freedom has played out in U.S. schools at the ends and beginnings of the last three centuries. I picked these points in the past because just as today, Americans then faced remarkable social, economic, and political changes, and I hope to connect the past with the present in ways that help us choose directions for current work as language educators in and out of schools.

From Revolution to a Republic

At its inception, the United States can be understood as a test of the practical validity of the political assumptions of the Enlightenment. Linking a great faith in reason to decipher the mysteries of the physical and social worlds in order to enhance human material comfort, an embryonic belief in the powers of capitalism to govern relations among men and families, and a pessimistic although wholly secular appraisal of human nature, Jefferson and other American intellectuals attempted to create a science of freedom. They encoded the lessons of history into a government of laws that would control and be controlled by its citizens. History had taught them that men (and they were concerned only with white men of means—landed yeoman, as Jefferson called them) need governing institutions in order to master their passions and to regulate their conflicts. Higher passions—pride, humanity, and patriotism—were often overbalanced by what James Madison called in *The Federalist Papers* "the propensity of mankind to fall into mutual animosities" (1787/1964, p. 18) and to form factions around many types of difference (such as race, class, gender, region, religion, political philosophy, language, etc.). Government, which was to be the focal point of national status after the American War of Independence, would guard the passions of individuals for the sake of order and guard the guardians for the sake of freedom. Without freedom, the natural taming of the physical and social worlds through science and capitalism would be impossible, and without government, science and capitalism would lead men to seek undue advantage over one another:

> Every government degenerates when trusted to the ruler of the people alone. The people themselves are its only safe deposito-

ries. And to render even them sage their minds must be improved to a certain degree. This indeed is not all that is necessary, though it be essentially necessary. An amendment of our constitution must come here in aid of the public education. The influence over government must be shared among all the people. (Jefferson, 1785/1961, p. 96)

The primary goal of schooling, then, became explicit—to improve Americans' minds to a certain degree. The definitions of *improvement* and *degree* were clarified in Jefferson's plan for schooling. The fundamentals of language education, arithmetic and history would be offered to all full citizens (not slaves or natives) during three years of publicly supported schooling. This education would improve the minds of these people in order to enable them to follow the arguments presented by those in authority. On completion of public schooling, a selection of no more than half of the white males of means would be permitted to continue their education for four more years in elementary schools at their families' expense so that they might become public school teachers and public servants (local magistrates, tax collectors, and the like). No more than half of *these* graduates would be enrolled at public expense in secondary schools (William and Mary College in Jefferson's original plan) in order to be educated to make and write the arguments to govern America. Jefferson's three-tiered system was organized to supply his vision of a republic with a "natural aristocracy" that was selected for its powers of rationality and with a literate citizenry whose white male members of some means were able to vote. Schooling as a means of separating individuals and classes of individuals was supported with Enlightenment philosophy. According to John Locke,

God has stamp'd certain Characters upon men's minds, which like their shape, may perhaps be a little mended, but can hardly be totally alter'd and transformed into the contrary. He therefore that is about Children, should well study their Natures and Aptitudes, and see, by often trials, what turn they easily take, and what becomes them; observe what their Native Stock is, how it may be want, whether they be capable of having it wrought into them by industry and incorporated there by Practice; and whether it be worth while to endeavor it. (1693/1964, p. 47)

The challenges to Americans at the turn of the eighteenth century were many: creating a government like no other before it, coping with the consequences of an economy in transition from agrarianism toward capitalism in which political equality had to be distinguished from economic and social inequalities, and assimilating streams of new immigrants from a variety of cultures. Schools were established to help meet these challenges through a series of formal exclusions and inclusions. In the U.S. Constitution, people of African descent were considered only three-fifths human, and American Indians had no status at all. Both at the time were excluded from schools, and laws were passed in many states which forbade the improvement of their minds to any degree. Women at that time had few property rights and no right to vote. Yet white women whose families had means enough to compensate for their loss to the family's economy attended public school, though rarely elementary schools. Of course, private tutors and schools were available to women in wealthy families.

Reports on the role of language education in addressing those challenges are bleak. From diaries, journals, and written reports of the early and middle eighteenth century, Barbara Finkelstein found that "most teachers of reading confined their activities to those of overseers and drillmasters" (1989, p. 26). Overseers left learning almost entirely to their students, limiting themselves to defining assignments and later listening to recitations. Drillmasters organized exercises that would help students memorize information, but without teacher explanation: "Teachers proceeded as though learning had occurred when their students could imitate the skills or reproduce the knowledge contained in each of the assignments" (p. 25).

These techniques appear to be founded on John Locke's proposed pedagogy in *Some Thoughts Concerning Education:* "By repeating the same action till it be grown habitual in them, and the performance will not depend on memory or reflection, the concomitant of prudence and age, and not of childhood; but will be natural to them" (1693/1964, p. 48). Supported by Locke's theories, educational leaders in this period believed they could create the good society through the proper molding of children from appropriate "Native Stock." Perfect schools would produce perfect political citizens, perfect moral beings, and perfect workers.

Noah Webster's series of textbooks, which he began to publish in 1783—and which sold over seventy million copies in less than one hundred years—were clearly part of the nation-building project:

> In the choice of pieces I have not been inattentive to the political interests of America. Several of those masterly addresses of Congress, written at the commencement of the last revolution, contain such noble, just, and independent sentiments of liberty and patriotism that I cannot help wishing to transfuse them into the breast of the rising generation. (qtd. in Rudolf, 1965, p. 85)

And Webster's ideas of perfection in governance were consonant with those of the founding fathers. For example, The Federal Catechism from the *Webster Elementary Reader* was a fierce defense of republicanism—rule by a natural aristocracy.

> Q. What are the deficits of democracy?
> A. In democracy, where people all meet for the purpose of making laws, there are commonly tumults and disorders. A small city may sometimes be governed in this manner, but if the citizens are numerous, their assemblies make a crowd or mob, where debates cannot be carried on with coolness and candor, nor can arguments be heard. Therefore a pure democracy is generally a very bad government. It is often the most tyrannical government on earth; for a multitude is often rash, and will not hear reason. (qtd. in Cohen, 1974, p. 50)

In "On the Education of Youth in America, Webster wrote, "education should be adopted and pursued which implants in the minds of American young the principles of virtue and of liberty and inspire[s] them with an attachment to their country." This attachment to country was forged by creating a national language and a national code of moral behavior as "summed up in the beginning of Matthew, in Christ's Sermon on the Mount," and would foster an emotional patriotism in which "every class of people should know and love the laws" (1790/1974, p. 51).

William Holmes McGuffey's textbooks were prepared for the common school system during the middle half of the eighteenth century. His readers were popular, selling 122 million between 1839 and 1922. "The Rich Boy" and "The Poor Boy," stories from his early readers, give some indication of how schooling helped address inequality. The rich boy explains what he will do with his inheritance and the poor boy proclaims his love of law and his lot in life:

> I would build a great many pretty cottages for people to live in, and every cottage should have a garden and a field, in order that the people might have vegetables, and might keep a cow, a pig, and some chickens; They should not pay me much rent. I would give clothes to the boys and girls who had not money to buy clothes with, and they should all learn to read and write and be very good.

> I have been told, and I have read, that it is God who makes some poor, and others rich; that the rich have many troubles which we know nothing of; and that the poor, if they are but good, may be very happy; indeed. I think that when I am good, nobody can be happier than I am. (McGuffey, 1843, p. 64)

At the end of the eighteenth century and into the nineteenth, the dialectic for schooling and language education was tipped decidedly toward nation building. The nation would protect political freedom from unreasonable rulers and economic freedom from restraint of capital or trade. A law-abiding, virtuous, and national citizenry who could read the arguments put forth by the natural aristocracy of the republic would be able to vote and to participate in the economy. Schools provided the methods and contents to develop these necessary patriotic, moral, and economic habits of rational action and mind. Webster's and McGuffey's textbooks were primarily designed to protect the property of the wealthy, promote Christianity, and produce a national language (Curti, 1935). Schools, at least the free public schools, were typically places where students learned to exercise reason for the sake of the nation, not for the sake of individual freedom: "If some were able to use the ability to read and write creatively, it was not because their schooling had taught them how" (Finkelstein, 1979, p. 133).

From Reconstruction to Progressivism

One hundred years after the Declaration of Independence, some limitations of the assumptions of the Enlightenment on which the nation was founded were becoming apparent. The economy was depressed while fortunes were amassed by a very few; the government was scandal ridden; the southern half of the nation was under federal military occupation; the army was at war with the country's natives in the West; many newly emancipated African Americans were still disenfranchised, illiterate, and unemployed; and the Declaration of Rights for Women demanded justice and equality for all citizens. Over the next fifty years, twenty million immigrants of many races, religions, and cultures would be added to the population of just under fifty million, challenging the Anglo-American national identity. Coupled with the shift in population from farm to city (from 30 percent in 1890 to over 50 percent by 1920), Americans faced new and different challenges than those the founding fathers had identified a century earlier.

The turn of the twentieth century is often labeled the Progressive Era, as many governmental reforms seemed designed to assuage the limitations of the assumptions of the Enlightenment. The Meat Inspection Act; the Hepburn Act to regulate railroads; the Pure Food and Drug Act; the Mann-Elkins Act, which put telephone and telegraph companies under the Interstate Commerce Commission; the Trade Commission to regulate monopolies; the Federal Reserve to regulate interest rates and banking; the Sixteenth Amendment, allowing a graduated income tax; the Seventh Amendment, providing for direct election of senators; the *Plessy v. Ferguson* Supreme Court decision of separate but equal schooling for African Americans; a variety of state laws regulating wages and work hours; workers' compensation and safety inspection of factories; and the Nineteenth Amendment, which allowed women to vote—all enlarged the role of the government in the everyday lives of citizens. Whether you judge the Progressive Era as the triumph of liberalism in the United States in restraining the owners of the business community (Schlesinger, 1968) or as the emergence of "political capitalism" to stabilize that system in a time of uncertainty and trouble (Kolko, 1963),

U.S. institutions, including schools, assumed greater responsibility in and for individuals' public and private lives.

Schooling for Individual Freedom

During the last quarter of the nineteenth century, Francis Wayland Parker complained that traditional schooling served "the aristocracy" rather than the masses at public expense: "The methods of the few, in their control of the many, still govern our public schools, and to a great degree their management" (1894, p. 436). He suggested that the myth of education as the means to social, economic, and political advancement was a mainstay in maintaining the gap between society's haves and have nots: "The problem [for the ruling class] was how to give the people education and keep them from exercising the divine gift of choice; to make them believe that they were educated and at the same time to prevent free action of the mind" (p. 408). Parker, a superintendent of schools in Quincy, Massachusetts, and later director of the Cook County Normal School outside Chicago, cajoled his teachers into reforming schools according to four tenets: (1) children have a right to be themselves, (2) learning is natural, (3) teachers should experiment in order to meet learners' needs, and (4) curriculum should be based on the individual's knowledge of the world around the school. The Quincy Method quickly became famous for its innovation, with nearly thirty thousand visitors between 1876 and 1880. What they witnessed is recorded in Lelia Patridge's (1885) *The Quincy Method Illustrated*, which offers detailed descriptions of teachers' and students' work, including transcripts of classroom dialogues. The wholesale changes in practice were captured in the remarks of then chair of the school board Charles Adams:

> As now taught in our schools, English grammar is a singularly unprofitable branch of instruction. It was now immediately hustled out of there; and the reader was sent after the grammar, and the spelling book after the reader, and the copybook after the speller. Reading at sight and writing off-hand were to constitute the basis of the new system. The faculty of doing either the one or the other of these could, however, be acquired only in one way—by constant practice. . . . Instruction in reading, writing,

grammar, spelling and to a very considerable degree history and geography were combined in the exercises—reading and writing. (1879/1935, pp. 502–3)

Quincy language education worked from two basic assumptions: "The process of learning to read, then, must consist of learning to use the written and printed word precisely as he used the spoken word" (Parker, 1894, p. 26) and "the association of words with their appropriate ideas aids the child in learning to read" (p. 27). Because literacy learning was based on function and association—speaking and extensive world knowledge—lessons were embedded in students' study of the social, physical, and biological worlds through guided observation, drawing, and discussion. Patridge (1885) recorded lessons about the dignity of the work in and around stone quarries, the absence of American Indians in the Boston area, a circus train that traveled through Quincy at night on its way to Providence, farm animals, bean plants, and students' adventures during the noon recess.

Schooling and Business Principles

Not all schoolteachers and superintendents rallied to Parker's position on schooling and language education. For example, the prestigious Committee of Fifteen's report on elementary school curriculum, chaired by William Torrey Harris (1895), proposed only slight changes from the eighteenth-century curriculum—reading (including literature after the fourth year): eight years with daily lessons; penmanship: six years, ten lessons per week for first two years, five lessons for third and fourth, and three for fifth and sixth; spelling: lists fourth, fifth, and sixth years, four lessons per week; grammar: oral with composition or dictation first year to middle of fifth, textbooks from middle of fifth to close of seventh, five lessons per week.

Moreover, the overwhelming changes in modes of production and the fortunes amassed by Carnegie, Rockefeller, Vanderbilt, and their like led to urging schools to apply business principles to their organization and instructional methods (Callahan, 1964). The success of social Darwinism in explaining social and economic inequalities and of scientific rationality in providing technological mastery of much of the environment through steam, electricity, and oil encouraged a search for the scientific laws of nature that underlie learning.

Business and science came together in the efficiency movement in schools during the first two decades of the twentieth century: "Primarily schooling is a problem of economy; it seeks to determine in what manner the working unit may be made to return the largest dividend upon the material investment of time, energy, and money" (Bagley, 1911, p. 2). Beginning in 1914, the Committee for the Economy of Time in Education applied means/ends rationality to all elementary subjects, culminating in three reports in 1919 entitled Principles of Method in (1) Teaching Writing, (2) Teaching Spelling, and (3) Teaching Reading as Derived from Scientific Investigation. These reports offered rules for economy in curriculum and instruction. Curriculum was reduced to objectively testable skills; speed and accuracy were reified as the primary criteria for success.

In the 1920s, textbook publishers combined these rules for efficient curriculum and instruction with E. L. Thorndike's four laws of learning to establish the basal reading series—a set of graded anthologies, practice books of skills for students, and teacher's manuals for the use of the anthologies and the teaching of skills. These materials were the technology of reading instruction that would standardize teachers' practices according to scientific principles in order to ensure efficiency and control the quality of student learning. The teacher's manual listed and sequenced the skills to be taught in order to ensure readiness, the workbook guaranteed skill exercise, and correct answers that were supplied in teacher's manuals encouraged teachers to reinforce students' good responses and to record student progress. Teacher's manuals were considered the correct stimulus to evoke the appropriate standard response from teachers in order to ensure that students received businesslike, scientific instruction.

Schooling for Democracy

At the turn of the twentieth century, John Dewey considered the mismatch between people's basically agrarian social knowledge and the demands of individualization and urbanization as a threat to U.S. democracy. The threat lay in the way the mismatch exaggerated the differences among social classes, the distinction between physical and mental labor, and the connection between social life and capital accumulation. Dewey argued that as urban life became more fragmented for the working classes, owners became even more politically powerful. In fact, Dewey accused the upper classes of using democracy as a slogan to better their circumstances: "in the name of democracy and individual freedom, the few as a result of superior possessions and power had in fact made it impossible for the masses of men to realize personal capacities and to count in the social order" (Dewey & Tufts, 1908, p. 443). Dewey lamented that most social decisions were made according to profit motives and condemned explicitly the commercialization of social life and the tolerance of others' misery for the sake of profit. Later, he concluded "that until there is something like economic security and economic democracy, aesthetic, intellectual, and social concern will be subordinated to an exploitation by the owning class which carries with it the commercialization of culture" (Dewey, 1928, p. 202).

True democracy, according to Dewey, is far more than a form of government or an expression of popular sovereignty; it should also be a means of living together that breaks down class barriers (Dewey, 1901). This democracy would present a way of life in which the self-realization of the individual in a community involves necessarily the self-realization of every other person (Dewey, 1891). At least at the beginning of his career, Dewey thought schooling was a powerful way to promote such realization of self and others:

> It remains but to organize all the factors to appreciate them in their fullness of meaning, and to put the ideas and ideals involved in complete, uncompromising possession of our school system. To do this means to make each one of our schools an embryonic community, active with types of occupations that reflect the life of the larger society, and permeated throughout with the spirit of art, history and science. When the school introduces and trains each child of society into membership within such a little community saturating him with the spirit of service, and providing him with the instruments of effective self-direction, we shall have

the deepest and best guarantee of a larger society which is worthy, lovely, and harmonious. (Dewey, 1897, p. 37)

At the University of Chicago at the turn of the nineteenth century, Dewey took Parker's pedagogy for individual freedom as a starting point to create that embryonic community at the Laboratory School. The school was community centered; that is, students, teachers, and parents were all considered community members who planned the programs and curricula together in order to "harmonize" the children's interests and lives with adult ends and values. Dewey's and the Lab School teachers' concerns that reading in the primary grades was a fetish created some disharmony in the community. According to Dewey, "It is not the purpose, as had been stated, of this school that the child learn to bake and sew at school, and to read, write and figure at home. It is true, however, that these subjects of reading, writing, etc. are not presented during the early years in large doses. . . . Books and the ability to read are, therefore, regarded strictly as tools. The child must learn to use those, just as he would any other tool" (1897, p. 44).

Because the processes of mental development were considered to be social processes developed through participation, teachers understood that a child's recognition of the functional value of literacy was gradual and likely to be embedded in the events of everyday activity. Thus teachers and students of all ages were expected to keep records of their progress on projects. Older children made notes to record their thoughts and descriptions of each day's events, and teachers took dictation for younger children. These written records were reviewed at the start of the next day in order to keep track of students' work on a day-to-day basis. During this as well as other literacy events, teachers talked about correct form, clarity, and accuracy of students' writing: "The desire to read for themselves was often born in children out of the idea that they might find better ways of doing and thus get more satisfactory results. With this interest as an urge, the child himself often freely set his attention to learning to read. A natural need thus became the stimulus to the gaining of skill in the use of a tool" (Mayhew & Edwards, 1936, p. 388).

Experimentalists and Expressionists: Problems Addressed; Problems Unaddressed

Progressive educators at the end of the nineteenth century and beginning of the twentieth were united only in their determination to change schools to better address society's needs. Thorndike and other experimentalists sought scientific and business rationality to ensure that a natural aristocracy would emerge, govern, and manage an educated populace efficiently and effectively. Although these experimentalists intended profound changes in classrooms and schools, they did little to alleviate the traditional imbalance which favored state building over freedom in school curricula and life.

Parker and other expressionist teachers focused on individual freedom and natural learning in order to enable each citizen to make choices while exerting greater control over his or her life. Expressionists challenged social and school hierarchies but left the contemporary problems of urbanization, immigration, and industrialization untouched. Therefore newly gained individual freedoms were limited to private matters, and the balance of social power remained unchanged also. Dewey and the teachers in *Schools of Tomorrow* (Dewey & Dewey, 1915) argued that numerous and varied interests must be consciously explored and shared among groups in a democratic society. Schools, then, should become environments in which individuals within various groups must defer their own interests and actions to the interests and actions of other groups in order to explore issues of diversity and common interests, preparing children and thus society to cope with modernity.

Social circumstances changed the types and strategies of inclusions and exclusions in schooling during the Progressive Era. Whereas language education for people of color was once considered a threat to the state—for fear of insurrection—it now became necessary to make "new" citizens into good patriotic workers for business and the state. Laws against teaching minorities to read gave way to pleas to prepare them for the literacies of the workplace. *Plessey v. Ferguson*, resident schools for American Indians, and harsh assimilation policies to make English the only language of instruction in public schools ensured that these

new inclusions would not increase access to the natural aristocracy. Necessities did, however, lead to debate about the appropriate curricula to serve these groups, such as the debate between
Booker T. Washington, who advocated vocational education for
African American males so that they might secure positions on
the bottom rung of the occupational ladder, and W. E. B. Du Bois
(see Lewis, 1993), who wrote:

> Is life not more than meat, and the body more than raiment?
> And men ask this today all the more eagerly because of sinister
> signs in recent educational moments. We shall hardly induce black
> men to believe that if their stomachs be full, it matters little about
> their brains.
>
> The tendency is here, born of slavery and quickened to re-
> newed life by the crazy imperialism of the day, to regard human
> beings as among the material resources of a land to be trained
> with an eye single to future dividends. Race prejudices, which
> keep brown and black men in their "places," we are coming to
> regard as useful allies with such theory. (Du Bois, 1903, p. 126)

Postindustrial to Information Age

During the last quarter of the twentieth century and now at the
start of the twenty-first, Americans still face the dialectic between
the state and freedom but in what appears to be a much broader
context. Scientific rationality brought material splendor for some
and military dominance for a few in the world but also wrought
havoc within the environment and made a human apocalypse
more than a possibility. The same technology that enables Americans to communicate with anyone in the world on any topic allows the government and business into our homes to build
demographic, preference, and activity profiles on each of us.
Capitalism, which in many respects now transcends national
boundaries, enables goods and services to travel freely and cheaply
around the world but increases gaps in wealth and income, heightening workers' anxiety over their livelihoods and lives. Today,
laying off workers from profitable companies means a rise in the
value of those stocks. Citizens' efforts to secure civic equality
under the law and access to the "natural aristocracy" within gov-

ernment and business have produced moderate gains for people of color, women, and gays and lesbians in these spheres. Those same efforts, however, have often succumbed to problems of identity politics and provoked an explicitly white male backlash, charging reverse discrimination in employment, proposing English as a national language and walls on our borders to keep out immigrants, and claiming survival of the fittest as our cultural credo.

Tipping the Scales Back toward State Building

Schools are still perceived as a primary institution to help individuals cope with the changing conditions of their lives at the turn of this century. All of the previous attempts to address the United States' problems through education are still with us. For instance, William Bennett argues that Americans have lost their moral compass, for which he blames unwed mothers, multiculturalism, and state-induced dependency. Americans have cast off "the moral moorings and anchors that have never been more necessary" (Bennett, 1993, p. 12), but if recaptured, "we can continue the task of preserving the principles, the ideals, and notions of goodness and greatness we hold dear" (p. 12). Drawing on E. D. Hirsch's (1987) *Cultural Literacy: What Every American Needs to Know* and Allan Bloom's (1988) *The Closing of the American Mind*, as well as Webster's and McGuffey's textbooks, Bennett suggests that the solution to the challenges ahead is to return schools, and therefore society, to the practices of the past through the use of his *The Book of Virtues, The Book of Virtues for Young People, The Moral Compass*, and a back-to-basics curriculum of skills and facts. For example, "Phonics improves the ability of children both to identify words and sound out new ones" (*What Works*, 1986, p. 21), and "Students read more fluently and with greater understanding if they have background knowledge of past and present" (p. 53). Similarly, "Memorizing can help students absorb and return the factual information on which understanding and critical thoughts are based" (p. 37). Bennett goes on to describe his *Book of Virtues* as a "how to" book for moral literacy (1993, p. 13). "Its contents have been defined in part by my attempt to present some material, most of which is drawn from the corpus of Western Civilization, that American school children, once upon a time, knew by heart" (p. 15).

Adopted as an educational position by several conservative groups, this back-to-the-future proposal for schooling resembles Jefferson's proposal for schools that would meet the challenges of the turn of the eighteenth century, and it has been used to prevent progressive alternatives from gaining much of a foothold in state and district educational policy. Bennett's position is clearly what many have in mind when they call for national curriculum standards.

A second approach, a version of the experimentalist movement from the Progressive Era, attempts to use schools to return the United States' faltering economy to its postwar glory: "It is now very important to think about our education and economic policies in tandem. If we do not, we will have to decide how to share among ourselves a swiftly declining national income" (Tucker, 1984, p. 1). According to advocates of this approach, schools have not kept pace with the rapidly changing demands of the workplace, which now requires a labor force that is creative, knowledgeable, and flexible to increase its productivity so it can meet the low-wage competition from other countries. Accordingly, schools are to be adjusted so that they produce an entire nation of workers who can "think for a living" and are continually on the cutting edge of technological innovation, whose expertise perpetually adds value to state-of-the-art products. Catching the interest of business and the fancy of both Republican and Democratic politicians, this approach led to the first national Governors' Conference on Education, America 2000, and, finally, the Educate America Act.

These three entities seek an increased role for the federal government in school curricula and teaching in order to establish fixed uniform goals on which their process/product logic can operate. For language education, this governmental insurgence has taken three forms. First, over the last twenty years the government has funded national language-education research centers with specific mandates to conduct particular types of research (Pearson, 1990). These centers have disseminated research findings supporting explicit systematic instruction in reading skills and the need for state-level competency tests of language. Second, in order to induce change in teachers' and schools' traditional practice, the federal government funded the development of national language-education tests during third, six, ninth, and eleventh grades. The results of these tests would be made public as school and state aggregate scores to enable businesses to base choices for factory and office locations on where they might find an educated workforce. Finally, the federal government called for national curricular standards in all subject areas and implied that federal financial aid would be tied to "voluntary" compliance with national tests and curricula. After seeding the International Reading Association, the National Council of Teachers of English, and the previous federal Center for the Study of Reading with funds to write the English/language arts national standards, the federal government induced these organizations to use over one million dollars of their own funds to complete the task. In the end, however, government officials found the professional organizations' product "vague and not what people are looking for" (Diegmueller, 1996).

Both neotraditionalists and experimentalists continue to apply basic Enlightenment tenets as they tip the dialectic between state and freedom decidedly in favor of state building. The resurgence of traditional curricula and instructional methods appears to be a reaction to the challenges presented by various racial, class, gender, and language groups to be represented in the school curriculum and to have their cultural patterns reflected within instructional methods. The traditional "natural" aristocracy seeks to maintain its control over political, social, and economic spheres through nonviolent means by reinstating preferential content and methods in schools. Certainly, recent attacks on affirmative action in admissions and employment can be read this way. Although the experimentalist approach seeks, at least rhetorically, to accommodate race, class, gender, and other diversity, its means to accomplish this—standardized curricula and tests as well as business rationality—necessarily continue the advantages already afforded white, middle- and upper-class, English-speaking males in their education and access to well-paying employment. In both approaches, Jefferson's natural aristocracy is maintained in fact, while being challenged by words.

Aligned with the neotraditional and new experimentalist positions on schooling is the recent movement to open up public schooling to economic market forces in order to bust the public school monopoly over education. For-profit public schools, individual tuition vouchers, and charter schools appear to invert the imbalance in the schooling dialectic, raising individual freedom to choose above the needs of the state. But even advocates admit that benefits are likely to accrue only to those with means:

> Opening competition with private schools will enrich the spectrum of choice for students. It is most unlikely that we are going to witness a mass transfer of students from public to private schools. Only motivated students or well-informed and educated parents will take advantage of choice programs. The inner cities and rural poor students' conditions will not significantly change in the short run. However, what is likely to occur in the longer run is that the existing private options will force the public schools to become more efficient, offer richer programs, make more efforts to satisfy their customers. (Hakim, Seidenstat, & Bowman, 1994, pp. 12–13)

Tilting toward the Individual

The recent version of the progressive expressionist movement began with a clear intention to reverse the dialectic of schooling from state building to individual freedom. According to Goodman, "Helping [students] to achieve a sense of control and ownership over their learning in school, over their own reading, writing, speaking, listening and thinking, will help to give them a sense of their potential power" (1986, p. 10). Whole language or process approaches to schooling were initiatives that began with issues of teacher and student empowerment through control over goals, curricula, and processes for learning in order to create citizens capable of defining and expressing their individual interests: "Whole language is not only a good idea; it is also a threatening idea for those with a vested interest in the status quo" (Edelsky, Altwerger, & Flores, 1991, p. 3).

According to new expressionists, schools should be organized to take advantage of how language works and how it is learned.

Rather than an established curriculum designed to lead students through a set of preordained skill exercises, advocates suggest schools and classrooms as sites of inquiry in which students investigate their own questions, simultaneously learning language, learning about language, and learning through language. Such curricula not only rework the relationship between student and curricula but also the relationships between students and teacher and students and the world. If students' inquiries are to direct curriculum, then the teacher's role changes from provider of information to demonstrator of the ways of learning. And if the student has an inquiring mind, then the world becomes a place of agency and nothing is beyond question. In this process, the struggle between social convention (the state) and personal invention (freedom) is tilted toward the individual.

Perhaps the best indication that the new expressionists are having an impact is the fact that commercial textbook publishers are incorporating their language into teacher manuals and workbooks (Shannon & Goodman, 1994). Teachers and administrators desperate to appear up to date are willing to overlook the contradiction between the medium and the message. The experimentalist position in textbooks has not changed (Crawford, 1995), but surface manifestations of expressionism have been added, creating a curious mix certain to confuse students and teachers and to undermine the currency of the new expressionist challenge. Perhaps more curious is advocates' attempts to use the bureaucratic apparatus of the state to formalize the spread of new expressionism within the state, school district, and classroom (Church, 1996). With these acts, a movement that stressed teacher and student control and individual freedom used state authority to force compliance from those who are not convinced through reason. This foray from a movement of resistance to one of state enforcement has pushed new expressionists into unfamiliar territory—the stronghold of new traditionalists and new experimentalists—and has brought an organized backlash from conservative Christian fundamentalists (e.g., *The Blumenfeld Newsletter)* and experts from colleges of education (e.g., Foorman, 1995).

Joining Freedom and Equity

Some theoretical descendants of John Dewey tie their expressionist curriculum-as-inquiry approach to investigations of systemic social inequalities. These teachers and students ask, "why are things the way they are?"; "what and who are considered important?"; and "whose interests are served by current social rules and events?" Questions of this sort challenge simultaneously the political neutrality of a Eurocentric male-focused neotraditional curriculum, the skills and testing promoted by the new experimentalists, and the uninterrogated "choices" which often reproduce social stereotypes within the new expressionism (Gilbert, 1991):

> Revision of the canon in itself will not suffice. . . . To achieve social power and skepticism, the logic of conventional texts needs to be demonstrated and deconstructed from the onset of literacy instruction. . . . In classrooms, this entails nothing less than naming and renaming, ordering and reordering, using and discarding of the parts. You can't play the game unless you know the rules. But to change the game, you gotta know that the rules are neither static nor non-negotiable. (Luke, 1993, p. 150)

To change the game of schooling and then society at the turn of the twentieth century, advocates propose to renegotiate its rules to "a curriculum grounded in the lives of students, dialogue, a question/problem posing approach, an emphasis on critiquing bias and attitudes, and teaching activism for social justice (Peterson, 1994, p. 13).

When examining students' lives, advocates acknowledge that many different discourses influence students' identities and lives. These discourses—ways of using language, of thinking, and of acting—identify one as a member of a socially meaningful group. Thus our choices, language, values, and actions are not solely our own; rather, they represent our discourse groups. As Gee puts it:

> It is sometimes helpful to say that it is not individuals who speak and act, but rather historically and socially defined discourses speak to each other through individuals. . . . Americans tend to be very focused on the individual, and thus often miss the fact

that the individual is simply the meeting point of many, sometimes conflicting, socially and historically defined discourses.
(1992, p. 23)

To these critical descendants of Dewey, language education becomes the exploration of various discourses encoded in printed
texts, films and other media, social mores, institutional charters
and organizations, and everyday language practices in order to
see how language can be used for and against various social
groups. Because all discourse groups do not possess the same
political, social, and economic power, language can offer opportunities for and constraints on social groups' abilities to participate actively in the civic life of their community and in larger
political units. Along the way, teachers and students explore their
differences, where those and other differences come from, and
how we can work together with those differences to enlarge the
corpus of groups engaged in civic life. Through these explorations, teachers and students seek to reposition the concept of difference in our lives. While previously in language education
difference was a means for dividing and sorting, now it can become a symbol of human rights in service of exposing contradictions between the social forms provided for us and the human
capabilities that could be encouraged in a free society.

Negotiating Cultural Freedom within an Economic State

New expressionist and new Deweyan positions are direct assaults
on Jefferson's configuration of the dialectic for schooling. Although new expressionists cling to the hope of the Enlightenment—that science will somehow justify their actions and beliefs
(e.g., Goodman, 1989)—they recognize that a science of freedom cannot be discovered. Rather, for new expressionists, freedom—like all social relationships—is negotiated locally among
individuals. The main tool for negotiation is an individual's ability to define and express his or her needs and desires within relationships. Within new expressionism, differences may be
recognized and acknowledged, but there appear to be few mechanisms developed to accommodate the unequal starting points of
different discourse groups (Delpit, 1988; Gilbert, 1991). Instead,

new expressionist learning communities seem predicated on personal structures for negotiation and inquiry that at best offer individual freedom while confirming the social status quo. If this is accurate, then the new expressionists have inadequate theories of both freedom and the state to meet the challenges of the twenty-first century.

New Deweyans maintain that negotiations of current social expectations, values, and norms are not conducted among equals, and therefore the resulting institutions, laws, and mores distribute benefits unequally among social groups. Even negotiations that appear to benefit the disadvantaged can be understood as acts in the best interests of elites (see Bell, 1992). Current inequalities, they argue, are based on past negotiations in which privileged positions have become regularized over time until social advantages appear to be natural and unchangeable rather than human artifacts and thus malleable. New Deweyans seek to expose and challenge these privileges as well as to describe and resist the way the social infrastructure works against the interests of the majority to the benefit of the few. Naming the source of these advantages has become a point of contention within this group, particularly since the "end of communism":

> The "struggle for recognition" is fast becoming the paradigmatic form of political conflict in the late twentieth century. Demands for "recognition of difference" fuel struggles of groups mobilized under the banners of nationality, ethnicity, "race," gender, and sexuality. In these "post-socialist" conflicts, group identity supplants exploitation as the fundamental injustice. And cultural recognition displaces socioeconomic redistribution as the remedy for injustice and the goal of political struggle. (Fraser, 1995, p. 68)

In this way, marginalized groups seek to move to the center of civic life in order to secure an equal share in social negotiations and benefits. These struggles for recognition have invited social groups to look inward to learn their own histories, cultures, and literatures and to act outwardly to demand the right to be represented accurately and fairly as well as to be acknowledged as different and equal. Advocates propose forms of language education that accommodate differences in language practices (e.g.,

Au, 1995), cultural patterns (e.g., Moll, 1992), and literary forms (Harris, 1993). These programs serve as a microcosm of wider struggles because the freedoms to be culturally different in language and literacy and equal participants in education are negotiated through and against the previously exclusionary policies and norms of schooling. That is, freedoms are found in group identities and power that simultaneously distinguish groups from and connect them with others. Moreover, the struggle for recognition within schools requires marginalized groups to attempt policy reform within an institution primarily organized around racist, sexist, homophobic, and the like projects to exclude groups or to standardize language, culture, values, and behaviors. Thus the challenge for recognition seeks to expand the theories of both freedom and the state in the Jeffersonian dialectic for schooling.

Yet, at the turn of the twenty-first century, the struggle for recognition on the cultural level is not sufficient, because it occurs in a world of exacerbated material inequality in income, property, access to well-paid work, education, health care, leisure time, caloric intake, exposure to environmental toxins, and even life expectancy. Although these inequalities are connected to cultural recognition, they are more socioeconomic in nature, predicated on issues of class interests, exploitation, and maldistribution. Solutions require redistribution of wealth within an environment that is openly hostile to such action—at least, if redistribution is downward. (The U.S. Congress exposes its class priorities in its current efforts to cut capital gains taxes, which will benefit only the richest 7 percent of Americans while reducing the welfare benefits of the bottom 15 percent.) These social issues cut across cultural boundaries, making larger coalitions of resistance possible. Blurring cultural boundaries, however, must be wed to recognizing and honoring cultural difference within classes—something that has been ignored in the past.

The central challenge we face today—how to negotiate cultural freedoms within a state constructed around economic and political justice—was the unacknowledged challenge which most Americans ignored at the turn of the eighteenth and nineteenth centuries. After two hundred years, the science of freedom put forth by Enlightened American thinkers has produced only a narrow legal equality (with recent wavering about the rights of the citizenship of children born in the United States to illegal immigrants) through a system of laws, policies, and institutions that has been used to exclude the majority of Americans from broader political and economic justice and cultural freedoms. Although these negotiations have been so lopsided that at times we become aware of the injustices, inequalities, and cultural control, we nevertheless believe ours to be the most equal and free society on earth.

The struggle for language educators, whether progressive or otherwise, is to find productive ways to make our work relevant to these challenges. Clearly, neotraditionals and new experimentalists favor the state over individual freedom. At present, the new expressionists seem captivated by individual freedoms or are unimpressed with the urgency of these dilemmas of justice. The strategies of both groups seem to further the social and political status quo. At this point, only the new Deweyans, with their attention to deconstruction of texts, recognition of discourse, and promotion of diverse civic agency, seem to be taking steps that may alter the dialectic between the state and individual freedom (see, for example, the collective work of the Rethinking Schools group at www.rethinkingschools.org).

With the advantage of over two hundred years of experience with Jeffersonian ideals, we face a new century with a tempered enthusiasm for the assumptions of the Enlightenment but with unbridled hope for the future. We know that we must redefine schooling as a public sphere of popular control in which dilemmas of recognition and redistribution are addressed seriously and openly by those directly affected by them. We must adapt C. Wright Mills's definition—"freedom is, first of all, the chance to formulate the available choices, to argue over them—and then the opportunity to choose" (1959, p. 162). Marginalized groups must have the chance to negotiate available choices *as they are formulated*—to be recognized as having that right, ability, and freedom. Schools, as representatives of the state, must become sponsors of this enlarged practice of cultural freedom. Under the rhetorical cover of Jefferson's original dialectic, such action would help redistribute power and cultural capital.

When we open our classroom doors to study and participate in the languages of the world, we begin to participate actively in the civic lives of our community and beyond—not in the three-tiered system that Jefferson proposed and condoned, but in concert with our students, working out what civic life ought to entail. We know we are not ignorant, just inexperienced. We know we are not free unless we participate actively in the decisions that affect our lives. And we know that civilization will become what we help to make it. Language educators can be at the center of the social dialectic between freedom and the state in the twenty-first century.

References

Adams, C. (1879/1935). The new departure in the common schools of Quincy. *Elementary School Journal, 35*, 495–504.

Au, K. (1995). Multicultural perspectives on literacy research. *Journal of Reading Behavior, 27*, 85–100.

Bagley, W. (1911). *Classroom management: Its principles and technique.* New York: Macmillan.

Bell, D. (1992). *Faces at the bottom of the well.* New York: Basic Books.

Bennett, W. (1993). *The book of virtues: A treasury of great moral stories.* New York: Simon & Schuster.

Bloom, A. (1988). *The closing of the American mind.* New York: Simon & Schuster.

Callahan, R. (1964). *Education and the cult of efficiency: A study of the social forces that have shaped the administration of the public schools.* Chicago: University of Chicago Press.

Church, S. (1996). *The future of whole language: Reconstruction or self-destruction?* Portsmouth, NH: Heinemann.

Cohen, S. (1974). *Education in the United States: A documentary history.* New York: Random House.

Crawford, P. (1995). *Reading bound: A deconstruction of the basal teachers' manual.* Unpublished doctoral dissertation, Penn State University.

Curti, M. (1935). *The social ideas of American educators.* New York: Scribner's.

Delpit, L. (1988). The silenced dialogue: Power and pedagogy in educating other people's children. *Harvard Educational Review, 58*, 280–98.

Dewey, J. (1891). *Outlines of a critical theory of ethics*. Ann Arbor: Michigan Register.

Dewey, J. (1897). The university elementary school: Studies and methods. *University Record, 1*, 42–47.

Dewey, J. (1901). The situation as regards the course of study. *Educational Review, 22*, 26–49.

Dewey, J. (1928). Progressive education and the science of education. *Progressive Education, 5*, 197–204.

Dewey, J., & Dewey, E. (1915). *Schools of to-morrow*. New York: Dutton.

Dewey, J., & Tufts, J. (1908). *Ethics*. New York: Henry Holt.

Diegmueller, K. (1996). A war of words: Whole language under siege. *Education Week, 15*(1), 14–15.

Du Bois, W. E. B. (1903). *The souls of black folks*. New York: New American Library.

Edelsky, C., Altwerger, B., & Flores, B. (1991). *Whole language: What's the difference?* Portsmouth, NH: Heinemann.

Finkelstein, B. (1979). *Regulated children, liberated children: Education in psychohistorical perspective*. New York: Psychohistory Press.

Finkelstein, B. (1989). *Governing the young: Teacher behavior in popular primary schools in nineteenth-century United States*. New York: Falmer Press.

Foorman, B. (1995). Research on "the great debate": Code-oriented versus whole language approaches to reading instruction. *School Psychology Review, 24*, 326–42.

Fraser, N. (1995). From redistribution to recognition? Dilemmas of justice in a "post-socialist" age. *New Left Review, 212*, 68–93.

Gee, J. P. (1992). What is literacy? In P. Shannon (Ed.), *Becoming political: Readings and writings in the politics of literacy education* (pp. 21–28). Portsmouth, NH: Heinemann.

Gilbert, P. (1991). Writing pedagogy: Personal voices, truth telling and "real" texts. In C. Baker and A. Luke (Eds.), *Towards a critical sociology of reading pedagogy* (pp. 27–46). Philadelphia: John Benjamins.

Goodman, K. (1986). *What's whole in whole language?* Portsmouth, NH: Heinemann.

Goodman, K. (1989). Whole-language research: Foundations and development. *Elementary School Journal, 90,* 207–21.

Hakim, S., Seidenstat, P., & Bowman, G. (Eds.). (1994). *Privatizing education and educational choice: Concepts, plans, and experiences.* Westport, CT: Praeger.

Harris, V. (Ed.) (1993). *Teaching multicultural literature in grades K–8.* Norwood, MA: Christopher-Gordon.

Harris, W. T. (1895). *Report on the committee of fifteen on elementary education.* Boston: New England.

Hirsch, E. D. (1987). *Cultural literacy: What every American needs to know.* Boston: Houghton Mifflin.

Jefferson, T. (1961). A bill for the more general diffusion of knowledge. In G. Lee (Ed.), *Crusade against ignorance: Thomas Jefferson on education.* New York: Teachers College Press. (Original work published 1779)

Jefferson, T. (1961). Notes on the state of Virginia. In G. Lee (Ed.), *Crusade against ignorance: Thomas Jefferson on education* (pp. 90–96). New York: Teachers College Press. (Original work published 1785)

Kolko, G. (1963). *The triumph of conservatism: A re-interpretation of American history, 1900–1916.* New York: Free Press.

Lewis, D. (1993). *W. E. B. DuBois: Biography of a race, 1868–1919.* New York: Henry Holt.

Locke, J. (1964). Some thoughts concerning education. In P. Gay (Ed.), *John Locke on education* (pp. 19–176). New York: Teachers College Press. (Original work published in 1693)

Luke, A. (1993). Stories of social regulation: The micropolitics of classroom narrative. In B. Green (Ed.), *The insistence of the letter: Literacy studies and curricular theorizing* (pp. 137–53). Pittsburgh: University of Pittsburgh Press.

Madison, J. (1964). Factions: Their cause and control. In A. Hamilton, J. Jay, & J. Madison, *The federalist papers* (pp. 16–24). New York: Washington Square Press. (Original work published 1787)

Mayhew, K., & Edwards, A. (1936). *The Dewey school: The laboratory school of the University of Chicago, 1896–1903*. New York: Appleton-Century.

McGuffey, W. H. (1843). *McGuffey's newly revised eclectic second reader*. Cincinnati, OH: Winthrop B. Smith.

Mills, C. W. (1959). *The sociological imagination*. New York: Oxford University Press.

Moll, L. (1992). Bilingual classroom studies and community analysis: Some recent trends. *Educational Researcher, 21*, 20–24.

Parker, F. W. (1894). *Talks on pedagogics: An outline of the theory of concentration*. New York: E. L. Kellogg.

Parker, F. W. (1902). Editorial. *Elementary School Teacher, 2*, 754.

Patridge, L. (1885). *The "Quincy Method" illustrated: Pen photographs from the Quincy schools*. New York: E. L. Kellogg.

Pearson, P. D. (1990). Introduction. In M. Adams, *Beginning to read: Thinking and learning about print* (pp. iii–ix). Cambridge, MA: MIT Press.

Peterson, B. (1994). Teaching for social justice: Making connections, examining the world. *Rethinking Schools, 8*, 10–13.

Rudolf, F. (Ed.). (1965). *Essays on education in the early republic*. Cambridge, MA: Belknap Press of Harvard University Press.

Schlesinger, A. (1968). *The American as reformer*. New York: Atheneum.

Shannon, P., & Goodman, K. (1994). *Basal readers: A second look*. Katonah, NY: Richard C. Owen.

Smith, N. B. (1934). *American reading instruction*. New York: Silver, Burdett.

Tucker, M. (1984, November). Readying future workers to move from challenge to challenge. Paper presented at the meeting of the Project on Information Technology and Education, Rochester, NY.

Webster, N. (1974). On the education of youth in America. In S. Cohen (Ed.), *Education in the United States: A documentary history* (pp. 94–96). New York: Random House. (Original work published 1790)

What Works. (1986). Washington, DC: U.S. Department of Education.

CHAPTER TWO

Progressivism, Critique, and Socially Situated Minds

JAMES PAUL GEE

University of Wisconsin at Madison

Progressive Ideas and Critique

Educational progressivism is built around a few core ideas. Each of these embodies a double-sidedness that has historically invited specific criticisms, many of which are still in evidence today. This double-sidedness stems from the fact that, for all their virtues, progressive ideas involve, in theory and practice, real dangers and risks. In fact, progressivism comes all the more clearly into focus when we consider the "sensitive" points to which its critics have historically been drawn.

In this chapter, after a brief consideration of several core ideas of progressivism, I concentrate my efforts on the idea of "immersion" as a form of teaching and learning. This concept is, I argue, central to progressivism and its contemporary embodiments. It is also at the heart of the two major contemporary critiques—beyond old-style, right-wing calls for "back to basics"—of progressive pedagogies. Using a particular perspective on mind and society, I argue that immersion of a certain sort is essential to learning, but that contemporary critiques of progressivism identify necessary supplements to immersion.

Before turning to a discussion of immersion, consider the ways in which core progressive ideas have inevitably invited specific criticisms. Take, for instance, the idea of "child centeredness." This idea, while honoring the child's goals, has always invited charges of cognitive and moral "permissiveness." It has also, in practice, encouraged some educators to refuse to provide direction, seeing teaching as a form of imposition (or worse, to use child-centered values to hide intellectual or pedagogical incompetence). Ironically, most of the other core progressive ideas have led, as we will see, to the reverse charge: the claim that they are built around a process of hidden indoctrination of learners.

The very notion of "reform," which connotes improvement and renewal, is itself historically double-sided for the progressive movement. Historically, starting in the 1890s and reaching its peak in the 1920s, the idea of progressive social and educational reform was tightly linked to the idea that modern science and technology, applied to every area of life, would lead to "progress," greater equality, and a better life for all (Montgomery, 1994; on the history of educational progressivism more generally, see Cremin, 1988; Cuban, 1984; Kliebard, 1986; Tanner & Tanner, 1990; Tyack, 1974). Progressivism was, at its outset, a modernist movement, and it has always invited attacks that decry modernism and its trust in the rational powers of "educated" people.

One wing of the reform movement, in fact, linked reform to the use of modern science and technology, as well as a new child psychology, to achieve greater "efficiency" (a highly valued word at the time) at work and at school (Montgomery, 1994; Pinar, Reynolds, Slattery, & Taubman, 1995). Tying education to the child's developmental stage, goals, and interests (as these were understood by psychology) was thought to make the child a more effective and efficient learner. In fact, Frederick Taylor, the man who pioneered the sorts of "efficient" control we associate with the industrial assembly line ("Fordism"), thought of himself as introducing reforms that would improve the lives of working people (by allowing workers to do their jobs more "rationally" and with less effort), not as augmenting the controls of bosses. The links between the core idea of reform and other ideas such as "progress" and trust in science, technology, and psychology have always been seen as problematic by some, more so today when such trust is at a historically low ebb.

Another core progressive idea whose double-sidedness has invited critique is the emphasis progressivists put on "growth" and on the "experience" of the child. In fact, these notions have historically invited a bevy of criticism (Pinar et al., 1995). First, they invite charges of individualism, of an overemphasis on the individual apart from the socializing forces of the group. Second, in their focus on the unfolding of the child's "nature," as well as on the child's "inner experience," they invite charges of covert manipulation of the child's development toward some "hidden" goal embodied in the teacher and his or her construction of the pedagogical environment. The image of a gardener, directing a plant's growth along certain domesticated lines, comes readily to mind.

Third, the progressivist movement always harbored a social wing that stressed the growth of the individual in the context of socialization within and adjustment to a democratic community. But this idea invited charges of hegemonically norming the individual to the values of a civic community that claimed "universal validity" while, in reality, representing the values of a specific group (e.g., the mainstream middle class). Indeed, this problem sullied the very notion of "democracy" itself—a key idea to the progressives (Dewey, 1916; Tanner, 1991). It also invited the charge that, in the guise of active participation on the part of the child, the classroom was made a replica of the existing order of inequality in the wider society and a fertile nursery for the tacit indoctrination of children into the norms and values of that wider society. The notion of "democracy" is ever more suspect (by the Right and by the Left) in our increasingly hierarchical, secular, and market-driven society (Gee, Hull, & Lankshear 1996).

Finally, the progressive emphasis on breaking down the boundaries between school and life—its stress on "learning as living" (Dewey, 1916)—has invited the charge that progressive schools co-opt the duties of the family (Montgomery, 1994). Worse, it has invited charges that progressivist reforms extend the reach of the school into nearly every aspect of the life of its students and their families. In our increasingly pluralistic and divided society, such schools are often seen as undermining family or cultural values that vary from the "mainstream."

The Attack of the Linguists

One recent criticism of progressive pedagogies is new. An analogy between language acquisition and other forms of later learning has been at the heart of many "progressive" pedagogies (see Cazden, 1972, pp. 139–42 for early and critical discussion of this issue; see also Edelsky, 1996). Children acquire their native languages not by direct instruction (indeed, overt correction seems to have little impact on them) but by being immersed in rich, meaningful, and natural communicative settings. So, by analogy, it might be argued that in other areas, outside first-language acquisition, humans learn best when their learning is self-motivated and self-directed in "natural" settings and not "imposed" on them by direct instruction.

This analogy was recently strongly attacked by a number of linguists in a letter to the Massachusetts commissioner of education (July 12, 1995) signed by "forty Massachusetts specialists in linguistics and psycholinguistics" (see also Melvold & Pesetsky, 1995; the controversy has continued in discussions on the Internet). And, indeed, I myself have argued that there are important aspects of first-language acquisition that are not analogous to other forms of later learning (Gee, 1994). One of these involves biology. Children acquiring language are confronted with lots of "data"—the language they hear everywhere around them—though of course these data always comprise a very small subset of the infinite set of sentences in any language (there is no longest sentence). A great many hypotheses can be made about or patterns identified in the "rules" that underlie the data (i.e., what generalizations there are in the data), especially given the creativity of the human mind and the infinity of language. Therefore, *something* must "constrain" the child's "search space" so that the child does not "waste" time considering fruitless or misleading hypotheses.

Many linguists argue that the "something" that "helps" the child out here is in the child's genes. While there are debates as to what and how much of language is biologically specified, few doubt that the course of human evolution has made us humans "motivated" and "good at" acquiring our first languages (Bickerton, 1981; Chomsky, 1986; Pinker, 1994; Scovel, 1988; see Gee, 1986, for an overview of some of the issues). For other sorts of learning—e.g., physics or literacy—evolution has not had enough time to build into human biology such a substantive and specific "step up," since things such as writing and physics have simply not been around long enough in human history.

The point put (too) bluntly is this: humans have an "instinct" for language, and this greatly aids them in its acquisition (as certain species of birds have an instinct that helps them build their characteristic nests or sing their distinctive songs). We humans have no such instinct for acquiring a school subject such as physics or literature, or for learning to read and write. As a result, there is far more variation in how people acquire these things than there is in how they acquire their first languages (the "failure rate," for instance, is dramatically different in the two cases).

It is important to bear in mind that modeling or overt correction by caregivers is, in all likelihood, not enough to "scaffold" children into grammar (and, in the case of correction, not necessary). When linguists make arguments about the biological capacity for grammar, they have in mind quite abstract properties of the system, properties not plausibly open to modeling or any form of "teaching" (however indirect).

For example, consider the following facts: The "subordinate clause introducer" ("complementizer") "that" is optional in English—e.g., both "Mary thinks <u>that</u> someone lied" and "Mary thinks someone lied" are grammatical. However, "that" *cannot* be present if the subject of the subordinate clause is "moved": "Who does Mary think <u>that</u> lied?" is ungrammatical, while "Who does Mary think lied" is fine (note that "who" is understood as the subject of "lied" but is not positioned before this verb). These facts, linguists argue, follow from rather deep properties of "language design," rooted in our biological capacity for language, and not from trivial properties of English alone. Indeed, such facts have striking (but sometimes abstractly defined) "resonances" across many (unrelated) languages. They are not, however, plausibly things that we all acquired (as uniformly and automatically as we have) by modeling or correction on the part of caregivers.

Linguists' argument about children's biological or genetic capacity for language and literacy addresses a very real problem. It demands that progressivists develop a coherent theory of instructional "guidance" for literacy and school subjects that can play the focusing ("scaffolding") role that human biology plays in first-language acquisition (Gee, 1994).

Some people, however, have taken the issue further than this and argued for a return to phonics and lots of direct instruction in literacy education. Unfortunately, when stripped to its bare essentials, the argument for this strategy is a simple fallacy, which takes the following form (David Pesetsky, personal communication, assures me that he does not hold this argument, though some people may have construed the linguists' claims in this way. Given the linguists' view on reading, however [discussed in the next section], there is ample danger of understanding their position in terms of just such an argument, and it has, in fact, been so understood.):

Premise 1:	Language is an "instinct."
Premise 2:	Anything that is an "instinct" is not acquired by direct instruction.
Conclusion 1:	Language is not acquired by direct instruction.
Premise 3:	Literacy is not an "instinct."
Conclusion 2:	Literacy is acquired by direct instruction (such as phonics, and not the sort of immersion characteristic of first-language acquisition).

Premises 1 and 2 are true and conclusion 1 is valid, but, although premise 3 is also true, conclusion 2 is most certainly not valid. To say that literacy is not an instinct still leaves open the question of whether it is acquired by immersion or direct instruction, since premise 2 addresses only instincts and is silent on noninstincts. Of course, the argument assumes (without explicitly stating) the premise that there is a "forced choice" here: either something is an instinct and acquired through immersion or it is not an instinct and is acquired through direct instruction. This premise needs an argument; it is not, on its face, obviously true.

For example, while language in the sense of "grammar" is biologically "programmed," cross-cultural variation in storytelling is not so obviously programmed. Nonetheless, storytelling is for the most part acquired through immersion in practice (e.g., consider the early linear "essayist" stories of not yet literate children from certain school-affiliated homes versus the "oral literature" sort of stories told by some other children

[Gee, 1996]). And, of course, there are many possible mixes between immersion and direct instruction; it is probably only these that are really worth arguing over.

Additionally, the entire issue raised by the linguists' argument is confused by the way in which the word *language* is used. The argument for the biological basis of language is an argument about *grammar,* not everything else that goes under the rubric "language." To a generative linguist, "grammar" names the *structural* properties of *sentences* (phonological, morphological, syntactic, and logical). It is about grammar in this sense that generative linguists make biological claims (and only grammar in this sense; even more specifically, only the parts of grammar relevant to the basic design of all languages). Properties of meaning beyond the "logical form" of sentences and nearly all properties of "discourse"(both in terms of how language is put to use in context and how sentences are connected to form "texts") do not fall under "grammatical theory" as generative linguists conceive it. But meaning and discourse are obviously crucial to literacy (Gee, 1996).

Let me point out as well that, unlike Hallidian linguists, Chomskian linguists are not functionalists. A functionalist is concerned with how the form (structure) of sentences and larger linguistic units (e.g., genres) align with various communicational and interactional functions they are designed to serve. Chomskian linguists are not concerned with this, because they do not believe that the basic design of language is primarily driven by the functions (communicative or otherwise) it serves (Chomsky, 1975). They make no claims, biological or otherwise, about communicational, social, and interactional functions. Clearly, however, the requisite analogy for progressives is between how children acquire the *functions* of language and how they learn to function with other sorts of representational, activity, and knowledge systems later in life, including at school (Halliday & Martin, 1993).

Linguists, then, in making their argument about phonics, are extrapolating from the acquisition of grammar (narrowly defined) to an enterprise—namely, the acquisition of literacy—that not only goes far beyond grammar, but is also ultimately rooted in function, discourse, and culture. Their argument does hold for the claim that nothing in our biology "helps" us humans acquire the "code" (i.e., the formal properties) of literacy, such as the ways in which sound and print as *formal* systems "match up." Thus, as I have already said, *something* is required to make up for this absence of biology. This still leaves wide open the question of what this *something* is or should be (i.e., what sorts of pedagogies are most efficacious for acquiring the code). It also leaves wide open the much larger question of how people acquire different "discourse systems"—that is, different socioculturally situated, functional "ways with words" in the world.

Reading and American and Australian Linguists

In their letter to the Massachusetts commissioner of education, the Massachusetts linguists claim that the state's new draft "Curriculum on Language Arts" "replaces the common-sense view of reading as the decoding of notated speech with a surprising view of reading as directly 'constructing meaning'." This remark misses decades of work on sociocultural approaches to language and literacy, as well as work on socially situated cognition (see Barton, 1994; Edelsky, 1996; Gee, 1996; and Street, 1995, for overviews of a copious literature).

At the heart of the matter is this: Is reading primarily the acquisition of a skill (the Massachuetts linguists' view) or the acquisition of a "culture" (the sociocultural perspective on literacy)? Sociocultural work holds that learning to read is a process of acculturation into different *social practices*, each of which recruits its own distinctive style of language, what we can call its own characteristic "social language" (in speech and writing). A focus on social practices and social languages changes the character of traditional debates about literacy. The phonics debate is about how people (should) learn the mapping between two formal systems: between phonemes (basic sounds like /s/ and /k/) and graphemes (letters such as "c"). But the problem of such form-to-form mapping is much more pervasive in language and literacy acquisition than the phonics debate lets on.

All social languages, whether the language of physicists or of street gangs, involve a mapping from the lexical, morphological, grammatical, and discourse resources of the language as a whole

("English") to the distinctive *configuration* of formal features of the particular social language. This point sounds a bit arcane, so let me make it concrete with an example. Consider the following sentence (adapted from Halliday & Martin 1993):

> Lung cancer death rates are clearly associated with an increase in smoking.

A bevy of linguistic features marks this sentence as part of a distinctive academic social language. These include a heavy subject ("lung cancer death rates"), deverbal nouns ("increase," "smoking"), a complex compound noun ("lung cancer death rates"), a low transitive relational predicate ("are associated with"), passive or passivelike voice ("are associated"), the absence of agency (no mention of who does the associating), an abstract noun ("rates"), and an assertive modifier to the verb ("clearly").

No one grammatical feature marks the social language of this sentence. Rather, all of these features (and a great many more, including many discourse-level features in longer stretches of text) form a distinctive *configuration*—a correlation or, better, co-relation that marks the social language. And, just like the mapping between phonemes and graphemes, this involves a form-form mapping: a mapping from formal features such as deverbal nouns, heavy subject, passive voice, etc., to a distinctive configuration of features that represents the social language.

This sort of form-form mapping is no easier for learners than phonics mapping. In fact, it is a good deal *harder. Far more people fail to acquire a distinctive type of literacy because they cannot master such "higher order" form-form mappings (mappings that lead to the recognition of social languages and genres of spoken and written language) than because they cannot master the phonics mapping.

This fact has led linguists in Australia to start the current "genre debate" (Cope & Kalantzis, 1993a, 1993b; Halliday & Martin, 1993). Some of these linguists claim that the grammatical and discourse features characteristic of genres (descriptions, reports, expositions, narratives, etc.) and social languages (e.g., various academic languages) need to be taught overtly through rather general rules. Their argument is a direct analog, at a higher level, of the Massachusetts linguists' arguments about the pho- neme-grapheme mapping.

But formal relationships, like those discussed in regard to the sentence about lung cancer, do not exist and therefore are not learned outside the distinctive social practices of which they are an integral part. They *are* part and parcel of the very "voice" or "identity" of people who speak, write, think, act, value, and live a particular way for a given time and place. Learning such rela- tionships is part of what it means to learn to recognize the social context one is in (and helping to create). What could it possibly *mean* to learn such things *outside* such contexts?

To their credit, the Australian linguists actually know this. They are simply at times overly optimistic about giving people an "overt grammar" of genres. Unfortunately, genres-in-action are too subtle, situated, and complex for this. The Australian linguists are also too optimistic in thinking that this overt in- struction will "stick" in practice. Unfortunately, learning does not work that way, as I argue in the following sections. Nonethe- less, they have pointed to the importance of getting teachers and learners to pay attention to "form-in-action-in-constructing-mean- ing-and-contexts." We just cannot take any one part of this "long word" out and still have "reading" or "language" in the sense of discourse.

In the end, we can say that general rules do not seem to pur- chase much. The configuration of features that mark a genre or social language is too complex and *too situated in the specific context they are helping to create* (after all, there is no such thing as a "general social science context") to be open to much gener- alized and rote learning. By all means, the mentor needs to focus the learner on, and scaffold the acquisition of, such features, but this needs to be done in situated social practice and as part of the acquisition of a socially situated identity.

Hiding the "Rules" and Indoctrinating the Child

Apart from right-wing calls for a return to "skill and drill," there are two important contemporary critiques of progressive pedagogies, both of which are variants on criticisms lodged repeatedly in the history of the movement. The first of these is the claim that progressive pedagogies "hide" the "rules of the game" from minority and lower socioeconomic learners (Cazden, 1992; Christie, 1990; Cope & Kalantzis, 1993b; Delpit, 1986, 1988, 1993, 1995; Freedman, 1993; Martin, 1990, 1991; Williams & Colomb, 1993). If we know rules and strategies about the sorts of thought, action, and language that bring success in school and "power" in the wider society, why not, critics ask, just *tell* learners, rather than leave them guessing amidst immersion in complex activities? This is particularly important for learners from families that do not already incorporate such "school-based" rules and strategies into the early socialization of their children.

The second critique is the claim that progressive pedagogies force learners to "expose" their "inner experience" so that it can be tacitly "disciplined" to ensure that they become—in thought, word, deed, and emotion—acceptable sorts of "middle class" people (Gilbert & Taylor, 1991; Gore, 1993; Cope & Kalantzis, 1993a; Kalantzis & Cope, 1993; Luke & Gore, 1992; Walkerdine, 1988). Progressive pedagogies, it is claimed, are a form of "soft" and indirect coercion. In encouraging learners to openly express their own "voice" and the nature of their "inner experience" as they develop in all aspects of life (for example, through personal journal writing), the teacher can tacitly inspect these voices and experiences to ensure that learners are becoming the "right" sort of people inside and out. And, the argument goes, "right" here is defined as being like those children whose families have traditionally affiliated their homes and hearts with school-based, mainstream ways.

Both of these critiques center on the very real fact that "immersion" learning, which is the heart and soul of progressive pedagogies, is in reality a double-edged sword. Any viable defense of progressivism must, I believe, involve a defense of immersion as central to successful learning (and the argument, as we have seen, cannot rely on facile analogies between acquiring a native language and later learning in life). At the same time, a viable defense must go beyond "pure progressivism"—immersion with little overt guidance and instruction—to squarely face the dangers and limitations of immersion. Any effective and moral pedagogy must be able to demonstrate how learners gain each of three things: (1) effective and efficient mastery in practice; (2) the ability to talk and think about practice accurately and explicitly (metaknowledge); and (3) the ability to critique practice and its relationships to larger systems of knowledge and power. It is to these issues I now turn.

Immersion: Perils and Possibilities

We acquire new concepts throughout our lives, and the concepts we have already acquired change dynamically as we acquire new ones since concepts are linked in complex networks of association and contrast. The way in which children acquire the concepts (meanings) associated with words can provide important insights into how the mind works in all efficacious learning.

Consider in this light the case of a little girl learning the word *shoe*. At first she uses the word only for the shoes in her mother's closet. Eventually, however, she "overextends" (E. Clark, 1993) the meaning of the word beyond the usage adults would employ. She uses it not only in situations where shoes are involved, but also while handling her teddy bear's shoeless feet, passing a doll's arm to an adult to be refitted on the doll, putting a sock on a doll, and looking at a picture of a brown beetle (Griffiths, 1986, pp. 296–97).

At this point, the little girl associates the word with a variety of different contexts, each of which contains one or more salient features that could trigger the use of the word. The picture of the beetle is associated with the word *shoe* presumably by virtue of features such as "shiny" and "hard" and "oval shaped"; the doll's arm merits the word *shoe* by virtue of features such as "fitable to the body" and "associated with a limb of the body," and so forth.

But this little girl must eventually come to realize that the features associated with a word are not just a list to be applied as they arise serially. Rather, they are *correlated* in certain ways and these correlations are important for applying the word (A. Clark, 1993). For example, in the case of shoes, features such as "hard," "shiny," "formal," "solid color," and "with thin laces" tend to go together to identify a certain set of shoes (formal shoes), and features such as "soft," "colored trim," "thick laces," and others tend to go together, identifying a different set of shoes (e.g., athletic shoes). Other feature correlations identify other sorts of shoes. Likewise, correlations such as "having a shape contoured to a human foot," "covering a significant amount of the foot," "flexible enough to fit on foot," but "relatively rigid" hang together in such a way that they identify a large class of the whole set of shoes, though even these features do not constitute a necessary and sufficient set of conditions for shoes in general. There are still borderline cases, such as moccasins (not really hard enough) and sandals (don't really cover enough). When the child reaches this point, she is finding *patterns* and *subpatterns* in the contexts in which the word *shoe* is used (Barsalou, 1992, chaps. 2 & 3).

But the child cannot stop with patterns. For adults, the concepts associated with words involve more than knowledge of feature correlations or patterns; they also involve a sometimes rather crude *explanation* of the correlations or patterns (Anglin, 1977; Keil, 1979, 1989): *Why* do these things hang together this way? That is, the correlated features (patterns) are required to make sense within some kind of cause-and-effect model or "theory" of the domain (here, feet and footwear). These "explanations," "models," or "theories," however, are very often tacit, partly or largely unconscious, or at least not easily articulated fully, and they are often incomplete in some ways. This does not mean that they are not also often very deep and rich in their own way.

In the case of the shoe example, the correlated features hang together as things to do with the fact that humans wear clothes (and shoes, in particular) for protection, but also for reasons of fashion. Different sorts of clothes are better or worse suited for different tasks and activities, and all these things vary with one's social or cultural group or subgroup. The child eventually comes to form a "theory" (really, we should say, comes to share with her community a more or less tacit "theory") of the shoe domain, a theory in which "higher-order" concepts such as "protection," "style," and "activities" play a role. This theory makes sense of the patterns the child has found, and in turn may well lead her to discern yet deeper or more complicated patterns. Since such theories are rooted in the practices of the sociocultural groups to which the learner belongs, they are sometimes referred to as "cultural models" (D'Andrade & Strauss, 1992; Holland & Quinn, 1987).

Because the world is full of potentially meaningful patterns and subpatterns in any domain, something must *guide* the learner in selecting which patterns and subpatterns to focus on (this is the same point drawn from the linguists' argument discussed earlier). Otherwise, given the creativity of the human mind, the learner will waste a great deal of time and effort dealing with spurious patterns. In fact, the learner could well never hit on the "right" patterns. This point is now well attested in computer simulations of pattern recognition: without guidance, such programs get lost amidst the wealth of possibilities (A. Clark, 1993; Dennett, 1995; Elman, 1991a, 1991b).

So a crucial question becomes, Where does the guidance come from when humans acquire meanings? The guidance resides in the cultural models of learners' sociocultural groups and the practices and settings in which such groups are rooted. Learners are guided to focus their attention and efforts in certain directions and not others; they are given feedback so that their patterns are adapted to the norms of their communities. Because the mind is a pattern recognizer, and because there are infinite ways to pattern features of the world, *of necessity,* though perhaps ironically, the mind is *social* (really, *cultural*), in the sense that sociocultural practices and settings guide and constrain the patterns of the learner's thoughts, actions, talk, values, and interactions. The point, then, is that in concept acquisition, immersion in experience and guidance are inextricably yoked.

Situated Meanings

Watching children who are acquiring concepts (word meanings) can help us to see that words fool us because they look general and make us believe that what the mind understands about a word is itself very general. But it is not. A word such as *coffee,* for instance, appears to be a "general term," standing for a general, decontextualized concept. But this is not true. Rather, the word *coffee* is associated with a number of more specific patterns of experience tied to particular contexts (Barsalou, 1987,

1991, 1992; A. Clark, 1993; Holland, Holyoak, Nisbett, & Thagard, 1986; Holyoak & Thagard, 1995). These patterns represent "mid-level" generalizations, not too specific and not too general, not totally contextualized and not totally decontextualized. The word *coffee* is associated with mid-level contextualized patterns such as the following: "coffee as a liquid that is found in various containers (e.g., coffee cups)"; "coffee as berries growing on a bush"; "coffee as a flavor of various foods, like ice-cream and candy"; and so forth. It is with these mid-level patterns—not a general, generic *coffee simpliciter*—that we operate in and on the world.

Although such mid-level patterns or "representations" are not referred to much in our everyday theories of the mind, nor in many formal theories in psychology and education, they are deeply important because they operate at the level at which the mind learns and works. Having been ignored until recently, such patterns do not even have an agreed on label as of yet. I call them here "mid-level situated meanings" ("situated meanings" for short). I also call them "assemblies" because human beings actively put these patterns together in their heads in response to features of the context they are experiencing or believe themselves to be experiencing. Situated meanings are crucial to learning; without them, learning is either too general or too specific and therefore useless for any "critical" or "deep" purpose.

Having argued that the meanings of words are not general concepts, we might very well ask why we have the *feeling* that the word *coffee* is associated with something more general, something that unites and rises above these mid-level patterns. Part of the answer is simply the fact that the single word exists, and we are misled by this to think that a single, general meaning exists. But another part of the answer is that the cultural model associated with the idea "coffee" gives us this feeling of generality. This model tells us that coffee grows, is picked, and is then prepared as beans or grain to be made into a drink, as well as into flavorings for other foods. It also tells us the when, where, who, and how of coffee from the perspective of our sociocultural groups (and their view of other groups).

It is important to realize that in order to "know" a situated meaning, it is not enough just to be able to "say certain words," e.g., "a cup of coffee." You must be able to recognize a pattern (e.g., a cup of coffee) in a variety of settings and variations—this is what makes situated meanings both contextualized and somewhat general. To see this point in another domain, one more important for education, consider the notion of "light" in physics. First of all, our everyday cultural model for "light" is not the same as the model (theory) of "light" in physics—that model is the specialized theory of electromagnetic radiation. It is more overt and articulated than most cultural models.

In physics, "light" is associated with a variety of situated meanings—e.g., as a bundle of waves of different wavelengths; as particles (photons) with various special (e.g., quantumlike) properties; as a beam that can be directed in various ways and for various purposes (e.g., lasers); as colors that can mix in various fashions; and more. If one wants to start "practicing" with light in order to learn physics, then one has to have experiences that lead to the acquisition of a few situated meanings (mid-level, contextualized patterns in one's pattern recognizer that can guide action). Otherwise, one cannot understand the theory of light, at least not in any way that could efficaciously guide pattern recognition, action, and reflection.

Although I have read and can recite much of the cultural theory behind light in physics, I must admit that I do not understand these various physically situated meanings sufficiently to have a deep understanding. To teach me, someone would have to ensure that I got experiences that allowed my mind/brain to recognize patterns at the level of situated meanings. And what does it mean to "recognize" these patterns? Situated meanings are correlations of various features: they are patterns that associate various features with each other, e.g., "light as a particle that behaves in terms of various sorts of contrived (experimental) observations in certain characteristic quantumlike ways." To recognize such things is to be able to recognize (reconstruct in terms of one's pattern-recognizing capabilities) and to act on and with these various features and their associations in a range of contexts. One's body and mind have to be able to be situated with—coordinated by and with—these correlated features in the world. Otherwise one has my sort of understanding. And, of course, the same is as true of literature (the study of textual worlds) as it is of physics (the study of physical worlds) or any other domain.

As it is, I cannot *really* understand what it means to say that light is a wave, even less that it is composed of various waves of different wavelengths, though I can *say* it. I simply have not had the action-and-reflection experiences that would have made this pattern, this correlation of features, meaningful and recognizable in a way useful for practice and thus for building on in the further development of patterns and theories. Likewise, I cannot be said to understand in any deep way the theory of light in physics (though I could pass some tests on it, perhaps), since that theory is what makes (partial) sense of the various patterns connected to the word *light*.

Situated meanings are, then, a product of the bottom-up action and reflection with which the learner engages the world and of the top-town guidance of the cultural models (theories) the learner is developing or being apprenticed to. Without both these levels, the learner ends up either with something too general (a cultural model or theory poorly connected to contextualized, mid-level patterns) or with something too specific and contextualized, something that functions too much like a proper name ("The word applies here; I don't really know why.").

I have demonstrated the absolute need for guidance (constraint, direction) as a supplement to being situated in experience. But I should be clear that this guidance, for any complex domain, rarely takes the form of explicit instruction, of putting everything into words. Given the embodied situatedness of meaning, the complexity of our cultural models, and their basis in our historic social practices, we can put only very small bits and pieces of our knowledge into words. We always do and mean far more than we can say; much of our knowledge is always tacit. Thus guidance often takes the form of the "master" saying, at the appropriate time and place, "Look at that" (see Schön, 1987, for excellent examples). Even our explicit wordings often have, in reality, a more demonstrative (focusing) function than an informational one.

For example, individuals who can recognize and write essays can articulate only a very small part of their knowledge. This is so in part because what they recognize and write are not "essays" in general, but always situated instances dovetailed to complex contexts, purposes, and specific communities. And whatever is general about essays is rooted in a complex and historically changing cultural model or theory, which is certainly not a set of rules, and much of which is stored in social practices and not individual minds. It would be a huge enterprise in its own right to uncover in overt form even a small part of this cultural model.

In the view of learning I am developing here, the vast portion of the "rules" are always "hidden." The key issue, as far as I am concerned, is to develop a theory of guidance and direction—of various forms of "scaffolding"—that goes well beyond "explicit instruction" and lists of overt rules (as in phonics). Educational theory has barely begun on this task. While in the next section I deal with the issue of immersion as a form of indoctrination, that discussion also speaks to, though by no means "solves," the guidance question. Let me also point out that in current simulations of learning as pattern recognition, as well as simulations of other sorts of adaptive systems, the guidance question is a problem at the leading edge of the field: amidst many complex, branching possibilities, how are learners, and other systems, helped to find and stay on "fruitful" paths (Dennett, 1995; Holland, 1995; Kauffman, 1995)?

Reflection and Critique

The Russian psychologist Lev Vygotsky famously argued that the way in which human minds are "furnished" is by "internalizing" (the interactional semiotics of) the social world. This is, of course, another way of talking about immersion: "Any higher mental function was external [and] social before it was internal. It was once a social relationship between two people" (qtd. in Minick, 1987, p. 21).

Humans use language and other sign systems as social *tools* to accomplish various interactional tasks and to eventually internalize patterns of tools-within-contexts-of-use as pieces of (intra-)mental furniture, furniture that still bears the hallmarks of its interactive uses. For example, by scaffolded participation in the conversational routines of their social groups, children get themselves mentally and physically "in sync" with ways of introducing, sustaining, controlling, and changing topics. Eventually,

they internalize "rules" (patterns) about topics and topic formation in conversation, though they could never explicitly state these
rules.

This process, like the more general process of immersion, is a
double-edged sword: On the one hand, it demonstrates how crucial cooperative sociocultural interaction is, how riven the mind
already is with the experiential, the social, the cultural, the interactive, the ideological. On the other hand, this process of translating the social into the mental does not allow children to gain
much, if any, reflective or critical insight into the "representations" they have "swallowed." For example, the intricate "rules"
and patterns that "govern" conversational interaction, so well
laid bare by ethnomethodologists (e.g., Schenkein, 1978), are not
"rules" and patterns that we consciously "know" as we use or
"internalize" them. Nor do children have much reflective meta-
awareness of their communities' "tacit theories" of shoes or anything else. Nothing in the translation of the social and experiential
into the (intra-)mental would give rise to much reflective or critical awareness. Indeed, this is the broader context to the historic
claims that progressive pedagogies lead to indoctrination and
conformity.

Vygotsky deals with this issue by making a distinction between two types of concepts: "spontaneous" concepts, those over
which the child has no awareness, and those the child is aware
of. He calls concepts over which the child *does* have reflective
awareness and conscious control "nonspontaneous" concepts
(also, using the term loosely, "scientific" concepts, the kind found
in academic disciplines). And these, Vygotsky argues, one gets
only through working collaboratively with others who "know"
more than one does *and* (simultaneously) by means of "overt
instruction" that focuses on (a) putting things into words, (b)
conscious and intentional use of the new concepts, and (c) the
relationships among forms and meanings.

By working with others to carry out joint tasks that require
the use of concepts—Vygotsky's "scientific concepts"—in such a
way that the child is focused consciously on conceptual connections, verbal links, and connections between form and meaning
(not typical of everyday learning outside the classroom), the child
achieves something that he or she cannot yet do alone, namely

using concepts in a reflective, controlled, and conscious way. Vygotsky argues that this process eventually leads not just to the acquisition of some scientific concepts, but also to the transfer of this ability (conscious control and mastery) to the realm of everyday spontaneous concepts. The child's everyday concepts eventually become reorganized so that the child discovers the links and connections among the concepts; he or she comes to see them, and to operate with them, as a *system*. The everyday spontaneous concept no longer hooks directly and singly to the world of experience, but to experience by way of an entire network of relationships with other concepts.

To take one of Vygotsky's (1987) examples, the concept of "because" no longer hooks directly to concrete instances, but instead reaches reality only through an intricate network of relationships with other concepts (e.g., physical causation, responsibility, contingency, various sorts of noncausal associations, and so forth). The child becomes aware that the concept has something of a life of its own and that it is related in various ways to other concepts. In turn, the child can now control attributions of causal relationships with more reflection and mastery.

The relationship between scientific and spontaneous concepts eventually becomes a reciprocal one. Just as scientific concepts help spontaneous concepts become reorganized and more consciously controlled, so too increasing contact with experience and with spontaneous concepts helps scientific concepts become "grounded" in practice, thereby becoming more and more like spontaneous concepts without losing their more overt connections to other concepts and conceptual networks.

We still have to delineate just what sorts of overt forms of instruction are fruitful—again, the issue of guidance. Vygotsky clearly does not believe that rote drill or working on "irrelevant" materials is efficacious—he explicitly disowns such approaches (see Vygotsky, 1987, pp. 198–200). He does believe that the sorts of guidance that are needed involve the learner actively working on problems with others in order to accomplish tasks the learner cannot succeed at alone. But beyond that, Vygotsky clearly believes that learners must overtly focus on words, relationships, and forms and functions to supplement mere collaborative problem solving if they are to obtain conscious control and reflective awareness. Educators have not as of yet done at all well in cataloging these necessary "scaffolds."

Let me give one example. A fourth-grade teacher teaching science feels that any overt guidance is an "imposition." Thus she has the children engage in discussion and activities ("experiments") they have selected themselves. In one session, the children are discussing what makes things rust, and they have placed a variety of objects in water to see which sorts of things will rust on exposure to water. Once they have drained the water, there is rust on a metal bottle cap, but also rust on a plastic plate that the cap had been sitting on:

> JILL: But if we didn't put the metal things on there [the plastic plate], it [the plate] wouldn't be all rusty.
>
> PHILIP: But if we didn't put the water on there [the metal bottle cap], it [the cap] wouldn't be all rusty.

The children's everyday language obliterates a crucial distinction, and it obliterates the "underlying mechanisms" (here, cause and effect) inherent in physical science. Jill's and Philip's parallel constructions—in particular, their uses of "all rusty" and "if we didn't put . . . on, it wouldn't be . . ."—obscure the fact that these two linguistic devices here mean (or could mean) two very different things. Rusty metal things "cause" things such as plastic plates to "be all rusty" (namely, by physical contact) in quite a different way than water "causes" metal things to "be all rusty" (namely, by a chemical reaction). Further, the plastic plate and the metal bottle cap are "all rusty" in two crucially different senses. In Jill's statement, "all rusty" means (or could mean) "covered in rust," while in Philip's statement it means (or could mean) "a surface which has become rusted." In other words, the distinction between "having rust" (a state) and "having rusted" (a process) is obliterated.

Everyday language, in creating patterns and associations, is less careful about differences and underlying systematic relations, which are crucial to science. I am not denigrating everyday language. The very weaknesses I am pointing to here are, in other contexts, sources of great power and strength. My point is that this is a case where an overt focus on language might well have rendered meaning more "public" for the other children in the class, who may have been misled by their classmates' language. It also might have led the children to reflect more overtly on different "ways with words" in different domains with different interests. This is by no means a call for a grammar lesson—it is a call for the teacher to focus attention on what is otherwise a "transparent" medium (i.e., language and its relationship to diverse social practices and interests). An effective guidance device here might well have been the one popularized by Socrates, asking "What do you mean?," "Can you say it in other words?" (Havelock, 1963). Another guidance device might have been an overt focus on the nature of ambiguity and communication.

There is, however, a further problem: while a focus on language may help learners gain the sort of reflective awareness that immersion alone cannot offer, such reflective awareness by no means guarantees "critical" awareness in the sense of the ability and willingness to critique the workings of power and inequality. Reflective awareness and conscious control do not guarantee "critical literacy."

One approach to this problem, which I cannot develop fully here, is this: On any occasion when we write or read, speak or listen, we coordinate and get coordinated by specific social identities; specific ways of using language; and various objects, tools, technologies, and sites and institutions, as well as by other people's minds and bodies. Think, for example, of a how a scientist does "being a scientist" when running an experiment or how a gang member does "being a gang member" when making a drug sale.

Words (oral or written) themselves are not important but rather the larger and specific sociocultural coordinations of which they are a part and in which they gain their significance. I have elsewhere referred to these coordinations as Discourses, with a capital *D* (Gee, 1992, 1996). Some examples of Discourses include (enacting) being an American or a Russian; a man or a woman; a member of a certain socioeconomic class; a factory worker or a boardroom executive; a doctor or a hospital patient; a teacher, an administrator, or a student; a student of physics or a student of literature; a member of a sewing circle, a club, a street gang, a lunch-time social gathering; a regular at a local bar.

The problem with Discourses is that you cannot readily critique them while you are participating in them. Showing clear doubts about or lack of allegiance to an identity you are attempting to display and be recognized as is an excellent way to exit the Discourse altogether. One way of mitigating this problem is to engage in a form of critique I call "juxtaposition." In juxtaposition, we take a bit of one Discourse (e.g., a text, an object, a tool, a place) and juxtapose it to related bits of other Discourses. The Discourses we juxtapose might be contemporaneously related (such as biology and medicine; police and gangs in L.A.), or they might be historically related, including earlier and later stages of the same Discourse (e.g., consider how biology has viewed the female body at different periods).

Such juxtaposition is an inherently "metalevel" act. That is, in comparing two things, we need to think and talk in a "higher level" ("meta-level") language, one that encompasses them both. Juxtaposition is a good way for learners to gain "metacognitive" and "metalinguistic" skills (as well as "meta-Discourse" skills). These skills are a part of what reflective awareness is about, and so this form of critique has the virtue of helping to facilitate the growth of reflective awareness. Because it exposes differences, juxtaposition also allows us to see more clearly the interests, desires, and identities embedded in Discourses, and their hidden (and sometimes not so hidden) assumptions about values, social relationships, and the distribution of goods and status. This is what renders juxtaposition a potential form of critique.

Conclusion

Immersion is the sine qua non of efficacious learning, inside and outside school. But, like other core progressivist ideas, immersion involves very real risks that have historically invited criticisms of permissiveness, hiding the rules, and soft-touch indoctrination. Immersion needs to be supplemented by forms of guidance that constrain the search space, develop reflective awareness, and lead to critical awareness ("critical literacy"). A contemporary progressivism must begin to theorize immersion-with-supplements in ways that transcend sterile reruns of skill and drill, memorizing schemas and rules, or overt telling cut off from socioculturally situated experience.

References

Anglin, J. M. (1977). *Word, object, and conceptual development.* New York: Norton.

Barsalou, L. W. (1987). The instability of graded structure in concepts. In U. Neisser (Ed.), *Concepts and conceptual development: Ecological and intellectual factors in categorization* (pp. 101–40). Cambridge: Cambridge University Press.

Barsalou, L. W. (1991). Deriving categories to achieve goals. In G. H. Bower (Ed.), *The psychology of learning and motivation: Advances in research and theory: Vol. 27* (pp. 1–64). San Diego: Academic Press.

Barsalou, L. W. (1992). *Cognitive psychology: An overview for cognitive scientists.* Hillsdale, NJ: Lawrence Erlbaum.

Barton, D. (1994). *Literacy: An introduction to the ecology of written language.* Oxford: Blackwell.

Bickerton, D. (1981). *Roots of language.* Ann Arbor, MI: Karoma.

Cazden, C. B. (1972). *Child language and education.* New York: Holt, Rinehart and Winston.

Cazden, C. B. (1992). *Whole language plus: Essays on literacy in the United States and New Zealand.* New York: Teachers College Press.

Chomsky, N. (1975). *Reflections on language.* New York: Pantheon.

Chomsky, N. (1986). *Knowledge of language: Its nature, origin, and use.* New York: Praeger.

Christie, F. (Ed.). (1990). *Literacy for a changing world.* Hawthorn, Victoria: Australian Council for Educational Research.

Clark, A. (1993). *Associative engines: Connectionism, concepts, and representational change.* Cambridge, MA: MIT Press.

Clark, E. V. (1993). *The lexicon in acquisition.* Cambridge: Cambridge University Press.

Cope, B., & Kalantzis, M. (1993a). The power of literacy and the literacy of power. In B. Cope & M. Kalantzis (Eds.), *The powers of literacy: A genre approach to teaching writing* (pp. 63–89). Pittsburgh, PA: University of Pittsburgh Press.

Cope, B., & Kalantzis, M. (1993b). *The powers of literacy: A genre approach to teaching writing*. Pittsburgh, PA: University of Pittsburgh Press.

Cremin, L. A. (1988). *American education: The metropolitan experience, 1876–1980*. New York: Harper & Row.

Cuban, L. (1984). *How teachers taught: Constancy and change in American classrooms, 1890–1980*. New York: Longman.

D'Andrade, R., & Strauss, C. (Eds.). (1992). *Human motives and cultural models*. Cambridge: Cambridge University Press.

Delpit, L. D. (1986). Skills and other dilemmas of a progressive black educator. *Harvard Educational Review, 56*, 379–85.

Delpit, L. D. (1988). The silenced dialogue: Power and pedagogy in educating other people's children. *Harvard Educational Review, 58*, 280–98.

Delpit, L. D. (1993). The politics of teaching literate discourse. In T. Perry & J. W. Fraser (Eds.), *Freedom's plow: Teaching in the multicultural classroom* (pp. 285–95). New York: Routledge.

Delpit, L. (1995). *Other people's children: Cultural conflict in the classroom*. New York: New Press.

Dennett, D. C. (1995). *Darwin's dangerous idea: Evolution and the meanings of life*. New York: Simon & Schuster.

Dewey, J. (1916). *Democracy and education: An introduction to the philosophy of education*. New York: Macmillan.

Edelsky, C. (1996). *With literacy and justice for all: Rethinking the social in language and education* (2nd ed.). London: Taylor & Francis.

Elman, J. (1991a). Distributed representations, simple recurrent networks, and grammatical structure. *Machine Learning, 7*, 195–226.

Elman, J. (1991b). *Incremental learning, or the importance of starting small* (Technical Report 9101). San Diego: Center for Research in Language, University of California at San Diego.

Freedman, A. (1993). Show and tell? The role of explicit teaching in the learning of new genres. *Research in the Teaching of English, 27,* 222–51.

Gee, J. P. (1986). Toward a realistic theory of language acquisition. *Harvard Educational Review, 56,* 52–68.

Gee, J. P. (1992). *The social mind: Language, ideology, and social practice.* New York: Bergin & Garvey.

Gee, J. P. (1994). First language acquisition as a guide for theories of learning and pedagogy. *Linguistics and Education 6,* 331–54.

Gee, J. P. (1996). *Social linguistics and literacies: Ideology in discourses* (2nd ed.). London: Taylor & Francis.

Gee, J. P., Hull, G., & Lankshear, C. (1996). *The new work order: Behind the language of the new capitalism.* Boulder, CO: Westview Press.

Gilbert, P., & Taylor, S. (1991). *Fashioning the feminine: Girls, popular culture, and schooling.* Sydney, Aust.: Allen & Unwin.

Gore, J. M. (1993). *The struggle for pedagogies: Critical and feminist discourses as regimes of truth.* New York: Routledge.

Griffiths, P. (1986). Early vocabulary. In P. Fletcher & M. Garman (Eds.), *Language acquisition: Studies in first language development* (2nd ed., pp. 279–306). Cambridge: Cambridge University Press.

Halliday, M. A. K., & Martin, J. (1993). *Writing science: Literacy and discursive power.* Pittsburgh, PA: University of Pittsburgh Press.

Havelock, E. A. (1963). *Preface to Plato.* Cambridge, MA: Belknap Press of Harvard University Press.

Holland, D., & Quinn, N. (Eds.). (1987). *Cultural models in language and thought.* Cambridge: Cambridge University Press.

Holland, J. H. (1995). *Hidden order: How adaptation builds complexity.* Reading, MA: Addison-Wesley.

Holland, J. H., Holyoak, K. J., Nisbett, R. E., & Thagard, P. R. (Eds.). (1986). *Induction: Processes of inference, learning, and discovery.* Cambridge, MA: MIT Press.

Holyoak, K. J., & Thagard, P. (1995). *Mental leaps: Analogy in creative thought.* Cambridge, MA: MIT Press.

Kalantzis, M., & Cope, B. (1993). Histories of pedagogy, cultures of schooling. In B. Cope & M. Kalantzis (Eds.), *The powers of literacy: A genre approach to teaching writing* (pp. 38–62). Pittsburgh, PA: University of Pittsburgh Press.

Kauffman, S. (1995). *At home in the universe: The search for laws of self-organization and complexity.* New York: Oxford University Press.

Keil, F. (1979). *Semantic and conceptual development: An ontological perspective.* Cambridge, MA: Harvard University Press.

Keil, F. (1989). *Concepts, kinds, and cognitive development.* Cambridge, MA: MIT Press.

Kliebard, H. (1986). *The struggle for the American curriculum, 1893–1958.* Boston: Routledge & Kegan Paul.

Luke, C., & Gore, J. M. (Eds.). (1992). *Feminisms and critical pedagogy.* New York: Routledge.

Martin, J. R. (1990). Literacy in science: Learning to handle text as technology. In F. Christie (Ed.), *Literacy for a changing world* (pp. 79–117). Hawthorn, Victoria: Australian Council for Educational Research.

Martin, J. R. (1991). Critical literacy: The role of a functional model of language. *Australian Journal of Reading, 14,* 117–32.

Melvold, J., & Pesetsky, D. (1995, October 29). Reading is not like speaking. *The Boston Globe* (Learning Section).

Minick, N. (1987). The development of Vygotsky's thought: An introduction, Introduction to Vygotsky. In R. W. Rieber & A. S. Carton (Eds.), N. Minick (Trans.), *The Collected works of L. S. Vygotsky: Vol. 1. Problems of general psychology.* New York: Plenum.

Montgomery, S. L. (1994). *Minds for the making: The role of science in American education, 1750–1990.* New York: Guilford Press.

Pinar, W. F., Reynolds, W. M., Slattery, P., & Taubman, P. M. (1995). *Understanding curriculum: An introduction to the study of historical and contemporary curriculum discourses.* New York: Peter Lang.

Pinker, S. (1994). *The language instinct: How the mind creates language.* New York: William Morrow.

Schenkein, J. (Ed.). (1978). *Studies in the organization of conversational interaction.* New York: Academic Press.

Schön, D. A. (1987). *Educating the reflective practitioner.* San Francisco: Jossey-Bass.

Scovel, T. (1988). *A time to speak: A psycholinguistic inquiry into the critical period for human speech.* Cambridge, UK: Newbury House.

Street, B. (1995). *Social literacies.* London: Longman.

Tanner, D. (1991). *Crusade for democracy: Progressive education at the crossroads.* Albany: State University of New York Press.

Tanner, D., & Tanner, L. (1990). *History of the school curriculum.* New York: Macmillan.

Tyack, D. (1974). *The one best system: A history of American urban education.* Cambridge, MA: Harvard University Press.

Vygotsky, L. S. (1987). *The collected works of L. S. Vygotsky, Vol. 1: Problems of general psychology.* R. W. Rieber & A. S. Carton (Eds.), N. Minick (Trans.). New York: Plenum.

Walkerdine, V. (1988). *The mastery of reason: Cognitive development and the production of rationality.* New York: Routledge.

Williams, J. M., & Colomb, G. G. (1993). The case for explicit teaching: Why what you don't know won't help you. *Research in the Teaching of English, 27,* 252–64.

CHAPTER THREE

What Is Progressive about Progressive Education?

JOHN WILLINSKY
University of British Columbia

Nobody can be progressive without being doctrinal; I might almost say that nobody can be progressive without being infallible (at any rate, without believing in some infallibility. For progress by its very name indicates a direction; and the moment we are in the least doubtful about the direction, we become in the same degree doubtful about the progress. Never perhaps since the beginning of the world has there been an age that had less right to use the word "progress" than we.

G. K. CHESTERTON, *The Heretic*

There can come a time when the ideas that propel an age reveal their shortcomings. The heretical G. K. Chesterton, for example, was ready at the turn of the century to call progress on its claims as a cure-all for being anything but progressive in its lack of direction and its doctrinal tendencies. With this cautionary note in mind, I consider in this chapter the course of progressive education in the twentieth century. And it seems perfectly proper, especially if we are to avoid the sins of the progressivism cited by Chesterton, for us—educators—to lift the skirts on our own thinking as part of the intellectual apparatus of our age, to ask what has buoyed our work, what has sped it along. Such inquiry is nothing less than we try to do for others. My contribution to this process is to ask what is progressive about progressive education by considering the historical play of ideas within notions of progress. The rather sweeping historical approach I cover in this chapter, from the Renaissance battle of the books to recent eruptions over Ebonics, offers a context for the specific progressive language education policies and programs treated in other chapters in this collection. I do so out of a belief that the classroom is a playing field of no small significance in the history of ideas such as "progress," with the struggle for progressive education driven by the not-always-compatible forces of science and democracy.

The Idea of Progress

When many of us were growing up not so long ago, progress was everything (certainly everything electric). You remember. There we were, gathered around the pale blue glow of the television set in our living rooms, with General Electric regularly reassuring us during *Howdy Doody* and *Ed Sullivan* that "progress is our most important product." We believed in progress as machinery and method in ways that have not diminished. But progress was always about something larger than living-room technology or child-centered classrooms. Progress defined the West as *modern*, and it did so in relation to a world that used just such ideas to dominate culturally and politically. Progress was represented as the product of Western freedom and reason, and as such could serve as a model for others. While the progressive changes in education described in many of the chapters in this book may seem removed from global concerns, we should not forget how our entire conception of progress developed not only in close association with education, but also during that era of global struggle and redefinition known as Western Imperialism.

In his history of the idea of progress, J. B. Bury (1932) describes how progress was originally equated in the West not with shiny new machines, but with forms of learning thought to lead, in an ever-upward ascent, to a mastery of the world's secrets. The progress of learning was seen as a form of power over the world or, as Francis Bacon put it in the seventeenth century, "the dominion of man over the things rests solely in the arts and sciences. For nature is not ruled unless she is obeyed" (1994, p.

131, Aphorism I, 129). Having achieved this progress of nature and the world through the arts and science, the West thought itself generous in contracting out to the rest of the world its hold on progress, largely through its educational initiatives abroad, making progress one of imperialism's most important products.[1]

Yet if Western education offers the rest of the world some form of progress, not all education within the West aspires to the label "progressive." Although "progressive education" names a specific movement (more on this below), a more general educational orientation toward progress and the future has long been a part of educational thinking in the West. The division between educators who hold up a past perfect as an ideal and those who look to a present future has its roots in the European Renaissance. Out of that era, and continuing into the eighteenth century, a learned and literary debate gradually emerged between the Ancients and the Moderns, as they were known. What had happened was that the European intelligentsia had been enriched by the great trove of Greco-Roman classical texts, which were acquired from Islamic scholars and by the scientific achievements of the imperial adventure, and this intelligentsia was soon divided on where best to direct its attention. Which was it to be: the wisdom of civilization's golden era or the new empire of reason? Against the respect for past glories there began a learned crusade on behalf of the progress of science, heralding a new age of empiricism and experimentation, led by the likes of Francis Bacon and shortly thereafter by the members of England's Royal Society, which was devoted to scientific and scholarly inquiry.[2]

A crucial move introduced in the early years of this century by John Dewey was the association of progressive education with the advancement of democracy. Dewey called for public schooling that would realize "the potential efficacy of education as a constructive agency of improving society—it represents not only a development of children and youth but also of the future society of which they will be the constituents" (1916, p. 79). He saw the work of education as nothing less than social transformation: "So that instead of reproducing current habits [of even the best educated], better habits shall be formed, and thus the future adult society be an improvement on their own" (1916, p. 79). If here and elsewhere Dewey is a little vague about the exact nature of the improvement, this can be taken as itself a democratic feature, with the "better habits" to be decided again and again in public forums. The danger here, of course, is that progressive educators may presume that improvement lies in teaching more people to be like themselves—progressive—in sense and sensibility. In such a case, the grand educational experiment and the earnest learning from experience would thus be directed at "reproducing current habits," which marks a more conservative approach to schooling.

To help us appreciate how progressivism stands against more conservative approaches to schooling, Dewey contrasts those who think education "can be treated as a process of accommodating the future to the past" with the progressive sort who seek "an utilization of the past for a resource in a developing future" (1916, p. 79). To insist that the past serve the future rather than command it invests the future, the yet-to-be, with a special authority. Note, however, how this does little to specify either the direction of progress or how it should be decided, to recall Chesterton's doubts about the claims of this age to progress. There can still be many futures, many ways of directing an education that is to be, as Dewey put it, "an instrument of realizing the better hopes of men" (1916, p. 79). In his last published statement, Dewey declares that "it should be a commonplace, but unfortunately it is not, that no education—or anything else for that matter—is progressive unless it is making progress" (qtd. in Tanner, 1991, p. 82).

The Progressive Education Association

When thinking about those possible futures, it is helpful to consider the three basic options teachers face in trying to achieve educational progress. The progressive educator can begin by teaching students in ways other than those by which he or she was taught. The next step may be to teach students to live outside the prejudices that govern the present world, as the teacher presumably does, believing that if more people battled biased thinking, they could change the world. The third difficult and daring step is to imagine with students a future that is not yet possible, even in the teacher's life, while experimenting with different ways of moving toward it, such as feminists pressing for a nonpatriarchal society or Moses leading his people to a promised land he would never be allowed to enter. This utopian regard for the future turns the progressive educator into a student of the future, with the risk of pursuing the wrong path to the desired future or, more likely, falling short of realizing it. But education is always an act of faith, and an education that seeks a new future is doubly so.

If we now have some sense of the progressive educator's commitment to progress in the future, we can begin to ask about the directions and developments most closely associated with this way of teaching over the last century. That is, in asking about progressive education, one is dealing with both an idea and a history, or, more accurately, the evolution of an idea within a history. Thanks in good measure to Dewey, the experimental bond between education and progress was fully tested in U.S. classrooms. With the formation of the Progressive Education Association (PEA) in 1918, card-carrying progressive educators had an impact on nearly every facet of education from life adjustment to literary analysis (Cremin, 1961). It should surprise no one that an educational movement was created in the United States out of the idea of progress.

Richard Hofstadter, always looking for the historical contradictions that beset this nation, has written that the United States is the only country that saw itself as starting with perfection while aspiring to progress. The United States' perfection, it must have seemed to many, was precisely its commitment to progress, not least of all in its educational efforts to support public education for all. As early as 1892, the journalist Joseph Mayer Rice, after a six-month fact-gathering tour of thirty-six cities, confidently proclaimed that "the great education spirit of this country is progressive" (qtd. in Cremin, 1961, p. 6). What led him to this conclusion was the professionalism he found among the teachers he met, many of whom were developing techniques to broaden and integrate the curriculum, while seeking to reach more and more children. The spirit of democracy, in its efforts to reach all children, and entrusted to the hands of dedicated professionals, set the direction for progressive education for the century to come.

The Progressive Education Association, formed on the heels

of the First World War, was eager to embrace the (human) sciences, which were seen as essential in adding a new level of professionalism to teaching. The "scientific study of pupil development" was the declared aim of the PEA in an unsigned restatement of the movement's goals in a 1930 issue of *Progressive Education* (Brown & Finn, 1988, p. 41). Curriculum was to be "based on the nature and needs of childhood and youth, with the idea of acquiring knowledge through the scientific method of first-hand observation, investigation and experiment and independent search for material"(p. 41). The school is ultimately cast as "an educational laboratory, where new methods are encouraged and the best of the past is leavened by the discoveries of the present" (p. 41). The PEA was prepared to extend the idea of science, as it infused society at large, to the entirety of the students' physical and psychic lives, and permeating the educational environment was a sense of adding to the individual's personal development and growth, with "self-mastery" seen as necessary to fostering a "group consciousness" that would allow for disciplined participation in "the school as community" (p. 41).

While the PEA statement recognizes "the spiritual forces and resources underlying all nature, life and conduct," the focus is largely on the individual and "the consciousness of [individual] achievement," which is said to motivate all work. Out of such a firm foundation could emerge a realization of "the interdependence of all peoples, and international goodwill" (Brown & Finn, 1988, p. 41). This may seem no more than the American philosophy of individualism: first we perfect ourselves and then we look outward to helping others. The important element of progressive education that does not show up well in this brief statement of goals, however, is its commitment to democracy, apart from depicting the school as a community of participation and the interdependence of humankind. These are the expected effects of education in general rather than explicit elements of the program, which is in the hands of the new, scientifically determined methods.

This PEA statement suggests that science will enable the school to best determine, and thus serve, the "individual needs and capacities of the child" (Brown & Finn, 1988, p. 41). Progress is defined through a two-step process which begins by determining the true nature of the child, physically and mentally, and follows with measures to ensure that this essence is fully realized. The scientific determination of children's "needs and capacities" is closely associated with the professional's selective enhancement of qualities that are judged to best prepare children for the world and all that they can be within it. As a result, the potential and progress of the child are largely defined through scientific and professional processes that, even as proponents claim they are rooted in the true nature of the child, undermine the democratic structures of education for child, family, and community. Consider, for example, what were thought to be the scientifically determined needs and capacities of girls, compared to those of boys, not so very long ago.

While one might counter that scientific progress has often had a democratic effect by, among other things, opening the workings of the world to a greater number of people, this is not necessarily, nor has it always been, the case. Scientific authority in the hands of professionals can be directed for or against what we might otherwise think of as the child's or the community's interests.[3]

For their part, progressive educators were wrestling with ways of applying scientific knowledge, largely dealing with the psychology of child development, to democracy's focus on individual rights and liberties. This issue came up with the resistance of members of the John Dewey Society to proposals of merger with the PEA in 1940, on the grounds that educators in the PEA were "possessed of a reformed psychological outlook" as opposed to that of the Dewey Society, where a "socio-economic-political outlook" prevailed (cited in Tanner, 1991, p. 55).[4, 5]

One point at which progressivism's embrace of the scientific spirit was decidedly on the side of democracy was in its early call for what we now refer to as "action research" among teachers. In a 1950 issue of *Progressive Education*, Stephen Corey called for "educational investigators" in the classroom who, given appropriate release time, would test their ideas in the midst of their teaching, and Corey gives the example of a Michigan school that allowed teachers half a day each week for this form of inquiry (1988, pp. 196–98). Much earlier, Dewey had called for the democratic participation of the teacher in educational decisions, as well as for the participation of the child in the curriculum. In a

1903 contribution to the *Elementary School Teacher,* Dewey insisted that the right of teachers to take charge of their work was essential to democracy:

> What does democracy mean save that the individual is to have a share in determining the conditions and the aims of his own work; and that upon the whole, through the free and mutual harmonizing of different individuals, the work of the world is better done than when planned, arranged and directed by the few, no matter how wise and good in intent that few? (1988, p. 200)

Action research on the part of teachers furthered that right, grounding it in an extension of the wisdom of those directly affected by the decisions. Progress was made through these research efforts, then, in increasing teachers' democratic participation in their own work while equipping them to take a stronger, more persuasive, and professional role in guiding the community. The risk with democracy is always that those who have become enfranchised may then reject progressive methods, or scientific inquiry for that matter, if it looks as though scientific inquiry is discovering that progressive initiatives are leading in unintended directions. The progressivist response to discouraging results may test their commitment to science, while their handling of popular resistance to progressive initiatives may try their notion of democracy.

A complicating and sometimes forgotten factor here is that democracy is not a fixed or given idea. It is an abstract idea dependent for its meaning on other abstractions such as equality and participation. The history of an idea continues to evolve our sense of what counts as democratic, but this idea can also, as we know only too well, take many, sometimes contradictory, forms. Think of the tensions that exist between the tyranny of the majority, as Tocqueville identified it well over a century ago, and the moral agenda that seeks greater equality for all, or the tensions between the asserted rights of individuals and collective identities that surface regarding affirmative action and other developments promulgated in the name of democracy. What is the role of educational leadership in realizing a greater degree of democracy in public education? How do professional expertise and professional self-interest figure in the democratic process? What are the different ways of interpreting the place of democracy in education? Some hold that democratic education is about extending the opportunity for education to a greater number of people, an education which is responsive to the values of the community, while others hold that forms of student self-governance are essential in making this commitment to democracy an educational reality.

The Progressive Way Ahead

To consider how the form of democracy comes into play in assessing the progress progressives would like to make, I turn to the contemporary advocacy of progressive education. Although the PEA collapsed in 1955, exhausted by internal fighting and the rise of a more conservative climate, the adjective *progressive* retains to this day its rhetorical force in promoting innovative approaches to teaching.[6]

Among those who would infuse progressivism with a fresh political impetus, Dennis Carlson (1995), in a discussion dealing with the threats posed by developments in national standards, voucher systems, and site-based management, proposes that progressive energies, once divided between psychological and political concerns, take up the cause of collective identities, whether of race, class, or gender. The intriguing dilemma here is that the neoconservative interests behind the initiatives Carlson opposes have carefully wrapped their ideas in the flag of democracy, a cause only strengthened by the degree of popular support they have garnered. On the question of standardized testing, for example, Carlson writes that

> instead of prescriptive standards tied to standardized testing, the state might require that local school districts engage representative constituencies in the community in a dialogue on educational renewal or find ways of making the curriculum more multicultural, making students more active learners, and so on. (1995, p. 347)

He fails to acknowledge how advocates of testing seek, through these measures, an equality of opportunity for every student by monitoring school performance and leveling the playing field, while presuming that standardized testing will lead to greater participation in the state through a language and curriculum shared by all.

However much these assumptions are vulnerable to critique, Carlson could do a better job promoting his progressive interests in multiculturalism and community dialogue by offering a more specific vision of the democracy and promised future that drive his project. He might argue for the democratic value of locally developed curricula, and for the value of exposing students to a variety of perspectives on what constitutes history or literature, which is typically discouraged by national testing; he might insist that students' learning to take greater responsibility for their programs is itself part of a democratic process, and point to how a diversely educated population enriches the range of possibilities for envisioning the future. It is not enough to assume that democracy and progress are on your side; progressive educators need to specify the nature of the progress and the democracy they seek to achieve in the name of progressive education.

Again, the lesson in all of this is that progress is multiheaded; it calls for dwelling on, rather than assuming, what the future might hold. Let the progressive educator name the markers of the intended progress that is to take place in the name of democracy. To recall the GE slogan, what are the important products to be? Where are the points of regress in those policies that progressives feel compelled to oppose? Despite Chesterton's warnings, the problem is not in being doctrinal regarding the progress of progressive education. The problem is in making the vision of the future explicit; it is about articulating the nature of the experiment, about making the lessons of experience plain, so that in democratic fashion one can participate in persuading and being persuaded in the process of establishing an educational direction for the future.

To recap my case to this point, I have proposed that, whether we are advocates or critics of progressive education, what is at issue in the claims of progressive education is its vision of the yet-to-be-realized future, its desire to make something more of the world through this form of education, which is informed by experiment and inquiry, and directed at achieving a greater degree of democracy. We have to ask, then, about this vision of the democratic future. To put this proposal to work, I conclude with two educational examples. The first is historical, looking back to the progressive legacy in the teaching of literature and literary analysis; for this, I draw from my earlier work in order to issue a retraction and an apology. The other example looks forward to forms of social action currently underway that are determining the future in ways that progressive educators with an interest in language might think it wise to participate in.

The Progressive Teaching of Literature

The teaching of literature certainly poses an interesting challenge to what it means to be progressive. The reading of a poem can be readily treated as an intensely private experience, an aesthetic and sublime phenomenon that can result in a moment of intense reflection and reverie, possibly allowing one to transcend the here and now. But does that make literature a source of progress and a producer of an improved humankind? Are we now to embrace the great Romantic poet Shelley's insistence that the world's true and unacknowledged legislators were poets? Are we to accept the argument that an education in English literature is itself an instrument of progress, an argument that was made on the initial introduction into formal education of English literature as a school subject? More than a century ago, Thomas Macaulay (1859/1971) successfully recommended the teaching of English literature in the colonial schools of India to make the natives British in all but color. Not long afterward, Matthew Arnold (1908) proposed the study of poetry for the children of the industrial classes of England, that their souls might be properly and unconsciously formed. These are not exactly the sorts of progressive uses of literature we would happily champion today.[7]

During this century, Louise Rosenblatt is first among those who have given serious consideration to how literature can be a progressive educational force; her landmark book, *Literature as Exploration* (1938), was sponsored by the PEA's Commission on Human Relations. This was the year *Time* magazine declared that no U.S. school had escaped the influence of progressivism, and Rosenblatt offered teachers a vision of progressive literary education in very pragmatic terms since it might supply the young "with tools and the knowledge necessary for a scientifically objective, critical appraisal of accepted opinion," as well as provide the basis of "working out a more fruitful living" (1938, p. 212). Here indeed was the enthusiasm and hope for the future which predicted the achievement of democracy through scientific thinking—the goal of progressive education. If there is a tendency to run a little flat and flabby toward the end of these promises, yet it remains part of the democratic gift to talk through the meaning of "fruitful living." And yet I am asking that we hazard an articulation of what *fruition* might look like in putting such promises forward. Rosenblatt did address how literature could help create, through its ability to generate vicarious experience, the necessary empathy to improve what were then known as "race relations."

In my review of Rosenblatt's work, I noted that her initial commitment to democracy, featured so prominently in *Literature as Exploration*, disappeared in the wake of the psychological and aesthetic dynamic that became known as reader-response, a theory highlighted in her second book published some forty years later (Willinsky, 1990, pp. 99–102; 1991). In *The Reader, the Text, the Poem*, Rosenblatt focused on what the reader "is living through during the reading event," with an emphasis on the aesthetic reading that rendered her work less progressive in its advocacy of democratic concerns (1978, p. 22). She was further developing a phenomenology of aesthetic experience, and this reader-response pedagogy was empirically grounded in close readings of students' classroom responses to literature. Rosenblatt did not agree that her work was any less engaged in opening democratic vistas, to use the term from Whitman that Rosenblatt cited. Although she objected to my interpretation of her later work, I felt that it risked encouraging a sense of self-absorption in literature, an abandoning of the world in favor of realizing the poem that lay in the text. This strategy seemed to promise little for the improvement of society, except perhaps for the heightening of sensitivity to the human condition that literature often evokes. When she wrote for the PEA in the 1930s, Rosenblatt's explicit treatment of democratic concerns was noticeably progressive at a time when the great literary figures of modernity—whether T. S. Eliot, Ezra Pound, or Wyndham Lewis—in their devotion to the aesthetic, were not strikingly democratic in disposition. The extreme self-cultivation of a literary sensibility does not always allow time for tapping into the common will so vital to the social contract of democracy.

For all my initial apprehensions, I should have been far more encouraged, I realize now, by the impact of Rosenblatt's reader-response theory on today's progressive classrooms (Willinsky 1991, pp. 125–37). In a democratic spirit, supported by opportunities for sharing and openly debating the vision of the literature's impact, students have indeed achieved a sense of arriving at their own reading (of one reader, one reading). Yes, readers can be swayed and "heartfelt" responses faked, but the opportunities are real, genuine, and demonstrably engaging. Progress was made through the democratic process of moving beyond the classroom scenario of the teacher dictating the meaning and significance of the assigned novel and of the symbols and metaphors in the poem. In this progressive setting, students learn to trust and offer their sense of the world, to become students, if not scientists, of their own sentiments in reading other's lives, beginning with the world contained within the syllabus of their literature class. Whether the students see this process as having any relation to the larger world, to the expansion of democracy and the shaping of the future, is doubtful. The articulation of this vision needs to begin in the classroom with the students, just as teachers need to be accountable for the way they teach. Still, I realize now, by virtue of this analysis, how wrong and hasty I was in judging that Rosenblatt's progressivism had lost its emphasis on building a future with a more democratic readership, and I apologize for that. One needs to learn to ask the right questions about what makes progressive education progressive.

A second manner of assessing the progress presumed by progressivism is to turn to current educational developments and ask, what is a progressive educator to do. On the question of language, for example, the United States is facing a particularly critical language question thanks to a recent bill, passed by the House of Representatives, that would make English the official language of the United States. This effort to enshrine and protect the "common" tongue, to ensure that the cultural values of the past are carried into the future, can be seen as fulfilling another item on the neoconservative agenda that is intent on enshrining what the United States once and should still stand for. The Official English movement wants to make sure that a common tongue, a national language, will be mastered in the schools and used in all government services. This new legislation threatens, among other things, Spanish-English bilingual programs in schools which serve as a bridge for Spanish-speaking students finding their way into an English-speaking education system.

Efforts to minimize this sort of damage to hard-won educational programs will call for arguments from progressive educators that refute the presumed necessity of a common language within a democracy, and remind the nation of its progress in building more tolerant and inclusive communities. Progressive educators could also ensure that the debate is informed by a history of successful attempts to discourage proposals for language academies to govern English. They could describe how much of the vocabulary of the English language has been enriched through its unregulated contact with other tongues. They could point out that the tensions found in multilingual communities are not dictated by communication problems but by other sorts of histories and disparities. This vision of progress draws on the past, as Dewey recommended, yet we should recognize that the past is no less an imagined place than the future. Progressive educators, as I am constructing them, are simply those who seek a future that is distinguished from the present by clear indications of democratic advances. The initiative to legislate English as a national language may seem to be other than that, but this is only to begin moving toward an educated and educational response for the progressive educator.

At the same time, and in a related issue that has garnered at least as much media attention, the Oakland Board of Education passed a resolution toward the close of 1996 that recognized the language spoken by many African American students as a distinct language. This language, commonly called Ebonics (merging "ebony" and "phonics"), was to be used in the classroom to facilitate the development of reading and writing skills in Standard English (Holmes, 1996). This measure, which included instruction in Ebonics for teachers, set off a controversy across the United States. The Linguistic Society of America endorsed the Oakland effort, pointing to the fact that Ebonics is "systematic and rule-governed like all natural speech varieties," and citing evidence that those who speak variations on Standard English are not inhibited from acquiring the standard when they are exposed to "approaches which recognize the legitimacy of the other varieties of a language" (Strosnider, 1997)[8, 9]

In my simpleminded approach to what progressive education stands for, one needs to articulate the progress—the shape of the future—sought. To be guided by the necessity of speaking only Standard English is to be directed by a principle that is far too sweeping to be scientifically warranted; but then it is also far too directed at the imagined current state of things to count as progressive thinking. While the language requirements that exist for many situations, such as written work submitted by students of the University of California across the bay from Oakland, can be stipulated, such situation-specific requirements are a far cry from assuming that a standard is necessary for communication. We know that our communities are sustained by a diversity of linguistic styles and that in critical situations, such as air safety, professional argots function best.

So the progressive educator, in projecting an imagined future, could well argue from an *educational* point of view that people will expand their capacity for and interest in linguistic variations while appreciating imaginative inventions and the social forces that shape them both up and down the social ladder, from the streets they do not visit to the pages of the *New York Times*. Progressive educators would ask that we become students of the English language, examining the claims made on its behalf, encouraging a critique perhaps of the Linguistic Society of America for defending Ebonics as a "natural language," an argument which fails to deal with the inherent identity issues of resistance and exclusion, even as the LSA accedes to the necessity of Standard English (first among natural dialects?), as if all who mastered it really did benefit and those who did not were duly punished. It is, after all, only progressive to believe that science is best at revising its own story of the world.

The progressive educator would work at identifying the democratic ramifications of the Ebonics debate as a means of addressing the underachievement of black students in the Oakland schools. After all, it was a committee of students, teachers, and parents that made the recommendations to the Oakland school board; the potential for Ebonics instruction to support greater participation by students in classrooms must be weighed against the potential for it to further proscribe the work of teachers. Certainly one needs to ask whether there can be a future in which the grammatical nuances that distinguish dialectics within a language will determine how the words are understood and taken. You may want to exclaim, No, grammatical distinctions, like other markers such as race and gender, will never fade, but however desirable in democratic terms it might be that such social distinctions fade, to teach as if this were true would only mislead students to direct their educational attention to this illusive end. To prepare students only for what we like to think of as the "real world" can be equally misleading, as that reality is also illusive in its myriad shapes and forms.

The educational exercise of "teaching the conflicts," which I here recommend, is fairly mundane and borrowed, at that, from Gerald Graff (1992). Because such controversies reveal a broad spectrum of opinion, as the Ebonics debate illustrates, turn the controversy into a lesson that informs and engages, insofar as it helps teachers and students clarify and shape their vision of the desired future. This, too, it seems to me, is the point of a progressive education—to be equally informed by the goals of reason and democracy. Progressive educational programs cannot rest on ready-made assumptions about what constitutes progress; they cannot rely on science to pave the road to democracy, just as they have to be wary of the tyranny of the majority, in Tocqueville's classic sense. Inquiry is part of the nature, as well as the advantage and responsibility, of education, although it may need to be adjusted so that we become, as I have recommended more than once, students of our own education.

To return to the epigraph at the head of this chapter, you might have sensed that G. K. Chesterton was no friend of progress, and I would add now that he also thought little enough of progressive education. The *Oxford English Dictionary*, in defining *progressive* in its educational sense, quotes Chesterton's view of

G. B. Shaw: "Shaw has always made this one immense mistake arising out of that progressive education of his, the mistake of treating convention as a bad thing." From a progressive point of view, there are times when the conventions by which a society is structured are decidedly a bad thing, and it is no mistake to work at changing them, whether through the theater or the schools. In fact, this is precisely what progressive education is about. It seeks to unsettle past conventions, not just in favor of a less convention-bound future, but also to establish new conventions. The progressive education tradition I consider in this chapter was dedicated to advancing democratic conventions of access to an education grounded in the recognition of individual rights. It sought to bring scientific reasoning to a new level of professional commitment. Although the PEA has collapsed, these elements of progressive education persist, along with some of the tensions that come from trying to strike the balance between science and society, individual and community. To give Chesterton his due, progressives can be doctrinal about progress, which is why we are under some compulsion to review without end these ideas of progress and the progressive. It is fair to ask, as he did at the outset of the Progressive Era, where exactly progressive educators are headed in their pursuit of sometimes ill-articulated visions of the future. To engage with what underlies these visions of the future in public forums such as this book seems to me to be about using the word and the idea of *progress* in its most hopeful, educational, and democratic senses.

Notes

1. Whether for a civilization or an individual, an increase in Western-style education represented a form of progress. So the number of years of formal schooling is a standard measure of progress or development for UNESCO and other agencies. For a fuller discussion of imperialism's educational legacy, see Willinsky (1998). Also, Shiv Visvanathan writes of Western science that "the West-as-modernity obtains the mandate of power and responsibility over this world left behind by history" (1988, p. 263).

2. The ensuing debate between the Ancients and the Moderns was, according to historian Bury, "the first clear assertions of the doctrine of progress in knowledge" (1932, p. 79). Certainly, Jonathan Swift had fun

with it in his 1697 pamphlet *The Battle of the Books,* where he set the two sides off against each other, he himself holding with the Ancients, whom he depicted, in what became a catch phrase of wisdom, as bees having "chosen to fill our hives with honey and wax; thus furnishing mankind with the two noblest of things, which are sweetness and light," which were opposed to the Moderns, mere spiders producing cobwebs, "nothing but dirt, spun out of your own entrails" (1891, p. 29). The conflict ever since has been between those honoring established authorities and those striking new claims on the world. The depth of this division can often be far more critical in keeping people at loggerheads than the particularities of a new program, even as it absorbs their attention and arguments. Bacon credited this progress in knowledge, at least in part, to the Age of Discovery, noting that in relation to

> the difference there is between the life of men in the most civilized province of Europe, and in the most savage and barbarous part of New India, . . . reflect that the difference is so great as truly to justify the saying "Man is a god to men," not only for the help and benefits he can bring, but also by comparing their conditions. (1994, p. 130, Aphorism I, 129)

3. Earlier in this century, for example, respected scientists proposed the perfection of the race as a decidedly progressive hope for the future of the United States through the eugenics movement, which had tragic and terrifying results that took on legislative force in a number of U.S. states and influenced developments in German science and society in the Nazi era (Kühl, 1994). Jatjinder K. Bajaj (1988) points to the tensions between the authority of science, with its Baconian focus on controlling nature, including humankind, and this scientific development then taken as integral to the development of democracy.

4. While Dewey held that self-fulfillment could only be realized in the social arena of justice, he was attacked for sacrificing individualism to social goals (Wain, 1995, p. 407). It may be worth noting that the John Dewey Society was then closely associated with *Social Frontier: A Journal of Educational Criticism and Reconstruction,* which ran from 1934 to 1938, while the Society now finds its publishing outlet home in *Educational Theory,* which might be thought to reflect its own form of encroaching professionalism.

5. This statement needs to be compared to the views of Dewey's current champion, Richard Rorty, who holds rather the opposite view, as Kenneth Wain points out, which is that the language of self-fulfillment does not lend itself to the sort of debate and sharing that the language of justice does, making it a strictly private matter compared to the imagi-

native solidarity we need to feel for others in the public realm (Wain, 1995, p. 404).

6. And yet, in a seemingly forward-looking collection like *Progressive Education for the 1990s,* Featherstone introduces his book with the irony that progressive educators today are looking back to a movement whose glories and heroes are in the past; this collection dwells on the Middletown study from the 1920s and the Eight Year Study from a decade later (1991). Still, a new generation of progressives has emerged that, after paying homage to its roots, seeks postmodern versions of progressivism (Silin, 1993; Carlson, 1995). See Cremin for a fine-grained analysis of the professional and political causes of what he finds to be the PEA's ready demise (1961, pp. 347–53).

7. This recalls Marshall McLuhan's quip that we often drive into the future with an eye on the rearview mirror. Dennis Carlson, for one, confirms the ongoing importance of this nostalgic progressivism to his own project: "The notion of progressivism seems to me worth maintaining because of the historical memories it invokes of that small but important strand of progressivism that has always stood for democratic reconstructionist approaches to curriculum and teaching" (1995, p. 338).

8. Critics of all races, however, have emerged, vehemently pointing to how only Standard English proves successful in the larger world, and declaring that to teach anything different or accept anything "less" from students is to shortchange them. Steven Holmes (1996) reports on earlier efforts at educational intervention, such as the 1979 landmark case in Ann Arbor, Michigan, which recognized how the schools disadvantaged those who spoke Black English. The case led to teacher training in Black English, but this training was dropped after two years, just as the earlier efforts of the Bridge project, which sought to introduce Black English into the classroom, quietly disappeared.

9. What does it mean, then, to be progressive in the face of this minor tempest? What future can be forged out of this conflict between the democratic assertion of nativism that demands a common language to ensure democracy and democratic efforts to recognize difference as a right of language? Henry Louis Gates Jr., chair of Afro-American Studies at Harvard, is quoted as calling the measure "obviously stupid and ridiculous" in its efforts to deal with "the sheer desperation of public schools in the inner city"; he promotes instead his *Norton Anthology of African-American Literature* ("I'd love for the book to be part of language training for inner-city black kids," which would show how African American writers "spoke vernacular and mastered the King's English"– precisely the goal of the Oakland resolution) (qtd. in Rich, 1997, p. A19).

References

Arnold, M. (1908). *Reports on elementary schools, 1852–1882*. London: HMSO.

Bacon, F. (1994). *Novum organum* (P. Urbach & J. Gibson, Trans.). Chicago: Open Court. (Original work published 1620)

Bajaj, J. (1988). Francis Bacon, the first philosopher of modern science: A non-western view. In A. Nandy (Ed.), *Science, hegemony and violence: A requiem for modernity* (pp. 24–67). Delhi, India: Oxford University Press.

Brown, S. I., & Finn, M. E. (Eds.). (1988). *Readings from* Progressive Education: *A movement and its professional journal* (Vol. I). Lanham, MD: University Press of America.

Bury, J. B. (1932). *The idea of progress: An inquiry into its origin and growth*. New York: Dover.

Carlson, D. (1995). Making progress: Progressive education in the postmodern. *Educational Theory, 45*(3), 337–57.

Corey, S. (1988). Teacher as investigator. In S. I. Brown & M. E. Finn (Eds.), *Readings from* Progressive Education: *A movement and its professional journal* (Vol. I) (pp. 196–98). Lanham, MD: University Press of America.

Cremin, L. A. (1961). *The transformation of the school: Progressivism in American education, 1876–1957*. New York: Knopf.

Dewey, J. (1916). *Democracy and education: An introduction to the philosophy of education*. New York: Free Press.

Dewey, J. (1988). Democracy and the teacher. In S. I. Brown & M. E. Finn (Eds.), *Readings from* Progressive Education: *A movement and its professional journal* (Vol. I) (pp. 199–201). Lanham, MD: University Press of America.

Featherstone, J. (1991). Foreword. In K. Jervis & C. Montag (Eds.), *Progressive Education for the 1990s: Transforming practice*. New York: Teachers College Press.

Graff, G. (1992). Teach the conflicts. In D. J. Gless & B. Herrnstein Smith (Eds.), *The politics of liberal education* (pp. 57–74). Durham, NC: Duke University Press.

Holmes, S. (1996, December 30). Black English debate: No standard assumptions. *New York Times*. Available: http://search.nytimes.com.

Kühl, S. (1994). *The Nazi connection: Eugenics, American racism, and German national socialism.* New York: Oxford University Press.

Macaulay, T. B. (1971). Thomas Babington Macaulay on education for India. In P. D. Curtin (Ed.), *Imperialism* (pp. 178–91). New York: Harper & Row. (Original work published 1859)

Rich, R. (1997, January 9). The ebonic plague. *Globe & Mail,* p. A19.

Rosenblatt, L. (1938). *Literature as exploration.* New York: Appleton-Century.

Rosenblatt, L. (1978). *The reader, the text, the poem: The transactional theory of the literary work.* Carbondale: Southern Illinois University Press.

Silin, J. G. (1993). New subjects, familiar roles: Progressive legacies in the postmodern world. In F. Pignatelli & S. W. Pflaum (Eds.), *Celebrating diverse voices: Progressive education and equity* (pp. 221–43). Newbury Park, CA: Corwin Press.

Strosnider, K. (1997, January 7). Linguistics scholars endorse use of Ebonics in schools. *Chronicle of Higher Education.* Available: http://chronicle.com.

Swift, J. (1891). *The battle of the books and other short pieces.* London: Cassell. (Original work published 1697)

Tanner, D. (1991). *Crusade for democracy: Progressive education at the crossroads.* Albany: State University of New York.

Wain, K. (1995). Richard Rorty, education, and politics. *Educational Theory, 45*(3), 395–409.

Willinsky, J. (1990). *The new literacy: Redefining reading and writing in the schools.* New York: Routledge.

Willinsky, J. (1991). *The triumph of literature/The fate of literacy: English in the secondary school curriculum.* New York: Teachers College Press.

Willinsky, J. (1998). *Learning to divide the world: Education at empire's end.* Minneapolis: University of Minnesota Press.

Visvanathan, S. (1988). On the annals of the laboratory state. In A. Nandy (Ed.), *Science, hegemony and violence: A requiem for modernity* (pp. 257–88). Delhi, India: Oxford University Press.

PROGRESSIVE LANGUAGE PROJECTS: SOME STORIES

CHAPTER FOUR

Schooling Disruptions:
The Case of Critical Literacy

BARBARA COMBER
University of South Australia

PHIL CORMACK
University of South Australia

JENNIFER O'BRIEN
University of South Australia

The last decade in Australia and in many postindustrial societies has seen the rapid development of increasingly sophisticated and changing literate practices arising from new media and technologies. This same period has been marked by increasing youth unemployment, underemployment, and poverty. In educational terms, this period has witnessed a polarization of debates in and around approaches to teaching literacy, calls for schools to be more publicly accountable, and the introduction of basic skills tests in most Australian states.

We argue that in times such as these it is increasingly important that the literacies we make available to poor and diverse student groups are complex, multiple, and useful to them immediately and in the future. Such literate practices have been described as "multi-literacies" (New London Group, 1996). Promises that basic literacy will lead to employment later are transparent falsehoods for children who witness firsthand the effects of long-term unemployment. But in an era when the media and politicians fuel public panic and anxiety about literacy and the need for basics, making time for complex, multiple, and powerful literacies in schools is by no means simple.

In this chapter, we describe and analyze instances of classroom teaching of socially critical literacies in order to examine tensions facing educators in a time of contradictory and increasing demands on their work (see Gee & Lankshear, 1995; Green, Hodgens, & Luke, 1994; Luke & Freebody, 1997; Nixon, 1998). In the midst of these demands, we wish to highlight both the difficulty and the urgency of maintaining a critical agenda for literacy education.

We focus on a group of teachers in South Australia who have found and exploited spaces for doing critical work, drawing attention to the tactic of operating within the opportunities offered by state and federal policies, programs, and curriculum documents. We consider how it has been possible for these teachers to operate within the social and political climate in order to further social justice agendas. We also consider the future of critical literacy and under what conditions it is likely to flourish in classrooms.

Critical Literacy in South Australian Classrooms

Critical literacy is disruptive—of assumptions about students' capacities and development; of traditional views of the literacy curriculum; and of the teacher's role as sole source of authorized knowledge. Therefore, it is fair to ask how critical literacy is received, how it got onto the agenda in South Australian classrooms, and what its prospects are for the future. Through discussion of three individual cases, we analyze the responses of students, teachers, school leaders, and parents to critical literacy and provide a selective view of contexts that make critical literacy possible.

Case 1: Racism—From the Global to the Local

We turn first to the examination of one literacy event from a classroom in which the teacher's explicit social justice agenda led to a discussion and writing about racism.[1] The context for this case is the work of Josie McKinnon, who was at the time of this lesson a grade 5-6-7 teacher in a Catholic parish primary school serving a diverse and socioeconomically disadvantaged community.

The transcript that follows shows McKinnon beginning a series of lessons on the subject of racism. She had informed students about the referendum on the voting rights of black people in South Africa and went on to talk about apartheid:

> TEACHER: It's basically about whether the country, or the people in the country, the white people in the country would like to move towards change . . . [inaudible] . . . I'm not sure how bad it is now, but it used to be much worse where black people had to walk on a different side of the street and they weren't allowed on buses and they weren't allowed to sit on certain seats or drink from the fountains or . . . [inaudible] . . . They virtually weren't allowed to do anything, and over the years they've, other countries said they don't like that and they tried to change it. But the people of South Africa who've lived that way for a long, long time are finding it very difficult to change. Now the white people who've got the white South African Parliament are the people who have the power and they're saying to the black people: No you cannot vote. You have no power in this country. You do what we tell you to do. Which also means they live where they're told to live and they find it very difficult to get work, they are paid less—all that kind of stuff that happens with racism.

In helping students understand the reason for the referendum and the effects of apartheid, McKinnon provided specific illustrations of the physical and economic consequences of racist policies on people's everyday circumstances—experiences to which some students could directly relate. She also described her personal investment in South African politics. She explained that she had friends in South Africa who feared the possibility of violent reactions or even civil war in the wake of the referendum. As she talked, students become extremely engaged, calling out comments and whispering to one other.

> TEACHER: What worries me and probably worries you is why does it ever have to get to that point? Why can't people live together peacefully? And where can we go? A

> bunch of people and a bunch of school kids and a
> bunch of teachers in one little place at B [school name]
> is just a speck on the world. Like we are just one tiny
> little speck. What can we do to make a difference? Not
> to the situation over there. How can we start the
> rippling effect from here? How can this little group of
> people cause a chain reaction?

At this point, McKinnon introduced the theme of local action and invited students to comment on forms of action they
could take. While she described the school community as "one
tiny little speck," she held out hope for transformative action.
Students suggested protest marches, letters, and petitions.
McKinnon accepted their suggestions but began her move to push
students to think and act locally:

> TEACHER: Yep, all those sorts of powerful things like writing
> letters and signing petitions are very powerful things.
> What about our attitudes? Could we have, what about
> our attitudes that we have in this classroom now
> towards each other and towards each other's differ-
> ences? Now come on. Someone give me a response to
> that question. What about us in this school and our
> attitude to each other and out of the school?

In making space and time for students to consider global
events in relation to the possibilities for local action, McKinnon
enacted a key principle of critical pedagogy. But when she invited students to talk about their attitudes toward each other, the
classroom erupted with simultaneous and overlapping conversations. The discussion became difficult for McKinnon to manage,
so she intervened by asking the students to write about questions
of racism (in both South Africa and Australia) in their journals.
Here the move to writing functioned both as a way of regaining
order and also as an attempt to capitalize on the students' energy
for this topic. After having students write for ten minutes,
McKinnon invited them to stand and share what they had written. Benjamith, born in Thailand and herself a person of color,
was the first to offer to read:

BENJAMITH: It doesn't matter if you are purple and green, orange or brown you live in this world too. So people should have the same rights as other people. To stop racism. It may be we all need to think about it and always try something new and pass down what you believe to your generation and their generation and perhaps something will happen. So why are people being so childish and selfish? And why not let Blacks have the same rights as Whites? It is just like children in the playground saying, 'I'm not going to play with you because you are a different colour,' Don't put people into categories because it doesn't matter if you're Black or White, purple or green. People still love each other.

Benjamith linked many of the key themes of the earlier discussion about intergenerational racism, equal rights, and the school context. Of particular interest is the way she related political racism to what children say to each other on the playground. Her use of rhetorical questions suggests she had written her text to be read aloud in the public forum. While Benjamith read her text with some passion and confidence, other students were reluctant to read their journal entries aloud.

A week later, McKinnon returned to the issue of who speaks in the public forum of the classroom. She referred to the kind of class community she was trying to construct—a place where students feel free to speak—and waited for students to respond. This is, after all, a key issue of contemporary citizenship and for educational communities committed to social justice. It is not enough for teachers to invite students to speak as though the space for them already exists. Speaking rights in classrooms do not depend solely on pedagogical decisions. The relationships between students are crucial to how the classroom forum is constructed and who can use it to what ends (see also Dyson, 1993).

JULIA: . . . and like you've got a really close friendship with some people but you've also got, I mean like everyone has enemies.

TEACHER: Have they?

STUDENTS: Yes, yeah, yes.

JULIA: Yes, everyone has enemies. I mean it's just if you hate those people and it's just, it's not like when your friends laugh at you, you know you sort of like it, but when you get enemies laugh at you it's really makes you mad.

TEACHER: Great, Julia, thanks. Now we're going to change topics.

STUDENTS: Why?

Here, Julia suggested an idea rarely talked about in school: that students have enemies within the classroom and that their reluctance to share relates not only to shyness or embarrassment, but also to relationships within the class community. McKinnon appeared flustered by Julia's revelation. This contrasted sharply with McKinnon's confidence in dealing with more global political issues such as apartheid. Issues of racism, local action, speaking out, and student safety led the class to a topic that was potentially explosive, and, not surprisingly, McKinnon interrupted a conversation that could have ended in personal hurt. What remained unexamined in this instance was the way race intersected with friendship groups within this classroom.

These lessons foreground some of the difficulties teachers may confront in talking about political issues such as racism. When students talked and wrote about racism in more global and distant terms, as in the case of South Africa, they produced what they know are the "right answers," those in line with an antiracism position. When they were invited to look at the micropolitics of their own classroom and talk about how they deal with differences, however, a conversation developed which the teacher was unsure how to manage.

Clearly, relationships between students affect what can be said by whom and in what situations. Thus the student who takes the risk of sharing his or her writing in front of peers is not simply displaying literate behaviors or confidence, but also making a strategic decision about what can be read and said in the public forum of the classroom (see also Dyson, 1993). These decisions relate in complex ways to the power relations and histories between students, which are affected by where students live, which churches they go to, which sports teams they play for, and so on. Family friendships, race, religion, gender, and class have unpredictable and changing effects on the playground and in classroom dynamics.

Two contextual issues are worth highlighting in relation to this case. First, the commitment of the Catholic school system within which McKinnon worked to issues of equity and social justice made it possible for her to take such risks. The second and connected issue is the context created for classroom discussion. McKinnon encouraged students to talk about the shaping of their conversation while at the same time ensuring that they could participate in that conversation in some safety. This case illustrates the complexities of what might be at stake in constructing critical literacies. As we have seen, such work can produce precarious scenarios in which the intersection of teachers' institutional locations and personal histories result in ambivalence and ambiguity. Ways of responding pedagogically to the anxieties, uncertainties, and angers that may be generated by opening the classroom space to talk about gender difference or racism is an urgent area for classroom research (see Cochran-Smith, 1995, for a discussion of related issues in university pedagogy).

Case 2: Revisiting the Local

It is the sixth week of the fourth term at Seaview Grove Primary School,[2] and the grade 1-2 students and their teacher have given little time or attention yet to Christmas, which is less than a month away. They are still fully engaged in research they began earlier in the term about trees. This research is not focused on the usual rain forest theme, though the students are certainly interested in the state of their environment. The students, who live in an area of high poverty and low employment that is the target of an urban renewal project, had become concerned about the poor condition and low numbers of trees in their local area. Their current literacy and math lessons have emerged from this interest and have been designed to help them actively research their local community.

What have the students been doing? On copies of local street maps, they have recorded the results of their fieldwork—the number and condition of trees. Physical fitness, observation, geography, science, reading and writing, and math came together as these young students, led by their teacher, walked their local area with maps and pencils in hand. They extended their investigations about trees into broader questions about the local area and called on the experience and knowledge of their families. As a result, they learned of the urban renewal project and conducted opinion polls with family members and neighbors about issues such as relocation. With their teacher's help, they wrote faxes to local authorities to obtain more information about plans for their local area.

This brief overview of the innovative and important work of this teacher and her students shows how this project incorporated attention to the environment, communication, mapping, number work, reading, writing, and inquiry. This was an integrated, not an add-on, curriculum. Learning literacy and numeracy in context had some tangible meaning for students in this instance. More than that, these forms of knowledge and skill were gained by exploring matters that concerned the quality of children's everyday lives. A teacher built a language and literacy curriculum around local issues and involved students as researchers and knowledge producers.

Clearly, a complex curriculum such as this was not fashioned in isolation. Among the network of personal, professional, and institutional conditions that make it possible, two elements can be highlighted—the involvement of the teacher in a university research project and the authorization by education policy of a critically oriented curriculum.

The teacher at this school is involved in a research project in which her efforts to open up new kinds of literacy for disadvantaged learners are an object of study and a point of discussion with a visiting university researcher. The research project links school system leaders and curriculum experts with university researchers, all of whom are committed to exploring the ways that school literacy practices can be better fitted to the social and cultural practices that students in diverse and poor communities can call on to succeed in school. Through her involvement in this project, the teacher's innovative practices can be acknowledged and supported. The teacher also has access to a wider network of ideas and people for evaluating and extending those practices.

The curriculum policies mandated for use in South Australian government schools are also relevant.[3] These documents, in the shape of sets of content statements and student achievement profiles, were initially produced in the early 1990s by a coalition of Australian federal government education authorities with Australian states and territories. Although the federal government's intended outcome was a comprehensive curriculum for Australian schools, not all states adopted the curriculum as produced. The policies, however, were adopted by the South Australian government as a basis for curriculum development throughout the state school system.

While these curriculum documents can be seen, along with other contemporary educational policies, as elements in the broader economic policy of the federal government at that time (Taylor, Rizvi, Lingard, & Henry, 1997), for our purposes their significance is that they explicitly engage at a number of points with social justice issues. For a start, the curriculum development enterprise was identified as a component of the federal government's equity programs, with the point made repeatedly that gender equity and the perspectives of indigenous Australians were integral to the new curricula (e.g., see Australian Education Council, 1994a, pp. iii, iv, 45). Moreover, a number of subject area curriculum documents signaled the possibility of a critical social analysis. The document outlining studies of society and environment (Australian Education Council, 1994b), for example, builds understanding, investigating, and eradicating discrimination and harassment into the official curriculum.

The most thorough development of a socially critical perspective is found in the subject of English language and literature. Beginning in the earliest years of schooling, students are encouraged to view texts as constructed objects open to deconstruction and reconstruction; to identify, discuss, and challenge social and cultural values implicitly and explicitly carried in literature and mass media texts; and to consider language as constitutive of social and political power relationships.

The point here is that a socially critical orientation such as that taken up by the teacher and students at Seaview was legitimated by official curriculum pronouncements. This is not to say that critical literacy was the norm, but rather that an official space was created within which innovative educators, including co-authors of this chapter, were able to take action.

Case 3: Researching Cultural Events and Familiar Texts

We turn now to the work of one early childhood teacher,[4] Jennifer O'Brien, in a suburban disadvantaged school in South Australia. In the first example, O'Brien and her students research Mother's Day and the junk mail which in South Australian suburbs and towns accompanies this familiar cultural event. In the second example, described in a later section, they critically examine a more conventional classroom text, a short novel written expressly for young children to read.

In the previous year, O'Brien had conducted an in-depth critical analysis of the Mother's Day fliers that she and her students had collected from the junk mail arriving in their mailboxes. She had worked with the students to analyze the versions of motherhood and mothers' desires represented in the marketing texts associated with this gendered cultural event. O'Brien's reports of this textual analysis of a large corpus of community texts had been influential, encouraging a number of teachers to explore similar territory with toy catalogs, cereal boxes, and other found texts (Luke, O'Brien, & Comber, 1994). O'Brien herself, however, remained self-critical about the usefulness of this deconstructive work in her bigger project about offering girls and boys opportunities to change the range of gendered subjectivities available to them. What is more, children's families, mothers in particular, were present only as topics of discussion.

The following year as Mother's Day approached once more, O'Brien decided to involve the students and their families in a broader piece of sociological research. Here are the key steps she took in examining Mother's Day as a cultural event. O'Brien

1. designed and produced a survey with the students to investigate their mothers', grandmothers', or female caregivers' views on Mother's Day.

2. collated and analyzed the survey responses in front of the students.

3. compared their mothers' views about presents with those portrayed in the catalogs.

4. compared the mothers shown in the catalogs with the students' mothers, particularly in regard to visible differences (such as those associated with race, age, and body shape).

5. scribed and produced a report of their research in a "big book" format so that students could read about and reflect on the process they had undertaken.

This project allowed the students to observe how surveys are designed and to watch and contribute as their teacher produced one in front of them. In step 1, for example, O'Brien scribed children's suggestions and organized the information, wording, spelling, ordering, and numbering of the questions. Teacher modeling, writing, and scribing for children were all in evidence here, as O'Brien demonstrated explicitly how and why to write a survey. She allowed the students access to her decision-making processes, thus giving them access to her metalinguistic thinking. And all of this work was done around a contemporary cultural event and its associated language practices and pictorial representations—the marketing of a version of motherhood.

Parents' responses to O'Brien's treatment of Mother's Day suggest that for them it was a legitimate element of educational practice. Most mothers made the time to answer the survey questions. Some listened as their children read the questions aloud; others helped inexperienced writers to record answers by supplying correct spelling or by scribing their answers. Further, many took the trouble to provide elaborate responses marked by tenderness, fantasy, and humor. Although it is unusual for young students in South Australian schools to study community texts such as Mother's Day catalogs or to research such a widely valued and generally unquestioned cultural event, parents did not question O'Brien or the school leadership about the project.

We suggest that two aspects of local educational conditions throw light on parents' responses. First, parents are generally not offered the chance to shape pedagogical decisions in government primary schools. At O'Brien's school, for example, decisions about what to teach and how and when were made by teachers at the classroom level, guided by, but not limited to, curriculum outlines developed at the state level. Teachers then informed parents about curricular decisions. Parents were encouraged to discuss their children's progress and happiness through a range of formal and informal mechanisms, but spaces for questioning content or perspective were not easily found. Second, O'Brien's pedagogy incorporated elements both familiar and highly regarded in the local context. For example, parents in the South Australian school system are often invited to join in classroom projects as informants, and reading and writing with children at home are valued practices. Further, O'Brien's attention to spelling and presentation of student written products matched current discourses in government and media spheres placing value on traditional literacy skills. Parents were in a sense co-opted by O'Brien to continue school-based pedagogical activities at home, a familiar position for parents in this setting.

Clearly, this was not an approach to teaching that could be called "anything goes" eclecticism, nor was it a step-by-step, formulaic approach to critical literacy. O'Brien put together the pedagogies that would assist her and her students in learning about the way their world worked and the way texts worked in their world. Teaching technologies such as teacher scribing, big book production, and teacher-parent newsletters were put to work in new ways on a socially significant local research project. The students in O'Brien's class discovered that there were discrepancies between what the fliers said their mothers wanted and what their mothers said they wanted. They discovered that the mothers in the catalogs looked different from their own mothers. In the catalogs, they noted an absence of Vietnamese, Aboriginal, and Lebanese mothers; more fair-haired and fair-skinned mothers; and more young than older mothers. The results of their analysis raised questions for them about why these texts were constructed to make motherhood appear the exclusive domain of middle-class, white, young, thin, women!

O'Brien was committed to making different positions available to students and to assisting them in contesting the taken-for-granted representations of gender and culture in the texts which shape everyday lives. In this case, she initiated the problem to be explored. She also decided on the kinds of textual practices that were likely to be of use, and explicitly showed the children how to produce the genre needed for the job at hand.

Lessons about Critical Literacy

The cases discussed here demonstrate that critical literacy is not formulaic; nor can it be characterized as a single approach or method of teaching (Comber, 1994). If anything, critical literacy is disruptive of many of the taken-for-granted assumptions (e.g., about curriculum, the teacher's role, appropriate texts) that drive most models of literacy teaching. But some principles underpinning critical literacy can be gleaned from the cases described.

Critical literacy is more than sets of activities. It takes seriously issues of content, especially those arising from local and daily sources. In each case described, the topics of the literacy lessons emerged from contemporary events and conditions in the students' and teachers' local worlds. McKinnon brought global issues from her own experience to local classroom relationships. The Seaview Grove teacher responded to students' observations about the lack of trees in their local area, and in following this lead took the students into new inquiries about the effects of urban renewal. O'Brien brought community texts and cultural events into the classroom as objects of study. These approaches also involved moving beyond the study of the standard, the mainstream, the accepted constructions (of good literature, of literacy) to include minority viewpoints. Here, critical literacy disrupted the apparently seamless presentation of literacy and literate practices as givens, as standards, to show that different perspectives were available and critique was possible.

The content covered connected local issues with broader social themes. As well as capitalizing on the opportunities which inevitably arose in daily life, the teachers here helped young students to research and analyze wider cultural events and artifacts that entailed various local representations and manifestations.

The students were engaged as language researchers. The students and teachers spent time researching how language worked in particular situations and through specific texts. Even very young children were involved in this. Students were placed in a different power relation with literacy. Rather than asking students to come to the study of literacy as neophytes, the teachers acknowledged students' knowledge about language and skill in its use and helped them use that knowledge to ask questions about, and analyze, others' use of language and its effects.

The teachers also made classroom and public texts objects of study and critique. Students and teachers questioned the assumptions behind texts and analyzed their taken-for-granted messages. Texts were not read as truth, nor as neutral, natural representations of the world, but as the products of decisions that served specific interests and shaped particular worldviews. In other words, rather than inviting the students to "get inside" texts, the teachers helped students to become distanced from texts, to treat them as objects, to consider how they were created and what would or could flow from them.

We argue that the kind of work summarized here is important in these times. These cases show that broader contexts such as government and education policy have an impact on what is possible, as do opportunities for teachers to connect to wider networks of support such as research projects. In these broader contexts, however, not all teachers take up the challenges offered by critical literacy. Other factors, more personal and local, also affect the fate of critical literacy practices. It is to this issue we now turn.

Critical Literacy: Personal and Local Contexts

Our presentation of responses to cases of critical literacy in South Australia has pointed to the disruptive potential of a critical perspective; to the diverse responses of teachers and students; and to the difficulties that critical literacy presents to teachers in classrooms. We have used these cases to note the broader contexts which have made this work possible, such as government and educational policy and curriculum development. We now turn to a case that illustrates some of the more local and personal contexts for work in critical literacy. Jennifer O'Brien provides a selective account of the local circumstances that supported her efforts to incorporate a critical perspective into the broadly whole language pedagogy that she, along with many teachers in South Australia, practiced with the five- to eight-year-olds in her classes. We asked, "What were the conditions that made a critical literacy possible in South Australian schools?" and "How does critical literacy get onto the agenda?" O'Brien now takes up the account in her own voice.

In 1990, while working on literacy assessment and reporting with teachers in disadvantaged school settings, I returned to postgraduate study and research. A significant part of the program and my reading was constructed around the theoretically based research of critical, feminist, and poststructuralist educators with social and political interests in challenging prevailing practices in the literacy curriculum and secondary English teaching. This work connected with my interest in the limits of contemporary anti-sexist educational practices (such as removing from the library books that stereotype girls and women as weak) to undermine the unequal educational experiences of girls (O'Brien, 1998). These educators suggested that literacy practices:

- ◆ be scrutinized for their potential to reproduce or challenge existing power structures (for example, Lankshear with Lawler, 1989)

- ◆ reposition students from their earliest years as critical analysts of school and community texts

- ◆ interrupt the subordination of readers to texts' representations of the social world (for example, Baker & Freebody, 1989; Freebody & Luke, 1990; Luke, 1991)

- ◆ examine gendered reading practices and writing practices

In response to these insights, I interrupted and complicated, rather than replaced, the literacy curriculum in my classroom. Into a predominantly whole language, progressivist practice, I incorporated a particular focus on gender and education. I made two key moves designed to question the taken-for-granted ways of doing literacy in junior primary classrooms: I expanded the range of classroom texts to include mass media and community texts, and I repositioned students and myself as critical analysts of texts.[5]

The moves were not taken in isolation. In fact, local institutional and political conditions were crucial in expanding space for me and other radical teachers to take up critical and feminist agendas. The work of curriculum officers in the gender and education and poverty programs set up by the South Australian Education Department made room for teachers to adopt critical positions. I was supported by a rapidly expanding literature in what came to be known widely as critical literacy. Also, my interruptions to assumptions about the way things ought to be between teachers and students and their texts were supported at personal and professional levels by a trusted colleague at a local tertiary institution.

Inequalities in girls' educational experiences and improvement in the educational participation of students living in poverty were on the agendas of both Australian and South Australian governments at that time. At the federal level, the Gender Equity and Curriculum Reform Project was funded by the Department of Employment, Education and Training. This project aimed to ensure that the gender equity principles of the national Policy for the Education of Girls in Australian Schools were "incorporated" into local policy development. In South Australia, the brief was taken up by the Education of Girls Unit. Officers of this unit collaborated with other sections of the educational bureaucracy contributing feminist, critical, and (in many cases) poststructuralist perspectives to publications and programs.

Similarly, the South Australian Disadvantaged Schools Programs and Targeted Populations Unit, funded by the Commonwealth National Equity Program for Schools, initiated equity-based programs in schools where poverty, isolation, gender, and Aboriginality were implicated in significant educational inequalities. Such officially sponsored moves carved out key places where local radical educators were able to contribute to policy development and simultaneously create spaces for social justice issues to be pursued by teachers coming from diverse positions.

The connections ran in all directions, bringing teachers in professional associations and educational bureaucrats with subject-specific curriculum briefs into a common space, creating and expanding new partnerships and places for critical inquiry. The elements of friendship and trust must not be forgotten. One example will make the point. Barbara Comber and I presented a collaboratively written account of critical literacy, including reflection on its practice in my early-years classrooms, at the annual conference of the (then) Australian Reading Association. This paper was published in a local university-based forum for critical educators (Comber & O'Brien, 1993a). It was subsequently taken up by an officer of the Targeted Populations Unit (a close colleague from previous teaching days) and republished in the series of discussion papers as part of the Social Justice Action Plan and distributed to all schools in the Disadvantaged Schools Program (Comber & O'Brien, 1993b). This group of friends and colleagues is still working together and with other partners across institutions and states to produce research, talks, papers, teaching resources, and chapters for books.

This case illustrates some of the personal and local contextual issues that have an impact on the fate of critical literacy. It should be noted, however, that this was not a universal experience. For many teachers, critical analysis was problematic. They contested the position from a number of viewpoints: that it would spoil students' enjoyment, that young students were manipulated into "unnatural" readings of texts, that students were too young to engage in this practice. Teachers questioned whether students' critically framed contributions to classroom discussion were their "real" responses, claiming instead that students were able to join in because we had "put words in students' mouths" or because students know "what the teacher wants to hear." Some teachers had difficulty with the position that textual and institutional authority could be the object of critical inquiry. In general, teachers' responses were marked by uncertainty not only about the meaning of critical literacy, but also about how to do it and what critical literacy looked like in the classroom.

On the other hand, a significant coalition of teachers did take up the challenges of critical literacy and used the opportunities provided by the introduction of new curriculum documents for English teaching in South Australian government schools. It became possible, for example, for educators committed to radical pedagogies to suggest to teachers reluctant to embrace the claims of critical literacy that the critical approach was now a required position. Thus critical literacy began to work its way into schools and tertiary institutions in South Australia, carried by flexible coalitions of tertiary teachers and students, classroom teachers, and members of English- and literacy-teaching professional associations in a variety of settings including seminars, workshops, and talks. Teachers familiar with socially analytic positions taken in media studies and literary studies and other kinds of new work such as antiracism studies and antisexism programs, showed strong interest and support for these approaches in the context of literacy.

Conclusions

Critical literacy is disruptive of taken-for-granted conceptions of literacy and its role in the school curriculum. By positioning students as language researchers, opening up the curriculum to minority constructions of language, and engaging students in critical analysis of texts, different kinds of authority relations are engendered—between students, between students and texts, and between students and teachers. As the cases described have shown, bringing critical literacy to the classroom also affects teachers through their personal histories, their beliefs about their role, and their professional and other networks.

These cases illustrate how critical literacy can work in classrooms. As O'Brien's retrospective analysis of the conditions that supported her actions demonstrates, however, it is important that this work not be cast as that of heroic individual teachers working in the privacy of their classrooms. Just as critical literacy emphasizes the social and situated nature of language and learning, we argue that the fate of disruptive curriculum practices is strongly connected to the wider social and power networks of educational settings.

The teaching and research referred to in this chapter reveal a number of common practices that have made critical literacy possible in the first place and sustained it over time. The fate of critical literacy will be determined by the ability of educators to sustain these practices in these new, uncertain, and changing times.

The first of these practices is collaboration between school and university colleagues. The research work of Comber referred to earlier has been marked by teachers and academics working together to inform practice with theory and theory with practice. Theories about literacy that are removed from the influence of teachers and the constraints and possibilities of classroom action tend to have little sustaining power. The work described in the case sections proves that teachers are important knowledge producers who can use their own experience and practice to inform, question, critique, and extend theoretical insights.

The second practice has been the cultivating of connections between classroom and university researchers and school system leaders and curriculum developers. The descriptions of the South Australian context described by O'Brien illustrate the way in which networks of educators, connected institutionally through study, research projects, and friendship, can form a "critical mass" of colleagues and influence policy and curriculum. The networking described here has been crucial in taking a practice from a stage of innovation and individual action into mainstream schooling where, exposed to debate, modification, and revision, it can be developed by teachers and adapted to changing contexts and times.

The third practice has been the involvement of educators committed to social justice in the sometimes tedious and difficult work of curriculum and policy development in state and federal government organizations. These people have also been connected to wider political efforts which have resulted in issues of equity, gender, poverty, and difference becoming objects of government policy and practice.

The fourth practice has been the emphasis on the local and avoidance of recipelike constructions of pedagogy. If critical literacy is to work for students of difference and contribute to more equitable educational outcomes, it needs to remain adaptable to local circumstances and the particular needs of different groups of students, their communities, and teachers. Thus critical literacy must mean different things in a tightly knit, isolated community with one television station, no library, and no daily papers but rich local oral language resources than it does in a school serving an ethnically diverse urban community, saturated with print and visual texts, where most workers commute. The illustrations we have provided do not imply that "anything goes" for critical literacy, but they do show that an enormous diversity of classroom talk, reading, and writing can arise from a commitment to students as language researchers, the foregrounding of minority uses of language, and the critical analysis of texts. What makes the practices we have illustrated count as critical literacy is, in part, that they engage with issues that are significant in the daily lives of students and their communities and that they are useful to them now as well as in the future.

Notes

1. An earlier version of this case appears in Comber and Kamler (1997).

2. The teacher in this case is not named here. This research is part of an ongoing collaborative research project with the South Australian Department for Education, Training and Employment (DETE) to investigate the acquisition of school literacies by children living in socioeconomically disadvantaged communities. The research team includes Barbara Comber, Helen Nixon, Lynne Badger, Jenny Barnett (University of Southern Australia), and Jane Pitt (DETE).

3. Curriculum documents were produced for each of eight areas of learning: English, mathematics, science, technology, languages other than English, health and physical education, studies of society, and the environment and the arts.

4. "Early childhood teacher" is a term referring to teachers who work with children in preschools, kindergartens, and the first two to three years of school.

5. Accounts of these moves are found in Comber and O'Brien (1993a) and O'Brien (1994a, 1994b).

References

Australian Education Council. (1994a). *A statement on English for Australian schools.* Carlton, Victoria: Curriculum Corporation.

Australian Education Council. (1994b). *A statement on studies of society and environment for Australian schools; a curriculum profile for Australian schools: A joint project of the states, territories and the commonwealth of Australia initiated by the Australian Education Council.* Carlton, Victoria: Curriculum Corporation.

Baker, C. D., & Freebody, P. (1989). *Children's first school books: Introductions to the culture of literacy.* Oxford, UK: B. Blackwell.

Cochran-Smith, M. (1995). Uncertain allies: Understanding the boundaries of race and teaching. *Harvard Educational Review, 65,* 541–70.

Comber, B. (1994). Critical literacy: An introduction to Australian debates and perspectives. *Journal of Curriculum Studies 26,* 655–68.

Comber, B., & Kamler, B. (1997). Critical literacies: Politicising the language classroom. *Interpretations, 30,* 30–53.

Comber, B., & O'Brien, J. (1993a). Critical literacy: Classroom explorations. *Critical Pedagogy Networker, 6*(1 & 2), 1–11.

Comber, B., & O'Brien, J. (1993b). Critical literacy: Classroom explorations. *Social Justice Action Plan Discussion Paper No. 4.* Adelaide, Australia: Targeted Populations Unit, Curriculum Division Department of Education, Employment and Training, South Australia.

Dyson, A. (1993). *Social worlds of children learning to write in an urban primary school.* New York: Teachers College Press.

Freebody, P., & Luke, A. (1990). "Literacies programs: Debates and demands in cultural context" in *Prospect: Australian Journal of ESL 5*(3).

Gee, J., & Lankshear, C. (1995). The new work order: Critical language awareness and "fast capitalism" texts. *Discourse, 16,* 5–19.

Green, B., Hodgens, J., & Luke, A. (1994). *Debating literacy in Australia: A documentary history, 1946–1990* (Vols. 1 & 2). Sydney: Australian Literacy Federation.

Lankshear, C., with Lawler, M. (1989). *Literacy, schooling and revolution.* New York: Falmer Press.

Luke, A. (1991). Towards a critical sociology of reading pedagogy: An introduction. In C. Baker & A. Luke (Eds.), *Towards a critical sociology of reading pedagogy: Papers of the X11 World Congress on Reading.* Amsterdam: John Benjamins.

Luke, A., & Freebody, P. (1997). Critical literacy and the question of normativity: An introduction. In S. Muspratt, A. Luke, & P. Freebody (Eds.), *Constructing critical literacies: Teaching and learning textual practice* (pp. 1–18). Creskill, NJ: Hampton Press.

Luke, A., O'Brien, J., & Comber, B. (1994). Making community texts objects of study. *Australian Journal of Language and Literacy, 17*(2), 139–49.

New London Group. (1996). A pedagogy of multiliteracies: Designing social futures. *Harvard Educational Review, 66*(1), pp. 60–92.

Nixon, H. (1998). Fun and games are serious business. In J. Sefton-Green (Ed.), *Digital diversions: Youth culture in the age of multimedia.* London: University College London Press.

O'Brien, J. (1994a). Critical literacy in an early childhood classroom: A progress report [Focus Issue: Critical Literacy]. *Australian Journal of Language and Literacy.*

O'Brien, J. (1994b). "Show mum you love her": Taking a new look at junk mail. *Reading 28*(1), 43–46.

O'Brien, J. (1998). Experts in Smurfland. In M. Knobel & A. Healy (Eds.), *Critical literacies in the primary classroom* (pp. 13–26). Newtown, New South Wales, Australia: Primary English Teaching Association.

Taylor, S., Rizvi, F., Lingard, B., & Henry, M. (1997). *Educational policy and the politics of change.* London: Routledge.

CHAPTER FIVE

Desegregation versus Bilingual Education: The Struggles of a School Community

CARYL GOTTLIEB CROWELL
Borton Primary Magnet School

ROBERT C. WORTMAN
Tucson Unified School District

For eighteen years, the Borton Primary Magnet School community has met every morning on the patio of the school for an opening ritual. Each week, one of the classes takes responsibility for leading the school in a favorite song, reciting the Pledge of Allegiance to the flag, and inviting adult announcements. It is impossible for most of the community even to think about beginning the day without this threshold ceremony (Peterson, 1992). This morning one of the bilingual classrooms is taking its turn on the patio stage. We can't help but notice that eighteen of the twenty-two students are Latino.

Our Dilemma

It is a disturbing realization in a court-ordered desegregated magnet school, established specifically to reduce minority isolation, that language policies have created de facto segregation. This, however, is not an unusual situation. Despite numerous court cases resulting in the forced desegregation of minority students, Latino students enjoy "the dubious distinction of being the most highly segregated group of America's children" (Menchaca & Valencia, 1990, p. 22). Many schools face difficult, if not impossible, decisions in attempting to meet the competing demands of both desegregation orders and mandates for bilingual education (Donato, Menchaca, & Valencia, 1991). Borton is no exception. On the one hand, we receive funding to further the integration of our classrooms and school community. On the other hand, in order for our district to receive funding for bilingual programs, Spanish-speaking students must be placed with teachers who have state-issued bilingual endorsements. There are not enough appropriately certified teachers at the school to both integrate and provide bilingually certified adults for all Spanish-speaking students. And in our zeal to provide what we believe is the best educational opportunity for our students, we have segregated them by language, and thus by ethnicity.

In this chapter, we share a brief history of Borton school and our early attempts to meet the contradictory demands of dual mandates, the conditions that motivated us to make fundamental changes in how we are rising to this challenge, and the roadblocks and paths we have encountered as we invent new ways to promote bilingualism for everyone in the Borton community.

Where We Began

Borton Primary Magnet School is a small school of 230 kindergarten through second-grade students located in an inner-city neighborhood surrounded by industrial sites and businesses. The high rate of substance abuse and related crimes in the area is exacerbated by the presence of several rival street gangs. The neighborhood buildings are regularly marked with gang graffiti, although the school itself is rarely touched.

Since 1979 and the advent of a larger districtwide desegregation court order, Borton has been a primary magnet school in a system of 102 school sites. The Borton neighborhood population is primarily lower-income minority: 80 percent Hispanic; 10 percent African American; 5 percent Asian American; 5 percent American Indian. Almost 45 percent of our students come from homes in which Spanish is the primary language. All kindergarten through second-grade students from the neighborhood attend Borton. By court order, neighborhood third- , fourth- , and fifth-grade students are bused to another school which is nine miles away in a predominantly European American neighborhood.

The court order requires that Borton maintain a student-body balance of 51 percent European American and 49 percent minority students by busing in European American students from across the district. The majority of bused students enter as kindergartners. Borton receives additional desegregation funding but no Title I or other compensatory program support. The court order provides for lower student to teacher ratios (20/1 in kindergarten and 25/1 in first and second grades), a fine arts specialist, a physical education specialist, a full-time counselor, a full-time librarian, full-time teaching assistants, and an extended day program which offers supervised enrichment activities before and after school.

A strong teacher association contract gives additional teaching assistant time to bilingual teachers who are assigned to classrooms identified as bilingual. The contract also provides for additional bilingual aide time for bilingual combination classes.

Over the years, our bilingual program developed in concert with our opportunities to add additional faculty and staff or fill vacancies left by staff members who moved on. Any open position was advertised as "bilingual required," increasing our endorsed bilingual faculty from three to five teachers. At the same time, the district's director of bilingual education was pushing schools to comply with state and federal guidelines for bilingual programs. It seemed our district was losing about half a million dollars a year due to noncompliance issues. At Borton we were delighted to be able to provide bilingual classroom placements for all of our Spanish-speaking students who were learning English. All of us believed that such children needed to study with endorsed teachers in order to continue developing their native languages while learning English at the same time. The bilingual teachers clung tenaciously to this belief while also arguing for better-integrated classes.

In complying with guidelines for bilingual education, we were "resegregating," filling the bilingual classrooms with minority students. For a couple of years, we attempted to cure this imbalance by first placing all the bilingual children with endorsed teachers and then adding enough European American students to the bilingual classrooms to reflect the court-required ethnic distributions. The result was very large bilingual classes—twenty-seven to thirty students as opposed to twenty-two or twenty-three in the nondesignated classrooms. But when we attempted to control for class size, we were faced with the same segregation problem: our bilingual classrooms then had about 85 percent minority enrollment.

Studies show that Hispanic students learn more English in classrooms that provide opportunities for Spanish-speaking students to interact with English-speaking peers (Merino, 1991). Within the highly segregated bilingual classrooms at Borton, English and Spanish speakers worked together when required; however, the students tended to sort themselves by language when they made their own choices of working groups. English was spoken mostly among adults and in adult talk directed to students. The small number of English-speaking students in the classes isolated themselves whenever possible. A few of the quieter Spanish-speaking students rarely put themselves in the position of having to speak English at all during the course of the entire year.

The problems with isolation and communication were not confined to the classroom. Groupings and relationships along language and ethnic lines also appeared during the lunch hour. The almost entirely minority neighborhood students, who qualified for free lunch, ate in the cafeteria; the English-speaking nonminority students, who often brought their own lunches, ate on the patio. The students who ate together tended to play together, too. In playground disputes, European American students complained about "those kids, those Mexican kids." Similar epithets were hurled from the other direction.

The school staff members were not the only ones concerned about the bilingual program. As the program became increasingly identified with minority students, fewer extended-community parents were requesting placements for their children in the bilingual classrooms. European American parents whose children were placed in the bilingual classrooms raised questions about the possibility that their children would not understand what was happening during the day. Lacking knowledge about and experience with bilingual education, English-speaking parents thought the bilingual classrooms used nothing but Spanish, and worried that their children would not have access to the curriculum. They saw the pervasive, but purposeful, oral language that characterizes bilingual classrooms as chaos and turmoil. Moreover, the children of the few parents who did want opportunities for their English-speaking children to learn Spanish did not have consistent access to bilingual education from one year to the next.

Committing to Change

We were caught between the proverbial rock and a hard place, perplexed by the conflicting mandates to desegregate our school and to provide bilingual education for all who qualified. By making the language needs of our students our top priority, we were perpetuating a view of bilingual education as compensatory education, intended only for minority children who spoke a language other than English. At the same time, we could no longer ignore the ethnic segregation of our students within a supposedly desegregated magnet school established under court order. We had arrived at the moment of change. None of our previous solutions had worked. We were loathe to initiate involuntary transfers of faculty in the hopes of acquiring more bilingual teachers since we saw the collegial community as one of the school's strengths. Something new had to be invented.

In the fall of 1995, Borton joined the Educational and Community Change (ECC) project. Created in 1990 by Dr. Paul Heckman of the University of Arizona, this project supported school communities in inquiry about the nature of schooling. The ECC project's work was based on the belief that change must be indigenous—that is, the invention of those most directly involved in the schooling of our students: teachers, administrators, parents, community residents, and the students themselves. With a combination of project and district funds, teachers and staff who chose to participate met once a week for a three-hour dialogue session, the ECC project's tool in the inquiry process. While substitute teachers covered our classes for half a day once a week, we gathered to examine the work we do with students and other adults. We hoped that the outcome of our inquiry would be a fundamentally different notion of "school," one built on our common interests.

Dialogue sessions during the first year often concerned problems related to segregation in the bilingual program. As our understanding of these problems deepened, we made a bold decision: we would place bilingual students in all of the classrooms the following year. Our inquiry in dialogue sessions would help us find new ways of working together both to foster integration and to meet the native-language literacy needs of all the students.

The next school year began auspiciously. Nonbilingual teachers were concerned but optimistic about having Spanish-speaking children in their classrooms. Only a few parents requested changes in their children's room assignments, including a few Latino parents who adamantly requested English-immersion placements for their children. These parents were not happy to hear that all the classrooms would offer bilingual education. The principal met individually with each of these families to answer their questions and to give them an opportunity to more fully voice their concerns. All parents were invited to observe in the classrooms and meet with the teachers, and they were provided with several articles on the benefits of bilingual education. Most parents, however, were happy that their children would have more opportunities to interact with speakers of a second language.

The reactions of the students to the changes in class composition were as varied as the students themselves. The Spanish-speaking students took everything in stride; they had always expected to learn to speak English. A few of the European American, extended-neighborhood students were noticeably annoyed at being expected to even listen to Spanish. One strong-willed kindergartner complained loudly whenever Spanish was used in his classroom. At the same time, however, his parents reported that he was teaching them the Spanish he was learning at school. Josiah, a first grader, shared his feelings that being in a bilingual classroom was "a little bit scary and a little bit cool." When asked by his teacher to explain his comment more fully, he replied, "It's scary because I don't always know everything that people are saying and it's cool because I'm learning Spanish." Other European American students were also delighted with their language-

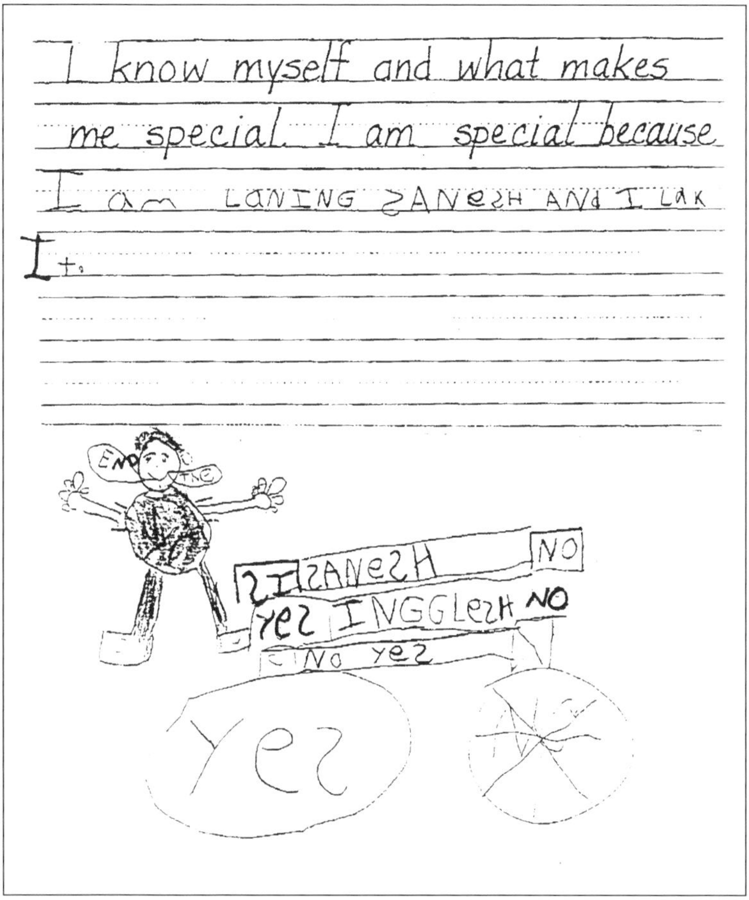

FIGURE **5.1.** *Student's response to learning Spanish.*

learning opportunities, and by fall conferences were writing in their self-assessments, "I'm learning Spanish and I like it!" and "I'm special because I'm bilingual" (see Figure 5.1). Classroom teachers continuously talked with their students about sensitivity to language learners, about the right to learn in one's native language, about the multiplicity of languages in the world, and about the importance and advantages of being bilingual.

We were aware of the need to provide opportunities for students to use their second languages in authentic ways (Wortman,

1991). In the classroom, students were encouraged to work together on meaningful projects, supported by the use of both Spanish and English languages and literacies. When language differences were pushed to the background and students' own language skills became resources for the group's meaning-making work, language proficiency developed almost as a by-product of the other learning taking place (Whitmore & Crowell, 1994).

Outside of the classroom, we also created contexts for natural and positive interactions between English and Spanish speakers. Given the groupings that evolved in connection with the free lunch program, we chose to purchase additional picnic tables for the patio so that students who ate hot lunches could carry their trays outdoors to join friends with lunchboxes. The result: more ethnically mixed groupings and leisurely conversation at lunchtime and fewer and less racially charged disputes on the playground.

Despite the presence of bilingual children in all our classrooms, a district site review team that evaluated the school's efforts to meet our self-identified and district goals noted that English predominated in many school contexts. As a result of the review team's observation, the staff made a concerted effort to increase the functional use of Spanish in the school environment. Our community representative made sure the seasonal displays she created for the front hallway made prominent use of Spanish. Teachers were encouraged to augment the visible Spanish print in their rooms (e.g., posters, labels, song charts, other environmental print), and they also ensured that their students had access to Spanish books and other materials. A second-grade English-speaking teacher drew on several resources to create Spanish posters of classroom norms and directions for daily activities. Her Spanish-speaking teaching assistant and even the assistant's mother offered spelling and grammatical support.

Examining Our Beliefs

The dialogue sessions proved to be a forum for critical discussion about issues related to the Borton School bilingual program.

At first some of the teachers who had limited experiences with bilingual learners were confused by the students' use of language. In one kindergarten, a Spanish-speaking child had invented a spelling for *conejo* (rabbit) to accompany his drawing. But when he read his work to the teacher, he read "rabbit," despite the teacher's insistent, "No, you wrote '*conejo*.'" In sharing with the dialogue group, that kindergarten teacher expressed her concern that the student was confused by his dual language environment. She viewed his language use as code switching, which to her meant not being able to communicate well in either language. One of the bilingual teachers brought another view of language to the discussion, explaining that bilingual speakers in her classroom were expected to make decisions about which language to use based on the needs of their audience. Perhaps, as Genishi (1981) wrote, that kindergarten child sensed that his teacher was more comfortable with English. The bilingual teacher also talked about the fact that many researchers and educators view code switching as a natural phenomenon in dual language communities, one that allows bilingual individuals to identify themselves as members of the same speech community through their use of both Spanish and English in the same utterance.

Participants brought their observations about students' second-language learning to the dialogue groups. For example, we noted a student's shifts from all Spanish to efforts to sometimes use English (occasionally with exhausted requests such as "*está bien si sigo en español?*" (is it okay if I continue in Spanish?) to explorations of English literacy and eventually to apparent comfort in both languages. We discussed examples of English speakers' decreasing requests for translations and one English-speaking student's growing fluency in Spanish as she pursued a friendship with a Spanish-speaking classmate. In fifteen months, Anna went from "inventing" Spanish (nonsense syllables with Spanish rhythm and intonation) to being proficient enough in Spanish to be used as a "Spanish consultant" by her mainstream peers. A few months later, Anna was beginning to read and write in Spanish (see Figure 5.2). Meanwhile, Anna's friend Jeanette had acquired considerable fluency in English, so both girls used both languages in their conversations and play with each other. Such special friendships and the opportunities they create for bilingualism have been

Anna:

Lo que yo aprendí en el Salón del Sol. Yo aprendí de rocas. Yo aprendí de las estrellas. Yo aprendí como leer. Y yo aprendí a escribir. A mí le gusta a matemáticas y subtracción. Y yo aprendí a cometa. Yo aprendí a las planetas. Yo aprendí mucho español y señales. Yo aprendí, aprendí escribir un cuentos.	[What I learned in the Sunshine Room. I learned about rocks. I learned about stars. I learned how to read. I learned to write. I like mathematics and subtraction. I learned about the comet. I learned about the planets. I learned a lot of Spanish and Sign. I learned, I learned to write stories.]

FIGURE 5.2. *Evidence of Anna's progress in Spanish-language acquisition.*

documented at Borton in other years as well (Whitmore & Crowell, 1994).

Seeing Ourselves as Language Learners

The dialogue sessions also helped us see the need to foreground ourselves as language learners: to demonstrate to our students the power that two languages offer us and the strategies we use in our language learning and our communication. Those of us who are learning a second language are doing so publicly. The principal, a native English speaker with three years of high school Spanish and nineteen years in a bilingual community, stretches himself to speak Spanish. He greets families and attempts to translate into Spanish at group meetings. He reads children's books in Spanish and organizes class discussions in two languages around his weekly read-alouds (Wortman & Matlin, 1995). He invites children to become language brokers (Whitmore & Crowell, 1994) by spotlighting bilingual children and their contributions to the school community.

Throughout the school, we have articulated the expectation that all members of the community can promote bilingualism even if individual members are less fluent than others. All classrooms send home a weekly bilingual bulletin about classroom curriculum and events. The office also publishes a weekly bulletin in English and Spanish. This expectation has increased the

> *Gracias por la carta. Me gustó. Me gusta la manera que se porta.*
> *Escribe bonito. Por cuántos años a trabajado en Borton? Me gustó la*
> *opera que hizo. Love, Raquel*
>
> [Thank you for the letter. I liked it. I like the way you act. You write
> well. How many years have you worked at Borton? I liked the opera
> that you made.]

FIGURE 5.3. *Student communication through the schoolwide postal system.*

need for collaboration. Bilingual adults who normally do not take responsibility for translating school documents have been pressed into service. They have found their language skills growing as they handle the tasks of translating the office bulletin and classroom newsletters and interpreting at parent meetings and office interactions. Teachers who once thought they could never manage sending home newsletters in two languages have been surprised by their success.

The students too have become capable language teachers. They write to the principal in Spanish through the schoolwide postal system (see Figure 5.3). Some gave their English-speaking student teacher homework in the form of vocabulary lists and sat her down regularly to read from predictable Spanish texts, like any emerging reader.

In response to our programmatic advocacy of bilingualism, some staff members have signed up for formal classes in conversational Spanish. Our community representative has organized ESL classes for parents at their request—classes that employ many of the same learning strategies evident in Borton's classrooms.

Supporting One Another

Once we decided to desegregate our bilingual classrooms, we created new problems for ourselves regarding Spanish-speaking students' access to native-language materials and instruction. Instead of having a concentration of bilingual students in just five classrooms, we now had bilingual students in all eleven classrooms, which meant we needed to have a rich collection of fiction, nonfiction, and reference materials in Spanish in all the classrooms. Teachers located all such resources and developed a long-term plan for spending priorities; the principal used funds creatively to systematically expand the collection.

The implications for staffing as a result of our decision to desegregate the bilingual classrooms presented a more difficult set of problems. For example, it meant that we had to redistribute teaching assistant time. According to district criteria, our school was entitled to sixty hours per week of such assistance, above and beyond any other teacher assistants provided by other funding. Distributing the extra help across all the classrooms was one way to provide support for nonbilingual teachers. But this solution violated the consensus agreement between the education association and the district about giving extra help to bilingual teachers. Some teachers accepted this situation and promoted it as an equitable way to provide support for non-Spanish-speaking teachers and our Spanish-speaking students. Not everyone was happy, however. One bilingual teacher felt the education association had fought hard to win the right to extra support for bilingual teachers and that giving it up could be interpreted to mean that bilingual teachers did not really need such support. Another bilingual teacher felt she needed all of the extra aide time that would normally be assigned to her because her class was unusually difficult. The issue of aide time provoked much tension in the school. Finally, we resolved it by agreeing as a staff to avoid a rigid, uniform policy and instead to redistribute the teaching assistant time according to the needs of individual classrooms, including the varying numbers of Spanish-speaking students in each classroom.

The bilingual teaching assistants themselves were divided in their opinions on this approach. Some found it difficult to be consistent and thorough in their work as they moved among multiple classrooms. Others found the daily changes refreshing, allowing them to know many children at the school and to see differences in teaching practices.

Some teachers supported each other in the effort to provide native-language instruction by teaming for part of each day. For example, the part-time bilingual resource teacher for the Literacy Assistance Project, an in-class tutorial program focusing on effective reading strategies, provided additional native-language literacy support for the Spanish-speaking children. Limited playground space and materials led two kindergarten teachers to collaborate on outdoor playtime activities, a collaboration that extended into areas of literacy and biliteracy.

Challenges for the Future

In our determination to integrate classrooms and promote bilingual education for all students, we have made many changes. Our biggest challenge is to maintain our momentum. Sometimes change is so slow and difficult that retreating seems to be the simplest and most comfortable alternative. Despite the difficulty, we are still committed to our dual goals of desegregating by race and also providing bilingual instruction for all.

So far the response seems mostly positive. Parents are noticing the improved ethnic balance in classrooms and are excited about their children's second-language learning opportunities. Students, parents, and staff members alike are quick to notice the few classrooms that remain unbalanced in terms of language and ethnicity. In the balanced classrooms, English-speaking parents in particular have commented that their children are learning the second language. Spanish-speaking parents have always expected their children to learn the second language at school, but they are nevertheless surprised at how easily the children now seem to be learning English.

The principal's support and academic leadership have been critical. If he were to leave, we would still require administrative support for our self-established goals in order to continue. Although our current assignment of bilingual students to nondesignated classrooms does not completely meet the district's preferred guidelines for placement, we still comply with state and federal requirements and receive support from the district Department of Bilingual Education. Over the years, certain individuals within that department and a few other district departments who share our beliefs have trusted us as professionals to provide the best bilingual educational opportunities for our Spanish-speaking students. They have made it possible for us to use our allotted resources creatively. We do not advertise the details of our solution to the wider district community. Other than what we have said as a result of our involvement in the Education and Community Change Project, this chapter is the first formal public sharing of our work on issues of desegregation and bilingual education.

Among the staff, a few of the English-speaking teachers retain deep-seated concerns about their ability to teach students who speak another language; they worry that they are not providing the best learning experience for the Spanish-speaking students in their classes. Rather than retreating from our current integration efforts, we see a need to examine our beliefs about how children learn. Even though we profess to understand that children do not learn by transmission from adult to child, it is difficult to break out of old patterns of behavior and to recognize that our students have many resources for learning, including each other—their classroom teacher is not the only source of language and knowledge. There are numerous opportunities in our school and in the larger Tucson community to develop and draw on bilingual resources in natural learning contexts, throughout the school day, and across the school year. If we take advantage of those moments and also create new ones whenever possible, we provide support for English-speaking teachers and enhance the possibility that we will meet our goal of promoting bilingualism for all.

Our response to our colleagues', the parents', and the students' approximations of their abilities to communicate in a second language is critical. It is not unusual for Spanish-speaking parents to avoid school-home interactions because they are not able to communicate proficiently in English, which is still perceived as the most important school language. When the English-dominant principal uses Spanish with Spanish-speaking parents, however, they often thank him for his efforts and tell him how well he is doing. We need to remind ourselves to point out and celebrate these moments for all members of our community, recalling how successful we feel ourselves when others are gracious and appreciative of our efforts, however humble.

As we continue to move forward in our effort to both desegregate classrooms and promote bilingualism, the need for collaboration among all members of the school community becomes even more imperative. We recognize the continued need to carve out the time and space in our workday necessary to engage in dialogue about the theoretical beliefs we hold and the decisions we make about how to best reflect our beliefs in our daily practice. The traditional nature of schooling and the difficulty teachers and principals have in reconceptualizing their work with students and parents both hinder and force change, making dialogue and true collaboration among any community of people with diverse expectations and experiences our greatest challenge.

References

Donato, R., Menchaca, M., & Valencia, R. (1991). Segregation, desegregation, and integration of Chicano students: Problems and prospects. In R. Valencia (Ed.), *Chicano school failure and success: Research and policy agendas for the 1990s* (pp. 27–63). New York: Falmer Press.

Genishi, C. (1981). Code switching in Chicano six-year-olds. In R. Durán (Ed.), *Latino language and communicative behavior* (pp. 133–52). Norwood, NJ: Ablex.

Menchaca, M., & Valencia, R. R. (1990). Anglo-Saxon ideologies in the 1920s–1930s: Their impact on the segregation of Mexican students in California. *Anthropology and Education Quarterly, 21,* 222–49.

Merino, B. (1991). Promoting school success for Chicanos: The view from inside the bilingual classroom. In R. Valencia (Ed.), *Chicano school failure and success: Research and policy agendas for the 1990s* (pp. 119–48). New York: Falmer Press.

Peterson, R. (1992). *Life in a crowded place: Making a learning community.* Portsmouth, NH: Heinemann.

Whitmore, K., & Crowell, C. (1994). *Inventing a classroom: Life in a bilingual, whole language learning community.* York, ME: Stenhouse.

Wortman, R., & Matlin, M. (1995). *Leadership in whole language: The principal's role.* York, ME: Stenhouse.

Wortman, R. C. (1991). *Authenticity in the writing events of a whole language kindergarten/first grade classroom.* Unpublished doctoral dissertation, University of Arizona.

CHAPTER SIX

The Struggle for Fratney School

BOB PETERSON
La Escuela Fratney

F idel Castro once said that organizing the Cuban revolution was easy. The hard part was building a new society. I have often thought of those words during the past decade while working to build an innovative, whole language school in the inner city of Milwaukee. It was relatively easy for a group of teachers and parents to out-vote the superintendent and win the right to establish a new school. The hard part has been building a school that really works in the midst of deepening urban crisis.

La Escuela Fratney (Fratney School) is a public school in the River West neighborhood of Milwaukee, one of the city's few integrated neighborhoods, serving 360 kindergarten through fifth-grade students (65 percent Latino, 20 percent African American, 13 percent White), about 70 percent of whom are eligible for the federal free lunch. In this chapter, I consider how we got La Escuela Fratney started and the reactions of people to our school over the years since its inception. First there was the struggle with the school board to establish Fratney School, which lasted a few brief but stormy months in 1988. Then there was the struggle over developing the school's initial curriculum and program, which lasted six months. Finally there is the ongoing struggle to run a quality school in a low-income urban area with an antiracist, child-centered philosophy based on respect and cooperation—a philosophy at odds with many of society's dominant values.

This chapter is a revised version of an essay that appeared in *Public Schools That Work: Creating Community*. Copyright © 1993. From *Public Schools That Work* by Gregory A. Smith. Reproduced by permission of Routledge, Inc.

Stage 1: The Struggle to Establish Fratney School

In late 1987, La Escuela Fratney was only the dream of a group of parents and teachers who gathered in each other's homes on the northeast side of Milwaukee, a city of 700,000. The central administration of Milwaukee's public schools had announced the closing of a ninety-year-old school building in the neighborhood. It meant little to the district bureaucracy that the neighborhood around the school was one of the few racially integrated, working-class neighborhoods in the city. In response, some parents, teachers, and community activists organized a group called Neighbors for a New Fratney. The group wanted to start a quality school in an integrated neighborhood governed by a council of parents and teachers, a school that children would want to attend, where youngsters would be taught progressive, antiracist values in a bilingual (Spanish/English) setting and where they would learn through cooperative and innovative methods. In a few short weeks, we developed a comprehensive proposal for a two-way bilingual, whole language, multicultural, site-managed, neighborhood, specialty school—La Escuela Fratney.

The school administration had another dream, however, a dream that was a nightmare to some community activists. The administration wanted to turn the empty building into an "Exemplary Teaching Center." The staff was to be comprised of "master teachers," defined as those with master's degrees and at least ten years of teaching experience, using the techniques of Madeline Hunter, an educator who has extensively marketed a "teacher-proof" instructional method. The goal was to have these "exemplary" teachers work with Milwaukee public school (MPS) teachers who were having classroom difficulties, bringing these teachers into the center for two-and-a-half-week training sessions. In response, parents questioned whether they wanted their kids taught by a succession of ineffective teachers. They also argued that such a center could be established anywhere, while the New Fratney proposal could only unfold as envisioned at its present site in a multicultural neighborhood.

Our posters went out on New Year's Day 1988. We called for community meetings and a public hearing. The public hearing coincided with a bitter snowstorm that forced all schools to close the next day. Still, the turnout for the meeting was so large that it convinced the school board to give our proposal serious consideration. Members of public and private schools, community groups, and parent organizations spoke in favor of the school board supporting our bold experiment. The board directed the district's school administration to meet with us and to try to come back with a revised recommendation.

From the beginning, the leadership at the central office did not appear to understand our project; the administration put forth a "compromise" proposal to combine their Madeline Hunter-type teacher-training program with our project. What we had proposed was, in fact, diametrically opposed to their plan. They wanted a top-down model for a teacher-training school organized and run by the central office. We wanted a program run by a council of parents and teachers. As members of Neighbors for New Fratney sat negotiating with the top administrators in the superintendent's conference room, the absurdity of the situation became evident. One teacher pointed out that the proposals could not be combined, that either a school was to be run by the staff development academy or by a group of teachers and parents. Moreover, the teacher continued, the central office's proposal for the teacher center had not mentioned the word *parents* once. "Wait!" responded one top administrator. "While it's true we didn't mention 'parents' once in our proposal, your proposal didn't mention 'Central Office.'"

The representatives of Neighbors for a New Fratney left that meeting almost in shock. Not only had the central office failed to understand the proposal, but worse yet, an atmosphere of fear had pervaded the meeting. The administrators spoke only after raising their hands and being recognized by the superintendent and then only in tentative fashion. More frightening was that in the hall after the meeting, three staff members came up to members of Neighbors for a New Fratney and, while glancing over their shoulders, urged them not to compromise—they thought that the proposal was sound and should be left intact. They said, however, that they could not say anything, out of fear of repercussions.

We stuck to our position and continued to mobilize the community. We did this in the midst of favorable political conditions. A few months earlier the school board had gone on record in favor of site-based management. Members of the African American community, led by Howard Fuller (who later served as Milwaukee's superintendent of schools from 1991 to 1994), were demanding an independent school district, charging, among other things, that the bureaucracy was incapable of listening to parents. School board members had become aware of the benefits of a whole language teaching approach, in part due to the previous efforts of *Rethinking Schools,* a quarterly newspaper whose editorial board included a number of members of Neighbors for a New Fratney. Eventually, the school board not only passed our proposal and established the first citywide specialty school with neighborhood preference—which meant giving children who lived in the neighborhood first choice in enrollment—but the board also directed the central office to cooperate with Neighbors for a New Fratney.

School board members were also influenced by the quality of the teaching of individual teachers. One member later remarked that during a key school board meeting he found himself in the back room discussing the Fratney proposal with a top MPS administrator and realized that the man hadn't the slightest idea what our proposal involved. "Quite honestly," the board member stated, "I didn't really know what you were talking about either, but I knew this much. My son had started first grade in a classroom of a teacher who used what she called whole language techniques. By Thanksgiving my kid was coming home and writing and publishing his own books, excited about reading and writing, loving to read and to be read to. I knew I had to support the Fratney proposal."

An important lesson from the initial stage of our struggle can best be summed up in the words of Margaret Mead: "Never doubt that a small group of thoughtful committed citizens can change the world; indeed it's the only thing that ever has." Both the progressive political community in Milwaukee and the educational community were surprised at our initial victory. People have become so used to losing social struggles—on behalf of civil rights, labor, women, and so on—in the last fifteen years that a clear victory was unexpected. When people asked, "How did you do it?" the simple response was hard work, solid organization, and acting quickly when opportunities presented themselves. Teachers and parents, having been inculcated during their own years of schooling with notions that only the rich and famous make history, have rarely understood the importance and power of organized grassroots movements in changing society. This is not to say such success is easy, particularly in a big-city school bureaucracy. But we knew what we wanted, we researched what was necessary, and we used all the resources, connections, and energy we had to make it possible.

A second lesson is that concisely written, quality position papers are instrumental in the success of specific school struggles. The Neighbors for a New Fratney circulated a twelve-page document summarizing the entire proposal, from the pedagogical rationale to enrollment statistics in the neighborhood. Especially in the educational arena, and if widely circulated as a part of an overall organizing strategy, such a document can have a huge impact.

A third lesson is that antiracism and equality are key factors in building multiracial unity. The organizing effort would have failed if African Americans, Latinos of various nationalities, and Whites had not worked closely together. Working with multiracial groupings in a racially divided society is difficult, with the success of such efforts often dependent on the underlying politics of the project and the individuals involved. We looked at "equality" in three different ways: first, as a value that we wanted to teach the students; second, as a way to define the relationship between parents and teachers as we strove to become true partners in raising children and running a school; and third, as a way to structure the balance of power between the two languages at our school, English and Spanish. In addition, the proposal explicitly called for antiracism to be taught as a value. Some activists of color saw this as a further indication that this project was serious about building multiracial unity.

The final lesson from this stage of the struggle was that winning is often harder than losing. Having won control of an entire school, we found ourselves in an unfamiliar position. We now actually had the power to do something about problems that in the past we as teachers and parents could only complain about. In addition, we faced an entirely new set of problems that teachers and parents without power do not have to deal with, from school security to staff members who did not "fit" with the program.

A victory for parent and teacher power on the school level therefore redefines many problems, allowing them to be approached in a fresh and broader manner. This is not to say that all or even most educational problems can be solved at the school level—for they cannot—but it refocuses problems where they should be addressed—collectively at the school. Then, when it is apparent that either district, state, or federal policy guidelines must come into play, parents and teachers will be in a much better position to influence such policies.

Stage Two: The Struggle Over Planning the School

The school board's approval essentially concluded the first stage of the struggle—the struggle for political power. It lasted only eight weeks. The next stage consisted of struggling over the program—from staffing, to selection of the principal, to renovation of the facility, to adoption of curriculum and materials. Unfortunately, what the district administrators failed to do politically at the board level, they attempted to do administratively.

Despite the school board's explicit order that district administrators cooperate with our group, a couple of weeks passed with no meetings or other contact between the central office and Neighbors for a New Fratney. Finally, by chance we learned about an important meeting to plan Fratney that was to take place the following day. Although uninvited, we asked a parent to attend. Because the parent had no idea where in the central office building the meeting was to be held, she waited until five minutes after the meeting was scheduled to begin. She then approached the secretary of the administrator in charge and asked to be taken to the meeting. The secretary, who did not know this parent had not been invited, escorted her into a room of surprised administrators. With the participation of that parent, a joint meeting was set up to start the planning.

This was not the end of our struggles with central office administrators. Between March and September, the administration tried to undo our work in a dozen ways including stalling, ignoring, and even sabotaging the efforts of our group. For example, to deal with the problem of recruiting faculty who wanted to be in this particular program we proposed that when staff openings were announced, all teachers be given a one-page explanation of our program. The Milwaukee Teachers' Education Association agreed, as did lower-level administrators. But the higher authorities thought otherwise and the proposal was never enacted. Similarly, when the community argued for a nationwide search for a principal, the administration refused and then proceeded to stall hiring altogether. Finally, a month before school was to open, and in opposition to the recommendations of a parent committee, the administration recommended the appointment of a woman whose only experience had been in suburban schools. Ironically, she was bilingual—as the community had hoped—but in English and German, not English and Spanish. This was seen as a direct affront to the community, particularly the Hispanic community, and once again Neighbors for a New Fratney mobilized. Holding picket signs bearing slogans such as "Remember Gallaudet"—in reference to a similar struggle at the famous university for deaf and hard of hearing students in Washington, D.C.—dozens of parents came to school board meetings. Bowing to pressure and publicity, newly hired Superintendent Robert S. Peterkin recognized the mistake made by his predecessor and hired an interim principal acceptable to the community.

Then there was the question of developing the curriculum. Five teachers wrote a draft curriculum at the central office in late June and into July. There are 240 administrators at the central office, and it was difficult working among people who had bitterly opposed our plan. Budgetary information was given only if we asked exactly the right question. Secretarial help seemed in extremely short supply when it came to our needs. One of the Fratney teachers remarked at the time that working on the Fratney project at central office was like being a peace activist with a job in the Pentagon.

Even minor issues became sources of antagonism for some central office personnel. For example, the old school contained desks called bicycle desks because the chair is attached to the desk. Needless to say, such pieces of furniture are not conducive to cooperative group work, which requires chairs placed together in a circle. Despite repeated requests, the administrator in charge refused to change the desks for newer ones, until one day a Fratney teacher announced to him that we had changed our minds. We wanted the old desks to stay because on the first day of school all the parents, teachers, and students were going to pile them up on the playground, call a press conference, and expose the administration for its failure to support our project. The next morning, two truckloads of new desks arrived at our school.

As a consequence of such administrative resistance, our whole planning process was too rushed. Even more important, the administration refused to appoint anyone to work on the project full time, so from approval by the board in February to the opening in September we had no one working full time or even part time on the matter. Since this experience, the administration has seen fit to put someone, usually an administrator, in charge of the opening of any new school at least a semester in advance.

When we returned to work in mid-August to make what we thought would be final preparations for an opening a few weeks later, we found that necessary renovation had only just begun and that the school still needed to be cleaned from the previous spring. Curiously, nothing we had ordered in July had yet arrived. We called vendors, who told us they had no record of our orders. We were chagrined to discover that, although the requisition forms had been signed on July 18 or before by an associate superintendent, the forms had sat in the purchasing division for a month because the department did not have an authorization card with the associate superintendent's signature. Ultimately, the forms were not sent out until August 15—a full month after we had completed them. The error was particularly annoying because most classrooms had been emptied when the school closed, and our two-way bilingual program needed new materials. The few library books that remained at Fratney were in boxes because of the delayed renovation of the library. We started school with virtually no materials. "Well, at least we ordered a decent

Xerox machine," one of my colleagues said hopefully. "We can rely on that for the first few weeks of school." But, of course, when we called to check on that order, somehow it had been lost.

This was the last straw. We wondered, was this all happening because of sabotage or incompetence? To this day, we do not know. We prefer to believe it was sabotage because the alternative is even more frightening. We did not sit back and wait for these problems to solve themselves. To make a long story a bit shorter, we stormed back to the central office. Fortunately, this time we had gained two allies, the new superintendent and his assistant, Dr. Deborah McGriff, now superintendent of Detroit public schools. McGriff was flabbergasted by our story and listened intently as we hinted that our next step would be a round-the-clock occupation of the school. She took immediate steps to get the administrators in line.

The next day parents and teachers met again in the superintendent's conference room, but this time the atmosphere had changed. Word had come down from the top that we should be helped in any way possible. Representatives from Neighbors for a New Fratney spoke openly and were in charge of the agenda. We agreed on how to overcome a host of problems. A couple of days later, after visiting on the first day of school, Superintendent Peterkin called Fratney a "model" of his version of school reform, referring to the need for both heavy parental involvement and a unified vision of what a school should be. Finally the tide had turned.

One lesson we learned from this stage of the struggle is that school districts planning new schools or programs within schools must allocate enough time and resources to do a decent job. The money invested up front, before a school opens, is well invested, reducing or eliminating confusion and problems. Specifically, the lead time to start a new program should be at least a year. Money should be allocated so that staff and parents can spend extended time over a period of several months to plan and revise the new program.

We also learned that new structures—task forces, committees, and so forth—have to be designed to allow for parent and teacher involvement. At the insistence of Neighbors for a New

Fratney, joint committees were established between central office administrators and parents and teachers. This was something new for many administrators, and it meant meeting after regular work hours. Internally, we patterned ourselves after a typical community organization with subcommittees and a steering committee. Unfortunately, because of our truncated timeline, things had to occur so quickly that the steering committee did more work than was originally anticipated.

Lines of authority within the school administration should be made clear, from the superintendent and school board on down. In the final six months of planning for a new program, this line of authority should include one person, preferably full time and paid, as the coordinator of the project. As indicated earlier, the Milwaukee public school system now appoints a principal or program coordinator to a new school a semester in advance; however, such appointments should not compromise the power of the broader planning body of parents and teachers.

School districts must assume the responsibility for training teachers, parents, and principals to run an entire school. This should include training in budgets, purchasing procedures, personnel policies, labor contracts, physical plant maintenance and repair, and a host of state and federal guidelines. Without such knowledge, even the most dedicated parents and teachers can have their efforts thwarted by administrators who can use obscure guidelines and policies as obstacles to change. An all-too-common bureaucratic tactic is withholding information that is not specifically requested. If parents or teachers do not ask the right question, they are kept in ignorance until it is too late. Parent and teacher groups should demand training and designate among themselves who will become an "expert" in certain areas so that as a group, their collective knowledge will be equal to or even deeper than that of their possible opponents.

Finally, through a number of incidents during the planning stage, we learned that at times it is necessary to "play hardball" with recalcitrant school officials. At times, public demonstrations and the judicious use of the press are necessary tactics in winning these kinds of struggles.

Stage Three: Running the School

The first day of school in August 1988 brought us to the third stage of struggle: the implementation of our program. We could now finally direct our energies and attention to the business of creating a new program at La Escuela Fratney. Unfortunately, the consequences of months of inaction and poor planning were acutely felt throughout the first year. But the problems had a positive effect, too; they brought parents and teachers closer together. The steady opposition from the administration forced regular meetings of people in homes, community centers, and even public parks to plan strategies and mobilizations. It taught us that a successful urban school needs an active parent-teacher-community alliance to sustain it, as well as a common vision of what is meant by a quality school. Differences, at times sharp, arose between parents and teachers during this early stage, but the common goal of creating a multicultural school run by parents and teachers held us together.

One difference of opinion emerged over the composition of the council that would run the school. From February through September, the steering committee of Neighbors for a New Fratney was essentially making all decisions for the school, but power needed to be transferred from that group to the teachers who would work there and to the parents whose children had enrolled. Members of the steering committee offered different ideas on the composition of the council, ranging from having two parents elected from each of the eleven classrooms with only two teacher representatives to an equal representation of parents and teachers. The matter was partially resolved when we learned of a new agreement between the school board and the teachers' union prescribing that all such councils needed 50 percent plus one teacher representation. After much discussion, Neighbors for a New Fratney decided that fighting the school board and the union on this issue would be futile, and that instead we should adhere to the agreement but include in our council's procedures a provision for parent alternates that would essentially ensure equal voice at site-based council meetings.

A year later we confronted another problem with parent representation. As in many schools, those parents who turned out for meetings were mainly middle class, and in our case, increasingly White. Even though only 13 percent of our school is White, it was not unusual for 50 percent of the parents at any particular gathering to be White.

We have dealt with this issue on a couple of levels. For a few years, we adopted a "quota" system for our site-based council, ensuring that there would be at least one African American and one Hispanic parent on the council. The quota system proposal caused considerable discussion among parents, including some negative reaction by a few White parents. The main thing it did, however, was educate people about the importance of our council and the need for multiracial unity. In the nine years of the council, all racial groups have been well represented.

But as important as representation is on the governing site-based council, general parental involvement is even more important. From the beginning, we decided to hire a parent organizer to help increase parental involvement, particularly among those parents not inclined to automatically participate in school affairs. We have provided child care at all major school activities and meetings. We help parents with transportation through car pooling or providing free bus tickets. Most important, we have attempted to develop personal relationships with parents so that they feel relaxed in coming into the school and comfortable when raising questions or concerns about a particular problem.

One of the issues of concern for parents was our whole language approach. Very few parents, if any, had attended a school where such techniques were practiced, so many parents had questions. These ranged from "Why doesn't my child have more textbooks?" to "What about spelling and handwriting?" Some parents were concerned that in our attempts to implement a child-centered whole language curriculum certain things dropped through the cracks.

Over the years, we have dealt with these concerns in two ways. First, we have held informational meetings for parents, oftentimes incorporated into school open houses, in which the philosophy and practices of our school are explained in concrete terms. Second, we have listened to parents' questions and modified our curriculum in certain ways. We did not take the easy route and simply adopt a spelling or handwriting basal, an approach that would have satisfied a number of parents. The more experienced teachers had worked with such texts in other schools and found them ineffective. Moreover, we were concerned that the less-experienced teachers would latch onto such texts rather than struggle with the hard task of incorporating skill lessons into whole language classrooms.

Nonetheless, there must be something in between a basal-driven curriculum and a curriculum based on the general writings of whole language and writing workshop advocates. Yes, we were opposed to mindless drill-and-kill worksheets on handwriting or in other subject areas, but we recognized the obvious: all children do not spontaneously learn how to form their letters or spell sight words. In fact, even though the most outspoken parent critics were middle class, those students most disadvantaged by a laissez-faire, whole language curricular approach were those children whose parents were unable to complement their schooling at home.

These parental concerns, along with the recognition that teachers had different conceptions about what "whole language" means in practice, compelled us to write our own draft curriculum that clearly established policies, guidelines, and, in some cases, scope and sequences in major curricular areas. The summer after our fourth year we paid teachers to work in committees to come up with draft curriculum. The following fall we held workshops for all staff on the new draft, and we discussed it at length at our site-based council meetings.

For example, some parents and staff raised the concern that while we call ourselves a multicultural, antiracist school, teachers had to decide on their own which cultural groups to emphasize at their particular grade level. The result was an overemphasis on certain things—such as Harriet Tubman and the Underground Railroad—and an underemphasis of other geopolitical groups, such as Asian Americans. After lengthy discussions, we established some general guidelines about acknowledging and reaffirming the cultural heritage of all children in a class, but then specified which geopolitical groups should be emphasized at which grade levels. This helped teachers avoid redundancy and ensure that children would be exposed to all groups.

The guide, shown in Figure 6.1 (see pp. 134–135),[1] does not answer all questions, of course, and it is viewed as a work in progress. As questions come up in response to particular curricular areas, we refer to the guide, use what we have written as a starting point, and then try to revise the appropriate section for greater clarity on the issue.

Other Problems We Have Confronted

As of this writing, we are moving into our tenth year of operation. We are on a much stronger footing than when we started, but we continue to struggle with the hard questions of how to provide a quality, antiracist, humane education to an urban student population. Several problems confronting our project have made our successes more difficult than we had anticipated:

1. Fundamentally negative features of school life in public elementary schools—such as overcrowded classrooms, inadequate physical facilities, lack of resources, and lack of time for teacher preparation, joint planning, parent-teacher conferences, and parent and teacher inservices—impede reform efforts. In four out of our nine years, we have had to mobilize our Fratney community to fight fiscal cutbacks to our program.

2. Moving from a traditional, text-centered, teacher-talk paradigm to a whole language, activity-based paradigm, and from a Eurocentric tradition of teaching to an antiracist, multicultural approach to teaching, is difficult even for the most experienced teachers, given the lack of resources for planning and preparation time.

3. The natural flow of people in and out of the program— parents, students, and teachers—has guaranteed that several people who helped start the school and shared the original vision have left. In addition, despite the written explanations of our school in a variety of media, new parents enroll their

K-4 to K-5 (four-year-olds and five-year-olds)
Children should be exposed to **all six geopolitical groups**: African Americans, Arab Americans, Asian Americans, European Americans, Hispanic Americans, and Native Americans. Teachers should utilize the concepts and lesson plans in *Anti-Bias Curriculum: Tools for Empowering Young Children* by Louise Derman-Sparks and the Anti-Bias Curriculum Task Force (1989), published by the National Association for the Education of Young Children, Washington, D.C.

First Grade
All groups within curriculum areas, with special emphasis on **Latino culture**. The diversity, traditions, and contributions of people of Latino descent should be emphasized. Teachers should utilize the concepts and lesson plans in *Anti-Bias Curriculum*.

Second Grade
Introduction to geopolitical groups through study of key ideas of shelter, clothing, language, food, and holidays, with an emphasis on contributions of each group to U.S. society. Ethnic groups to be focused on are **Native American** and **African American**, with emphasis given to their diversity and traditions. For African American study, emphasis should be placed on African heritage and the modern civil rights movement. For Native Americans, emphasis should be placed on diversity, contributions, and current struggles for justice. Teachers should utilize the concepts and lesson plans in *Anti-Bias Curriculum*.

Third Grade
Reference will be made to all major ethnic groups, particularly in the context of the study of world geography. A special emphasis will be placed on **European American, Puerto Rican, and Asian American history and culture**. Emphasis should be placed on the diversity of these cultures. In our European American study, emphasis should be put on diversity, contributions, struggles of immigrants, and the contradictory role they have played in relation to the issue of race in this country. In our Puerto Rican study, emphasis should be given to the diversity of Puerto Ricans, their history and struggle for independence, and their traditions. In our Asian American study, emphasis should be given to the diversity of Asians and their histories of immigration and struggles for justice once they arrived in the United States.

Fourth Grade
Native Americans of Wisconsin and **Latin American** history and culture, with an emphasis on **Mexico and Mexican Americans**. This emphasis is in accord with the new Wisconsin state statute mandating the study of Wisconsin Native Americans in fourth grade. Other

FIGURE **6.1.** *Multicultural/antiracist focus, by grade level, at La Escuela Fratney.*

Figure 6.1 continued

geopolitical groups should be looked at in the context of the study of Wisconsin and in the general curricula.

Fifth grade
How people of color have faired within the U.S. experience: Asian Americans, Latinos, Native Americans, African Americans, Europeans (immigrant and working class). A special emphasis will be given to the **Asian American** and **African American** experience. In the study of the African American experience, emphasis will be given to the period 1620–1882 (slavery, resistance, abolitionism, and reconstruction).

Note: Teachers will make a special point to learn the ethnic/national background of all their students at the beginning of the year. Special sensitivity and emphasis should be given to those children and their national origin in connection with pertinent topics of study. A word of caution, however, is that while a child and his or her family may be from a certain country or ethnic group, we should not make the assumption that they have extensive knowledge of that group or country.

children in our school for a range of reasons, and some are unclear about our methodologies. Also, new students regularly transfer into our school (the only criterion is that after first grade the student needs previous Spanish-language experience, so most of our transfers are Spanish-speaking immigrant children), and because they have not had the same experience with student-centered approaches, they sometimes have difficulty adjusting.

4. Providing truly bilingual services is challenging in a society that is so English-language dominant/biased. There is an obvious "English pull" in our country, and placing Spanish on an equal level with English in our school has not been easy. Moreover, a two-way bilingual school faces some unique problems in terms of how much of which language should be emphasized.

5. We underestimated the negative influence that our violent

class- and race-stratified society has had on children and how much it takes to overcome such influences.

6. Maintaining a high level of parental involvement, particularly among those people who have been traditionally alienated from school—people of color and poor people—is difficult.

7. There is a contradiction between needing teachers and parents to be involved at the district level to change policies which could directly affect conditions at Fratney and needing the same committed teachers and parents to put their full effort into running and improving Fratney school.

A Community That Fosters Reflection

We have often said to visitors that while we do not have all the answers, we do think we are asking the right questions. We also have learned that as with many curricular questions, there is no one set "right answer," and that, in fact, one of the secrets to a successful school is to have a community of staff, parents, and students who are continually reflecting and struggling with these questions.

We have tried to create structures within our school and our district to encourage such discussions. For example, we pioneered "banking time" days, which meant getting permission from the state Department of Public Instruction to add ten minutes onto each school day and then "banking" the time so that we could have a periodic afternoon or full day off to do curricular planning. This eventually became the norm throughout the district, but we have yet to figure out a way to provide child-care services to parents during those days when staff is planning at school.

As part of creating a community of parents, staff, and students committed to our vision of education, we found it advantageous to gain more school control over the introduction of new staff into our building. In Milwaukee, interschool staffing transfers are dictated on the basis of districtwide seniority, which at times can mean that new staff are not in accord with the philosophy of the school. We arranged to be one of two of the 150 schools in the district to have a memorandum of understanding between the teachers' union and the school district so that we are exempt from the seniority provision for transfers. Instead, a committee of parents, staff, and the principal interviews each prospective teacher, and we then make a decision.

We also have helped create within the district the political climate that allows our kind of pedagogical approach to flourish. Our staff members and parents serve on a variety of districtwide committees and councils and have helped shape districtwide policy, including a major K–12 curriculum reform effort that has, among other things, the explicit goal of practicing antiracist, antibias teaching in all classrooms in the district. While such districtwide goals are ignored in some schools, for a school like ours it provides the umbrella under which we can work even during larger political storms. So instead of our school being signaled out for political criticism, the district as a whole must confront those who question more progressive educational policies.

District- and statewide mandates tend to be pendulum-like, however, susceptible to political pressures that have nothing to do with sound educational practices. For example, Milwaukee has embarked on a system of performance-based assessment in writing, oral communication, science, and art. Students are expected to perform tasks that are "more authentic" than multiple-choice tests, and their work is graded holistically, using a rubric. One purpose of such a districtwide policy is to push teachers to adopt more activity-centered instructional strategies. While this is good in general, for a classroom teacher already engaged in such practices the imposition of numerous performance-based assessments can disrupt an already packed curriculum. For the oral language assessment, the task for fifth, seventh, and tenth graders was participation in a mock job interview, which was to be videotaped. The administration made it known that such assessment fit nicely in line with the "school-to-work" priorities of the district. Some teachers and parents, from Fratney and other schools, felt that the task unnecessarily restricted classroom practices and narrowly focused students' attention on one aspect of school-to-work connections. Ultimately, the district expanded the options for oral language assessment.

Confronting Serious Attacks

Regardless of the quality of the work done in individual schools or districtwide, nothing will stop those who are out to attack progressive education. The best way we have found to deal with such attacks is to have done a good job educating parents and community members so that when such attacks come they will be ignored or responded to by those most directly affected. Two pertinent examples come to mind. One had its origin in a fifth-grade social studies project in which my students write an extensive research report on someone in U.S. history who worked for social justice. One year, two female students came to me upset because while Thomas Edison had a long entry in the CD-ROM encyclopedia, Harriet Tubman rated barely a mention. This concern led to a combined math and social studies project in which kids analyzed the CD-ROM encyclopedia for bias, sharpening their analytical skills so that in the future they might recognize and act against other forms of bias. Interestingly enough, it was this lesson, which I subsequently wrote up in the journal *Rethinking Schools*, that caused local radio talk show host Charlie Sykes to claim that my teaching is a form of child abuse; he made this claim the day after it was announced that I had been selected as Wisconsin Elementary Teacher of the Year. In subsequent days, he and a talk show host on another radio station continued to criticize me.

On the day of the attack, a couple of parents called me at school to let me know what had happened. On subsequent days, more parents and staff talked to me about what they had heard secondhand. I distributed the *Rethinking Schools* article to all interested persons, gave more details about the project to those who were curious, but not once did I receive a negative reaction from any parent. The staff of our school wrote a letter to the station managers inviting the talk show host to visit our school and my classroom before he made further comments. Of course, the talk show host ignored the invitation.

In another case, the local papers had run a number of articles about studies which allegedly show the superiority of phonics-based reading instruction over whole language–based reading instruction. When such articles occur in the daily press, we often wonder what the reaction is among parents. In a recent case, a former Fratney parent wrote back to the press in response to an anti–whole language letter to the editor:

> Why would the *Journal Sentinel* publish this [anti–whole language] letter? My child attends a whole language program at La Escuela Fratney, from K-4 [kindergarten for four-year-olds] through fifth grade.
>
> Starting in K-4, the empirical evidence began mounting that our daughter was in a good program. She was bringing home "stories," drawn out, that followed a complete story from beginning to end.
>
> By first grade, she was telling similar stories with a combination of pictures and words. By third grade, the teachers began to concentrate more on spelling, and by fifth grade, I was extremely impressed by her ability to think very complex thoughts and place these thoughts on paper.

While specific attacks on Fratney, our teachers, or whole language can be countered on a case-by-case basis, ultimately our program will be judged by the quality of learning that takes place by our students. For our school to be perceived as one that "works," we believe we must make sure that our students do well on district- and state-mandated measures, while at the same time have public opportunities to demonstrate what they have learned and what they can do. We have fought for district measures to be more authentic, and we have created other mechanisms so students have more opportunities to show what they have learned. For example, we are developing a schoolwide portfolio system, student-led "parent-teacher" conferences, and student exhibitions for that purpose.

By focusing on student achievement in a way that allows us to foster children's multiple intelligences, we know that parents and the broader community will see that indeed the Fratney experiment demonstrates that in an urban setting schools not only can work but also flourish and be a cause of hope.

Note

1. This guide is an example of what one school did in figuring out the emphasis to be placed on geopolitical groups, grade by grade. Note that over 65 percent of students at Fratney are Hispanic. I am not suggesting that this listing be copied; it simply illustrates curricular preferences that account for the goals of the school and the population of the community.

CHAPTER SEVEN

The Dool School Story

JANE S. CARPENTER
Dool Elementary School

ELENA R. CASTRO
Dool Elementary School

Dool Elementary School, with a population of seven hundred students, is located within walking distance of the international border at the point where Mexicali, Baja California, touches Calexico, California. The fact that Calexico, a city of 25,000 built next to both agricultural fields and unirrigated desert, is so close to the Mexico/U.S. border has been an important factor in the history of Dool School.

Still, it was not until the late 1960s that the Calexico Unified School District, comprising three elementary schools and one high school, began to recognize and try to account for the needs of its Spanish-speaking students in the Calexico schools. Until that time, from kindergarten through high school, the only option for Spanish-speaking students was English immersion, a sink-or-swim approach. There was no attempt to provide for the special needs of Spanish-speaking students or even a recognition that these students might have special needs. The majority of teachers and administrators in the district were mainstream monolingual English speakers. Georgeann Gretencord recalls, "In the fifth grade I knew that all the Mexican kids were placed in the back of the room and the Anglo kids were in the front." The placement of mainstream children at the front of the class was a powerful metaphor for the marginalization of Spanish-speaking children and the inequities that were visible to everyone living in this desert community.

Also in the 1960s, Elena Castro was herself a first grader. As a monolingual Spanish speaker, she remembers with pain being placed outside the classroom by a mainstream teacher because she did not speak English. She remembers being made to feel that she was worthless because she could not speak or understand the teacher's language. She even remembers being called "Helen"— not Elena—by her teacher because "Elena" was a Spanish name. "We don't speak Spanish in *this* classroom," said Miss Johnson as she pinned on Elena's nametag. "This girl doesn't listen. She's a behavior problem" was what was told Elena's mother at parent conferences. Of course, how could Elena listen to a language she could not understand?

These were not isolated instances of discrimination. Many of the students in Calexico at that time experienced or witnessed being deprived of a sensitive, culturally relevant environment for learning, and being denied the right to social and academic success because of limited proficiency in English. Certainly, many Spanish-speaking students made it through the system despite such discrimination, but it is impossible to know exactly how many more students were denied the opportunity to develop their full potential in a "tracked" school system.

In time, however, the pressure of the growing number of Spanish-speaking immigrants, the increased availability of federal monies for bilingual education, and the growing social consciousness of the 1960s prodded the school district to take a more responsible position toward its Spanish-speaking students. As did many other districts, Calexico successfully applied for a federal grant under the auspices of Title VII in an effort to find a better solution to educating Spanish-speaking students. The current superintendent, Roberto Moreno, now refers to that first Title VII project as a "mini-version" of a bilingual program, implemented only at the high school and even then only in a limited form.

In 1969 the district expanded its sights; it received a Title VII grant for a three-year bilingual program to phase in seventh, eighth, and ninth grade students at the junior high level. The program was set up on a voluntary basis, in one classroom at each grade level, on the "simultaneous translation" model. Many of the monolingual English teachers responded to this program with relief. Now they could shift the Spanish-speaking students onto someone else. But the volunteers for the program were the "wrong" students. Those with limited proficiency in English—the targeted population—who were supposed to be helped by the bilingual program design did not enroll. Those who did choose to enroll tended to be students who were already speaking enough English to quickly become bored with tedious translations of curricular materials. Most Spanish-speaking parents at that time were generally indifferent to this district innovation. Since they had experienced the "sink-or-swim" approach themselves, the old way—for all its limitations—was at least familiar.

By the mid-1970s, following renewal of the earlier grants, an additional Title VII grant and a state-funded "1329 Grant" were awarded to two elementary schools: Dool and Rockwood. The newly funded bilingual programs at these schools were to be "transitional"; that is, students were to be exited from them and moved into all-English programs as soon as possible. The principal feature of these programs was the allocation of the two languages on an alternate-days plan (sometimes this was alternate weeks): Spanish days were to be conducted all in Spanish and English days all in English. The rationale for this language-allocation model was that it would not be advantageous for language learners to mix the two languages. Classes were labeled as either monolingual English or bilingual English-Spanish. Not surprisingly, the monolingual classes rated the higher status in the eyes of everyone in the district, and they had better resources. Spanish-language materials were limited since most publishers were not willing to invest the money required to develop such materials before they were certain of a well-established market. Therefore the bilingual teachers in the project often had to translate materials. In addition to the extra work at home such translation required, the bilingual program teachers were often subjected to a difficult social situation at school; many were criticized or even shunned by other teachers who did not understand or believe in the program.

These early bilingual programs did little to improve the quality of educational opportunities for Spanish-speaking students in Calexico. The district continued to segregate students by language, and Spanish-speaking students continued to do poorly in academic subjects and on standardized achievement tests. Moreover, the programs did little to challenge the prevailing idea that Spanish-speaking students were simply deficient and therefore "earned" their status as low achievers.

Parents were understandably reluctant to allow their children to be placed in bilingual programs, which were viewed by the community as remedial holding tanks for "low students." In addition to parents' memories ("I don't want them to have to go through the same things I went through"), many parents did not recognize the educational value of Spanish (*"Mi niño/a puede aprender español en la casa"* [My child can learn Spanish at home]; "They need to learn English. That's why they are in school"). And there was yet another misunderstanding. Many parents believed that in a bilingual program everything that students hear and learn is in Spanish. So when parents were asked which program they preferred, they chose the English-language monolingual program. No matter how often teachers tried to explain the various components of the bilingual program, the response from the Spanish-speaking parents was usually an emphatic *"No."*

Until 1979 the bilingual program at Dool Elementary was well supported financially and administratively. Then a new elementary school opened in Calexico with a bilingual strand at all grade levels. Teachers were recruited who valued bilingualism. Many of these teachers lived in the community and had been educated in the school district. The majority of the Title VII staff and the funding were transferred to the new school. Dool School was left with a bilingual program that had few financial underpinnings and fewer resources. From 1979 through 1984, lacking funding, support, and direction, Dool's bilingual program withered. But a small cadre of teachers remained committed to bilingual education.

A Turning Point

In the spring of 1985, district administration began to look more closely at Dool School. Standardized test scores—always the bottom line—were lower than expected. Teachers were clearly working hard, but their students were not making much progress. It was at this time that an Imperial County educational office director, George Parrish, approached the Calexico district office. He had met some educators in Arizona who were working with an innovative program they called "whole language." That program, according to Parrish, was working wonders with bilingual children in the Phoenix area. Roberto Moreno, then assistant superintendent of Calexico School District, thought such a program might be something Dool School teachers would be interested in exploring. Soon, a group of teachers (including the authors of this chapter) and parents traveled to Arizona to observe these innovative classrooms. They found bilingual children reading stories and writing and publishing books in kindergarten and first grade. Students were writing in interactive journals as early as kindergarten. The Dool teachers also noticed the stance the Arizona teachers took toward their students. All spoke about high expectations for *all* their students. There was no talk about deficits. We still recall how excited we were to see these classrooms, how energized we felt.

That excitement grew as we returned to Dool School and began to share what we had seen with our teaching colleagues, staff, and parents. The wheels were in motion. With help and support from the district office, a plan began to form for the next year. Our excitement was tempered by nervousness, however. To whom would we go for training? At what grade levels should we start? Will it really work? How do we fund this venture?

A proposal for a Title VII grant was submitted by the county office with the assistance of Dr. Barbara Flores, who over the next five years was our mentor and friend. The plan was to establish whole language as the basis for a Dool School alternative bilingual program, beginning with the kindergarten and first grades and phasing in second and third grades in subsequent years. At first, educators from Arizona worked with Dool teachers on Fridays after school and during all-day Saturday sessions and weeklong sessions in the summer. It took a while, but finally we began to concentrate on what we *knew* rather than on "how to do it." We began to see that the more we knew about how children learn, the better we could reach each student. We began to see our students' successes no matter what language they were using. In those early years, curiosity, renewed excitement, and enthusiasm seemed to be everywhere.

Struggles Along the Way

Change is difficult and uneven. A new principal arrived at Dool School who did not believe holistic instruction was the right approach and therefore did not support the program or the teachers' efforts to shift their own understandings and practice in that direction. Actually, "did not support" hardly captures the situation. The relationship between the bilingual program faculty and the new principal was thick with hostility, and the atmosphere throughout the school was tense. Still, those teachers who had taken part in the intensive professional development work on weekends and during the summer and who had been part of the effort to develop a bilingual program over the prior decade maintained their direction despite the principal's disapproval. At one particularly strained meeting during which Dool teachers presented an update on the program along with some evidence of its benefits to the Board of Education, the principal publicly discounted their presentation and denigrated the program. Fortunately, the board rejected the principal's position, but more fortunately still, for personal reasons the principal left the district.

At the same time that teachers were coping with the new principal, they were still trying to convince parents that the changes taking place at Dool were in their children's best interests. Interactive journals, alphabet books, literature logs, guided reading, and book publishing—all strategies for teaching the conventions of written English and Spanish in a meaningful context—were unfamiliar to these parents. Parents expected phonics worksheets; they did not expect to participate in homework assignments that asked them to listen to their children read. And they did not understand that phonics could still be an integral part of teaching children to read even if the format did not resemble the phonics instruction they had experienced in school.

In an effort to help parents understand the "new" methodology, the staff at Dool School began to offer evening sessions to familiarize parents with whole language. Parents were invited to hear teachers present different strategies such as journal writing, theme cycles, and integrated content in both languages. Teachers demonstrated reading aloud and shared reading so that parents could use these techniques at home. They shared samples of students' work and pointed out markers of learning. Most persuasive of all, parents began to see, for the first time, that their children were developing a love for reading.

In 1987, yet another new principal was appointed. Unlike the former principal, William Cudog liked what he saw almost immediately. The teachers believed, however, that the principal's initial reaction needed to be strengthened, so we set about dialoguing with Mr. Cudog about learning and providing him with as much information about the program as possible. Some teachers shared books with him while others invited him to their classrooms for special activities. Eventually, Mr. Cudog became a roving reader, going from classroom to classroom to read to children. Within a year, Mr. Cudog was an *informed* supporter of the whole language programs at Dool School.

Meanwhile, as a result of the teachers' outreach to parents and the students' responses to whole language instruction, many parents began to support the program. Parents whose children were not in the program began to ask why their children were not publishing books or writing journals. Many requested that their children be moved to the bilingual program.

Success

Soon after Mr. Cudog arrived, Dool School started to see positive results of the whole language approach. As teachers and parents began to understand how the learners' language and cultural backgrounds were powerful resources for learning, that very understanding increased opportunities for students to perform at higher levels. The Dool community could see the results up close in the work students were doing from day to day—discovering and learning in two languages in a context in which both languages now had social value and an authentic academic function.

Others started to take notice when standardized test scores at Dool School began to rise. Districts from around the state and even out of state began to recognize Dool School's program as a successful bilingual program. Teachers, administrators, professors, and authors from around the United States came to observe Dool classrooms to see what was happening and how it was happening. Dool teachers became consultants to other districts and shared their success stories. Parents also began to revise their views of bilingual education. Instead of viewing bilingual education as a remedial program, parents began to perceive Dool's version as an enrichment program.

The program had in fact been transformed from a "mini-bilingual" program for the high school in the 1970s to the holistic bilingual program at Dool. From a focus on "What do we do with these Spanish-speaking kids?" to an attitude of "Look how much we can we do to develop biliteracy in today's students." From a program segregated by language to a dual language program that demonstrated that English speakers and Spanish speakers could learn academically through the others' language.

The last shift from one-way bilingual to dual language had been institutionalized in 1987 as the Dual Language Biliteracy Program. The teachers had recognized the need for English speakers and Spanish speakers to be integrated into one classroom so that English speakers could serve as models for the Spanish speakers acquiring English and vice versa. With the shift to a dual language program, monolingual English speakers, monolingual Spanish speakers, and bilingual students interacted more socially; it was this social interaction that provided real reasons for learners to use the new language.

In 1991 the California Association of Bilingual Education presented Dool School with an Exemplary School Award for its whole language program and the positive effects it had on bilingual children. In 1997 the state of California recognized Dool School as an Achieving School for its work with Title I students and for its gains in reading and mathematics. In May 1997, at the annual meeting of the International Reading Association in Atlanta, the United States Department of Education concurred and named Dool School a Distinguished School.

One obvious irony is the public criticism of the whole language, dual language programs that were the basis for the awards. The current controversy in California pitting phonics against whole language has put pressure on Dool to return to the "basic skills" model and to treat phonics as the panacea for all aspects of literacy, including biliteracy. Clearly, many changes are taking place right now. What we hope will not change are certain hard-won beliefs that now prevail in the Dool School community, beliefs that were not part of that first-grade teacher's worldview in 1961 when Elena Castro and Georgeann Gretencord attended elementary school: (1) all students are capable of academic and social success; (2) a child's primary language is a valued resource in developing a solid foundation for becoming biliterate; (3) children's academic strengths can be enhanced through authentic language use; and (4) learning through two languages is of great social and academic value (98 percent of the current Dool School staff is bilingual).

Right now, Georgeann Gretencord's young son is in a bilingual second grade at Dool School, but he is not sitting at the back of the classroom. He sits in the middle, surrounded by English and Spanish speakers in a print-rich environment containing a variety of books and resources in both languages, and he feels quite comfortable there. But we are not hopeful that we can say the same for the classroom situation that may be available to his younger family members in the next century given the anti-immigrant, English Only climate that underlies the current push to mandate phonics and eliminate both whole language and bilingual education.

CHAPTER EIGHT

A Dual Language Program in Phoenix and How It Grew

JOHN W. WANN, IRMA RIVERA-FIGUEROA, JUAN SIERRA,
BRENDA HARRELL, AND MARTHA R. ARRIETA
Valley View School

This chapter tells the story of an evolving language policy in a prekindergarten through eighth-grade school in Phoenix, Arizona. The school is located in a semirural neighborhood, although developers are building subdivisions on the horizon. (It is still possible to smell cut hay, manure fertilizer, and orange blossoms at certain times of the year.) The school serves a primarily Latino population (80 percent) with 11 percent African American, 8 percent White, and 1 percent American Indian students. With prodding from a new principal in 1990, Valley View School staff began working with a variety of "alternative" practices: writing process programs, aggressively inclusive practices in special education, literature-based reading, a school-based curriculum, the creation of a "teaching/learning facilitator" position, and a dual language program. Each of these efforts has involved different sets of staff members and students, but each also has an effect on—and often aims to eventually include—the entire school. In this chapter, we focus on the dual language program (DLP), though the other efforts are interwoven.

While not everyone participates directly in the DLP, the entire school community is affected by it programmatically. In fact, the proposal for Title VII funds to support the DLP included support for the development of curriculum and professional practice for all Valley View teachers, not just those in the DLP. That Title VII proposal was tied to a collaboration with Valley View's Title I program to support reflective practice structures (e.g., formalized professional discussion formats and child-study practice and assessment based on the work of Pat Carini [1986], team planning sessions, and book study groups)—all in the service of planning schoolwide changes in curriculum and assessment. Other programs strengthen and support but are not directly tied to the DLP; e.g., in-home community libraries, parent and family workshops in curriculum and computers, a foreign-language component (SSL/ESL) for all students, a teacher exchange project with Mexico open to all teachers, and a Hands Across the Border experience open to all fourth- through eighth-grade students. Thus by design the DLP offers benefits to and is benefited by other efforts at Valley View. Unfortunately, the DLP has also had an unintended and somewhat problematic effect on the total school climate.

The Dual Language Program

The basic intent of the dual language program is to promote bilingualism and biliteracy for both Spanish-speaking and English-speaking students. To that end, we attempt to recruit kindergarten students whose families value bilingualism and biliteracy taught in a multicultural environment. "Dual language" implies that native speakers of the usual school language (English in the United States) and native speakers of a second language (Spanish in our case) are recruited in equal numbers for each incoming kindergarten class. Our language model for kindergarten and first and second grades is 80/20—80 percent Spanish and 20 percent English. The only language spoken and taught by the teacher in those early years is supposed to be Spanish. English is reserved for special area classes and ESL instruction.

Our dual language model, adapted to the language environment in the United States and our community in particular, requires that two different types of bilingual education programs be implemented simultaneously. For the Spanish-speaking kindergarten child (referred to as an English learner), the program is maintenance bilingual.[1] For the English-speaking kindergartner (henceforth referred to as a Spanish learner), it is a language immersion program.[2]

The dual language program at Valley View is unique in that it is based on a neighborhood school design. Most dual language programs are magnets, "importing" Spanish learners from more affluent, usually mainstream neighborhoods. These more affluent students add status and sometimes resources to those programs. In Valley View's program, however, the Spanish learners are not "imports," and 86 percent of the students—both Spanish and English learners—are eligible for free or reduced-cost lunch. The Spanish learners are mostly Chicanos, one or two generations removed from Spanish, whose families are trying to "recapture" Spanish. Therefore immigrant students who are learning English study alongside students who are trying to learn the lost language of their ancestors who, a generation or two ago, were in the same shoes as these immigrant students. This has had the unintended effect of accentuating an existing cultural or social status conflict within the community.

Another unusual feature of the DLP at Valley View is its staff. Early on, the director and the principal decided to recruit native speakers of Spanish from Mexico to fill some of the teaching positions, especially at the early grades. These Mexican teachers not only provide language and cultural models for both the students and the staff, but some are also English learners themselves.

Getting Started

Prior to the development of the DLP, bilingual education at Valley View had been almost completely extinguished. Only one bilingual teacher remained on the staff when John Wann, the current principal, was hired. In an effort to resurrect services for language-minority students, the dual language concept evolved. Wann talked with parents and teachers, received approval from the district, wrote a proposal for federal funds, and the DLP was on its way. Beginning with one kindergarten and one first grade class, the DLP has added a new grade each year. Our first students in the program entered the sixth grade in the 1997–98 school year. The program has also expanded horizontally. Currently, nearly half of the students and teachers in grades kindergarten through 6 are in the DLP.

We are often asked how we dealt with "selling" the project. How did we convince parents, teachers, and school board members? Did native English-speaking parents want to enroll their children in this program? Although newsletters to parents, staff bulletins, and memos to district personnel described the program and invited participation in program development and enrollment, almost all of those who actively participated at first were already supporters of the idea of dual language. There were few recruits. Neither were there many supporters. It was a small but enthusiastic group of teachers, parents, and administrators who signed the proposal and also "signed up." (It is fair to say that none of us really understood the complexity of what we were doing.) Surprisingly, there was no significant opposition. It was as though personnel in the district office and also many of the staff at Valley View, having seen reforms come and go, assumed "this too shall pass" and generally ignored what was happening. Even the governing board members, who maintained a policy of supporting the development of two-way bilingual programs, showed little interest. They gave our first grant (and our subsequent follow-up funding grant) full approval but asked virtually no questions.

The Early Days

That first year was a mix of eagerness and confusion on the part of the DLP teachers and cynicism and resentment on the part of those outside the DLP. Irma Rivera-Figueroa, the one bilingual teacher remaining at the school from prior administrations, recalls that

> help from consultants and the administration that first year was focused on the wrong things—e.g., on whole language issues and "authentic learning"—but nothing and no one was answering questions related to dual language education. By midyear, problems were already arising. The two new teachers [from Mexico] felt that their teaching methods were being attacked [because of the contrast with whole language], while I was trying to prepare myself for the new group the following year.

The 80/20 model for language use was a particular problem. Martha Arrieta, a student teacher at first and then a regular first-grade teacher during the first year of the DLP, remembers that

> the language policy was heavily weighted in Spanish for the entire day. It was not supposed to be supported by translation of any part of the content or conversation. That first year the Spanish learners won the Spanish/English tug of war as soon as they learned that if they persisted in acting as though they were not comprehending, I would come through with the English version. At the end of that year, when the children preferred English to Spanish, I knew there was a problem.

As the DLP grew the second year, the divisions between Chicana and Mexicana teachers within the DLP staff became more obvious. Juan Sierra, a consultant to the DLP during the first three years, reflects on those divisions.

> On the surface, the divisions were pedagogical, but I believe they were rooted in deeper cultural beliefs about learning, teaching, and socialization. I was brought in from California as a consultant, supposedly to train all the teachers regarding literacy events. My real assignment, however, was to initiate dialogue among teachers about their practices. The guise didn't work. The Chicana teachers were familiar with practices associated with whole language and were comfortable with dialoguing about methodologies and theoretical knowledge. They were willing to share philosophies and practices. When we got together to discuss pedagogies, the Mexicana teachers were defensive about their practices and unwilling to discuss the theoretical basis for those practices. They gave scant accounts or refused to participate, even when pushed. Worse yet, the conflicts spread to other areas of school and formal encounters. Mexicana teachers complained about the perceived lack of professionalism among the Chicana teachers (i.e., dressing too casually, presenting themselves much too informally at parent meetings and performances, etc.). The Chicana teachers were at a loss to explain any *intended* mistreatment or misconduct.

The problems of cultural discontinuity between Chicanas and Mexicanas surprised everyone. After all, both groups are of the same historical cloth and are linked culturally through the Spanish language (Mindiola & Martinez, 1986). In addition to history and language, both groups share the same religion, food, music, and family ties. John Wann remembers that the conflict pointed up the complexity of the project, that the program was entangled with inter/intracultural and class issues stemming from the structures of racism in our society. The conflicts the first few years were an immediate obstacle, but they were also to provide an opportunity for growth during the settling-in years.

Meanwhile, teachers and some district personnel who were not participating in the DLP began to complain from the sidelines. Irma Rivera-Figueroa remembers hearing evidence of resentment: "We DLP teachers began traveling to conferences to learn about dual language 'best practices.' To some of the staff and district personnel, we became known as 'the travel club.' People would ask, 'Where did you go now? Hawaii?'"

Because of the DLP, the invitation to Spanish-speaking parents to become active in school life, and the decision to hire teachers from Mexico, the role of Spanish on campus changed—seemingly overnight. Spanish-speaking parents were welcomed, and therefore accepted invitations to participate. In response, a simmering racism, long a part of the perspectives of some staff and parents, surfaced. Statements were heard such as, "When is Mr. Wann going to do something for *our* kids?"; "This school is starting to look like Little Mexico"; "He'll let *them* into our school and even provide the transportation"; "He supports the Mexican parents more than us teachers."

The Settling-in Years

The project and its language policies were supported by families, as evidenced by the growth in enrollment. Parents were then, and continue to be, intrigued by the idea of their children becoming bilingual, linking bilingualism with economic opportunity. Even some African American parents, who in our neighborhood tend to be opposed to bilingual programs, approved of the DLP. What has frightened some parents away is the 80/20 model. English-speaking parents and teachers would rather have a second language introduced a little at a time rather than through a "scary" immersion model. Spanish-speaking parents want more of the second language than dual language offers. Given the poor academic success in the Latino community (high school dropout rates approaching 50 percent, college graduation rates of 1 percent), one can understand parents' wariness of any program that might further complicate their children's school careers.

Parental choice of the DLP for their kindergarten child has not been entirely a matter of language issues or program design, however. Short-term child care is often the parents' first concern. Arizona funds only a half-day kindergarten. We have been successful in creating one all-day kindergarten class in the DLP. Hence, many parents choose to enroll their child in the DLP because of what they see as free baby-sitting. Because we wanted parents to make an informed choice for the DLP, not just a pragmatic day care–driven choice, we soon made it mandatory that parents observe a DLP class before being allowed to select the DLP for their child. Nevertheless, even though the program is explained at great length before, during, and after the visit, parents often end the conversation with, "Yeah, but does my child get an all-day class?"

The reaction to the DLP from the Chicano community became noticeably mixed during these years, yearning and satisfaction dwelling sometimes literally next door to resentment and dissatisfaction. Chicano parents with children in the DLP applauded it. Several program parents with children too old for the program have expressed regret that these children missed out. Many others seek out the program—and particular teachers—when their younger children approach kindergarten age. The most common reasons for support are based on language and culture: "My parents speak Spanish; I don't want my kids to lose it." On the other hand, the strongest parental resistance to the DLP has also come from the Chicano community—parents who do not and have not had children in the program. The complaints have focused on exclusion ("You're keeping secrets from us," in reponse to the school marquee being in Spanish); favoritism ("You're spending all your efforts on *those* kids"); linguistic nationalism ("When will they learn English?"); and curriculum ("What about the basics?")

The settling-in years saw changes in the teaching staff. A few teachers transferred to other districts, claiming salary and transportation reasons. Martha Arrieta, however, believes there was something more, that they felt either

> the language policy was fine but that something yet in its "experimental stages" has too many problems still to be worked out, or that the Spanish speakers were not being serviced in English early enough and English speakers were missing out on early skills in their native language. Some teachers can't deal with a long-term program like ours.

Those who stayed and learned to adhere to the "teachers speak only Spanish" policy saw their Spanish learners make great strides. As Arrieta said, "I began to see the development in the students unfold before my eyes. That was the first year I really felt successful with what the proposal actually called for."

The Mexicana/Chicana dynamic also shifted. To an outside observer, the practices of all the teachers in the DLP seemed fairly similar, even though the teachers themselves still identified great differences according to "country of origin." Nevertheless, both sets of teachers began to relax their defenses and share with each other. Juan Sierra took advantage of this improved relationship and invited the Mexicana teachers to instruct the rest of the staff on Mexican teaching practices. They accepted and offered an excellent account of Mexican educational practices, along with explanations of regional and class differences. The stereotypes began to break down.

At the district level, personnel remained either indifferent or resistant to the DLP. The business department knew little about Title VII funding; therefore trying to obtain certain services and materials was a time-consuming effort. Even the bilingual department did not accommodate its categories and procedures to this "unusual" program: it listed the DLP erroneously as "transitional bilingual," bureaucratically unable to add the category "dual language."

When the DLP program received the Golden Bell Award by the Arizona School Board Association, our entire district governing board was present. They asked questions and gave congratulations, but their interest was piqued only momentarily; they have not yet acted on their promises to visit "such a wonderful program."

The DLP teachers' interest, on the other hand, remained constant. Teachers continued to be concerned about their teaching, not so much about the "slant" of their practice as about their work with the language policy. Martha Arrieta offers this insider perspective:

> I have come to realize that I am a practitioner of our language policy. During my five years at Valley View, there have been disagreements over teaching methods but not over the language policy. We've agreed about the need to keep close to the required percentages outlined in the grant. That doesn't mean we've all actually carried out this plan. There's been some talk about the children's need to warm up to Spanish in the younger grades by using more English than 10 percent for the first few weeks. Also, the ongoing argument about literacy development in the first language crops up yearly in the fall as kindergartners and first graders begin to show strong interests in reading and writing.

Carrying out the language policy in the classroom has been hard enough. Maintaining the policy of 100 percent Spanish by teachers has been even more difficult in meetings and other professional DLP gatherings. The employment of Mexican teachers has helped to bring Spanish into the context of the teachers' meeting, but it is still often the principal's deliberate use of Spanish that prevents English from dominating in meetings.

The division between the DLP and the rest of the staff at Valley View remains a huge problem. In the fifth year of the DLP, Brenda Harrell began a study of non-DLP teachers' perceptions of the DLP. Teachers responded to a survey and were also interviewed. Admittedly, the questions on the survey, written by non-professional survey writers, were slanted negatively (focusing on known "sore points"). Still, the results were sobering. The non-DLP staff members were generally displeased with the quality of the communication about the goals and procedures of the DLP. Most felt excluded or at least not aware of what was going on in DLP classrooms. Many believed that other programs at Valley View took a backseat to the DLP. Non-DLP teachers reported job insecurities if they did not have the credentials to teach in an ESL or bilingual classroom. Most reported they saw no differences in students as a result of the DLP. The only positive comments, shared by almost all of the non-DLP staff, were that becoming bilingual would be valuable for all students and that Spanish speakers did indeed want to learn English.

Brenda Harrell's interviews with teachers revealed even more clearly the non-DLP teachers' sense of exclusion and some of its consequences.

> Some teachers told me they feel excluded when parts of the daily written announcements are in Spanish without English translation. Of course, no one likes to feel excluded. But the idea of printing the announcements only in English or with Spanish translated into English contradicts the DLP philosophy that equal status be given to English and Spanish on campus. Since every class has at least one child who can read and translate information provided in Spanish, announcement reading would be another opportunity to equalize Spanish and English on campus. Ironically, a number of non-DLP teachers said they were not aware that reading the announcements was supposed to be done by students as a way to promote literacy, so if they as teachers could not read the Spanish parts, they simply skipped them. Thus non-DLP classes sometimes missed assemblies and other activities because the teachers didn't read that part of the announcement.
>
> After Dr. Sarah Hudelson came to Valley View to explain the requirements for obtaining an Arizona ESL or bilingual endorsement, some teachers felt that this "opportunity" was really a demand, that soon, teachers who speak only English will be replaced by bilingual teachers through transfers to other schools or by other means.

Many non-DLP teachers told Brenda Harrell in interviews that the number one priority of the administration is the dual language program, that

> when something involves "dual language"—but not anything else—everyone is expected to drop everything—change schedules or adapt in any way in order to meet the demand. These teachers believe there is favoritism toward DL teachers and toward supporters of the DLP.

Staff demographics perhaps play a role in this division between DLP and non-DLP teachers. Resistance to the DLP—and to bilingualism itself—is heavily concentrated in the older, vet-

eran teachers, some of whom are minorities themselves. Therefore issues of class and ethnicity are part of the mix leading to
dissension. Additionally, pedagogical differences surface. The
older teachers are generally more traditional in instructional orientation; the bilingual teachers are more progressive. In general,
non-DLP staff is largely unaware of the extra obligations DLP
teachers have in terms of curriculum development, testing in two
languages, staff development and conferences, and additional
meetings. But whatever the reason for the division, it has to be
bridged if the DLP and related projects are to continue to benefit
the entire Valley View community.

Overall, DLP parents continue to support the program, participating in classroom activities and attending meetings and
classes (e.g., meetings about the DLP, computer literacy classes
taught in English and Spanish, adult language classes). If parents
have any concerns, they center on English. Spanish-speaking parents worry about too little English being used in the classroom.
English-speaking parents, while impressed with their children's
developing abilities in Spanish, worry about whether their children are at the "right" level of English literacy. Few parents (Spanish or English speaking) mention any concerns about literacy in
Spanish, though English-speaking parents are impressed with,
even awed by, their children's progress in this area.

The English-speaking parents most supportive of our language policies are usually actively working on furthering their
own education. Some lost their Spanish through their early schooling and wish to regain some of the language, if only through
their child. Literacy is what concerns them at first. What they
notice most, however, often around the middle of first grade, is
how much Spanish their child is understanding or using to communicate. Several parents have reported that their child understands the Spanish channel on television or understands and "can
talk with Nana at home." One mother said, almost enviously,
that her child watches the *novelas*, and "when I ask her what
they are saying, she can tell me."

Most of the Spanish-speaking parents express their gratitude
for a program that offers their children the familiarity of the home
language. But many also feel that it is much too long before En-

glish is emphasized. They are not so impressed with their children's development of Spanish literacy; they want their children to read and write in English in order for them to be successful in the U.S. school system.

Although African Americans are not represented in the DLP in proportion to their numbers at Valley View (11 percent of the total school population), the few African American students in the DLP have had unqualified success in learning Spanish and becoming biliterate. To our chagrin, however, the racial animosity that exists between African Americans and Latinos in our school community persists. The bridges that have been built within the DLP have not extended outside it.

Brenda Harrell surveyed third- through fifth-grade DLP students about the program, their language use, and their beliefs about the value of each language. Of the seventy students surveyed, fifty-one spoke Spanish as their first language and nineteen spoke English, but when asked which language they prefer to speak, half said Spanish and half said English. When asked which language is more important, all but three answered that both were equally important. Most consider themselves literate in both languages. Some of the things students said they like about the DLP include learning two languages, teachers who speak both languages, singing and dancing in the school programs put on by the DLP classes, being able to help other students in two languages, being the only one at home able to speak Spanish, learning about different countries, meeting people who speak different languages, and being able to take exams in both English and Spanish. Some of the things students said they dislike about being in the DLP are not understanding when someone speaks their second language, not having enough English in the classroom, making mistakes in their second language, and teachers refusing to translate.

The governing board continues to be supportive in policy and rhetoric, but it has not sought to learn more about the program or to visit the school. At the board meeting in which our current five-year grant was approved, the board president expressed pleasure that the grant included a Hands Across the Border component. Yet, when we began the Hands project last year and requested board permission for students, faculty, and parents to travel to Sonora, Mexico and vice versa, the item was approved by being placed on the no-discussion "consent" agenda. We were never granted an opportunity to report the details of the upcoming experience.

Spanish on Campus

The most unusual element of our program is the genuine internal shift in the status of the two languages. The administration and the DLP staff do everything they can to create a status-equal language situation within a larger context that is decidedly unequal. It is reasonable, then, to ask whether and how students, teachers, parents, and other Valley View community members respond to this change of status. We have already referred to several aspects of this response (e.g., students learning Spanish in class and using it at home, teachers having some difficulty using Spanish for professional discussions, etc.). Here, we want to mention a few other particularly visible changes we can attribute to the DLP.

As soon as the invitation was given to the Spanish-speaking community to become a part of campus life, it responded, beginning with the sale of snacks to children and extending to committee participation, site council membership, and volunteering in classrooms. At the time the proposal for the DLP was being written and submitted, parent meetings had begun to be conducted in both languages; soon they were being conducted in Spanish with English interpretation.

The contexts of Spanish-language use by students have increased both within and outside DLP classrooms. It is common to observe bilingual students conversing with the staff in Spanish in informal settings (e.g., in sidewalk conversations, counseling, discipline or Talk It Out sessions, community events, and so on). The shift in the acceptability of Spanish on campus is not lost on students who are not in the DLP. In the seventh and eighth grades, where dual language classrooms do not yet exist, students often speak to teachers in Spanish, and this appears to be acceptable now to their non-Spanish-speaking peers. At our recent eighth-grade promotion ceremony, the student addresses were presented in both English and Spanish, according to the student speaker's choice. The speeches were well crafted; the speakers were articulate and fluent—and they were delivered by students who have not been in bilingual classrooms. Such student-supported use of Spanish was not visible a few years ago.

Where Do We Go from Here?

We believe the DLP is at Valley View for the near future, though its long-term prospects are much less clear. It is not yet institutionalized. Even though our staff now has fifteen bilingual teachers, compared to only one bilingual teacher seven years ago, and even though stability is improving, there are obstacles. Finding enough qualified bilingual staff is a problem. In our low property-wealth district (funded through property taxes, as are all districts in Arizona), the pay is not competitive. Moreover, colleges of education, even those with bilingual teacher preparation programs, are not able to meet the demand for teachers either in sheer number or in the level of preparation that a progressive language curriculum demands.

Establishing credibility for the DLP so that it can withstand personnel changes is another challenge. Administrative turnover is high; John Wann, now in his eighth year as principal at Valley View, is the senior principal in the district (of eighteen schools). Further staff and administration changes are inevitable. To offset the risk of diminished administrative support, we are working on broad-based assessment and changes in reporting. We are attempting to develop an honest, comprehensive, carefully monitored assessment plan to monitor academic growth in both languages. Our plan includes portfolios, standardized testing, and performance-based assessment in order both to report to others (demonstrating that our decisions are "assessment driven") and to help us revise our practice. There is strong evidence that dual language programs are successful in achievement measure, but we have not yet tracked Spanish learners from low-income families for long enough to know whether the immersion model helps or impedes their literacy development in the long run. Nor do we have data on whether an 80/20 (Spanish/English) model or a 50/50 model is more appropriate for this population.

Not only do we need to continue to educate parents about language learning (the more knowledge parents have about language learning, the more they support the program), but we must also find ways to hear the different voices of diverse parents. For example, African American perspectives and experiences regarding Spanish-language learning are different from Chicano perspectives and experiences, which in turn are different from recent immigrants' perspectives. Hearing these separate voices, *in addition to* integrating our populations, will be essential for long-term success.

Major continuing obstacles are the tensions within the community and between DLP and non-DLP staff. We are working hard to improve relations among the entire staff. The plan now (though it may well change in the future) includes improving communication about the program to all staff, continuing professional development for all staff with careful attention to non-DLP programs, and increasing offerings in SSL (Spanish as a Second Language) throughout the grade levels, so that all of our students will have an opportunity to learn a second language, if not through a dual language model then through a foreign-language teaching model.

Despite the obstacles, we are optimistic about the continuation of the DLP. In two and a half years, our first students will leave eighth grade, having completed their entire pre-high school education through a dual language program. As we consider their future educational prospects, we worry about how the local high school will react. Will the high school appreciate bilingual fluency and grant our students admission to advanced placement classes, or will grammar test scores continue to be the sole basis of both administrative and curricular decisions? Thus, with both optimism for our own prospects and concern for our students as they move on, we plan to initiate a dialogue with the local high school about programmatic possibilities for DLP students. From its beginnings, the DLP has been an evolving language policy program. It continues to be.

Notes

1. "Maintenance bilingual" means that (1) the language of the non-English-speaking child is used as a language of instruction; (2) as the child learns the dominant language (English in the United States), both languages will continue to be used in teaching; and (3) the culture(s) of the non-native speaker is clearly evidenced in the curriculum.

2. "Language immersion" means that a speaker of a dominant language is immersed in the nondominant target language. For our program, this means that all primary content including literacy is presented to the Spanish learner in Spanish.

References

Carini, P. (1986). Building from children's strengths. *Journal of Education, 168*, 13–24.

Mindiola, T., & Martínez, M. (1986). Introduction to Chicano-Mexicano relations. In T. Mindiola & M. Martínez (Eds.), *Chicano-Mexicano relations*. University Park, TX: University of Houston.

CHAPTER NINE

Power, Politics, and the Demise of Progressive Education

FRANK SERAFINI
Saguaro School District

CAROLYN J. ROGERS
Saguaro School District

The Saguaro School District (SSD) is a medium-sized district in southwestern United States comprising thirteen schools and approximately nine thousand students. The district had a regional and national reputation in the educational community for its extensive staff development program. This program was the sole responsibility of the curriculum director, whose vision and progressive direction were instrumental in creating the types of classes and opportunities offered for the professional development of teachers in the Saguaro district. Saguaro offered at least twenty to thirty district inservice classes each semester, taught by such notable educators as Yetta Goodman, Ken Goodman, Carole Edelsky, Barbara Flores, and Ralph Peterson. Even more important, many of the classes were taught by classroom teachers from both in and outside the district.

SSD was committed to the professional development of its staff and recognized the role inservice opportunities could play in promoting progressive language policies and practices. Teachers new to the district were required to take at least nine district classes during their first three years as contract employees. These classes often dealt with holistic approaches to literacy instruction, documenting individual student growth through the use of observational checklists created by a district committee, and collecting samples of student work.

To further support the growth of teachers and progressive language practices within the district, the curriculum director sought our help in designing a summer institute for district teachers, later called the Reflective Assessment Institute. It was to be an extensive, week-long summer inservice program designed to extend assessments already in place to include teacher and student reflection. Approximately forty teachers, three from each of the thirteen schools in the district, attended this summer institute. The Reflective Assessment Institute (see Figure 9.1) reflected our own constructivist philosophy of teaching and learning that aligned with the progressive language policies already in place at SSD. We felt that in order to teach children more effectively, to place them in the center of the curriculum, teachers needed new ways to come to know their students. Using ethnographic procedures such as portfolios, observational field notes, interviews, audio- and videotapes, and observational checklists, teachers would learn to collect information about each child that would be passed on from year to year. The students would also begin to create portfolios of their own that could be used for reflection and self-evaluation.

In this chapter, we tell the story of the dismantling of progressive education in the Saguaro district schools. To tell our tale, we draw on our own experiences as teachers in SSD and participants in school board meetings, board documents, letters to the editor in local newspapers, media accounts, and conversations with parents and school board administrators.

Saguaro District School Board Belief Statements

Up to the mid-1990s, the school board appeared to have been supportive of progressive language policies and practices. The SSD board, for example, was comprised of five members with a history of involvement in the district, both with their children and as advocates for change. They had fought against censorship that had threatened the district and supported the arts as a necessary part of the curriculum for every child. Three of the current board members had been instrumental in removing another board

---

Reflective Assessment Institute

Day 1   Foundations of Assessment
         Effective Classroom Environments

Day 2   Sources of Information
         Windows to Learning

Day 3   Treasuries—Portfolios
         Promoting Student Reflection

Day 4   Grading and Reporting
         Student-Led Conferences

Day 5   Teacher as Inquirer
         Trustworthiness/Accountability

Philosophy Statement

The purpose of reflective assessment is to help teachers bring lasting improvements to curriculum, classroom environments, and instructional practices. Effective change occurs when teachers begin to ask: Is this activity working for my students? Does this assessment procedure fit with my beliefs about assessment? Does current research support my practice? When teachers reflect on the effectiveness of their instructional and assessment practices, and then judge these ideas against their own philosophy, they can improve the quality of the educational experiences afforded their students.

Our summer assessment institute allows teachers to begin with what they already know about learning and assessment. The institute is designed to help teachers critically reflect upon their practice, to understand themselves and their students better, and to use these reflections to guide their instructional decisions. Teachers will be involved in presentations and hands-on engagements that will help them understand crucial aspects of assessment and learning.

FIGURE **9.1.** *Schedule and introduction from the first year's institute.*

member who had threatened progressive language policies and practices in SSD in the past. This group of school board members adopted the following belief statement in 1995:

Saguaro School District Mission and Philosophy

WE BELIEVE:

1. Learning is nonsequential; students construct higher-level meaning when they are not restricted by a predetermined set of lower-level skills.

2. Assessment, as an aspect of learning, should be an authentic and purposeful experience, focusing on growth over time and providing opportunities for self-reflection.

3. Students learn best when they are engaged in authentic self-expression as part of their literacy development.

4. Students learn best in a noncompetitive environment where all feel confident that they are valued and appreciated for their knowledge, talents, accomplishments, and individuality.

5. Learners construct their own meaning when they understand that taking risks and making mistakes are part of learning and they that are free to take risks, investigate, hypothesize, and test their hypotheses.

Reflecting the school board's progressive position, this document was intended to guide all decisions made by the board and by the individual schools. In fact, it was this guiding philosophy that eventually led us to accept teaching positions within the district for the 1995–96 school year.

Homogeneous versus Heterogeneous Groupings

Early in the 1995–96 school year, a conflict arose at one of the middle schools regarding the math program—specifically, how students were grouped for instruction. The administration and teachers at this school were proposing, for a second time, to eliminate homogeneous grouping in math in favor of heterogeneous grouping. This proposal encountered strong resistance from a group of parents concerned that their children would no longer be able to take advanced math classes. The first time the middle school had tried to introduce heterogeneous grouping for math, this group of parents appealed to the superintendent, who overruled the principal's decision. This led to the resignation of the principal and the continuation of homogeneous grouping. The teachers, however, along with the new principal, continued to push for heterogeneous grouping in math classes and, once again, the same group of parents resisted. This time the teachers, the principal, and supportive parents took their fight to the school board, attending board meetings and speaking out in support of heterogeneous grouping. Teachers and parents questioned the superintendent's actions, concerned that she was overruling the school's decision to have heterogeneous math groupings simply to appease a small group of disgruntled parents. Many expressed their concern that decisions being made by the administrative team were not in the best interests of students' education, and they requested open forums for dialogue on this issue. The board was divided on the issue.

Changes in Saguaro's Belief Statements

During a summer retreat for board members and Saguaro's administrative staff, the issue of heterogeneous grouping led to a broader discussion of the district belief statements. It was noted that the middle school's use of homogeneous grouping contradicted the section of the Saguaro school board's belief statements that asserts that students learn best in a noncompetitive environment.

Some administrators at this retreat also noted that physical education teachers and coaches objected to taking competition out of the district's guiding philosophy. Some principals also expressed their fear that students would not be able to function in society, where competition in the workplace is prevalent, if they were not educated in a competitive environment. In response to these concerns, the administration suggested removing the word *noncompetitive* from the board-adopted belief statement.

During the retreat, it was also proposed that the section reading, "We believe that learning is nonsequential; students construct higher-level meaning when they are not restricted by a predetermined set of lower-level skills" be removed as well. Some on the board and administrative team felt that students must learn some things sequentially, offering as examples students' need to learn the alphabet before they can read books, and the need for basic math facts before attempting more complicated mathematical problems. This change in the proposed belief statements allowed teachers and schools to follow scope and sequence programs in the adopted basals and content-area textbooks.

The few dissenting voices at this meeting (including those of the curriculum director, two principals, and a board member) were unable to influence the rest of the administrative team and school board to reconsider the proposed changes to the district's belief statement. School administrators throughout the district opened school doors that fall by sharing with the staff the proposed changes to the SSD belief statements. Many teachers and parents on the school advisory councils were visibly upset. They complained that the proposed changes represented a complete turnabout from where they had thought the district was headed. Other parents and teachers, however, supported the administration and the proposed changes.

Requests for Dialogue

Teachers began to request forums in which staff members from across the district could discuss and offer their own input to the proposed changes in the belief statements. The superintendent, however, made no effort to arrange any meetings or public forums around this issue that was dividing her district and instead restricted dialogue to local school campuses. Time after time, teachers and parents were told that only principals would attend; they would report the results of these discussions to the superintendent during her cabinet meetings. Many teachers protested that having principals represent their views was not the same as having an opportunity to personally voice their concerns. After all, it was not at all certain that principals would give equal weight to all of the teachers' concerns. More seriously, this process denied teachers the opportunity to engage in any kind of meaningful dialogue with their colleagues. From our perspective, at least, it was clear that the superintendent was enacting a policy that limited district dialogue to three arenas—administrative cabinet meetings, board meetings, and the Superintendent's Advisory Council (SAC)—none of which permitted significant teacher or parent involvement. SAC consisted of district administrators, a teacher from each school (chosen by the principal), and a representative of the teacher association from each school (chosen by the association president).

As it turned out, the revised belief statements never went to the board for formal approval. But although they lacked official board approval, the statements appeared in their revised form in many of the school's handbooks and publications.

Saguaro School Board Meetings

District staff, embroiled in the controversy over the changes to the belief statements, began to attend school board meetings where their voices might be heard. Public debate at board meetings often continued until midnight. Often these teachers were critical of both the superintendent and board members who chose to side with her. In response to the increasing number of speakers who wanted to address the board, the board president enacted a policy limiting individual public comment at the meetings to three minutes per person. When this policy failed to reduce the number of potential speakers or the critical tone of comments during the public comment phase of board meetings, the board president took the extraordinary action of reading a statement at each and every board meeting indicating that only positive comments should be made at the public podium. More seriously, his statement routinely included the ominous warning that remarks critical of school officials or board members could result in legal action.

Not satisfied with restricting the content or the time available for remarks by individual citizens attending school board meetings, the board president eventually enacted a policy limiting to thirty minutes the total amount of time allotted for public comments. To make matters worse, the board president began to insist that those who wished to address the board had to fill out a form prior to the public comment section of the meeting stating their name, address, and a brief description concerning the agenda item they wished to speak to. These forms were generally filled out before the board meeting and turned in to the board secretary. This action enabled the school board president to control who spoke at board meetings during the thirty minutes allocated to public comments. Of course, this practice also gave the president control over who had *no* opportunity to speak at these meetings. The president did not take speakers in the order of form submission. Instead, it soon became obvious that citizens who regularly spoke out against the board or the superintendent were pushed to the end of the agenda, often having no opportunity to speak at all.

Time for public comment at school board meetings was also taken up by principals who used this time to make presentations about their respective schools, claiming that the community needed to see positive images of schools at these meetings. We were among those who viewed this claim as an obvious ploy to control public comment at board meetings since the principals making these presentations had made their support of the superintendent and her positions well known.

Administrative Reactions to Conflict within SSD

At one school in the Saguaro district, individuals who spoke out against the school board's actions at board meetings were being called into the principal's office the next day and told that board meetings were not the appropriate arena for these particular discussions. These teachers sought the counsel of their teachers' organization because they were also being denied representation during these meetings with their principal. Grievances against this principal, however, did not alleviate the pressure placed on these teachers to refrain from writing letters to the editor or speaking at board meetings. The principal at our school reported to us that he was instructed by the superintendent to control his teachers—including us. He refused, however, to follow that directive. It proved to be a costly decision for him, since his advocacy for progressive language practices (as well as his own beliefs) would eventually cost him his job.

At the same time, individuals who had spoken at board meetings in support of board policies and in other ways demonstrated their loyalty to the superintendent were being promoted to positions within the district office administration. A principal who was often the target of criticism by parents at school board meetings announced her resignation and was immediately given a job at the district office in a newly created position. One classroom teacher who was a vocal supporter of board policy was promoted to assistant principal at one of the district schools. Supporters of the superintendent working at the district office were also being given new titles and salary increases. Several principals were given newly created positions after their retirements were announced. These movements were the subject of much inquiry in the newspapers as the superintendent took action against two of those who did not publicly support her position: the curriculum director and our principal. Their contracts were recommended for nonrenewal, a decision that was eventually upheld by the board in a four to one vote. One reporter looked into school board campaign contributions from the previous election and found that many who had contributed to the current board members' campaigns held their positions or received promotions. The two administrators who had contributed to opposing campaigns were the ones up for nonrenewal of contract.

Parents speaking out at board meetings claimed that they feared reprisals against their children at school. At one board meeting we attended, a parent from one of the schools complained that she felt she and her children were the subjects of discrimination by the principal and assistant principal of her children's school. During the next meeting, this same parent approached the podium in tears, saying that she was brought to the meeting by her child's principal and told to apologize for lying about the discriminatory behavior she had allegedly experienced. We sat in horror as she stood at the podium and made her statement. She told the board that she was afraid for herself and for her children at the school. She stated that the principal had threatened to call Child Protective Services if she did not withdraw her statement. Although it was difficult to ascertain if her accusations were true, it was widely believed among parents and teachers that vocal opposition to administration would meet consequences and vocal support would meet rewards. By this time, it was obvious that two camps had developed and firmly established themselves—those who supported the superintendent and those who were trying to protect the progressive language policies.

The majority of the board supported the superintendent, although one board member regularly took a stance opposing the superintendent and other board members (votes of four to one became common on most board decisions). It was the subject of much speculation amongst community members and teaching staff that the set of board governing policies adopted in 1996—described in the following section—were established in an effort to control this dissenting board member.

Development of Board Governing Policies

The superintendent recommended that board members participate in an educational development program taught by a nationally known advisor to nonprofit organizations. John Carver was brought in to help create new board governance policies. With Carver's help, a set of operating procedures was developed that was meant to help the Saguaro board focus on the job of setting goals for the school district. After looking at the actual policies that had been written, however, many began to oppose their adoption in letters to the editor and at the public podium at board meetings. Opponents felt that these policies would isolate the board from the schools, parents, and teachers. A section from these policies reads:

> No individual board member may be in the schools except
> (a) when engaged in organized Board visitation or monitoring of system performance,
> (b) after notifying appropriate staff, and
> (c) when fulfilling a role distinct from being a board member, such as parent or invited volunteer.
>   No board member can place himself or herself between staff members in their disputes or negotiations. No board member can serve on staff committees, engage in solving staff problems, or interpret anything to staff.

Many community members wrote to the local newspaper saying that requiring board members to announce themselves before coming to schools was not appropriate given their governing roles. We were concerned that not involving board members in staff discussions and committees would alienate them from the actual school environment. These kinds of informal interactions are necessary for board members to develop an understanding of the complex problems facing their district. During staff meetings, many other teachers expressed their concern that if board members were not present on committees and did not interact with the staff on a regular basis, their perspectives would be limited, and the district administration and superintendent could control the information the board received.

Another part of this document that caused us concern stated:

> Although all members are obligated to register differences of opinion on board issues at the board level as passionately as desired, individual members may not direct their differences of opinion to staff in a manner which would create polarization in the organization or undermine a decision of the Board majority.

Since only one board member regularly voted against the majority and continued to support progressive language practices, we suspect that this particular policy was directed at that member in an effort to muzzle her. Whatever the superintendent's intentions, her actions and those of the school board only confirmed the impression of many teachers and parents that the creation and implementation of school board policy was becoming a private matter between the superintendent and the school board. All indications were that input from parents, the general public, and district staff was neither encouraged nor welcome. For example, the revised board policies included a new language for the superintendent's job description which was explicit about her role in defining the relationship between the board and district staff:

1. As the Board's single official link to the operating organization. . . . All board authority delegated to staff is delegated through the superintendent, so that all authority and accountability to staff—as far as the Board is concerned—is considered to be the authority and accountability of the superintendent.

2. The superintendent, as CEO, is accountable to the Board acting as a body. The Board will instruct the superintendent through written policies, delegating to him or her interpretation and implementation of those policies.

Many teachers and parents criticized the board for considering policies that would in effect turn over much of their power to the superintendent, putting them in the position of having to rely on her to report to them on the state of the district. Teachers, including the two of us, spoke out against these policies at subsequent board meetings. Community members wrote letters to the editor stating that this transfer of power could and should be challenged in court. One parent, for example, referring to the expense of $15,000 to have a corporate consultant help write the new board policies, wrote:

> Are these new governance policies even legal if they allow the above actions and others to be taken without question or even without the knowledge of every board member? I understand that these policies allow board members to receive all types of information in private without the sharing of it with other board members. I would be really interested if an attorney would read these policies and challenge the legality of these policies. (SSD parent in a letter to the editor, published in the local paper)

After three readings and much public opposition, however, the board passed the operating policies in yet another vote of four to one. We feared that the superintendent would use these policies in ways detrimental to the district, and we feared that the progressive practices that had drawn us to seek teaching positions in SSD were on their way to extinction. With the superintendent controlling district operations and establishing a stranglehold on the channels of communication, things began to change for the worse.

Saguaro District Administrators Fired

These new policies left many personnel decisions up to the superintendent, and we were among those teachers who worried that investing so much power in the hands of the superintendent would lead to wholesale personnel changes throughout the district. As it turned out, in the spring of 1997 the curriculum director of Saguaro School District, a longtime advocate of progressive language policies and practices, found himself in the superintendent's office facing a demotion. As a result of the new board policies, the superintendent did not have to take the curriculum director's demotion to the board for approval. In demoting this educator, the superintendent had effectively eliminated all advocates of holistic instruction from her cabinet of central office administrators.

Parents, community members, educational leaders, teachers, and students spoke at board meeting after board meeting urging school board members to reverse the superintendent's decision to demote the curriculum director, but the board did not act. A majority of teachers at one particular school, Agave, were vocal at board meetings and in the local paper in their opposition to the superintendent's decision to demote this highly respected educator. It was probably no coincidence that the principal of Agave School found himself on the agenda of the next board meeting for nonrenewal of his contract, along with the curriculum director, who had been demoted to bilingual coordinator. Interestingly, the reason given for not renewing the contracts of these popular administrators was that they were not "team players." Despite the support of four hundred parents, teachers, students, and community members in attendance at the school board meeting, many of whom offered public testimony in support of these educators, the board accepted the recommendation of the superintendent not to renew their contracts.

Perhaps because of the outpouring of public support for this principal and the curriculum director, the local news media began to inquire into these cases. The response repeatedly given by the board and the superintendent to the media was that board policy prohibited discussing personnel matters publicly despite the request by the administrators whose contracts had been terminated that the board discuss these particular personnel decisions publicly. But the board steadfastly refused to make public its rationale for the firings, despite repeated calls for public discussion.

Amongst the approximately four hundred people who attended the public board meeting in support of these two administrators were the students of Agave School. Student after tearful student approached the board, pleading with them not to take away their much beloved principal, who knew all their names and was in their classrooms and on their playgrounds every day. Incredibly, supporters of the superintendent used this student support to make a case that students were being "used" in an effort to evoke sympathy. Students' feelings and opinions were negated, where they had once been heralded as an important part of the district's assessment. The child-centered curriculum that had drawn us to SSD only two years earlier had shifted that quickly to a curriculum controlled more and more by the central administration. This shift was evidenced by a newsletter to all district employees that appeared shortly after the firings with this headline: "SSD Launches Effort to Establish Plan for Developing Curriculum with High Standards and Aligned Assessments."

Revisions in SSD Curriculum, Student Assessment, and Staff Development Opportunities

The newly promoted district office administrative staff set on a course to revise all district curricula in one school year through the use of curriculum cadres of teachers and parent representatives appointed by the school principals. With the firing of the former curriculum director and the principal of Agave School, the administration could control the makeup of these district committees, thereby undercutting holistic practices that had been in place in SSD. A total reworking of the curriculum—away from the progressive child-centered practices that had attracted us to the Saguaro School District—was based on the claim that teachers were asking for specific grade-level objectives that would tell them what to teach. Staff members were also told by their principals and central office administrators that new teachers were floundering under a curriculum that gave them so much latitude over what to teach, when to teach, and how to teach. These teachers needed more comprehensive guidelines. The new curriculum director said that the SSD curriculum had "holes" and that students were not learning the same things from classroom to classroom. Worse, some teachers said that the curriculum was "too whole language" or progressive in orientation and that it did not allow them the freedom to teach their students in the way they desired.

In 1996, Saguaro School District's assessment plan highlighted student portfolios as an assessment tool. The district staff was implementing a separation of those portfolios to include a teacher-created portfolio and a student-created portfolio for each student in the district. But the superintendent demanded more quantitative data concerning student achievement. In her view, portfolios, although useful for classroom teachers, students, and parents, did not provide the information necessary for large-scale accountability. From her perspective, quantifiable assessment provided information that was readily communicable in numerical form to the newspapers, the public, and the school board. Therefore district office personnel moved to deemphasize staff development on portfolio assessment and instead worked to develop more standardized assessments. The superintendent wanted technical reports to present to the board, and these classroom-based assessments did not provide the necessary data.

Staff development began to take the form of inservices directed at the new textbook adoptions and master's degree classes taught in cooperation with one of the major universities in the state. District inservice opportunities used to be published in book form, with at least thirty course offerings per semester, and included teacher study groups as well as training in new instructional techniques. New inservice publications, however, were limited to two pages and included only courses offered by a local university to teachers seeking their master's degrees and course work to support the textbook adoption. The new direction of staff development was being sold to the school board as being more rigorous than the professional literature study groups, the Reflective Assessment Institute, and the portfolio classes that had been offered under the now demoted curriculum director. Individuals who proposed classes for staff development were told that they were required to take a class instructing them how to teach inservice for adults, including a Saturday morning class on effective charting. This enraged many teachers, who for years had been developing their inservice courses and refining their abilities to teach teachers. In taking control of the inservice education of district teachers, the central office administrators were attempting to control the content of what teachers were being taught. We, along with many of our colleagues who had been teaching district inservices, simply refused to teach the classes or were not asked to teach them again, and in the end, the Reflective Assessment Institute and teacher inservice development classes we had so highly valued in SSD were discontinued.

Accusations and Reactions

It was apparent from their actions that the board was unwilling to question the superintendent's actions and, more seriously, they supported the silencing of dissenting opinion. In 1997, however, the board and superintendent found themselves the object of legal scrutiny when the state attorney general's office was informed that the school board was violating the state's open meeting law. Charges were subsequently filed against four of the five board members for many open meeting law violations. Videotapes of board members meeting at private homes with the superintendent also began to appear on the evening news with some regularity. School board members, however, denied the allegations and continued to function in their elected offices while under investigation.

Throughout these events, parents and teachers who had helped with school board members' previous election campaigns repeatedly asked board members why their beliefs about effective educational policies had changed. Again and again, individual board members said they had not changed their beliefs or philosophy of education. One board member, however, after resigning in a plea agreement with the attorney general's office, wrote to the local paper stating that her beliefs on some things had changed because she had been talking to her best friend who had a child in private school, and she could no longer defend our district's policies on progressive language instruction. She also stated that she realized that Saguaro's district administration was correct in wanting to make changes.

Epilogue

In the end, a new principal was appointed to Agave School, and despite pleading from parents and teachers to have a voice in interviewing and selecting candidates for this position, the board made it clear that the power to hire and fire principals rested solely in the superintendent's hands. And, of course, new board policies had indeed given the superintendent that power. These policies also made it possible for the board to avoid any responsibility for decisions made by the superintendent. As we were writing this chapter, however, four of the board members resigned under pressure from the attorney general's office, and they have been prohibited from holding public office for the next three years. The state superintendent appointed four new members to serve on the board until the next election. Litigation brought by the two administrators whose contracts were not renewed is still pending against the district.

The superintendent took an extensive leave of absence after the board members were charged with violating the state's open meeting law, and she eventually sued the district for $4 million for alleged pain and suffering due to the testimony of one of Saguaro's board members. In a settlement agreement with the newly appointed board, she received $40,000 and paid medical insurance to the end of her contract in exchange for her resignation. Fittingly, the settlement was passed in a four to one vote.

The assistant superintendent acted as superintendent during the leave of absence. He was then promoted by the new board to the position and given a two-year contract. In the media release regarding his promotion, the new superintendent was quoted as saying that the accomplishments of the district staff over the past year were a legacy to the past superintendent's excellent leadership. The new board president also wrote an editorial for the local newspaper echoing the applause for the past superintendent. And so it begins again. . . .

Chapter Ten

Politics and the English Language Arts

Sheridan Blau
University of California Santa Barbara

California's Progressive Language Arts Assessment: A Brief History

In the spring of 1993 and again in 1994, all public school students in California in grades 4, 8, and 10 took a new language arts test— a test designed to assess student performance in reading and writing. The test was sponsored by the California Department of Education and funded by a bill that created the California Learning Assessment System, known as CLAS. Late in the fall of 1994, the bill that would have provided funds for the continuation of the CLAS tests for the next several years was vetoed by the governor, after barely surviving repeated assaults in both legislative chambers. The veto was the finale to a massive statewide campaign by conservative pressure groups which had convinced large segments of the public that the language arts tests—particularly the reading test—and the instructional goals that these tests supported, were morally unhealthy for students, unreliable in their results, and subversive of the kind of literacy that schools, employers, and the public have traditionally valued. The story of the development of those tests and their political demise reveals a good deal about current and historical tensions in the teaching of literature and literacy in schools and about a growing cultural gap between the discourse of well-informed professionals in the language arts and that of the public and legislative bodies they serve.

The CLAS language arts test, which was under development for almost nine years, was designed by a team whose membership rotated over the years, but in its last several years consisted at any one time of about twenty-five teachers, representing fairly evenly the three levels of schooling tested—elementary, middle school, and high school. The team was assisted throughout its operation by two or three advisors who were curriculum specialists in the English language arts or representatives of the university research community. From 1991 through 1994, when the bill authorizing the test and the entire statewide testing program were canceled by a gubernatorial veto, I served as a senior advisor to the Language Arts Test Development Team.

Many of the teachers on the test development team in its final years were veterans of the earlier team that had, under a previous state administration, done the initial development work for California's groundbreaking direct assessment of writing, when the state testing program was known as the California Assessment Program, or CAP. The CAP writing assessment, introduced statewide in 1987, had been a forward-looking attempt to move beyond multiple-choice tests for the large-scale assessment of writing by asking students to actually produce writing.

Just as important, the CAP writing test was a matrix-sampling test, designed not so much to assess children as to assess instruction. It consisted therefore of a battery of tests designed to assess writing at designated grades across a spectrum of genre or writing types appropriate for the target grades (based largely on Moffett's [1981, 1983] discourse typology, including such types as "autobiographical incident," "report of information," "problem-solution," "interpretation," "controversial issue," and so on. Thus, within any classroom to be tested, the students would be writing on a number of topics representing the eight types of writing specified for that grade (see Dudley, 1997; Claggett, 1999). Scores, derived from a holistic scoring procedure overseen by the Educational Testing Service (ETS), were then given to schools and districts, informing them about how well students were writing in each of the designated genres.

Working from the premise that testing will drive teaching, the legislature funded the expensive CAP writing assessment program to improve the teaching of writing in California schools and supported it with an extensive staff development program spearheaded by the state-funded California Writing Project. Some sixteen sites of the California Writing Project were also kept busy throughout the state conducting inservice programs on the teaching of writing, funded by schools and districts that wanted to ensure a credible performance by their students on the new writing assessment. By the end of the decade, it appeared that testing was driving teaching in a healthy direction as schools and districts invested heavily in professional development programs in the teaching of writing, and English classes throughout the state typically called for more writing and a greater variety of types of writing than had been observed previously in California classrooms. Encouraged by the apparent success of the new assessment program in writing, the state superintendent of instruction charged the test development team in language arts to turn its attention to developing a test in reading that would complement the writing tests as an "authentic assessment," and that would drive instruction in reading—as it had in writing—in a direction representing the current state of knowledge about best practices. In the interest of these goals, development team members rotating off the team were replaced by teachers drawn from the newly created California Literature Project as well as the Writing Project, until the team consisted of members representing both projects in approximately equal numbers.

The teachers selected to serve on the newly charged Language Arts Test Development Team were ultimately appointed by a joint committee of team members, advisors, and Department of Education officials after a rigorous review process that began with nominations from leaders in the professional community (especially from site directors of the California Writing and Literature Projects) and that included a lengthy application with sample lessons and an interview. In appointing new members, the selection committee tried to ensure that the team represented the various regions as well as the ethnic diversity of the state, but the primary consideration was always that of selecting teachers who were themselves expert classroom practitioners and accomplished readers and writers.

Sample Reading Test and Scoring Guide

With this introduction, let me now present a model of the reading test whose development I have been describing and an account of the scoring guide that was used to assess student performances. To save space, I have developed a sample test (Figure 10.1) that is unrepresentative only insofar as its reading selection is shorter than those typically used and in which the blank space that would be ordinarily provided for responses (including a full page drawing of the "open mind") has been largely eliminated. The text and questions I am using here would probably be appropriate for a tenth-grade test, but could possibly be used with eighth graders as well. Even the fourth-grade test used similar questions or test items. And performances at all grades were assessed according to the same scoring guide.

A couple of additional prefatory remarks are also in order about the reading selection I have chosen for this sample—a short poem. In fact, poems were often used on the administered tests, usually paired with a second poem or with a short prose piece. More often, the reading selection was a short story or passage from a work of fiction or nonfiction. Virtually all the reading selections included in the test, however—including nonfiction pieces—were drawn from the reservoir of writing that is usually classified as "literature," so the reading selections were almost all belletristic rather than informational pieces, even if they were rich with information. The rationale here is that the development team was charged with testing reading as it is taught within the framework of the language arts curriculum, a curriculum that distinctly favors literature. Hence the reading test included none of the commonplace, nonliterary reading that ordinary citizens do on the job or in the conduct of civic or domestic life—no typical newspaper articles, instruction manuals, voter pamphlets, or bus schedules. Nor did it include the sort of pedestrian textbook prose that students might be called on to read in a science or history class. Conventional news articles or commonplace informational writing were found to be insufficiently rich or insufficiently challenging to call on the strategic and cognitive strengths that distinguish the reading performances of the most accomplished readers. The maxim among critics that great literature requires great readers logically applies in complementary fashion in the domain of testing: powerful readers require complex and challenging examples of writing in order to demonstrate their accomplishments as readers (see also Claggett, 1999).

Read the poem that appears below and answer the questions that follow. Feel free to make notes in the margin as you read.

Introductory Note: This poem by Emma Lazarus (1849–1887) was selected in 1886 to be inscribed on the pedestal of the Statue of Liberty, which stands in New York harbor (between New York City and Jersey City, New Jersey) at the entrance to the Port of New York. Every boat entering the Port of New York passes within view of the statue. For generations New York was the port of arrival for most immigrants entering the United States by boat, so that for most immigrants the Statue of Liberty was the symbol of welcome to the United States. The original "Colossus," one of the seven wonders of the ancient world, was a huge statue that straddled the harbor of Rhodes in ancient Greece.

The New Colossus   (1883)   *Your Notes*

Not like the brazen giant of Greek fame,
With conquering limbs astride from land to land;
Here at our sea-washed, sunset gates shall stand
A mighty woman with a torch, whose flame
Is the imprisoned lightning, and her name
Mother of Exiles. From her beacon-hand
Glows world-wide welcome; her mild eyes command
The air-bridged harbor that twin cities frame.
"Keep, ancient lands, your storied pomp!" cries she
With silent lips. "Give me your tired, your poor,
Your huddled masses yearning to breathe free,
The wretched refuse of your teeming shore.
Send these, the homeless, tempest-tossed to me,
I lift my lamp beside the golden door!"

1. What is your initial reaction or response (your thoughts, feelings, observations, questions, ideas, etc.) to this poem?

2. Pick a line in this poem that seems to you especially important or interesting. Write out the line and then explain your reasons for selecting it.

3. How do you interpret the name "Mother of Exiles" in line 6? What is the significance of this name in the poem?

4. The last part of the poem says, "Give **me your** tired, **your** poor."

   a. Who is "me" and who is "you" or "your?" Who is speaking in the last five lines of this poem and to whom are these lines addressed?

   b. Using the "Open Mind" outline provided [on a full page in the actual test], show with drawings, symbols, or words what the speaker of these lines is thinking or what a person hearing these lines might be expected to think.

   c. Explain your graphic.

5. Use the opportunity provided by this question to say anything else you might want to say about this poem. You might want to talk about its form or language, its meaning to you personally or as a member of a group, its cultural or historical or ideological or aesthetic significance, or anything else you haven't already said about the poem.

FIGURE **10.1.** *Sample reading test.*

Reading Scoring Guide

Reading performances were ranked on a six-point scale according to the degree to which they matched the descriptors for each score point and the model papers that demonstrated the range of performances within a single scorepoint. In general, readers were seen as demonstrating more advanced levels of achievement by the degree to which they attended to increasingly more complex structures of meaning. The least skilled readers (scorepoints 1 or 2) seemed able to make meaning only of parts of a text (individual words or phrases for a score of 1 and whole sentences or concepts or plot elements for a score of 2). Readers judged to perform at what was seen as the lower range of the middle level of performance—scorepoint 3—showed they were able to gather the meaning or gist of a whole text, at least at a literal level. Somewhat more accomplished readers were able to construct interpretations that elaborated on the meaning of a text or moved beyond the surface features and boundaries of the literal text to suggest more implied meanings or to draw some generalized principle from the text (scorepoint 4). The most advanced readers produced interpretations that analyzed as well as explicated a text and reflected persuasively on its wider significance or value (scorepoints 5 and 6). Thus reading performances at scorepoint 1 were designated "minimal"; at scorepoint 2, "limited"; at 3, "literal"; at 4, "thoughtful"; at 5, "discerning"; at 6, "exemplary."

Training for the assessors was based on a fully elaborated rubric and on a generous sampling of "benchmarks" or "anchors" used as examples of each scorepoint and of the variety of responses typically falling within a single scorepoint. The conception of reading that governed the construction of the test and the assessment of student performances will be evident in the full description of a reading performance at scorepoint 6:

> *An exemplary reading performance is insightful, discerning, and perceptive as the reader constructs and reflects on meaning in a text.* Readers at this level are sensitive to linguistic, structural, cultural, and psychological nuances and complexi-

ties. They fill in gaps in a text, making warranted and responsible assumptions about unstated causes or motivations,
or drawing meaning from subtle cues. They differentiate between literal and figurative meanings. They recognize real or
seeming contradictions, exploring possibilities for their resolution or tolerating ambiguities. They demonstrate their understanding of the whole work as well as an awareness of
how the parts work together to create the whole.

*Readers achieving score point 6 develop connections with
and among texts.* They connect their understanding of the
text not only to their own ideas, experience, and knowledge,
but also to their history as participants in a culture or larger
community, often making connections to other texts or other
works of art. Exceptional readers draw on evidence from the
text to generate, validate, expand, and reflect on their own
ideas.

These readers take risks. They entertain challenging ideas and
explore multiple possibilities of meaning as they read, grounding these meanings in their acute perceptions of textual and
cultural complexities. They often revise their understanding
of a text as they re-read and as additional information or
insight becomes available to them. They sometimes articulate a newly developed level of understanding.

Readers performing at level 6 challenge the text. They carry
on dialogue with the writer, raising questions, taking exception, agreeing or disagreeing, appreciating or criticizing text
features. They may sometimes suggest ways of rewriting the
text. They may test the validity of the author's ideas or information, by considering the authority of the author and the
nature and quality of evidence presented. They may speculate about the ideology or cultural or historical biases that
seem to inform a text, sometimes recognizing and embracing
and sometimes resisting the position that a text seems to construct for its reader.

What Was Accomplished in the Development of the CLAS Reading Test?

Putting aside the failure of the CLAS test as an enduring instrument of state educational policy in California, the CLAS reading test represents an important contribution to the art of assessment in the language arts and to the repertoire of teaching and testing strategies available nationally to teachers of reading and literature. Its achievements as an innovative instrument for assessing reading include the following:

1. It captured the complexity of reading, assessing reading as it is practiced by literate persons in academic and other settings.

2. It honored multiple possibilities for interpretation while demanding plausibility for any interpretive claims.

3. It honored the possibility of a literate yet resistant reading, a reading that takes an oppositional stance to the ideology inscribed in the text being read.

4. It honored reading as an experience, especially as an aesthetic experience (Rosenblatt, 1938, 1978).

5. It honored alternative styles of learning and of representing knowledge.

6. It demonstrated respect for the professionalism of teachers by putting test development and scoring in the hands of teachers, thereby also promoting teacher reflection on the activity of reading and interpreting texts, and providing a rich professional development opportunity for teachers of reading and literature.

7. It provided a workable model for conducting a valid and highly reliable (Dudley, 1997) large-scale assessment of reading, using a holistic scoring instrument that is credible for the professional community of language arts specialists and consistent with the instructional goals and practices of well-informed English and language arts teachers nationwide.

Given Such Accomplishments, Why Did the CLAS Reading Test Engender Such Powerful and Widespread Opposition?

The answer is largely because it was so good. That is to say, the test was opposed by its most passionate detractors for precisely the same reasons it was so widely appreciated in the community of language arts professionals. For example, the fact that the test honored multiple interpretations of reading selections was seen by its detractors as evidence of a kind of moral relativism on the part of the educators who were responsible for producing the test and of a deliberate policy of dumbing down standards for reading so that the answers of all children could be equally valued.

The fact that the test honored reading as an experience and therefore invited students to describe their own responses to literary works and that the scoring guide directed assessors to evaluate the thoughtfulness and complexity of a student's engagement with a text was all seen as evidence of an attempt on the part of the state educational apparatus to control the thoughts and feelings of students. Such a view was not entirely unreasonable, given the further assumption on the part of the test's critics that every question on a test ought to have a correct answer. Therefore the presence of questions asking students to reveal their thoughts, feelings, or ideas presupposed for the test's detractors a correct set of thoughts, feelings, and ideas toward which the test could be said to direct students or toward which their teachers would presumably direct them so that they might perform well on the test. Hence the test was attacked as an attempt on the part of a state educational agency to control the thoughts, feelings, and values of students statewide.

Moreover, all questions about responses, thoughts, feelings, ideas, or values (especially questions that mentioned "feelings") were seen by the test's detractors as belonging more properly to the realm of psychological testing and the field of counseling than to the domain of literacy, and were therefore seen as intrusions into the private lives of students and their families. In some two dozen jurisdictions in California, parents (supported by lawyers from fundamentalist or right-wing pressure groups) instituted suits against school districts to stop the administration of the CLAS reading test, citing article 60650 of the California education code, which requires parental permission before a child is subjected to psychological tests or any test inquiring into family practices or beliefs in matters of sex, morality, or religion. (The suit was found to have no merit in the only court—the District Court of Los Angeles—in which the case went to trial.)

Additionally, the fact that the test was developed and scored by teachers using a holistic scoring system meant to its detractors that the assessment process was entirely subjective and that the test was an instrument of ideological manipulation through which teachers could impose their liberal prejudices and atheistic and humanistic (as opposed to religiously pious) values on students.

Given the attempt on the part of the testmakers to provide readings that might interest and engage students in genuine literary discussion, it is hardly surprising (in retrospect) that much of the most vigorous opposition to the test also derived from reports and rumors about the content of the test's literary selections. Since the literary selections and test questions actually used or planned for use were matters of the strictest confidentiality, neither the state Department of Education nor the members of the test development team could comment on the accuracy of the reports (most of them false or largely false) that circulated wildly around PTA groups, neighborhoods, religious congregations, school boards, and the state legislative chambers. These rumors referred to the sexually explicit, graphically violent, antifamily, racist, linguistically degenerate, anti-American, morbid, and antireligious literary selections that children were said to be forced to read and write about on the CLAS test (see also Dudley, 1997). Not only were children required to write about such selections, but they were also, according to the popular mythology which many parents and school board members believed, required to write about similar topics (sex, violence, generational conflicts, gender conflicts, parental abuse) in their own families.

Nor would the opposition to the test have been much ame-liorated if the public had been given access to all the reading selections actually used or planned for use. Indeed, in a belated and unsuccessful attempt to regain public confidence and com-bat the wildfire rumors about the immorality of the reading se-lections on the CLAS reading test, the Department of Education released to the public all tests used in the 1993 and 1994 CLAS reading test administrations. Aside from the fact that some crit-ics then claimed that the Department of Education was continu-ing to hide the most offensive reading selections, the real reading selections proved hardly less controversial for the simple reason that any reading selection used on a required state test will be offensive to some segment of the public, and a large collection of such readings will therefore find a large collectivity to be offended.

In fact, the public debate over California's reading assess-ment served as a laboratory demonstration of a principle of poststructuralist literary theory—i.e., that all texts and reading methods are ideological and that all readings are partial. There-fore even the most apparently innocuous stories and essays in-spired opposition on the part of some parents or public officials, such as the well-educated state education officials who objected to a test form that included an autobiographical selection by Joan Didion in which she recounts a childhood event of throwing a snowball at a car and finding herself chased by foot all over her neighborhood by an angry motorist who eventually catches her and does nothing more in his helpless anger than call her a "stu-pid kid." The passage was offensive to these officials because they regarded it, first, as violent (largely because the escaping child imagines a violence which never materializes), and then as an implicit endorsement of a dangerous and unlawful activity—throwing snowballs at cars (see also Dudley, 1997).

In many cases far more outrageous than this one, we discov-ered (much to our surprise—a measure of our naiveté) that for a significant segment of the public, any action represented in a lit-erary work printed on a test was assumed to be endorsed not only by the author but by the authority of the testmaker—no matter how the act might be treated within the text, no matter what context might qualify it or moral judgment might implicitly or explicitly frame it. Similarly, any language usage represented in reading selections on the test was seen as exemplary for student use, including all passages of dialogue that might include speech in various nonstandard dialects. Thus many parents, seeing test forms with literary texts that included realistic representations of the speech of speakers of nonstandard dialects (including immigrant speakers speaking fractured English), objected to the fact that the tests (or any books that included such stories) were teaching their children to use improper English.

The Sources of Opposition

The kinds of charges against the test that I have been describing do not by any means represent merely the paranoid fantasies of some lunatic fringe group; it is clear they were promulgated widely through a propaganda campaign funded largely by nationally organized right-wing pressure groups. All across the nation these groups were particularly active in 1993 and 1994 in the service of an agenda that was generally opposed to the national reform movement in education and that specifically sought to discredit state educational agencies, undermine public confidence in public schools, oppose performance-based assessments wherever they appeared, and stop any proposals to adopt outcomes-based education programs (apparently because the outcomes proposed or adopted in some states tended to deemphasize substantive knowledge while foregrounding psychological or ideological outcomes that represent such liberal values as self-esteem, tolerance for different beliefs and lifestyles, and respect for other cultures). Having mistakenly identified California's "authentic assessment program" with the national outcomes-based education movement, conservative pressure groups targeted the California assessment program as a threat to traditional educational values and goals.

Thus national organizations, in collaboration with state and locally organized groups of concerned citizens, arranged for the publication and widespread distribution of pamphlets and fact sheets purporting to reveal the truth about California's new assessment program and to expose for public scrutiny what they claimed were actual copies of test forms used in the reading assessment and smuggled to them for public exposure by individual outraged and courageous teachers. Some of the test forms were copies of pilot tests, a few were of genuine tests, but many were practice tests made up by publishers or by well-intentioned but not always well-informed teachers or district language arts coordinators (see Dudley, 1997).

What is most striking about these exposed tests and the commentary provided on them is not the degree to which they misrepresented the actual tests used in the CLAS reading assessment, but how much the same features that I have described as strengths of the test were described with a fair degree of accuracy by the opposition. The opponents cited these same features, however, as evidence of the test's academic flabbiness and intrusiveness into the private lives and thoughts of students and their parents. Moreover, the reading selections reproduced to demonstrate the inappropriateness of the test reading materials were drawn almost exclusively from approved textbooks, even when they were selections that would not have survived the rigorous CLAS vetting process, and usually consisted of stories or essays by African American or Mexican American authors. These reading selections (including those actually used on CLAS tests) were typically found objectionable for their nonstandard language (dialect in dialogue), their negative accounts of American life (descriptions of inner-city neighborhoods or rural poverty), their indifference to traditional family values (portraits of single-parent households), their promotion of racial conflict (accounts of incidents of racism), or their representations of violence or cruelty (story conflict). What was objectionable, in other words, was any realistic literary representation of the American experience of people of color.

The published accounts of the grounds for opposing the CLAS tests sound almost sweetly reasonable, however, compared to the attacks on the tests that were frequently offered in public meetings by outraged parents and representatives of various organizations with right-wing educational, political, and religious agendas. In legislative hearings, meetings sponsored by civic groups, school board–sponsored hearings, and the like, where people gathered mainly to protest the new state tests, one could repeatedly hear that one form of the reading test required children to speculate about what most adults do on their wedding night or that another form of the test asked students to tell about a time they had been abused by their parents. Such meetings were also frequented by well-dressed, well-spoken people who would confide in me in all seriousness and with unshakable certitude that the state of California maintained a computer file with every child's answers to the CLAS reading tests in it, so that teachers would have access to the way each of their students thought and would be able to correct the thinking of any students whose test responses showed that they needed an attitude adjustment—particularly in their attitudes toward sex, family life, multiculturalism, the environment, politics, and religion.

As I have suggested, however, California's progressive assessment program was not defeated by the political power of the lunatic fringe in the state nor by the epidemic of statewide paranoia or by widespread sympathy with the political or educational agenda of extreme right-wing pressure groups. Rather, it seems to be the case that large segments of the middle-of-the-road public in California found features of the new reading test unsettling or unfamiliar enough to lend credibility to the more plausible attacks on the test advertised so widely by the right-wing propaganda machine and featured so prominently in newspaper and TV reports on public opposition to the test. In fact, some of the most damning criticism and misguided but influential ridicule of the test came from the presumably liberal press, including journalists who had not otherwise seemed bent on discrediting public education or the Department of Education.

Columnists at influential newspapers, for example, wrote with contempt of what they took to be an absurd feature of the CLAS reading test: the fact that every test form included at least one question which asked students to produce a drawing or other visual representation of the meaning of the reading selection or some part of it. This unconventional feature of the test—the use of the open mind, in particular, where a student is asked to use drawings within the outline of a head to represent what is going on in a character's mind at a crucial moment in a story—was widely mentioned in the press as evidence that the test demanded no intellectual rigor and would call for none in the scoring of it. Yet anyone who is willing to reflect thoughtfully on such test items would recognize that they characteristically entailed asking students the most conventional literary questions (about the unspoken motives of characters, for example) and that they were innovative only in their attempt to make the assessment more accessible to students for whom writing is a less comfortable medium of expression than drawing. In fact, the one defect of the test, troublesome to the testmakers and to other educators but never mentioned by the critics of the test, is the fact that it requires writing to demonstrate performance in reading. And it is this defect that questions like the open mind and others calling for drawing instead of writing tried to ameliorate if not correct.

The test was particularly vulnerable to criticism and attack, of course, because it was unlike other tests that most people had seen, and it asked questions about reading that were unlike the questions most people were inclined to expect on a reading test. The degree to which it violated conventional expectations about the teaching or testing of reading was dramatically revealed to me in an exchange I engaged in with a conservative senior state senator who was genuinely interested in learning about the test and understanding (rather than merely pandering to) the complaints of his constituents. This was one of the few senators who responded to an invitation by the Department of Education to legislators to review the full battery of reading tests that were to be given to students in the spring of 1994. Senators willing to sign a pledge of confidentiality about the test content were invited to come to a small (guarded) antechamber just off of the Senate floor where the tests were available for inspection and where consultants would also be available to discuss the tests. In this context, I sat next to this particular senator as he read through a test form that included a story by Gary Soto. As the senator read, he muttered aloud to himself, noting the nonstandard ("ungrammatical") language represented in the dialogue and expressing disgust with the attitudes toward school and authority that he saw displayed by the story's narrator and some of its characters. Then, when he finished reading the story and came to the first question on the assessment ("What is your initial response to this story: what ideas, thoughts, observations, or questions does this story raise for you?"), the senator turned to me and, pointing to the test question, asked, "What the hell do you care?"

It was a stunning and revealing inquiry. Fortunately, I had been sitting next to the senator as he read the story and could point out to him that he had been a very critical reader of it, commenting unfavorably on its language and on the attitudes and political values he saw endorsed by or represented in the story. I told him that his running commentary as he read showed me that he was an active, engaged reader and that he therefore would have a good deal to say in response to a question asking him for his initial response. A weak reader, I pointed out, would have to struggle to make sense of the bare plot of the story and would not be engaged enough in it to respond critically or to make political or ideological observations or to register much of a thoughtful or reflective response of any kind.

The senator may have come, as a consequence of this experience, to understand what we were after in the first question on the test, but his initial response to the test item reveals why so many parents were so easily convinced that questions asking students about their responses to their reading—about their own ideas, thoughts, feelings, or confusions—indicated that the test was not a test of reading at all, but an invitation to produce some kind of New Age feel-good blather that substitutes in contemporary schools for knowledge. That is to say, for the senator and perhaps for most adults in the United States without special literary interests or background, reading is almost solely a matter of acquiring information, and it can therefore only be tested by asking factual questions which have correct answers. To depart from the realm of those facts in a reading assessment is to inquire into entirely subjective matters that are the private business of individuals, not subject to evaluation by teachers and especially not by the state.

This is not a stupid or paranoid view of what it means to read or to evaluate reading, even though it represents an unsophisticated model of the reading process and a reductive conception of the problem of textual meaning and the process of constructing an interpretation. Surely it owes a great deal to the way in which reading—including literary reading—has been taught and assessed in most U.S. classrooms until quite recently, and the way it may still be taught in many schools. What else is one to conclude about reading, when it is tested on schoolwide and state-sponsored assessments through multiple-choice tests in which each test item has only one correct answer? How long has it been, moreover, since teachers of literature stopped leading students to the one and only correct interpretation of a literary text or stopped testing reading by asking anything other than factual questions or highly interpretive questions for which, according to the teacher and the teacher's scoring system, there is only one correct response (What is the theme of Shakespeare's *Julius Caesar*? What word best describes the character of Mark Antony?)?

Moreover, the very idea of a reader's response being of any possible interest to a teacher or critic intent on producing an authoritative interpretation of a literary work would have been condemned in many universities until fairly recently (surely until the 1970s) as an instance of the "affective fallacy" (Wimsatt & Beardsley, 1954), an interpretive move that was said to confuse the psychological state of a reader with the objective meaning of a text. And how many teachers reading this essay would have been inclined, only a few years ago, to tell students who resisted the sentiments and ideology informing the Emma Lazarus poem that they were not reading the poem in the proper spirit and could not understand it "correctly" if they were to insist on criticizing it from a political point of view different from that of its implied reader?

Only a couple of years ago one of my students in an introductory literature course told me that he could not complete the assignment to write about his reading of a widely anthologized seventeenth-century poem by Richard Lovelace, "To Lucasta on Going to the Wars" (beginning, "Tell me not, Sweet, I am unkind / That from the nunnery / Of thy chaste breast and quiet mind / To war and arms I fly"), because the poem spoke for an attitude toward war and male duty that the student found objectionable and for which he could have no sympathy. Of course, I told him that he appeared to be a highly competent reader of the poem and that he might have a good deal more to say about his reading of the poem than students less hostile to and possibly less engaged by it. But his response to the assignment shows that his literary education had trained him to believe that a correct or acceptable reading of a poem must be one that does not merely recognize but accepts the view or position constructed for the reader by the poem. Parents who make that assumption about what it means to read a piece of literature correctly might therefore feel extremely wary about having their children evaluated as readers on the basis of responses to literary works that speak for values or ideas different from or opposed to their own.

What Can Language Arts Professionals Learn from the California Experience?

Given the fact that public opposition to the test reflected the way most citizens had experienced literary instruction in schools, the fate of the CLAS reading test might be cited as an instance of karmic justice. We reaped as an educational community what we had sown. A more sanguine way of making the same observation is to say that as an educational community we need to do a better job of selling any new kind of test to the public that funds it and to the parents whose schools and children will be ranked or graded by it. We do not know whether it would have been possible (it surely would have been wise) for the Department of Education in California to have conducted an anticipatory public relations campaign that could have successfully inoculated the public against the hysteria fomented by the propaganda machine of extremist pressure groups. Departments of Education in other states, having learned from California's experience, seem to be paying much more attention to the need for such proactive educational campaigns, but it is not clear that they will succeed. It also appears that one of the preventive steps being taken in most states is that of avoiding the elements of the CLAS test that would be most likely to invite criticism—an avoidance that appears to be producing tests that hardly differ from traditional reading tests.

Costs versus Benefits

Such caution, however, is surely the safest policy and it may well be the wisest. For one of the most important lessons that the teaching community in California learned from our recent history with statewide tests of literacy is that good teachers, who have not in the past been hurt by bad tests, can be hurt badly by good tests. It is questionable, on the other hand, whether weak teachers can best be helped by good tests. That is, the rationale for a new California reading test which would model best practices and therefore promote exemplary instruction may have been based on faulty or naive assumptions. The actual impact of the California fiasco was to drive the best teaching in many communities underground because practices that had long been honored in schools and communities, particularly the practices of the most professionally active and expert teachers, suddenly became controversial and subject to censure by watchdog groups of parents.

Thus many teachers reported that as a consequence of the controversy over the CLAS tests, such classroom practices as having students keep literature logs or reading journals, having them write responses to their reading, inviting them to make personal connections to literary texts, encouraging them to make (and explain) drawings in response to literary works, and asking them to work in collaborative reading groups in which students explore multiple ways of interpreting texts—all of these practices—fell under suspicion and were feared by many parents as New Age techniques, part of the general movement to dumb down the curriculum and teach attitudes and values in place of substantive knowledge. In some schools, parents visited classrooms to assure themselves that such practices were not being imposed on their children. Many of the best teachers I know—particularly at the elementary level—confided to me in the midst of the CLAS controversy that in spite of their support for everything the CLAS reading test represented, their classrooms and schools were damaged by the new test, while they had hardly been affected at all by the former innocuous multiple-choice tests.

Nor is it clear that in the first year of the CLAS reading test, when there was no controversy over the teaching techniques it modeled, that it had any lasting or significant impact on classroom teachers who were not about to experiment with new teaching techniques anyway. Without the opportunity to develop an understanding of the principles underlying new teaching practices or to reflect on those practices in conversation with colleagues, how meaningful or lasting would any change in practice be to a teacher who felt forced by a test to experiment with a strategy that ran counter to familiar and conventional practice? The relevant lesson here may be that extensive, thoughtfully conceived professional development programs and not statewide tests are the proper venues for improving classroom teaching practice.

Public and Professional Conceptions of Reading with a Historical Perspective on Competing Paradigms

Perhaps the most important lesson to be learned from the defeat of California's progressive reading assessment is one I have already alluded to about how wide the gap is between the way reading—particularly literary reading—is construed by well-informed professionals in the language arts and the way it is construed by the wider lay public, including most parents. We can characterize the difference between professional and popular conceptions of reading as representing two different and oppositional paradigms which apply to reading both as a private activity and as an academic discipline to be taught and evaluated. The oppositional character of these paradigms may be quickly and perhaps not reductively apprehended by the chart in Figure 10.2, which shows contrasting sets of assumptions.

These conflicting conceptions of literacy and literacy practices may seem to reflect irreconcilable ideological differences, but they may also reflect the evolutionary history of literacy practices in the United States and the tendency of older models of literacy to survive in a period when they are being challenged and replaced by newer models. Myers (1996) identifies five conceptions of literacy that have emerged one after the other in U.S. history, each overlapping with its neighbors to shape for a period of time the teaching and assessment of reading in schools and the way literacy is understood in the workplace, in public policy, and in the popular mind. Moments of contestation, like our own, he sees as the inevitable result of clashes between different versions of literacy that are overlapping and that therefore remain current for different groups of Americans, much as linguistic

The Professional View	The Public's View
1. Reading is a transactional and experiential process. Readers may be seen as engaged in a transaction with a text—a transaction to which they bring their own background knowledge, values, and prior experience (their culture), and, guided by the language and structure of the text, they undergo a new experience out of which they construct a meaning for the text and a sense of its value to them (Rosenblatt, 1938, 1978).	1. Reading is essentially a process of information retrieval. Texts give information. Readers may be said to understand a text when they can show that they have received the information given.
2. Meaning is negotiated and subject to change. The meaning of a text is seen as something a reader arrives at through a problem-solving process, working with a text, asking questions, obtaining contextual and background information, and consulting other readers, including readers who may perceive the same text differently. Each construction of a sense of the meaning of a text is tentative because it is subject to change with subsequent and better-informed and increasingly mature readings.	2. The meaning of a text (especially canonical literary texts) is not negotiable or tentative; it is known and fixed by authorities (who have usually discerned the intentions of authors). Teachers and other authorized sources (e.g., CliffsNotes) are responsible for transmitting these meanings to students, and students are responsible for knowing them. That (and technical terms and descriptions of technical elements about texts) is what constitutes literary knowledge, and it is testable through multiple-choice tests.
3. Interpretations of texts are subject to evaluation by the criterion of plausibility. Interpretations are always subject to challenge, and the process of adjudicating between competing interpretations is a process of weighing textual and contextual evidence.	3. Interpretations may be evaluated by the criterion of correctness. Correct interpretations are those that represent (usually) the intentions of authors and that are known and transmitted by authorities.
4. Critical reading (which is built on or follows from interpretive reading) may entail resistant reading or reading against the ideological or ethical grain of a text. Strong readers often talk back to texts, challenging their ideology or values. Texts selected for study, including classic or canonical texts, command our attention, but not necessarily our belief or endorsement.	4. Critical reading means appreciating the artistry of a work and its moral vision. All texts worthy enough to be taught are to be revered. And (for a smaller yet still sizable segment of the public) whatever is textually represented is thereby endorsed. Furthermore, students may be said to be encouraged to imitate any action represented in an assigned or recommended text, because every action, thought, or event represented, even in a work of fiction, is at least tacitly recommended by the author and by the teacher or school that approves or requires the reading of the text.

FIGURE 10.2. *The professional versus the public view of reading.*

changes or changes in fashion take place at a different pace in different regions of the country and among different cultural groups.

The forms of literacy that Myers (1996) identifies as dominant in shaping literacy practices in schools and in the workplace begin with what he calls "signature literacy" in the colonial period, when in the context of what remained largely an oral culture a person was thought to be literate if he could sign his name to a document as a witness or to certify that a document had been read to him. This form of literacy is followed in the period from the Revolutionary War to the Civil War by what Myers calls "recording literacy," which defines a person as literate if he or she can write his or her full name legibly, read and write short common words, and copy short texts accurately. Such a literacy enabled those who possessed it to make and read lists and records of sales or inventories and read and write public signs and simple notices (often using invented spelling).

Recording literacy gave way in the period roughly between the Civil War and the First World War to what Myers (1996) and other scholars have called "recitation literacy," a literacy which was exercised in schools largely in recitations of memorized poems and passages and prepared and rehearsed oral readings of morally uplifting and patriotic texts, with instruction focused largely on elocution—correct pronunciation, pacing, and emphasis. These practices gave way in the period between 1916 and 1983 to a form of literacy Myers calls "decoding/analytic literacy," which entailed a shift from oral reading to silent reading and a shift from the memorization or rehearsal of texts for oral performance to the study and "comprehension" of texts not previously read. For more advanced students, it also entailed a shift from treating literature as a transparent medium for the transmission of patriotic and religious values to treating literature as an art form to be analyzed according to an established protocol and understood "correctly," which is to say, according to an authoritatively preestablished interpretation (see Blau, 1994).

The current phase of literacy, or the phase that is still coming into dominance for language arts professionals, Myers calls "critical literacy," which he describes in precisely the terms I have used to describe the reading and teaching practices fostered by the

CLAS test in reading and by most well-informed contemporary specialists in the English language arts. It is also the form of literacy desiderated in recent English language arts standards documents and similar statements authorized by such professional bodies as the National Board for Professional Teaching Standards (1994), the National Council of Teachers of English and the International Reading Association (1996), and the College Entrance Examination Board (Wolf, 1995).

From the perspective of Myers's historical-cultural analysis, we may be inclined to read the conflicts over literacy practices in schools more generously than if we view them merely as evidence of irreconcilable political and ideological differences among competing constituencies within the political bodies that govern schools. The historical-cultural perspective invites us, instead, to read the challenges to instruction in critical literacy as expressions of the cultural survival at this moment in history of former models of literacy, all of which, it might be argued, deserve the same respect we are inclined to confer on other forms of cultural difference within the diverse communities served by public schools.

Yet there are surely some ideological differences inscribed in cultural differences that do not equally command our respect or even our tolerance. We do not in policy or practice pretend that the ideologies of racism or anti-Semitism—though they may represent cultural norms for sizable population groups and cultural constituencies who send their children to public schools—deserve equal respect and attention among a number of competing ideologies in shaping curricular and pedagogical decisions. Some cultural values and practices literacy educators have an ethical and professional responsibility uncompromisingly to oppose.

Coda: The Ethical Responsibility of Language Arts Professionals

As respectful as we may be about cultural differences that divide communities in their definitions of literacy, we can still justify the claim that some versions of literacy are at least more advanced than others intellectually and implicitly represent more inclusive versions of democracy. We must also recognize that critical literacy is not an invention of the late twentieth century. Rather, it has always been practiced by an elite class of persons upon whom all other practitioners of literacy have depended and whose practices are presupposed by all other conceptions of literacy.

In fact, each of the culturally constructed versions of literacy that Myers (1996) describes presupposes and requires in its moment of cultural dominance practitioners of all the forms of literacy that become dominant subsequently. People who acquire only signature literacy must depend on those who have attained higher forms of literacy to read them any documents they may be asked to witness or certify as having heard. And such readers depend on the presence of other persons literate enough to have composed such documents and so on. Practitioners of recitation literacy are similarly dependent on the prior activity of analytically literate persons who know the qualities of canonical texts which make them aesthetically and morally fit for inclusion in the canon of works to be recited. And these more highly literate persons are in turn dependent on critically literate people who at some point had to read fit and unfit texts in order to select some and deselect others and provide authoritative interpretations of those entering the canon.

Thus, throughout the history of literary culture there has been a population of persons who have practiced something like late-twentieth-century critical literacy and who have conceived of literacy in a way that resembles what I have described as the contemporary progressive version of literacy. This is surely the form of literacy practiced by all the authors whose works have become canonical, by practitioners of biblical exegesis in the early Middle Ages, by Talmudic scholars in the tenth century in Spain, by the educators who have theorized in every age about literary education, by critics, by diplomats, and by other members of the ruling or intellectually authoritative classes. It is also the form of literacy practiced by the chief theorists and polemicists of the very groups who have argued most vigorously in California and elsewhere against critical literacy as a proper educational standard for children in schools. For in opposing the CLAS reading tests and the ideology they found inscribed in those tests and in related Department of Education documents, the critics of the tests were enthusiastically engaged in resistant readings, in strong and independent interpretations, and in a very modern form of ideological or cultural criticism.

The difference between professional and public views of literacy is more than a difference between two currently competing conceptions of curriculum and assessment in the English language arts or even between versions of literacy deriving from different cultural traditions. It represents instead two different visions of students and of human beings—of the capacity of ordinary people to learn to exercise reasonable judgment and produce discerning interpretations on their own behalf. That there are cultural traditions supporting a partial and diminished version of literacy argues no more for the validity of that version or that tradition than the argument that some cultural traditions sanction slavery for captives or corporal punishment for wayward children and disobedient wives.

What is controverted in the current debates about the assessment and teaching of literacy is, then, largely a question about the nature of students and how much we want to respect and nurture their capacity as fully human agents in their exercise of the essential tool available to them for learning—that of reading—or how much we want the education of children in our schools to be one that renders them permanently dependent in matters of interpretation and judgment on the authority and values of an aristocratic class of readers—readers who demand respect and compliance (not merely a hearing in a process of negotiation and discussion) by virtue of their cultural position and their presumably superior education and refined sensibilities.

The present battle being fought on the political front over the proper form of assessment and instruction in literature for the mass of students in public schools pits language arts educators as a professional group against large numbers of parents and policymakers who wish to see literary education return to the texts and practices of previous generations. Those who would march backward would do so, moreover, in the name of morality and the wisdom of tradition. Against that nostalgia and the hypocritical tradition it longs for, language arts educators have an ethical responsibility to stand firm for the more fundamental values of our democratic tradition and for a version of literacy that treats all students as potential aristocrats or as agents and exercisers of power in a democratic society.

References

Blau, S. (1994). Transactions between theory and practice in the teaching of literature. In J. Flood & J. Langer (Eds.), *Literature instruction: Practice and policy* (pp. 19–52). New York: Scholastic.

Claggett, F. (1999). Integrating reading and writing in large-scale assessment. In C. Cooper & L. Odell (Eds.), *Evaluating writing: The role of teachers' knowledge about text, learning, and culture* (pp. 344–65). Urbana, IL: National Council of Teachers of English.

Dudley, M. (1997). The rise and fall of a statewide assessment system. *English Journal, 86*(1), 15–20.

Moffett, J. (1981). *Active voice: A writing program across the curriculum.* Upper Montclair, NJ: Boynton/Cook.

Moffett, J. (1983). *Teaching the universe of discourse.* Boston: Houghton Mifflin.

Myers, M. (1996). *Changing our minds: Negotiating English and literacy.* Urbana, IL: National Council of Teachers of English.

National Council of Teachers of English & International Reading Association. (1996). *Standards for the English language arts.* Urbana, IL, & Newark, DE: Authors.

Rosenblatt, L. (1938). *Literature as exploration.* New York: Appleton-Century.

Rosenblatt, L. (1978). *The reader, the text, the poem: The transactional theory of the literary work.* Carbondale: Southern Illinois University Press.

Wimsatt, W. K., & Beardsley, M. (1954). *The verbal icon: Studies in the meaning of poetry.* Lexington: University of Kentucky Press.

Wolf, D. P. (1995). *Reading reconsidered: Literature and literacy in high school.* New York: College Entrance Examination Board.

CHAPTER ELEVEN

First-Language Support in the Curriculum

NANCI GOLDMAN
Toronto District School Board/Upper Canada College

JOYCE ROGERS
Toronto District School Board

BRIAN A. SMITH
Toronto District School Board

Toronto, Canada, known disparagingly in the early 1800s as "muddy York," began as a largely British colonial town. Now it is one of the most diverse, multicultural cities in the world. A recent article in the *Toronto Star*, for example, indicated that over half the people living in Toronto were born outside of Canada. Paralleling this change in demographics has been an evolution of social and political ideas in government offices and agencies directly responsible for education. The Toronto district school board, for instance, has moved away from earlier policies that reflected blatant bigotry to more enlightened policies and practices that demand and respect inclusivity.

In the early 1900s, Toronto school board documents and curricular materials emphasized exclusion and an unquestioned commitment to British English and British culture. The *Ontario School Geography* textbook (authorized by the Minister of Education for Ontario for use in the public schools and in the continuation and high schools) in use in Toronto schools in 1910, for example, reveals a disturbing attitude toward non-White, non-English people, expressed in startlingly racist language:

The largest number of people belongs to the Caucasian (Indo-

European), or White Race. . . . They are the most active, enter-
prising, and intelligent race in the world. . . . The next largest
number of people belongs to the Yellow Race. . . . They include
some of the most backward tribes of the world, and as a rule, are
not progressive. . . . The third great race is the American Indian,
or Red Race. . . . Most of the Red Race are but little civilized.
The fourth and last great group of people is the Black, or Negro
Race. . . . As a race they are somewhat indolent. . . . They are
often impulsive in their actions, but they are faithful and affec-
tionate to anyone for whom they care. (pp. 60–62)

Similar attitudes were evident in Toronto school board policies regarding the use of languages other than English. In 1919,
for example, the board decreed that "no language other than the
English language be used at any meeting held in our school buildings." The following incident recorded in the minutes from a
meeting of the school board in January 1919 is clear about the
board's commitment to this exclusionary policy. Mrs. Ida Siegel,
president of the Hester Howe School Mothers' Club, appeared before the board to request a limited exemption from this regulation:

There had been no intention of using any language but English
except for the interpretation to those who did not understand
English. . . . [She noted] that they had some Yiddish speakers,
but had not been informed that it was not in accordance with the
wishes of the Board and that she had always translated the
speeches into English. (Toronto Board of Education Archives,
January 16, 1919)

A subcommittee was formed to report on the matter "before any
change is made in the present regulations," but in the end, the
subcommittee recommended no change in the regulation concerning the mandatory use of the English language in meetings in
the Toronto public schools.

After World War II, the Toronto Board of Education found
itself in the position of having to respond to a wave of new immigrants from non-English-speaking countries and to pressure from
various language groups that were demanding that the schools
address the issue of the use of languages other than English. The
next twenty years were witness to an ongoing struggle between
the board and various linguistic communities, each requesting
that its language and culture be recognized and valued in schools.

As thousands of families from a great variety of cultural and linguistic backgrounds settled in Toronto in successive waves of immigration, the Toronto Board of Education endeavored to identify and respond to their diverse needs and to provide appropriate support in the schools. This included, for example, support for students whose first language, dialect, or culture "interfered" with their progress in regular programs so that students could enter the mainstream program as quickly as possible. The Board of Education also provided specially qualified teachers to help students make this transition. And school officials began to recognize the importance of hiring interpreters, without whom communication between teachers and parents was sometimes impossible.

Recently, upheavals and conflicts around the world have led to dramatic changes in the population of immigrants settling in Toronto. During the past decade, Canada has admitted large numbers of refugees who have experienced the traumas of war, family dislocation, the inability to attend school, lengthy stays in refugee camps, and/or moving from country to country. The children of these families have posed new and difficult challenges to the Toronto schools.

Toronto public schools began this century openly hostile to the needs of its non-White, non-English-speaking students. Over the years, however, the Toronto Board of Education has responded to its increasingly diverse student population with increasingly inclusive curricula and teaching practices that recognize the importance of students' first languages and cultures. Responding to these needs, Toronto schools have created what is quite possibly the largest variety of systemwide school first-language support programs in the world.

First-Language Supports

In Toronto schools, first-language supports include the provision of services, materials, and resources to assist students in becoming active and successful participants in their schooling and to create an environment that promotes inclusion, equity, and access to curriculum. These supports enable students to draw on their first language, providing them with opportunities to demonstrate what they know and have learned, and in turn help teachers capitalize on students' background knowledge and experience.

The following are examples of first-language supports that reflect the Toronto Board of Education's commitment to inclusivity and equity.

First-language tutor/mentors are recruited from students' language communities to provide intensive, short-term help for those students who are experiencing academic and adjustment problems. Students have the assistance of a tutor/mentor supervised by a teacher for approximately fifteen hours over a period of four to six weeks. Older students not literate in either their first language or in English benefit from having new concepts explained in their first language. Other students may need only direct translation of text materials to establish meaning. For students experiencing adjustment difficulties, tutor/mentors provide the necessary comfort by relating to students in their first language.

International language programs (formerly called "heritage" language programs) promote the maintenance of students' first languages or, in some cases, facilitate proficiency in the first language. International Language Programs are available for students aged four to fourteen and are offered during the regular school day, after school, and on weekends. Instructors provide support to students during the adjustment process. International Language Program teachers and first-language tutor/mentors help facilitate the blending of content and language learning during the regular school day for students not yet proficient in English.

As part of **student and family support services,** the Toronto Board of Education employs psychoeducational consultants, social workers, psychiatrists, and school community advisors, many of whom have facility in the languages of students or have knowledge of their cultural and educational backgrounds. These people support students and their families by acting as liaisons between home and school, facilitating understanding among families, students, and teachers, and explaining how the school system works.

The Borrow-a-Book Program allows children to borrow books daily from their classroom libraries to read at home or to be read to by siblings or parents. The program also stocks classrooms and school libraries with age-appropriate books in students' first languages and English. In addition, it supplies translations that can be affixed to selected primary-grade English-language books, permitting these to be converted to multilingual texts. The program offers teachers access to bilingual audiotapes of children's books for use in their language arts programs or for sending home with children along with accompanying books. The program also makes available a handbook for helping parents share books with their children.

Extensive **interpretation and translation services** are available to promote communication and involvement with families who do not speak or read English.

Professional development, in the form of English as a Second Language (ESL) courses, is provided so that educators can study system, school, and classroom issues related to Toronto's culturally diverse environment. As a result of an Ontario Ministry of Education's ESL course designed and provided for the entire staff of one school, the staff developed a school-based welcoming center; a school handbook translated into four languages; a school video produced by students for parents and available in four languages; a program facilitating the inclusion of students learning English as another language into the mainstream with the support of the International Language Program teachers; and an intergenerational program that involved inviting grandparents into the classroom to share, in their first language, their stories, experiences, and skills.

Orientation and cultural background resources are available to teachers who wish to increase their knowledge of the students in their classes and may be used to help students understand and appreciate fellow students who have come from other countries. The Toronto Board of Education also produces and makes available resources—print and video resources such as posters, research documents, information brochures, and CD-ROMs, many of which are available in a variety of languages—that help to acquaint families and their children with their new country, society, and educational system.

An annual multilingual, multicultural, multiracial book/resource fair and curriculum showcase enables teachers and parents to view the wide range of inclusive curriculum materials available from the Toronto Board of Education. Parents and teachers can review storybooks, dictionaries, curriculum texts, CD-ROMs, and videos in English, bilingual formats, and languages other than English. Many of the subject textbooks are well-illustrated versions of regularly used texts, modified to make the curriculum more accessible. Curriculum subject departments, local bookstores, distributors, and publishers are invited to display and sell their materials.

A Whole-School Approach

To fully implement these first-language supports, it is essential that teachers and parents become an integral part of a whole-school approach. Therefore, the Toronto board encourages the staffs of entire schools to meet regularly to ensure that minority-language students are adjusting to their new culture; that minority-language students' first languages and cultures are maintained and respected; that minority-language students are taught language and content concurrently and are supported in the mainstream classroom; that minority-language students receive long-term support in both English and their first language; and that minority-language students are not inappropriately labeled as exceptional and requiring special education service.

Responses to First-Language Supports and Prospects for the Future

Teachers and administrators have generally been remarkably accepting of the first-language support initiatives. Many have regularly taken part in educational activities to increase their knowledge of languages and cultures in Toronto, antiracist practices and policies, and ESL pedagogy. In some cases, they have established reception/transition classes to support students suffering from culture shock, trauma, or interrupted schooling. Some schools have held regular meetings for teams of International Language Program teachers, ESL teachers, first-language support educators, classroom teachers, principals, and social workers to discuss students' progress and ensure that needed supports are in place. Toronto teachers have developed a variety of assessment methods including observation, conferences, journal writing, portfolios, and teacher narrative notes to gather information about incoming minority-language students. Many have developed content and instructional practices informed by a multicultural perspective. It is not at all unusual to find classrooms in which students and their backgrounds constitute the content of the social studies curriculum.

Students too have responded well to—and with awareness of—the first-language support initiatives. Ismael, for example, arrived in Canada from Lebanon when he was ten years old, after a two-year interruption in his schooling. Later, when asked by his seventh-grade teacher to write an autobiography, Ismael reflected on his experiences as a newly arrived immigrant in a school that supported the needs of students new to Canada and who were learning English as a new language:

> As my parents and I entered the school, we felt somewhat hesitant and intimidated. Once we went through the front door, the first thing we saw was a very large poster which said "Welcome" in many languages including Arabic. We proceeded into the school and according to another sign in Arabic, we found and entered the school office. On the office bulletin board we saw a large map of the world. On this map were the countries of origin of all the students in the school. Each student's name was recorded on the map. A thin string attached their country of origin and their mode of travel to Toronto.
>
> In the school office we were introduced to the principal. She welcomed us to Canada, to Toronto, and to my new school. She invited us to the school Welcome Room and gave us a copy of the school handbook translated into many languages. We saw this year's updated school video produced by senior students and

translated into Arabic. The video described all the school programs. I was given a school Welcome Bag which included school supplies, a map of the school, pictures and names of all the school staff members and a list of special school days. A translator was called to help my parents with my registration. The ESL teacher asked a lot of questions about my education before I came to Canada. I hadn't been to school for two years and I remembered being very frightened. But the ESL teacher was really nice. She said she would help me get to know the school and learn English.

My grade 5 teacher introduced me to the whole class and especially to Ahmed who came to the school four years before. He sat beside me and told me that after class he would take me on a tour of the whole school. He introduced me to all the teachers and classes. I remember my teacher saying that after recess we would hear about my country and my customs. She had many books and pictures of my country. Only one week after being in the school, I was asked to help with the morning announcement. I welcomed a new student from my country.

The Threat

The positive responses to first-language supports within the system governed by the Toronto district school board is not mirrored in the actions of current provincial policymakers. During the 1980s, the ideological climate and a booming economy made it relatively easy to support language-minority students like Ismael in Toronto schools. Educational supports and practices that embraced and respected the diversity of our students were widely encouraged, well funded, and enthusiastically implemented at the local, provincial, and national levels. The current political and economic climate, however, is limited and restrictive. In general, educational funding is being drastically reduced by Ontario's neoconservative government. Instead of educational priorities dictating funding, decreased funding is dictating educational priorities. What the board classified as "supports" essential for successful learning are now classified by current funding models as nonessential. Toronto is now at risk of losing its ability to provide the support and resources to meet the needs of all its students.

Historically, the Toronto Board of Education funded programs through its ability to levy property taxes as needs arose.

Thus the board was able to increase programs to meet the needs of its increasingly diverse student population. Provincial legislation (Bill 160) stripped Ontario school boards such as Toronto's of their ability to levy taxes by limiting funding to provincial grants. Present Ministry of Education funding does not take into account welcome rooms, interpreters, translated materials, the provision of bilingual texts, first-language tutors, or the support of "international" teachers working with regular classroom teachers. The province also makes no provision for the extensive inservice education needed by teachers if they are to provide inclusive curricula and programming. Nor does the current provincial government acknowledge the time required for students to learn English. The new, rigidly prescriptive, grade-by-grade, outcomes-based curricula being implemented by the Ontario government make no provision for students who do not learn English "quickly." The ESL provincial government grant only funds ESL students for a three-year period, ignoring extensive research conducted right here in Ontario that has determined that students often require support for between four and seven years to achieve academic success. In general, the "back-to-basics" programs favored by the Ontario government make no room for first-language support services and programs that have taken decades to develop and implement.

What have been recognized as some of the best first- and second-language support programs in the world are now threatened by an unsympathetic provincial government that views these programs as either "frills" or special privileges. Deep budget cuts and an unwillingness to compromise threaten the very existence of these programs.

References

Ontario School Geography. (1910). Toronto, Ontario: The Educational Book Company.

Toronto Board of Education Archives. (1919). Minutes of the Board.

CHAPTER TWELVE

The Rainbow Curriculum: Politics over the Rainbow

BARBARA GERARD
New York City Board of Education

In 1991 the New York City Board of Education introduced the *Children of the Press,* a multicultural curriculum and resource guide for first-grade teachers. The *Children of the Rainbow* grew out of an earlier *Statement of Policy on Multicultural Education and Promotion of Positive Intergroup Relations* that was formally adopted by the New York City Board of Education in 1989. The policy was intended to be inclusive, going beyond ethnicity and race to include age, class, gender, disabilities, and sexual orientation. To attain the goals stated in the policy, *An Action Plan for Multicultural Education* (NYC Board of Education, 1990a) was developed to address goals in curriculum, program, and professional development; technical assistance; parent and community involvement; affirmative action; bilingual education; and program assessment and evaluation. The goal that grabbed the attention of the public and the media was the redesigning of curriculum, particularly the *Children of the Rainbow* kindergarten guide (NYC Board of Education, 1990b).

The *Children of the Rainbow* kindergarten guide was developed on the assumption that multicultural education should begin with the young child and continue up through the grades, engaging students' minds, providing opportunities for hands-on experiences, encouraging student interaction, and building social action skills (Baker, 1994). When the *Children of the Rainbow* first-grade guide was published in 1991 (NYC Board of Education, 1991), it offered guidance to teachers in the use of culturally diverse materials and in creating classroom environments that were intended to build respect and understanding among students of various cultural backgrounds. It was supposed to help teachers design developmentally appropriate (Bredekamp, 1987), multicultural instructional programs for young children that included overlapping elements—home, school, and community partnerships, with each element contributing its culture and language to the classroom experience. The guides were also supposed to aid professionals in their own development—in their awareness, acknowledgment, and affirmation of the ethnic, linguistic, and religious affiliations, as well as family customs and traditions, that are present in family life.

Not long after its publication, however, *Children of the Rainbow* became the source of a community political power struggle that attracted national media attention. A curriculum that had been intended to promote respect for all families instead spawned one of the fiercest, nastiest—and disrespectful—political battles in the recent history of the New York City Board of Education.

Rationale for the Rainbow Curriculum

The U.S. Bureau of the Census statistics for 1990 indicated that only 23 percent of families were "traditional." During the decade from 1980 to 1990, the "Norman Rockwell" family—consisting of a working father, housewife mother, and two school-age children—accounted for just 6 percent of all households (Hodgkinson, 1992). In response to these demographic data, the *Children of the Rainbow* tried to address alternate family structures, such as grandparents as parents, teenage parents, blended families (consisting of children from two or more different families), biracial families, adoptive families, and single-parent (male or female) families, as well as a variety of others.

Not only did most families not match the idealized norm, but students' backgrounds and teachers' backgrounds in New York City were also largely mismatched. For the 1992–93 school year, the New York City Public Schools was the largest school system in the United States, with 972,146 students attending the 1,057 schools in five boroughs. Over 80 percent of these students were children of color, with the Latino and Asian communities the fastest-growing segments of the population. But the diversity of the teaching staff did not reflect the diversity of the student population (see Table 12.1). For all ethnic groups except Whites, there was a smaller percentage of teachers than students. The percentage of African American students in the public schools, for example, was about twice that of African American teachers. The percentage of Latino students was over three times the percentage of Latino teachers, and the percentage of Asian students was more than four times that of Asian teachers.

Pressure from the Press, Confusion and Conflict in the Community

Children of the Rainbow was assaulted by the press. The media focused the public's attention on two books dealing with gay and lesbian families, *Daddy's Roommate* (Willhoite, 1991) and *Heather Has Two Mommies* (Newman, 1989), although these two books were listed in the bibliography only. *Heather Has Two Mommies* especially became the target of widespread condemnation. Sections of this picture book were reproduced daily in the print media and shown on television, with claims that it— and the *Children of the Rainbow* generally—was evidence that the New York City Board of Education was teaching young children about and promoting homosexual lifestyles. There were

TABLE 12.1. Students Attending/Teachers Employed, New York City Public Schools, 1992–1993

Racial Classification	# of Students/Percent		# of Teachers/Percent	
American Indian	1,680	0.02	53	0.1
Asian	80, 377	8.3	1,110	1.9
Latino	343,297	35.3	6,320	11.0
African American	367,369	37.8	11,167	19.4
White	179,423	18.5	38,877	67.6
Total	972,146	100.0	57,527	100.0
Source: (NYC Board of Education, 1992).				

numerous articles in the *New York Times, New York Newsday, New York Daily News*, and *New York Post,* as well as a number of local community and union newspapers. The "Rainbow Curriculum" story blared in the headlines for weeks: "Somewhere Over the Rainbow"; "Queens Grandmother Challenges the Chancellor Over the Rainbow"; "The Cardinal Blasts 'Rainbow'"; "Whose Agenda Is It Anyway?"; "Rainbow Curriculum Promotes Homosexuality"; "*Heather Has Two Mommies* Used in First Grade."

There was also some (though far less) publicized support for the *Children of the Rainbow* and its goals. The United Federation of Teachers (UFT), for example, declared its full support of the curriculum in its educational newspaper, in media interviews, and through letter writing campaigns. Unlike many of the critics of the Rainbow curriculum, UFT officials had done their homework—they had read all 443 pages of the curriculum guide. Advocacy groups for and against the guide gave public testimony, appeared regularly on local radio and television, and verbally and even physically assaulted each other over this conflict. For its part, the media, which understands well the degree to which conflict "sells" (see Tannen, 1998), fueled the controversy by reducing the discussion of complex questions raised by the Rainbow curriculum ("How do we create schools that make room for the voices of all our citizens?") to a series of oppositions, polemics, and antinomies.

Parent and community groups were split on *Children of the Rainbow.* Teachers were mostly supportive of the teacher guide. Many parents, on the other hand, believed that the *Children of the Rainbow* conflicted with their values and religious beliefs. In the minds of many in the public, the issues of multicultural content, same-gender parents, and sexual orientation were conflated. Gay rights activists and conservative church groups staged demonstrations and counterdemonstrations, which were highlighted in the media as front-page news. Religious groups, including Moslems, Pentecostals, various Jewish denominations, and Roman Catholics, coalesced and organized demonstrations, distributed literature, and conducted media events demanding the chancellor's resignation. As often happens in sensational censorship cases, many of the most strident and uncompromising critics of the Rainbow curriculum had never actually read the curriculum guide, but instead based their opinions on media reports and rumor; nor did they have children in the system (DelFattore, 1992).

The effort at the New York City Board of Education headquarters to address the flood of media and public attention to the Rainbow curriculum was all consuming. I was pulled to press conferences, speak-outs, and parent meetings all over the city. On one occasion, less than an hour after I had arrived in Washington, D.C., for a conference, I was called back to New York so that I could address a group of "concerned parents" in the borough of Queens. I attended another particularly dramatic meeting in Washington Heights, a largely Hispanic neighborhood in Manhattan. In attendance were a priest, a minister, a rabbi, two sets of same-gender couples, and an array of families, primarily Dominicans. After a while, the shouting actually had a calming effect.

One incident, which demonstrates how quickly local conflicts can have international repercussions, still makes me laugh. A friend who is a member of the Italian parliament was flying into New York from Rome to join me and some other friends for dinner. When she finally arrived, she greeted everyone and sat down at the table with a worried look on her face. I recall wondering which of her many governmental and political responsibilities was causing her such concern: Difficulties in unifying European economies? Recent political upheavals in her country? A pending trade pact? After a moment, she turned to face me and, placing her hand on my arm, asked somberly, "So, what is this 'Rainbow curriculum' controversy all about?"

Then-Chancellor Joseph Fernandez had his own view of the Rainbow curriculum controversy:

> There was pressure from the mayor's office, from the borough presidents, from the unions. . . . We took more heat in 1992 with our "Children of the Rainbow" multicultural curriculum, which included a small segment (two pages out of 443) dealing with tolerance of non-traditional (including homosexual) family structures. My supporting opinion was that if we're ever going to get this country together, we have to deal with such biases early, even in the first grade. (Fernandez, 1993, p. 239)

Chancellor Fernandez further stated that the Board of Education did not back him on the curriculum because, in his opinion, board members were more concerned about the issue of condom availability. Regardless of the board's positions, the community was shouting as loud as it could. Comments "on the street" were telling, and included accusations of conspiracy and a "homosexual agenda."

What's the Problem? "Rainbow" or . . . .

It was in this context that, in the fall of 1992, I reviewed a survey of responses to the *Action Plan for Multicultural Education* from community school districts' multicultural education coordinators. Based on these interviews, I identified two possible causes of—and also dimensions to—the *Children of the Rainbow* "problem." The first problem was pace and breadth. *Children of the Rainbow* was developed in a relatively short period of time by too few people. That is, although a few parent leaders had been consulted on its development, the vast majority of parents were not involved in the process, despite strong evidence that parents might well see the new curriculum guide as a threat to their beliefs. Not enough time was given to collaboration among educators and community members over content. The curriculum guide was also introduced and disseminated too quickly, thus excluding too many views at early but crucial points. It was distributed to the community school districts' coordinators after only a one-day conference. Nor was sufficient time allocated for finding ways of preparing personnel throughout the system, teachers in particular, and parents and others in the community. Staff development was clearly inadequate. For instance, twenty-one of the thirty-two school districts under the purview of the New York City Board of Education never conducted *any* training for teachers in the Rainbow curriculum. Therefore, when the media offered inaccurate and misleading information that played largely on the public's homophobia, coordinators and teachers were not familiar enough with the guide and had not used it for a sufficient period of time in the classroom to respond adequately.

The second problem I identified through the interviews may have fueled the uproar over *Children of the Rainbow* but was just as likely a dimension of its aftermath. The widespread controversy generated by this curriculum gave those districts in which multicultural education was not a priority an excuse to resist the new curriculum and to reject the overall goal of educating *multiculturally*. The *Children of the Rainbow* affirmed pluralism in ways that demanded changes beyond those that could easily be incorporated without fundamental restructuring of or contradiction in traditional curricula. Many schools—indeed, entire districts within the affected board—were not ready for a pluralism that went beyond a superficial bow to ethnic holidays and foods.

The Rainbow Project

The Rainbow Project, initiated in 1993, attempted to overcome the *Children of the Rainbow*'s problems of pacing and insufficient involvement of key constituencies. Like the earlier work on *Children of the Rainbow*, the Rainbow Project was intent on having multicultural education implemented strategically and comprehensively (throughout city schools, throughout a classroom day); that is, included in that notion of comprehensive implementation was not only the use of certain materials but also their integration into social action activities. For at least some of us involved in the project, multicultural education—what was to be implemented—had not changed; it still reflected Nieto's view that:

> Multicultural education is a process of comprehensive school reform and basic education for all students. It challenges and rejects racism and other forms of discrimination in schools and society and accepts and affirms the pluralism (ethnic, racial, linguistic, religious, economic, and gender, among others) that students, their communities, and teachers represent. Multicultural education permeates the curriculum and instructional strategies used in schools as well as the interactions among teachers, students, and parents, and the very way that schools conceptualize the nature of teaching and learning. Because it uses critical pedagogy as its underlying philosophy and focuses on knowledge,

reflection, and action (praxis) as the basis for social change, multicultural education furthers the democratic principles of school justice. (1992, p. 112)

But this time there would be adequate staff development and collaborative planning. In fact, a major goal of the Rainbow Project was to have central-level, district-level, and school-level personnel involved in planning the systemwide staff development for such an undertaking. But while the implementation would, of course, be at the specific school sites, the revision of the Rainbow curriculum was to take place at the central and district levels.

The Rainbow Project looked to the literature on staff development and attempted to account for what *Children of the Rainbow* had missed: that systemic change is made by communities of people, not individuals (Joyce & Showers, 1988). A systemic initiative (like implementing multicultural education) is complex and requires integrating staff development within an organizational climate (Williams, 1993). The plans to be developed would have to focus on change at the school (i.e., grassroots) level over a period of time (Joyce, 1990), but the change itself would need to permeate the culture of the entire organization (Fullan, 1993). *Children of the Rainbow* resulted in a bloodbath before the waters were ever tested; the Rainbow Project would test those waters as part of its slower-paced attempt at educational change.

I conducted a pilot study during the 1993–94 academic year to explore the attitudes and feelings of school teams—which included teachers and parents—about the *Children of the Rainbow*. The pilot study had two parts. The first was a series of conversational assessments ("one-leg interviews") with teachers and parents prior to revising the *Children of the Rainbow*. Later on in the project, these same teachers, as well as other teachers and parents, were asked for their reactions to the curriculum. In the second part of the pilot, I conducted in-depth interviews with one teacher and a parent to document the initial reactions of teachers and parents. I subsequently used what I learned from this process to revise the curriculum and to work with school team members on its application in the classroom. Most meaningful, however, was team members' input and involvement in the process.

I began interviews by asking teachers and parents two questions: "What was your initial reaction to *Children of the Rainbow* when you read about it in the newspapers?" and "Had you seen *Children of the Rainbow* before?" A second-grade teacher's response was typical:

> I didn't know at first what [the media] was talking about or referring to. I had the curriculum in my possession. . . . I looked it over and at first I could not find any reference to *Heather Has Two Mommies*. It was not until later, when one of my colleagues told me that the book was a reference, not in the text itself, but listed in the bibliography.

Another teacher's response confirmed this teacher's experience. "The whole business was a sham, a joke. All the media coverage was about a few books on homosexual families that were listed in the bibliography. None of these books or their contents appeared in the curriculum." Like this teacher, a first-grade parent I interviewed was puzzled by the controversy over the Rainbow curriculum, but also more than a little concerned: "I heard and saw all about the controversy and I became alarmed. I called the principal and the district office immediately to ask them about the guide, the books, and asked what was going on." Parents were more easily alarmed by the media coverage than were teachers, although this parent was ultimately reassured by the principal:

> I was really concerned about those books that they kept flashing on the television. I went to school to speak to the principal to see if he had copies of the books. . . . I did not like the books. . . . The principal said that since they were just resource books they would not necessarily be used in the classroom. The principal decided to [obtain] copies . . . to be able to show them to the parents and indicated that they were separate from the curriculum. The principal's response assured and relieved me.

Another parent, however, was more willing to accept the media's representation of *Children of the Rainbow*, commenting, "I don't want the school teaching my child about homosexuality."

The general pattern in these interviews was that teachers indicated bafflement over media reactions to the Rainbow curriculum, while parents tended to be more concerned. One parent I interviewed took productive action:

> When I first heard about *Children of the Rainbow* and all the media coverage it was given, I was not sure what the controversy was about. . . . As the controversy grew, I became more concerned and alarmed. . . . I decided to follow up with the principal.

This parent did go to the principal's office the next day and asked to review a copy of the curriculum, but by this time the reaction among some of the parents had reached the level of hysteria. The principal told me that:

> the parents kept coming and calling the school each time a newscast appeared on television, or a new article appeared in the newspapers. I personally was getting very tired of the whole event, and I wanted to get back to the regular routine of the school.

Eventually, this mother, who was a leader in the school community, decided to help organize a group discussion with parents who were concerned about the curriculum during which they could review it and then discuss it as a group with the principal. Once these parents were able to express their dismay over the controversy surrounding the Rainbow curriculum, the teachers I interviewed were able to discuss the potential use of the *Children of the Rainbow* in their classrooms. They talked about the general information offered:

> I especially like the information for educators on such topics as "Planning for the First Grade," "The Multicultural Learning Environment," and "Instructional Approaches and Strategies." The themes are well constructed, especially "What Is in a Name?"; "Families"; and "Numbers Around Us"; the advice about how to create multicultural curricula in their classrooms; and how to adapt curriculum for the bilingual and ESL classroom. Some applauded the thoroughness of plans, clarity of goals, and abundance of suggested activities.

The administrators I interviewed were also positive about the potential of the Rainbow curriculum, if somewhat more cautious, perhaps due to concern about the possibility of continued political fallout. They were generally pleased with the detailed plans and also the range of current problems and concerns addressed by the resource information. One of the principals concluded: "I found the curriculum to be bias-free and culturally balanced. [But] I believe some activities might not be appropriate for first graders who bring different experiences and values to inner-city schools."

While expressing his support for *Children of the Rainbow,* a local school board superintendent offered a few suggestions for revision:

> The section on homework might include recognition of differences in home environment that may impact on completion of assignments (i.e., working parents, "shelter" children). The "Learning to Read through the Arts" section would be more helpful if it included specific age-appropriate trip suggestions.

Not everyone I spoke to was so positive, however. A local school board president, perhaps either rejecting or misunderstanding the goals of multicultural education, had the following suggestions for revising the curriculum:

> The statement on bilingual education and material should be referenced. The current research on multicultural education should be deleted, including all references. What about mentioning American holidays (i.e., Thanksgiving)? The curriculum should [also] include lessons on values.

In-depth interviews also gave me a chance to talk to parents and teachers about their thoughts on revising the curriculum in light of their experience (and the media controversy). One first-grade teacher felt that "the curriculum is fine as it is. Why does it have to be revised?" Of course, not everyone shared this view, although in general teachers were pleased to have the opportunity for local input: "Finally, teachers are being asked about their opinion on something to do with students." Another teacher I interviewed agreed:

> Being on the inside . . . [of] curriculum reform might be good since that is the way it should be. As educators, classroom teach-

ers know what the children need. We are always the last ones to be asked our opinion, advice, or participation.

Parents seemed to feel the same way. "As far as the curriculum," one parent said, "I don't know what skills I have to contribute, but I will participate in whatever way I can, since I really want to be involved in the project." She also believed that what she learned working on the team would expand her ability to work with her daughter at home.

The Revised Curriculum

Over time, staff development sessions centered increasingly on revising the content of *Children of the Rainbow*. The ensuing draft, now titled *Teaching First Grade: A Comprehensive Instructional Program*[1] (NYC Board of Education, 1994a), was disseminated for piloting in 1994. The revision removed the two questionable pages on lifestyles in the resource section and also some trade and picture books on same-gender families (e.g., *Gloria Goes to Gay Pride*, *Daddy's Roommate*, and *Heather Has Two Mommies*). Another "two mommy" book, *Belinda's Bouquet* (Newman, 1991), survived the revision, although another battle ensued over another "two daddy" book—until the protesters realized that the two daddies in the book were a birth dad and a stepdad.

During that school year, work continued on the second-grade guide, now titled *Teaching Second Grade: A Comprehensive Instructional Program* (NYC Board of Education, 1994b), which was subsequently disseminated for review and pilot testing. At the end of the year, in June 1994, a team composed of parents and central office, district office, and university personnel continued the development of the multicultural curriculum. At planning meetings, a conceptual framework, including the development of curricular themes, was designed for a third-grade multicultural curriculum. Teams of early childhood teachers and parents, under the supervision of early childhood and multicultural specialists, began writing this third-grade curriculum in July 1994. The third-grade curriculum resource guide includes a framework for an interdisciplinary approach based on an infused multicultural education approach. It addresses the ability to develop social action skills in students and provides for a wide range of learning styles. It says nothing about gay and lesbian families.

The Final Outcome

For me, the final outcome of this process was loss—loss of time, effort, energy, creativity, proactivity, and a belief in the possibility of real change (not change for change's sake but for doing the right thing). At the beginning of this decade, I believed that we were creating an agenda, an education that was multicultural in a linguistically and culturally diverse city, with the hope of eventually influencing a nation. It was a heady time. My sense of excitement abounded. Now there is this sense of loss.

But from the beginning, I have been in this struggle for the long haul; therefore I felt (and feel) disappointment, not frustration. I have been down this road before with bilingual education. I know that sometimes it is necessary to move forward five steps and then take ten steps back. I have learned, on the one hand, that no matter how important an innovation may seem, true change has to go through a process that takes time, and on the other hand, that the contemporary news media can color people's perceptions instantaneously.

James Baldwin said, "Not everything that is faced can be changed, but nothing can be changed until it is faced" (qtd. in Stanford, 1977, p. 201). My hope is that the need for inclusivity, for the New York public schools and for society in general, can be both faced and changed. If it is, Nieto's view of multicultural education remains a possibility, just one that will take time and struggle:

> Our knowledge of the change process and insight into the dynamics of change have become considerably sophisticated. At the same time, the problems of society have become more complex. . . . We have learned that understanding ever more complex change processes is only half the battle. Doing something about it is far more of a challenge, which should occupy us for years to come. (qtd. in Fullan, 1993, p. 132)

Note

1. A revised edition of *Teaching First Grade: A Comprehensive Instructional Program* (New York City Board of Education, 1994a) was finally officially distributed in October 1997 as *Grade One and Growing: A Comprehensive Instructional Resource Guide for Teachers* (New York City Board of Education, 1997).

References

Baker, G. C. (1994). *Planning and organizing for multicultural instruction* (2nd ed.). Menlo Park, CA: Addison-Wesley.

Bredekamp, S. (Ed.). (1987). *Developmentally appropriate practice in early programs serving children from birth through age 8*. Washington, DC: National Association for the Education of Young Children.

DelFattore, J. (1992). *What Johnny shouldn't read: Textbook censorship in America*. New Haven, CT: Yale University Press.

Elwin, R., & Paulse, M. (1990). *Asha's mums*. Toronto: Women's Press.

Fernández, J. A. (1993). *Tales out of school: Joseph Fernández's crusade to rescue American education*. Boston: Little, Brown.

Fullan, M. (1993). *Innovation, reform, and restructuring strategies*. In G. Cawelti (Ed.), *Challenges and achievements of American education*. Alexandria, VA: Association for Supervision and Curriculum Development.

Hodgkinson, H. (1992). *A demographic look at tomorrow*. Washington, DC: Institute for Education Leadership/Center for Demographic Policy.

Joyce, B. (1990). *Changing school culture through staff development*. Alexandria, VA: Association for Supervision and Curriculum Development.

Joyce, B., & Showers, B. (1988). *Student achievement through staff development*. New York: Longman.

Newman, L. (1989). *Heather has two mommies*. Boston: Alyson Wonderland.

Newman, L. (1991). *Belinda's bouquet*. Boston: Alyson Wonderland.

Nieto, S. (1992). *Affirming diversity: The sociopolitical context of multicultural education*. New York: Longman.

New York City Board of Education. (1989). *Statement of policy on multicultural education and promotion of positive intergroup relations.* New York: Author.

New York City Board of Education. (1990a). *An action plan for multicultural education.* New York: Author.

New York City Board of Education. (1990b). *"Children of the Rainbow," kindergarten.* New York: Author.

New York City Board of Education. (1991a). *"Children of the Rainbow," first grade.* New York: Author.

New York City Board of Education. (1992b). *New York City public schools facts and figures 1992–1993.* Unpublished manuscript.

New York City Board of Education. (1994a). *Teaching first grade: A comprehensive instructional program.* New York: Author.

New York City Board of Education. (1994b). *Teaching second grade: A comprehensive instructional program.* New York: Author.

New York City Board of Education. (1997). *Grade one and growing: A comprehensive instructional resource guide for teachers.* New York: Author.

Stanford, G. (1977). *Developing effective classroom groups: A practical guide for teachers.* New York: Hart.

Tannen, D. (1998). *The argument culture: Moving from debate to dialogue.* New York: Random House.

Willhoite, M. (1991). *Daddy's roommate.* Boston: Alyson Wonderland.

Williams, R. (1993). Initiatives for systemic change. *Journal of Staff Development, 14*(2), 16–20.

CHAPTER THIRTEEN

Two News, Two Views of Toronto Schools: Learning from Broadcast News (or, Lessons on Becoming Articulate)

DON DIPPO

York University, Toronto

Public schooling has been the subject/object of considerable media attention in recent years. Sometimes identified as the source of all that ails us socially, politically, and economically, other times touted as the only solution to the social, political, and economic problems we face, broadcast media versions of what is really going on in schools find their way into the always lively, often overheated public discussion of what to do with a nearly 150-year-old system of tax-supported, compulsory public schools. And while media stories are not the only source of information, analysis, and opinion, they have an impact that is the stuff of dreams for parent groups, teacher unions, "concerned citizens," academics, ratepayers, and civil servants who want to be seen, heard, understood, and believed by the "public-at-large." Creators of news and current affairs programs would, of course, have us believe that the stories they generate are objective reports or investigative accounts of school matters that serve an increasing public interest in (or appetite for) education-related issues. To achieve some semblance of "balanced coverage," they often employ a pattern of good news/bad news. Stories about illiteracy, violence, and dropouts are interspersed with reports of computers in the classroom, peer counseling, and school-business partnerships.

This chapter focuses on two news reports featuring the greater Toronto public schools. The "good news" report is from *ABC World News Tonight* (Blakemore, 1990) and tells the tale of a system that has not sold itself short by emphasizing only "the basics." Here in Toronto, ABC News reports, students are encouraged to think deeply, feel passionately, and act wisely by exercising some measure of control over the curriculum. They are engaged in what the reporter discovers is called "whole language" and "active learning." The "bad news" story comes from *CBC Monitor* (Kofman, 1989). In this report, the viewer is taken into the same schools, observes the same whole language classrooms, and is informed that this approach to teaching and learning is thought by some to be hazardous to the well-being of students.

This chapter is not about which version of "what's really going on" is more true or false, more right or wrong. Instead, both ABC's and CBC's construction of progressive education are viewed as the creations of newsmakers, designed to shape views about public education generally and about certain educational practices in particular. Both documentaries are also themselves reactions to language practices viewed in this volume as progressive. As calls to action, however, they operate from very different sets of assumptions. In this chapter, I explore how news reports such as these participate in a public discourse about schooling and rely for their intelligibility on taken-for-granted assumptions about the nature of knowledge, the imperatives of pedagogy, the work of teachers, and the aims and purposes of schooling. I conclude with a discussion of the implications of such an analysis for educators, especially those interested in participating in the public, media-mediated discussion of the future of public schooling.

Articulateness in Teacher Education

I teach a course in the social foundations of education at York University in Toronto. The Faculty of Education at York has, since its inception in 1973, been seen as an institution unapologetically supportive of progressive pedagogy. I take pretty much for granted that in their practicum-related classes most of my students will be exposed to, and will eventually buy into, whole language approaches to literacy, constructivist mathematics, inquiry-based social and environmental studies, activity-based science, and so on. What I do not, and cannot, take for granted, however, is that in the process of becoming more competent practitioners of progressive teaching, my students are also becoming more articulate about their practice.

The problem of "articulateness" in teacher education is one that has been explored by Liston and Zeichner (1991), building on the work of Margaret Buchmann (1986). They begin by expressing dissatisfaction with notions of reflection and reflective practice so widely used in teaching and teacher education today. Concerned with promoting a level of self-consciousness and self-understanding, these ideas pay little explicit attention to the importance of exploring the assumptions, perspectives, and commitments that underlie teaching practice. As teaching is increasingly scrutinized and teachers are more and more often called upon to justify what they do, it becomes even more important that they be able not only to explain themselves to themselves, but also to explain to others and give good reasons for the decisions they have made and the actions they have taken.

> We sense that teacher education ought to aim directly at developing teachers who are able to identify and articulate their purposes, who can choose the appropriate instructional strategies or appropriate means, who know and understand the content to be taught, who understand the social experiences and cognitive orientations of their students, and who can be counted on for giving good reasons for their actions. (Liston & Zeichner, 1991, p. 39)

One of my aims, then, in the social foundations course I teach is to help my students become more articulate about their practice. I do this by making the giving of reasons a topic in class; by expecting them to give defensible justifications for the curricular and pedagogical decisions they make; and by making explicit the links between justification, the social context of schooling, and personally held social, cultural, and political beliefs. Two resources I have found particularly useful for framing discourses of legitimation and exploring assumptions about teaching, learning, and schooling are "Child's Play," broadcast on CBC's *Monitor* program, and "The American Agenda," broadcast on *ABC World News Tonight*. These two shows provide contrasting versions of what are essentially the same school settings and programs by appealing to two very different sets of assumptions about the aims and purposes of schooling. Not only does the intelligibility of each of the programs rest on these sets of assumptions, but the shows themselves are also organized in such a way as to make the aims and purposes they assume seem the only reasonable positions viewers can take.

CBC Monitor: "Child's Play"

Monitor was a locally produced and locally broadcast current affairs program. As implied by the name, *Monitor* was supposed to be a kind of watchdog program modeled after high-profile, nationally (and internationally) broadcast investigative shows like *60 Minutes*. More than reporting (or at least as much as reporting), the show was interested in revealing and exposing the foibles of local celebrities and the misdeeds of municipal governments. This "investigative" orientation helps explain why the show chose to focus on (or create?) a particularly conspiratorial narrative thread in its show on active learning. The program "Child's Play" is comprised of three separate but related stories which are intercut with one another. The first story is about active learning and is told by several students and their teacher. The second story is about a group of parents who have organized to oppose active learning in their local school, and this story is told by a couple who claim to speak on behalf of other families as well as for themselves. The third story is about a missing research report commissioned by the Board of Education in the early seventies which allegedly proves that active learning is less effective than traditional teaching methods. So the central questions around which the show is organized are: What is active learning? Why are these parents opposed to it? Where is the research report which shows active learning to be less effective than traditional methods? Why does the board continue to push active learning when it knows that traditional methods work better?

The program opens with the sounds of children singing, "Down by the bay, where the watermelons grow, back to my home, I dare not go, but if I do, my Mama will say . . . ." The camera records kids singing, kids at a board game, kids at a water table. The voice-over begins: "Some things never change . . . like kids and kindergarten. They're still singing songs and playing games." Cut to a shot of older students gathered around a table. "This is a sixth-grade class at Islington Elementary School in Etobicoke. Used to be that kids at this level played games after school. But today games are what you play *in* school. When it started, they called this 'play learning.' Now the buzz-words are 'active' or 'child-centered' learning." And so begins this investigative report into why "they" continue to do "it" to kids.

In the next segment of the program, the reporter talks to that group of sixth-grade students who have just been shown playing a board game. He asks them what they are doing, and they explain that they are learning about Marco Polo's journeys. They say that the game they are playing is a more effective and more interesting way to learn than copying notes from a book or from the board. The reporter concludes this segment with the ominous warning, "Active learning is taking over in classrooms across Ontario."

Viewers are then introduced to a group of six parents sitting around a dining room table. The reporter's voice-over explains that there is a "counterrevolution" going on and that this revolution is made up of "concerned parents" who are opposed to active learning. He asks one parent if the group isn't simply asking for a return to "the three 'R's." The reply is an emphatic "No!" What parents want is "balance" and the assurance that their children will learn to read and write. "Wasn't your son being taught to read or write?" asks the reporter. "We didn't see him progressing," is the father's reply. When asked if they had ever visited the school, the mother responds that yes indeed they had visited and witnessed what can only be described as "chaos" and "aimlessness."

The camera pans around a kindergarten classroom. Students are working at tables and common activity centers with sandboxes, hollow blocks, tape recorders, easels, and the like. Many are talking to each other. Some are walking from one activity to another. The reporter intones, "This kindergarten class looks chaotic . . . but we were assured this is *organized chaos*."

"All kids love to play. They have a good time playing but that doesn't mean they'll learn how to read." The speaker is identified as a retired principal who for twenty years ran what *Monitor* describes as some of the best schools in the city. "If you want children to learn to read," he advises, "you teach them directly. If you want them to learn math well, you teach them directly."

Cutting back to the sixth-grade class shown earlier in the program, viewers are introduced to the teacher, who is evidently in the midst of explaining something to the reporter. "These children are learning," she is telling the reporter. "They're learning through active learning. Look at their faces . . . see the involvement?"

The retired principal, however, is skeptical. Like the concerned parents, he thinks a "balanced approach" is what is needed. "I would say if they took child-centered learning and combined it with structured learning, we'd have a good system."

Meanwhile, back in the classroom the reporter is still struggling with the basics. He understands that students in this class help each other, but what happens if one of them approaches the teacher and asks, "How do I do this?" The teacher here might be thinking about exemplary practice. She might be thinking about colleagues watching this report on television. She might be thinking about the reporter, who seems unable to comprehend what he sees. What she is not thinking about, because she has not been a party to the conversation, are things like "chaos," "aimlessness," and the redemptive qualities of "direct instruction," and so she answers in a way that seems reasonable to her but which plays into the emerging theme that organizes the rest of the show. She says, "First, I'd tell him to try to think about the problem from a different point of view. If that didn't work, I'd suggest discussing it with someone else or brainstorming with some others." The reporter asks about spelling and grammar: "Are they getting it? Do you think so?" The teacher replies, "I know that they are where I'd like them to be."

This implied crisis of accountability leads the reporter to ask if there is or isn't any proof that, in his words, "toys are better than textbooks." He puts the question first to the concerned parents. "Have you ever asked the board if they had research?" The mother replies, "They were asked by concerned parents on a number of occasions to back up what they're doing. Finally, we asked them in writing. They said, 'There is no research.'" The reporter, however, knows otherwise. There was a report, commissioned by the Board of Education, which compared "traditional methods" with "an early version of the active learning methods now used here in Etobicoke." What researchers found, according to the reporter, was that "with active learning, kids were actually *learning less* than those in traditional classrooms." What's more, we are told that the board never released the study and that they never even showed it to their own trustees!

On camera now, a professor of educational administration at the Ontario Institute for Studies in Education states that it was a "good report, good research" but that "the powers that be" didn't want it to be published. The board didn't say it was bad research, according to the professor, but "hid it" and then "proceeded, on a compulsory basis, in all schools, to implement a method which was less successful."

A superintendent from the board is called to account. The reporter asks, "Why was the report not released?" The superintendent, like the seemingly irresolute teacher, responds, "I'm not sure. I wasn't in administration at that time." And then, echoing the teacher's suspect confidence, the superintendent responds to a query about literacy: "The teachers say it's there. And what better instrument [for evaluation] than a teacher saying, 'Here's the criteria the Ministry [of Education] has set down for that grade level and yes, my kids can do that'?"

The professor will have none of it. He characterizes progressive education as a "cult." "The ideas are not rational," he declares. The superintendent, evidently asked to respond to the professor's characterization, says, "It's not a cult. It's not a fad. These are trained teachers." Cutting back to the retired principal, "For twenty years I pleaded with 'the powers that be' to go slow."

Viewers are shown an image of an eleven- or twelve-year-old boy doing homework at a dining room table. The voice-over laments, "Jason is reading and writing now, but his parents have given up on public schools. He now attends a private school."

Cut to Jason's father, one of the concerned parents: "I know people who have had worse experiences than us. One family I know only found out in grade 4 that their child can't read!"

On the screen, the sixth-grade class goes about its business. The reporter, in his most ominous voice, concludes, "Active learning is government policy in Ontario. In a few years it will be in classrooms all across the province."

My students respond to this tape in much the same way that teachers in Toronto responded when it was first broadcast—with outrage, indignation, and a sense of betrayal. The first comments are usually intended to cast aspersions on the concerned parents: "What parent who's paying attention wouldn't notice that a kid is having reading difficulties until grade 4?" They take exception to their classrooms being described as chaotic and aimless. They resent being characterized as members of a cult. They feel terrible about the way the teacher was set up by the reporter and made to look and sound ridiculous. They wonder how parents and the public can believe that teachers would knowingly do harm to children. And then they ask questions about the research. Was there such a study? What happened to it? Aren't there any studies that prove that active learning, or whole language, or constructivist math, or inquiry science, or other progressive methods are as effective or more effective than traditional methods? What they do not usually ask about at this point are the dangers of talking about any of these approaches as methods that can be compared to so-called traditional methods and be found better or worse. Neither do they pay sufficient attention to how the concerned parents and the retired principal invoke the goodness of "balance" in their talk, or how the retired principal and the professor conjure up the evils of "the powers that be." This video puts my students very much on the defensive, and the more defensive they get the less articulate they become. To the extent that they buy into the terms of the argument set out by the concerned parents, the retired principal, and the professor, they are stuck defending themselves against charges of being duped by a sinister educational bureaucracy, unable to talk thoughtfully, reasonably, and persuasively about what they do and why they do it. So we watch the second video.

ABC World News Tonight: "The American Agenda"

The show opens with the anchor/host sitting at the news desk. She tells viewers that the president has determined that "real improvement in American schools is not simply a matter of spending more money." Rather, it is a matter of setting goals, of "asking more of our schools, our teachers, our students, and ourselves." Tonight, she says, an ABC reporter visits a big city school district that set a goal of excellence fifteen years ago, "and it worked."

"School on a chilly morning. Lockers are opening and closing all over town." The shots are of elementary school students outside on the playground, standing in groups, walking in hallways. The voice-over continues, "Outside or inside, they're talking about school. Even before the bell rings, they're focused on learning." The national anthem begins the school day and, in what must come as a surprise to U.S. viewers, the anthem is "O' Canada." "Here in Toronto," continues the reporter, "the school system is remarkable." He describes students as "intent," "engrossed," and "focused on learning all day." "Schools focused on learning are not the exception but the rule all over town," he exclaims. Over the past fifteen years, when schools in the United States have emphasized a return to "the basics" of reading, writing, and arithmetic, in Ontario they tried something else. They set some general goals about the kinds of people they wanted to come out of their schools. These goals included people who would "like to learn"; who would "think clearly," "feel deeply," and "act wisely"; who would "enjoy working with others"; who could "problem solve"; who were "self-reliant"; and who showed "respect for a wide variety of cultures"—all of this in addition to the basic knowledge and skills of literacy and numeracy. "To accomplish this," the reporter explains, "they are concentrating on what they call 'active learning.'"

The scene is of a fourth- or fifth-grade classroom. Students are working at tables with beakers, cans, lengths of surgical hose, scales, pencils and paper, and lots of water. A quick cut to someone identified as the director of education: "What takes root in children's minds," she says, "is what they do, what they talk about, what they experience." Cut back to the classroom and a conversation with a teacher. "The children are doing the work. I'm supervising, keeping them on track." The camera cuts to another classroom where the students are younger. They are working at tables with paper and pencils. "Listen to the noise," the teacher tells the reporter. "It's a constructive, solid, happy noise." Cutting back to the classroom of older students, the reporter explains that teachers view this as a more efficient use of their time. They can make sure that they are teaching each student. "I can see how they're working," says a teacher. "I can see the logic and the sequence they're using to reach conclusions." This individual attention is important, the reporter continues, because of the racial and cultural complexity of Toronto's exploding population. In schools, students are taught to be proud of their heritage, proud of themselves, and proud of their work.

The reporter is in conversation with two boys who appear to be in third or fourth grade. He asks the boys what they are doing. "We're writing a novel." "And what will you do with it when you're finished?" "Publish it at the library," they reply. Cut to a scene of the library where students are sitting on sofas, comfortable chairs, and on the floor reading self-published as well as commercially published books. The reporter remarks, "Their book will be kept in the library where others can read it, learn from it, and critique it."

Cut back to the classroom: "And how do these teachers know if kids are learning?" the reporter asks. "They keep samples of their work throughout the year," he answers, "to keep track of improvement. And through observation." A teacher explains that if you observe and keep watch over what's going on you'll know if a student is learning or not. What's more, she continues, children tell you what they have learned and what they are having difficulty with. "What better system do you need," she asks, "to evaluate learning?"

Visiting U.S. educators have been impressed by what they have seen in Toronto, according to this report. A visiting U.S. educator is interviewed in the corridor of the school where the opening sequence was filmed. He says that several years ago in Ontario people decided that they wanted students to learn to think. At the same time, in the United States people decided they wanted to "keep the lid on things" and teach "low-level," "threshold," and "basic" skills. "We ask for less, and we get less," he concludes. "In Ontario they ask for more," announces the reporter, "and then leave it to the district and the schools to decide how to do the job." The person who appears next on the screen is identified by subtitle as the deputy minister of education for Ontario. He quips, "I don't believe that anyone knows the answer to the question 'What is the best way to do *X*?'. . . What works, works." The reporter returns to his previous line of thinking to conclude his report from Toronto: "In Ontario they set goals and kept insisting on them until they got what they asked for. They asked for well-educated people, ready to engage the world, [*pause*] and they're getting them."

Learning from Broadcast News

My students are always exuberant after watching this program. The first thing they want to know is how they can get a copy of the videotape. I feel somewhat Grinch-like when I begin to ask students to adopt a more critical stance toward the video, but the point of the exercise is not merely to pit pretense against pretense. What my students easily saw and objected to in the first video they now grudgingly recognize in the second: that these are simplified and constructed (even contrived) accounts of complex and contested settings; that they conform, each in its own context, to media versions of and predilections for being "oppositional"; and that they are calls for action designed to provide parents and the public not only with information but also a line of argument with which to begin to engage teachers, school officials, and "the powers that be" in discussions about what goes on and should go on in schools.

In addition to these common features, other points of comparison are usually taken up in class. One of these concerns assumptions about students as credible and informed spokespersons about their own experiences. In both videos, students are asked by reporters to comment on what they are learning and doing. In both videos, students talk about the worthwhileness of their experiences and the enthusiasm they have for this approach to teaching and learning. In the ABC report, students' words stand as testament to the value of active learning. The pleasure they take in, and the benefits they derive from, participating in the curricular and pedagogical decisions which will affect their own learning are taken for granted. By way of contrast, in the CBC report students' assessment is dismissed by the retired principal's comment, "Sure they like it. But do they *learn*?" The assumption here seems to be that the acquisition of basic skills and knowledge requires some measure of discomfort, even drudgery, and that students will not learn (will refuse to learn?) unless taught directly.

Assumptions about teachers as responsible adults and reliable evaluators provide another interesting point of contrast. In the CBC video, "They are where I'd like them to be" comes across as vague, unreliable, and self-serving. Yet in the ABC video, the question, "Who better to judge?" seems rhetorical, with an answer that is self-evident—the teacher, of course. Once again these differences signal conflicting understandings and expectations regarding the work of teachers. On the one hand, teachers are seen as professionals responsible for providing resources; structuring activities; extending learning opportunities; and assessing, recording, and reporting students' progress. On the other hand, they are seen as functionaries responsible for carrying out the directives of a misinformed ministry. What they should be, according to the concerned parents, are technicians who use the most efficient methods to achieve standardized, quantifiable results.

Parents in CBC-land, especially concerned parents, are portrayed as waging a "counterrevolution" and beginning to demand effective instruction for their children. The assumption here is that, as "consumers" of education and on behalf of their children, parents should have the last word about what is taught and how it is taught in schools. There is no acknowledgment that schools might serve public purposes which extend beyond the demands of particular parent groups. Also missing in this account is any willingness to recognize that teachers themselves have a legitimate stake in determining how their work is organized. ABC, on the other hand, must assume that children in Canada have no parents (insofar as none were interviewed for the program) or at least have no "concerned" parents. Avoiding the issue of parental preference altogether, they posit instead a more generalized public that, fifteen years ago in ways that are never described, began "to ask more of schools."

Finally, educational institutions in general and the educational bureaucracy in particular are characterized very differently in the two videos. The central narrative thread in the CBC report is the story of how "the powers that be" continue to insist on what they know to be inferior methods of instruction and enlist the support of duplicitous teachers who inflict active learning on students for their own mysterious, cult-like purposes. The educational establishment in the United States, according to ABC, is more complacent—hoping mainly to "keep the lid on" things at school and willing to settle for less from students. In Ontario, by contrast, according to ABC, the Ministry of Education is enlightened, full of plans, and responsive. When the public began to "ask more of schools," the ministry responded by setting goals and insisting on them until they got the results they asked for. "They asked for well-educated people prepared to engage the world—and they're getting them."

Lessons for Becoming Articulate

What can be learned by paying attention to the juxtaposition of these two news reports? If in one teachers come across as confused and self-serving and in another they appear thoughtful and committed, what can be said about interpretive frames and discourses of legitimation that would help teachers and student teachers express themselves more clearly and more persuasively? Are there lessons here for becoming more articulate about what is being done and why? The first point I try to make when talking about these accounts in class is that the issues cannot be reduced to questions of method or technique. To become embroiled in the kind of technical debate set out (or set up) along CBC lines is to grant legitimacy to a position that can only imagine schooling as a question of choosing between most effective and least effective methods as determined by test results. It is to confer "reasonableness" on a position which appeals to "balance" as if progressive pedagogies (whether active learning, whole language, or child-centered) and basic knowledges and skills such as literacy and numeracy were incommensurable. Rather than thinking about these positions as dichotomous, irreconcilable, or requiring balance, they can be understood as reflecting differences in scope, with progressive pedagogies encompassing a broader view of what education could and should be about. I am not suggesting that concerns about and interest in basic literacy and numeracy skills be ceded to those with the narrowest possible conception of education. Rather, I am suggesting that it is futile to be drawn into deliberations in which the terms are limited to technical concerns about effective methods. Progressive approaches will inevitably come across as indirect and imprecise because their primary pedagogical concerns are with education more broadly conceived.

When the terms of the discussion are enlarged to include a consideration of the basic aims and purposes of education, as happens in the ABC report, progressive approaches fare much better. One need not go so far as to invoke the ministry goals of "feeling deeply" or "acting wisely." Progressive pedagogies seem much more reasonable when literacy and numeracy are understood in relation to other aims and commitments such as developing problem-solving abilities, collaborative skills, and an interest in finding ways for students to work with and learn from others who are different from themselves. These are, after all, the qualities that even the concerned parents want for their children because they will enable them to become productive, contributing, and active members of society. What we learn then from the ABC report is that the legitimacy of progressive pedagogy and its intelligibility for parents is best understood when presented against a backdrop of socially recognized and valued aims and purposes. As educators, we can begin to address the concerns of concerned parents only if we can assure them that literacy and numeracy are not at risk but, in fact, are paramount in progressive educational practice, and that education for employment is not ignored but incorporated within a larger vision of education for active citizenship. Rather than becoming defensive or evasive when approached by those who question or oppose a particular classroom practice, teachers must be able to give the kinds of reasons and provide the kinds of explanations that will enable others to see order and purpose in their own and their students' activities. They must be prepared to talk about *what* they do and *why* they do it. They must be prepared to monitor, evaluate, and report to parents regularly. What they must avoid is getting drawn into arguments about what someone has seen or heard on television, read in the newspaper, or remembered about their own "golden days" in school.

Conclusion

In the years since I started using these videos in my class, George Bush—the self-proclaimed "education president"—lost his job at the White House to Bill Clinton, whose "progressive" agenda as set out in the Goals 2000 Program includes making standardized testing a national priority. In the province of Ontario, where a Conservative government has been elected, the situation for progressive educators is not as rosy as it was when ABC came to visit. Indeed, standardization, centralization, so-called "accountability," and a return to "the basics" have become the hallmarks of the new Ministry of Education and Training. Cuts to health care and welfare, antilabor legislation, an end to equity initiatives, and a return to "the competitive spirit" have come to characterize the actions of this provincial government more generally. Education for active citizenship in this context is not likely to be found on the list of educational outcomes or objectives produced by this much criticized and much protested government and its ministers. Yet active citizenship is precisely what was being taught when the teachers of Ontario closed the schools for two weeks in the fall of 1997 to protest the government's attack on public education (which in Ontario includes both public and Catholic schools). One thing the protest action demonstrated was that the battle for public opinion and popular support can be won. Contrary to government expectations, support for teachers actually increased as the strike went on. This was due in no small measure to the articulateness of those teachers who walked the line and talked to parents and reporters about the effects of underfunding and elimination of preparation time, the implications of centralized decision making and curriculum development, and the distortion (many would say the destruction) of authentic, purposeful learning environments brought about by provincewide standardized testing. The struggle, as they say, continues in Ontario, but the burden of resisting the conservative attack of progressive education should not rest only on the shoulders of classroom teachers forced to take such drastic action to make their point to the public. All progressive educators, whether they work in elementary schools, high schools, board offices, or universities, must bear some responsibility for resisting the dumbing down of the curriculum—the expecting less which is called "demanding more"—and for rearticulating a progressive vision of what public education could be. For those of us no longer immersed in the day-to-day work of public school teaching, and here I am talking about administrators, teacher educators, and educational researchers in particular, the time has come (the window of opportunity has been open for thirty years) to enter the fray—to risk being misrepresented, misinterpreted, and misunderstood—and to begin to engage in a much more deliberate, focused, and committed way to challenging the conservative agenda for education by writing letters to the editor, giving interviews to reporters, appearing on television, speaking at parent council meetings, and participating in all manner of public forum and debate.

Articulateness for teachers, while never sufficient, has become more important than ever. What I want for my students, then, is for them to be able to teach and to be able to participate effectively in public discussions, debates, and political actions which affect their professional lives. Those who will be successful, who will be consulted by colleagues and have the confidence of parents, may be those who have learned not merely to name what they do (these days *not* naming might be a better strategy), but also to describe the curricular and pedagogical choices they have made, to explain the aims and purposes behind those choices, and to do these things in ways that not only make sense to fellow educators, but also are persuasive and compelling to a larger public.

References

Blakemore, B. (1990, November 13). The American agenda [Documentary, with intro. by Diane Sawyer]. In *World News Tonight*. New York: ABC.

Buchmann, M. (1986). Role over person: Morality and authenticity in teaching. *Teachers College Record* 87(4): 527–43.

Kofman, J. (1989, November 27). Child's play [Documentary]. In *CBC Monitor*. Toronto: CBC.

Liston, D., & Zeichner, K. (1991). *Teacher education and the social conditions of schooling*. New York: Routledge.

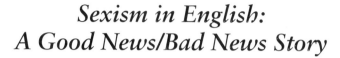

CHAPTER FOURTEEN

Sexism in English:
A Good News/Bad News Story

ALLEEN PACE NILSEN
Arizona State University

The old maxim about politicians seeing which way the people are moving and then jumping in front and running as fast as they can is descriptive of the actions of the National Council of Teachers of English (NCTE) in relation to sexism and English. When in 1976 the Council distributed its *Guidelines for Non-sexist Use of Language in NCTE Publications,* we were neither the first nor the bravest with our guidelines, but the prestige of the Council and its large membership nevertheless made us leaders in the struggle to make speakers aware of how their language was often unfair to women and, in some cases, to men.

Simone de Beauvoir's *The Second Sex* (1953), Betty Friedan's *The Feminine Mystique* (1963), and Germaine Greer's *The Female Eunuch* (1971) set the scene for new kinds of thinking. As early as 1970, the question of sexism and language was being discussed in the mass media, as well as in scholarly journals. Ann Bayer (1970) prepared a photo essay for *LIFE* magazine illustrating such obviously sexist terms as *clinging vine, wallflower,* and *cupcake.* In 1971 Casey Miller and Kate Swift published "One Small Step for Genkind" in the *New York Times Magazine.* Their article, which has been frequently reprinted and quoted, was the groundwork for their 1976 book *Words and Women: New Language in New Times.* In July 1974, Robin Lakoff published "You Are What You Say" in *Ms.* magazine as a forerunner to her book *Language and Woman's Place,* which came out in 1975.

It was in the midst of this kind of interest and activity that NCTE founded its Women's Committee. At the 1971 Annual Convention in Las Vegas, the Executive Board approved the founding of a Committee on the Role and Image of Women in the Council and the Profession, a name soon shortened to the Women's Committee. Janet Emig, who later became NCTE president, was appointed as the first chair. No formal committee meeting was held that year, but the program listed a discussion group on "The Status of Women in the Teaching Profession." Among the speakers who became important in the early work of the committee were Elisabeth McPherson from Forest Park Community College in Missouri; Lou Kelly from the University of Iowa; Alpha Quincy from Mt. Diablo Unified School District in Concord, California; and Nancy Lauter from NCTE Headquarters.

In NCTE's 1972 Annual Report, Emig wrote that she spent the year trying to organize a committee that would accurately represent "not only women in the four-year colleges and universities but also the range of women who teach the language arts and English in the elementary and secondary schools and in the two-year colleges." She also sought diversity in age, race, geography, and nature of academic responsibility. The hardest part was finding women who were in administration, and she was especially pleased when one of the few women principals in New York City joined the committee.

Perhaps because the next committee chair, Johanna DeStefano of Ohio State University, was a linguist, the committee's attention began to focus heavily on language. Or it may be that a linguist was chosen as chair because the committee members already felt obligated as English teachers to join what was rapidly becoming a national debate.

An important fact about the Women's Committee is that it was formed out of an already established need, and most of the people chosen for membership had already been involved with issues of sexism and language, and remained involved long after their formal terms on the committee ended. For example, I had just finished writing my dissertation at the University of Iowa on the topic of pronoun usage, and from 1969 to 1973 Alpha Quincy was on the California State Curriculum Commission, where she noted the sexist language in the textbooks the committee was evaluating. As she said years later in a letter of October 24, 1996, the issue was ripe for discussion, as shown by the response from television, newspapers, and state legislators. As a result, fifteen major publishers of reading textbooks made changes to eliminate gender and other biases, and the state legislature codified the need for nonbiased textbooks.

As editor of *Elementary English* (now called *Language Arts*), Iris Tiedt solicited articles for a special issue on the topic of women, girls, and the language arts curriculum (October 1973). Other members of the Women's Committee worked in cooperation with NCTE's Committee on Public Doublespeak to produce a book, *Sexism and Language,* which the Council published in 1977; co-authors included Haig Bosmajian, H. Lee Gershuny, Julia P. Stanley, and myself. Stanley later dropped her surname and wrote extensively under the name of Julia Penelope, publishing in 1990 *Speaking Freely: Unlearning the Lies of the Fathers' Tongues.* Other early committee members included Carolyn Allen, who later became the editor of *Signs: Journal of Women in Culture and Society,* and Joyce Penfield, who in 1987 published *Women and Language in Transition.*

A second reason for the committee's early success was widespread cooperation among NCTE, the Modern Language Association (MLA), and the Linguistic Society of America (LSA). Women from all three organizations joined in a range of activities to which they brought their insights and enthusiasm. One of the earliest activities called for NCTE members to work with the already established Commission on Women of the Modern Language Association to sponsor several sessions at the 1970 MLA meeting in New York. In an unusual example of cooperation, the papers from these MLA sessions were printed in the May 1971 issue of *College English* and in that same year were expanded into the NCTE monograph *A Case for Equity: Women in English Departments,* edited by Susan McAllester.

A three-hour panel discussion was one of the highlights of the 1972 NCTE Annual Convention in Minneapolis. Participants included Margaret Mead, from the Museum of Natural History; Florence Howe, president of MLA; Elaine Reuben, University of

Wisconsin; Charlotte Croman, City University of New York; and Harriet W. Sheridan, Carleton College. In her annual report for that year, Emig wrote that Mead "characterized the meeting as the most intelligent and stimulating session on women in which she had ever participated."

The following February, NCTE's Women's Committee met for two days at the Palmer House in Chicago. The chief outcome was a decision to produce a series of guidelines in key areas involving professional women: publications, programs, textbooks, teaching and teacher preparation, women's and girls' studies, and the profession itself. The first to be prepared was the guidelines on publications, which was distributed at the 1973 meeting of the Conference on College Composition and Communication, then mailed to the membership. The MLA Women's Committee also mailed out 3,000 copies.

These publication guidelines were written in two parts, with the first part supposedly addressed to publishers and editors and the second part addressed to readers. These guidelines were not specifically on sexism and language, but they prepared people for the next step and did much to increase awareness of how language choices can contribute to sexism. Suggestions to editors included:

◆ Solicit and publish articles dealing with women's problems.

◆ Ensure a fair balance of articles by women as well as for and about them.

◆ Refuse advertising which discriminates against women or which purports to be representative when in fact it is not.

◆ Become consciously aware of unconscious sexist bias and hidden assumptions in every manuscript, whatever its subject matter.

◆ Refuse to publish articles which contain such hidden biases and assumptions, not in an attempt to limit controversy, but to see that conflicting views are presented openly.

In the section addressed to readers (who among the guidelines recipients must have outnumbered publishers and editors a hundred to one), advice included:

- Watch for expressed and implied sexist biases and assumptions in language choice in comments about women's roles.

- Protest biased articles with letters to the editor, to the organization that sponsors the publication, and to the author.

- Congratulate editors who adopt these guidelines and praise them when they print good material on the role and image of women.

For the 1974 NCTE Annual Convention in New Orleans, the Women's Committee organized a preconference workshop for the purpose of going a step further than the publication guidelines—drafting a statement about sexism and language directed to the general membership. At the same convention, the Women's Committee brought a resolution to the Board of Directors asking for the preparation of guidelines that would curtail sexist language in NCTE publications. The committee did not think it was asking for anything revolutionary because other publishing houses already had such guidelines, such as Scott Foresman's 1972 *Guidelines for Improving the Image of Women in Textbooks* and McGraw-Hill's 1974 *Guidelines for Equal Treatment of the Sexes.* In an organization as large as NCTE, however, progress is slow. Even after the resolution was approved, a policy still had to be developed and voted on. At the 1975 meeting, the board adopted a formal policy stating, "The National Council of Teachers of English should encourage the use of nonsexist language, particularly through its publications and periodicals."

At the time the policy was passed, the Council had a somewhat timid brochure that had grown out of the 1974 preconference workshop. It asked such questions as:

- Do you expect or promote a different kind of written and oral expression from boys than from girls?

- Do you refer to teachers as *she* while principals, professors, and department heads are *he*?

- Are doctors and lawyers automatically *he*, while nurses and secretaries are always *she*?

- Do you personify bad practices in English teaching as always female (i.e., *Miss Fiddith* or *Mrs. Grundy*)?

◆ Do you give the impression that female writers are somehow apart from the mainstream with the titles *poetess* and *authoress*?

◆ Do you mentally exclude women from the business world and teach your students to do the same by heading letters to unknown people with either *Gentlemen* or *Dear Sirs*?

It was 1976 before NCTE's official guidelines were developed and distributed to the membership. They were organized around the three major problems of:

omission of one sex

demeaning women

sex-role stereotyping

These guidelines, which were revised in 1985, were never voted on. Their development was considered to be a response by NCTE's editorial staff and the Women's Committee to the policy statement approved in 1975.

Today, the guidelines more or less languish in the warehouse at NCTE Headquarters. They consist of eight half-sheet pages of small type. Single copies are free on request, and they are also available in bulk at 100 for $7.00.[1] This is a far cry from their treatment twenty years ago, when they were widely distributed for free, printed and reprinted in all the journals, and the subject of workshops and discussions, as well as of heated debates, at various conventions. The guidelines were brought to participants' attention by NCTE conference organizers, who included a statement in program invitations encouraging the use of nonsexist language by speakers and session chairs. This put a personal responsibility on hundreds, if not thousands, of individuals. But the biggest controversy was over whether editors had the right to change what they considered to be sexist language. Harold Allen, former NCTE president and professor emeritus at the University of Minnesota, was especially adamant against what he viewed as censorship. He successfully sponsored a policy that served as an amendment to the original policy on nonsexist language. The new policy stated that NCTE editors should obtain the permission of contributors before changing language they considered sexist.

As noble as this sounds, for most of the journals this was not a practical solution. Between 1981 and 1987, Ken Donelson and I co-edited the *English Journal* on what was basically a volunteer basis with a half-time secretary. There was no way we could communicate with authors about editorial changes. Early during our editorship, I checked the original and the edited manuscripts for a couple of issues chosen at random and discovered that in one-third of the published manuscripts we had made a change that in some way related to sexism.

To accommodate what came to be known as "Harold Allen's amendment" and still survive as volunteer editors and full-time faculty members while living up to our promise of making *English Journal* "a model of inconspicuous, but at the same time sex-fair language," we printed a boilerplate statement to the effect that we would abide by the NCTE *Guidelines for Nonsexist Use of Language in NCTE Publications,* and that anyone who objected to those guidelines should let us know when submitting an article. Out of the 3,000 submissions we handled during our seven years of editing, only one was accompanied by a note asking us not to change the pronouns to *he/she,* which the author considered an abomination. As editors, we quite agreed with her opinion and did whatever we could to avoid dual pronouns.

Today's NCTE journal editors do not seem to be as sensitive to the Harold Allen amendment as we were. The masthead for the most recent *College English* simply reads, "The editor reserves the right to edit essays so that their usage conforms with the *Guidelines for Nonsexist Use of Language in NCTE Publications,*" while on the *English Journal* "Call for Manuscripts" page, the editor has written, "Prospective contributors should obtain a copy of the National Council of Teachers of English *Guidelines for Nonsexist Use of Language in NCTE Publications* by writing to Don Robbins, NCTE, 1111 W. Kenyon Road, Urbana, IL 61801-1096."

The amendment, however, was one of the reasons the *Guidelines* were revised in 1985 and are currently being considered for a new update. They are printed as Appendix 14.1. Note the concluding four-paragraph discussion on the "Implementation of

Guidelines": It is mostly a defense of the role of editors and their right—and duty—to edit. But then in what sounds almost contradictory, the section ends with the statement, "In the case of language inconsistent with the guidelines, it is the editor's duty to question the author's use of a particular term; on the other hand, the author has the right to insist on its use, but a footnote will be provided to reflect such insistence." In fifteen years of reading NCTE journals and books since the Harold Allen directive was approved, I have never seen such a footnote.

Another difference between the original and the revised version of the *Guidelines* is that while the original was almost glib about the ease with which sexist language could be changed, the 1985 revision at least hints at the complexity of the matter by tackling the rewriting of a paragraph that includes references to "a Vassar-trained Miss Fidditch," "a cute and perky cheerleader type," and Somerset Maugham's declaration that "Good prose should resemble the conversation of a well-bred man."

Twenty-Five Years of Progress

As I look back on the past twenty-five years, I have mixed feelings about our success. The images that come to mind include a sweating Sisyphus pushing his rock up the hill only to have it roll down again, while in a nearby woods, I see the exhausted Alice being dragged along by the Red Queen and told that her efforts have only been adequate for staying in the same place: "If you want to get somewhere else, you must run at least twice as fast as that." And finally I think of the good news/bad news cliché, which is perhaps the most accurate way to describe the situation.

It is good news that over the last three decades several groups other than feminists came to realize the power of language in shaping how groups view themselves as well as how they are viewed by others, but it is bad news that so much attention was placed on various aspects of language that many speakers began to feel overwhelmed by all the proscriptions and dismissed the entire idea as "political correctness." Once the easy and startling observations had been made, the media grew tired of the issue. Thankfully, newspaper columnists and comedians have quit making up ridiculous words like *personhole covers* and *personhattan,* but unfortunately they have lumped sexism in with all the other -isms and joined in a general backlash. The negativity that has come to be associated with the term *political correctness* serves as a gathering point for those who are hostile to ideas of social reform, while it is falsely reassuring to less involved individuals who feel they can now relax because the term vindicates their niggling suspicion that things had gone too far.

In the 1970s, one of the key messages feminists tried to convey to the public was that as a culture we exaggerated or even created many of the supposed differences between males and females. Now in the 1990s, the pendulum is swinging the other way. Such linguists as George Lakoff are writing about the effects of embodiment on language perception; there is a surge of interest in Jungian psychology and in the work of Joseph Campbell about old archetypes which put males and females at opposite ends of various spectrums; and the bestselling books about gender are those that stress differences between males and females, such as Deborah Tannen's (1990) *You Just Don't Understand: Women and Men in Conversation* and John Gray's (1992) *Men Are from Mars; Women Are from Venus.* The worry is not that we have relapsed into the attitudes that were pervasive in the 1950s and 1960s, when general beliefs glorified male roles and denigrated female roles. But society does seem to be circling back around to the belief that males and females are inherently different—not better or worse—but different.

It is generally good news that in some areas, speakers made more dramatic changes than those of us preparing the NCTE *Guidelines* ever dreamed of. We apparently did not recognize the inconsistency between the titles of *Mr.* and *Mrs.,* where one shows marital status and one does not. *Ms.* came into the language with little help from us, but in the revised *Guidelines,* we acknowledge its existence with a reference to *Mr. Burger* and *Ms. O'Connor.* The *Guidelines* have also been silent on family naming patterns. Nevertheless, many women began to view the loss of their family name upon marriage as institutionalized sexism and so began working to provide themselves and others with the option of choosing whether or not to take their husband's surnames. In 1994 a survey reported in *American Demographics* magazine showed that 14 percent of married women under the age of forty had kept their birth surnames. The figure was 10 percent for women in their forties and 5 percent for women over fifty. The statistics were cited in the *Arizona Republic* by Karen DeWitt (1995), a *New York Times* reporter, who claimed the trend had already peaked. The stumbling block has been over what to name the children.

Probably the biggest good news/bad news aspect is the success we have had in convincing writers of the importance of inclusive language, juxtaposed against the fact that we are still working toward solutions, some of which have been abysmal failures. One of the least successful pieces of advice we gave, which thankfully is not in the 1985 revised version of the *Guidelines,* was to achieve inclusiveness by taking turns, sometimes referring to males and sometimes to females. My favorite example of a failure is this paragraph from a doctor who wrote a syndicated health care column. This paragraph was brought to one of our Arizona State University humor conferences by Betty Lou Dubois and Isabel M. Crouch, who found it printed in the *Albuquerque Journal* (February 19, 1976) under the title "Injuries to Head Need Prompt Aid":

> Following a head injury, have the patient lie down and remain completely quiet no matter how she feels. Have him do this even though he acts all right and insists that you leave her alone. Keep the patient flat on his back (or face down if he's vomiting) if her face is gray, blue, or pale.

Dr. Spock took turns, writing the first several editions of his famous *Baby and Child Care* book using masculine pronouns to refer to the baby, and then in the last edition, apologizing and changing to feminine throughout. The authors of one of the psychology textbooks used at Arizona State University alternates pronouns by chapters, but my students complain that such a use is misleading, and they cannot keep from thinking about gender in relation to the chapter's subject; for example, masculine pronouns were used exclusively in the chapter on juvenile delinquency and feminine pronouns throughout the chapter on adolescent emotions. The forced pronoun usage kept interfering with an accurate portrayal of the subjects.

Another unusual approach to taking turns was tried at the University of Ottawa in Canada where the collective bargaining agreement for 1990–93 had to be written in both French and English. This statement appeared in the *Bulletin of the Association of Professors*, May 1990:

Use of Gender in the Text of the Collective Agreement

By agreement of the University of Ottawa Administrative Committee and the APUO Executive Committee, the matter of gender will be handled as follows in the official text of the 1990–93 collective agreement. The English text will be written using the feminine gender throughout (except when dealing with paternity leave) and the French text will be written using the masculine gender throughout (except when dealing with maternity leave). The French version of the *note* presently appearing on page 4 of the agreement will remain unchanged while the English version will state that "a word used in the feminine gender shall include both genders."

On a more positive note, these unusual examples stand out because they are so different from most professional writing, in which inclusive language is used without attracting attention to itself. But counterbalancing my pleasure that many people have learned to be inconspicuously inclusive and sex-fair is the realization that people who are good at this have had to do it pretty much on their own, and I am not sure that students and the general public are motivated enough or able to learn such skills without help. Sadly, producers of textbooks and teaching materials are noticeably silent on the matter. While new texts—at least the ones I have seen—no longer teach the so-called generic *he*, they remain silent on most aspects of nonsexist language lest someone on a textbook selection committee should vote against the book because of tell-tale signs of "liberalism."

Where Do We Go from Here?

A logical question to ask is, where we go from here? In answering such a question, I must stress that all I am offering are my own opinions, and that after twenty-five years of seeing how futile some feminist efforts have been, I speak with due humility.

If we should revise the *Guidelines* again, the first change I would campaign for is to delete the term *nonsexist* from the title. A better title would be something like *Guidelines for Language That Is Fair to Both Sexes*. I dislike the term *nonsexist* because many people interpret it to mean we are advocating that speakers no longer distinguish between males and females. Some people may believe this is desirable or possible, but I am not one of them. All languages have ways to distinguish between references to males and females, and I seriously doubt that we could or even should try to change what is truly a language universal.

In preparation for the 1985 revision, I campaigned to replace *nonsexist* with *sex-fair*. I lost the argument when critics said the term would make readers think of a festivity in Denmark where pornography and leather bindings were sold. When the final version appeared in print, I was surprised to see a footnote appended to the first page reading, "Although *nonsexist* is the word traditionally used to describe such language, other terms have come into common use, namely, *gender-neutral, sex-fair, gender-free*." That my *sex-fair* was squeezed in between someone else's *gender-neutral* and *gender-free* showed that I had failed to get my point across. There is a big difference between rejecting the unfair "rule" that indefinite pronouns are singular and should be referenced with the "generic" *he* or *him*, and going to the extremes of advocating a gender-neutral or gender-free pronoun system, as illustrated by a letter I received from a man complaining about a Florida school publication which printed the following dialogue:

> "Who was E with?"
> "E was with Ir self."

The explanation for this usage was that because of a federal ban on language excluding one sex or the other, this particular school district had adopted *E* for *he/she* and *Ir* for *him/her*. I am suspicious that people who promote such nonsense are more interested in fueling the flames of ridicule against political correctness than in supporting feminist causes.

The second change I would campaign for in the title is to drop the prepositional phrase reading "in NCTE Publications."

When the *Guidelines* are cited, many people already leave it off because from the beginning it was a compromise. Those of us who originally campaigned for the *Guidelines* wanted to influence general language usage, not just NCTE style manuals; note this sentence from the original policy statement: "The National Council of Teachers of English should encourage the use of non-sexist language, particularly through its publications and periodicals." Putting a title on the *Guidelines* that in effect limits their applicability to NCTE publications can be viewed as both a mark of humility and evidence of political expediency. We quite rightly thought there would be fewer objections if we appeared to be looking after only our own shop, rather than setting out to change how the world talks. Nevertheless, anyone reading between the lines of the document and looking at the tone of the sample sentences and suggested revisions can see that much of the advice is aimed at student writers rather than at editors of NCTE's professional publications.

As to the actual *Guidelines*, I would make them more of a teaching tool. In addition to goodwill, using language that is fair to both sexes requires skill and training. If a national organization of English teachers will not provide guidance, who will?

The area that needs the most attention is that of pronoun choice. In 1984 I was so optimistic that I wrote an article for *College English* entitled "Winning the Great *He/She* Battle." Today I would be more likely to entitle such an article "Losing the Great *He/She* Battle" because the advice I gave, along with the examples I cited from *English Journal* manuscripts, was fine for formal writing overseen by two diligent editors, but it was too complicated for everyday use and speaking.

It is counterproductive for us to recommend practices that require extensive teaching or editorial supervision because new technologies and changing conditions are lessening the influence of both teachers and editors on the "niceties" of English.

♦ Writing teachers no longer go on error hunts. Instead, they encourage "process writing" in which teachers serve as background supporters and directors of prewriting, drafting, peer editing, conferencing, and finally publishing.

♦ Because so much communication is now by e-mail, which is hard to edit or rewrite, written messages are coming to resemble oral messages.

♦ Even at professional levels, where writers submit their books electronically as well as on paper, editors are tempted to send material on to the typesetter with only a quick read-through instead of the thorough going-over that used to be part of the production process.

♦ Today's students get much of their research material from the Internet, which contains materials that have not been professionally edited.

The easy accessibility of photocopy machines also has an influence. In my Methods of Teaching English course this past semester, we had a unit on personal names and went through the writing process, finishing off with a published booklet. One student who was absent on the days we did peer editing and conferencing brought her paper in when I was literally on the way to the photocopy shop. I slipped it into alphabetical order and "published" it without noticing this dreadful opening paragraph:

> I think we can all agree that a person's name and their identity go hand in hand. Can we also assume, then, that if a person intensely hates her/his name, it might severely damage how that person views his/her identity? Can we then further assume that if a child hates his/her name, it can ruin their childhood?

Writing like this deserves to be ridiculed for trying too hard. Besides its unwieldiness, the paragraph fails as communication mainly because the author was trying so hard to be nonsexist that both she as a writer and the class as readers could not concentrate on her message but instead focused on sorting out the pronouns. And in spite of her best efforts to be fair, even alternating between *her/his* and *his/her,* she slipped into what was obviously a more natural way to make her point in both her beginning and ending sentences, where she used *their* as a singular pronoun. I know this is blasphemy to purists, but can anyone honestly argue that her opening and closing units ("I think we can all agree that a person's name and their identity go hand in hand," and "[a child's hatred of a name] can ruin their childhood") are infinitely preferably to the gobbledygook in the middle?

If today we were as brave and as committed as we were twenty-five years ago when we first developed the *Guidelines for Nonsexist Language,* we would take a stand to say that English speakers often use *they* and *their* in a singular sense, especially when referring collectively to referents who may be either male or female. The present *Guidelines* give a gingerly approval to such a usage in relation to indefinite pronouns by writing as point 6 under "Generic *He* and *Him*": "When the subject is an indefinite pronoun, the plural form *their* can occasionally be used with it, especially when the referent for the pronoun is clearly understood to be plural." One sample sentence is given, "When everyone contributes their own ideas, the discussion will be a success," followed by the statement, "But since this usage is transitional, it is usually better to recast the sentence and avoid the indefinite pronoun." The sentence is then changed to: "When all the students contribute their own ideas. . . ."

This suggestion of changing the indefinite pronoun to "all the students" may work in carefully edited writing, but in effect we are asking people to remove from their vocabularies some very basic words: *anyone, anybody, someone, somebody, no one, none, nobody, everyone,* and *everybody.* If we are not asking speakers to remove these words from their vocabularies, then we are asking them to make several split-second decisions every time they use one of them:

◆ They must decide whether the underlying semantic reference is plural or singular.

◆ They must plan ahead to see whether they will need to refer back with a pronoun.

◆ If so, they must quickly choose a replacement word or phrase so that *they* or *their* can be used "legally."

All that most educated speakers can do is remember the first lesson that we have helped teach the world, which is that *he, him,* and *his* are indeed masculine rather than generic, and so as they look for something that will include female as well as male referents, they use *they* or *their.* Sensitive speakers would rather make a "mistake" with number reference than with gender. Also, today's speakers have learned about deep structure and surface structure, and they recognize that in most instances when we use indefinite pronouns, the deep structure is actually plural.

When we were in junior and senior high school, my generation was taught the prescriptive rule about indefinite pronouns requiring singular, so-called generic masculine pronouns. But many of today's college students—even English majors who are almost ready to graduate—are ignorant of the rule. And those who have heard of it have not internalized it. Even most of my generation did not internalize the rule. My seventh-grade teacher made us come to the chalkboard and write "single" in the midst of each indefinite pronoun. This was a good mnemonic device, but as twelve-year-olds we still knew that we were talking about thirty kids when the teacher had us write, "Every*single*body is supposed to pay his dollar by tomorrow."

Simply because this is a school-taught—rather than a naturally absorbed—rule, not everyone learns it, and so along with other things that are hard to acquire, it has snob appeal. It serves less as a tool of communication than as a shibboleth. Those of us who know the rule feel superior to those who do not. But in speech, the rule is broken so often that we usually do not even notice, especially if we like the individual. For example, when Ambassador Jeane Kirkpatrick was forced to change a vote she had cast at the United Nations because of conflicting advice from President Reagan and Secretary of State Alexander Haig, she responded to a question at a news conference with, "Of course I was embarrassed. Anyone would have been, wouldn't they?"

The press reported this without comment, but when President Clinton's former adviser Dick Morris said in relation to his $2.5 million book contract with Random House, "I believe that anyone who has had the unique opportunity to work closely with the president of the United States for a significant period of time should write their memoirs and share their experience with the public . . . ," *Los Angeles Times* columnist Paul Greenberg (1996) used Morris's use of "the plural *their* when referring back to the singular *anyone*" as evidence that "slovenly language is the surest sign of slovenly thought." This was his lead to a downer column about all the things wrong with today's political leadership.

I am no fonder of Dick Morris than is Paul Greenberg, but I disagree that Morris's use of *their* is evidence of slovenly language and thought. I think that as a skilled politician Morris purposely chose to use *they* in a grammatically singular (but deep-structure plural) sense to help women feel included as possible advisors to the president of the United States. *They* reveals careless or slovenly thinking only when it is used without an antecedent, as in complaints such as "They're raising taxes again!" and "They've decided to build a freeway through my dad's ranch."

Even in these two sentences, *they* indicates a kind of collective. It is like *whoever*, which depending on other references in the sentence can take either a singular or a plural pronoun, as in "Whoever left their cars in Parking Lot A . . ." or "Whoever left his car in Parking Lot A . . . ." *They* is also like *you*, which can be used when speaking to a single individual, as when on an elevator I might say to the person closest to the buttons, "Will you push '2' for me?" or to a whole nation, as when in his inaugural speech President Kennedy said, "Ask not what your country can do for you; ask what you can do for your country."

What I am proposing is that we become descriptive rather than prescriptive linguists and follow the lead of the general public in realizing that the easiest and most natural way to solve the "Great He/She Battle" is to simply acknowledge that speakers use *they* in a singular sense as well as a plural sense. Table 14.1 outlines the English pronoun system as speakers actually use it.

I am not underestimating the outcry that teaching such a paradigm will cause from language purists, but neither have I forgotten all the scoffing we got from those leaders in our profession who swore they would never be called a piece of furniture, but now comfortably answer to the title of *Chair*. Bringing about an acceptance among our colleagues will be harder than among the general public because fellow English teachers are the ones who as good students learned the unnatural rule about "generic" pronouns and have spent a lifetime tiptoeing through the intricacies that such a rule requires. It is hard to give up even such a small indication of our own superiority.

Our English department here at Arizona State University is currently revising its bylaws. When the sixty plus members met to go over the suggested changes, the first item brought up was that on page 3 the committee had committed a grammatical sin by writing:

> Every faculty member should determine the percentages of work time each year to represent appropriately their contributions to the Department. . . .

My comment that we all know that "every faculty member" is plural in concept and so *their* is perfectly acceptable was met with a chorus of "No, it isn't!" Of the afternoon's proceedings,

TABLE **14.1.** English Pronoun System as Pronounced by Speakers in Everyday Use

SINGULAR			
	Nominative	Accusative	Possessive Possessive-Substantive

	Nominative	Accusative	Possessive	Possessive-Substantive
1st person	I	me	my	mine
2nd person	you	you	your	yours
3rd person	he	him	his	his
	she	her	her	hers
	they	them	their	theirs
	*it	it	its	its

*Note that *it* represents lack of gender (i.e., nonhuman), which is why speakers feel uncomfortable in using *it* as a nongendered pronoun to refer to people.

PLURAL			
	Nominative	Accusative	Possessive	Possessive-Substantive
1st person	we	us	our	ours
2nd person	you	you	your	yours
3rd person	they	them	their	theirs

changing the sentence to read "All faculty members . . ." instead of "Every faculty member . . ." was the only item on which the department came to consensus.

In contrast to this experience, ever since I was asked to write this essay, I have been pondering and talking about the matter so much that both my husband, linguistics professor Don L. F. Nilsen, and I have been watching for pronoun references in our reading. Don is writing a research guide on humor in British literature and I am gathering a collection of essays for a college language reader. Outside of academic (what some people would call "stuffy") journals, we have run across virtually no writers who make use of the double *he/she* pronoun pattern, but we have seen several instances of *they* used in a singular sense. This inspired Don to offer the candid advice that if I want to take credit for this language change, I had better get this essay published fast because the change is coming regardless of what we English teachers decide to do.

I guess he was saying that we can choose to stand in opposition to the people's choice of how best to solve the problem that we brought to their attention, or we can turn around and do what we did twenty-five years ago when we felt inspired to get in front and play a leadership role. I, for one, choose the latter approach, and when I grade a set of papers I will no longer waste red ink on arguing with students over whether *they* and *their* are singular or plural. I will write letters to people whose reasoning resembles that of Paul Greenberg's, and I will recognize such sentences as

> Anybody born before 1970 needs to bring their proof of vaccination.
>
> Every faculty member should select their preferred method of evaluation.
>
> Anyone would have been embarrassed, wouldn't they?

as gracious and natural solutions to a language problem that we professionals could describe but could not solve. I will save my red pen for stilted uses of *he/she*, *hers/his*, and *s/he*.

Appendix 14.1

Guidelines for Nonsexist Use of Language in NCTE Publications (Revised, 1985)

Introduction

During the 1971 Annual Convention of the National Council of Teachers of English in Las Vegas, Nevada, the Executive Committee and the Board of Directors approved the formation of an NCTE Committee on the Role and Image of Women in the Council and the Profession. As the result of a resolution passed by the members of NCTE at the 1974 Annual Convention, one of the committee's responsibilities was to assist in setting guidelines for nonsexist* use of language in NCTE publications.

Suggestions were elicited from editors of Council journals and from professional staff members at NCTE, as well as from members of the Women's Committee. Copies of the guidelines also went to all members of the Board of Directors. At the 1975 Annual Convention, the Board of Directors adopted a formal policy statement that read in part: "The National Council of Teachers of English should encourage the use of nonsexist language, particularly through its publications and periodicals."

Ten years have passed since these guidelines were created, and although language usage has begun to change, the importance of the guidelines has not diminished. Because language plays a central role in the way human beings think and behave, we still need to promote language that opens rather than closes possibilities for women and men. Whether teaching in the classroom, assigning texts, determining curriculum, serving on national committees, or writing in professional publications, NCTE members directly and indirectly influence thought and behavior.

As an educational publisher, NCTE is not alone in its concern for fair treatment of men and women. The role of education is to make choices available, not to limit opportunities. Censorship removes possibilities; these guidelines extend what is available by offering alternatives to traditional usages and to editorial choices that restrict meaning.

Language

This section deals primarily with word choice. Many of the examples are matters of vocabulary; a few are matters of grammatical choice. The vocabulary items are relatively easy to deal with, since the English lexicon has a history of rapid change. Grammar is a more difficult area, and we have chosen to use alternatives that already exist in the language rather than to invent new constructions. In both cases, recommended alternatives have been determined by what is graceful and unobtrusive. The purpose of these changes is to suggest alternative styles.

---

*Although *nonsexist* is the word traditionally used to describe such language, other terms have come into common use, namely, *gender neutral, sex-fair, gender-free.*

Generic "Man"

1. Since the word *man* has come to refer almost exclusively to adult males, it is sometimes difficult to recognize its generic meaning.

Problems	*Alternatives*
mankind	humanity, human beings, people*
man's achievements	human achievements
the best man for the job	the best person for the job
the common man	the average person, ordinary people
cavemen	cave dwellers, prehistoric people

2. Sometimes the combining form *-woman* is used alongside *-man* in occupational terms and job titles, but we prefer using the same titles for men and women when naming jobs that could be held by both. Note, too, that using the same forms for men and women is a way to avoid using the combining form *-person* as a substitute for *-woman* only.

Problems	*Alternatives*
chairman/chairwoman	chair, coordinator (of a committee or department), moderator (of a meeting), presiding officer, head, chairperson
businessman/businesswoman	business executive, manager
congressman/congresswoman	congressional representative
policeman/policewoman	police officer
salesman/saleswoman	sales clerk, sales representative, salesperson
fireman	fire fighter
mailman	letter carrier

Generic "He" and "His"

Because there is no one pronoun in English that can be effectively substituted for *he* or *his,* we offer several alternatives. The form *he or she* has been the NCTE house style over the last ten years, on the premise that it is less distracting then *she or he* or *he/she.* There are other choices, however. The one you make will depend on what you are writing.

1. Sometimes it is possible to drop the possessive form *his* altogether or to substitute an article.

Problems	*Alternatives*
The average student is worried about his grades.	The average student is worried about grades.
When the student hands in his paper, read it immediately.	When the student hands in the paper, read it immediately.

2. Often, it makes sense to use the plural instead of the singular.

Problems	*Alternatives*
Give the student his grade right away.	Give the students their grades right away.
Ask the student to hand in his work as soon as he is finished.	Ask students to hand in their work as soon as they are finished.

*A one-word substitution for *mankind* isn't always possible, especially in set phrases like *the story of mankind.* Sometimes recasting the sentence altogether may be the best solution.

3. The first or second person can sometimes be substituted for the third person.

Problems	*Alternatives*
As a teacher, he is faced daily with the problem of paperwork.	As teachers, we are faced daily with the problem of paperwork.
When a teacher asks his students for an evaluation, he is putting himself on the spot.	When you ask your students for an evaluation, you are putting yourself on the spot.

4. In some situations, the pronoun *one (one's)* can be substituted for *he (his)*, but it should be used sparingly. Notice that the use of *one*—like the use of *we* or *you*—changes the tone of what you are writing.

Problem	*Alternative*
He might well wonder what his response should be.	One might well wonder what one's response should be.

5. A sentence with *he* or *his* can sometimes be recast in the passive voice or another impersonal construction.

Problems	*Alternatives*
Each student should hand in his paper promptly.	Papers should be handed in promptly.
He found such an idea intolerable.	Such an idea was intolerable.

6. When the subject is an indefinite pronoun, the plural form *their* can occasionally be used with it, especially when the referent for the pronoun is clearly understood to be plural.

Problem	*Alternative*
When everyone contributes his own ideas, the discussion will be a success.	When everyone contributes their own ideas, the discussion will be a success.

But since this usage is transitional, it is usually better to recast the sentence and avoid the indefinite pronoun.

Problem	*Alternative*
When everyone contributes his own ideas, the discussion will be a success.	When all the students contribute their own ideas, the discussion will be a success.

7. Finally, sparing use can be made of *he or she* and *his or her.* It is best to restrict this choice to contexts in which the pronouns are not repeated.

Problems	*Alternatives*
Each student will do better if he has a voice in the decision.	Each student will do better if he or she has a voice in the decision.
Each student can select his own topic.	Each student can select his or her own topic.

Sex-Role Stereotyping

Word choices sometimes reflect unfortunate and unconscious assumptions about sex roles—for example, that farmers are always men and elementary school teachers are always women; that men are valued for their accomplishments and women for their physical attributes; or that men are strong and brave while women are weak and timid. We need to examine the assumptions inherent in certain stock phrases and choose nonstereotyped alternatives.

1. Identify men and women in the same way. Diminutive or special forms to name women are usually unnecessary. In most cases, generic terms such as *doctor* or *actor* should be assumed to include both men and women. Only occasionally are alternate forms needed, and in these cases, the alternate form replaces both the masculine and the feminine titles.

Problems	*Alternatives*
stewardess	flight attendant (for both *steward* and *stewardess*)
authoress	author
waitress	server, food server
poetess	poet
coed	student
lady lawyer	lawyer . . . she
male nurse	nurse . . . he

2. Do not represent women as occupying only certain jobs or roles and men as occupying only certain others.

Problems	*Alternatives*
the kindergarten teacher . . . she	*occasionally use* the kindergarten teacher . . . he *or* kindergarten teachers . . . they
the principal . . . he	*occasionally use* the principal. . . she *or* principals . . . they
Have your mother send a snack for the party.	Have a parent send a snack for the party. *occasionally use* Have your father . . . *or* Have your parents. . . .
NCTE conventiongoers and their wives are invited.	NCTE conventiongoers and their spouses are invited.
Writers become so involved in their work that they neglect their wives and children.	Writers become so involved in their work that they neglect their families.

3. Treat men and women in a parallel manner.

Problems	*Alternatives*
The class interviewed Chief Justice Burger and Mrs. O'Connor.	The class interviewed Warren Burger and Sandra O'Connor. *or* . . . Mr. Burger and Ms. O'Connor. *or* . . . Chief Justice Burger and Justice O'Connor.
The reading list included Proust, Joyce, Gide, and Virginia Woolf.	The reading list included Proust, Joyce, Gide, and Woolf. *or.* . . Marcel Proust, James Joyce, André Gide, and Virginia Woolf.
Both Bill Smith, a straight-A sophomore, and Kathy Ryan, a pert junior, won writing awards.	Both sophomore Bill Smith, a straight-A student, and junior Kathy Ryan, editor of the school paper, won writing awards.

4. Seek alternatives to language that patronizes or trivializes women, as well as to language that reinforces stereotyped images of both women and men.

Problems	*Alternatives*
The president of the company hired a gal Friday.	The president of the company hired an assistant.
I'll have my girl do it.	I'll ask my secretary to do it.
Stella is a career woman.	Stella is a professional. *Or* Stella is a doctor (architect, etc.).
The ladies on the committee all supported the bill.	The women on the committee all supported the bill.
Pam had lunch with the girls from the office.	Pam had lunch with the women from the office.
This is a man-sized job.	This is a big (huge, enormous) job.
That's just an old wives' tale.	That's just a superstition (superstitious story).
Don't be such an old lady.	Don't be so fussy.

Sexist Language in a Direct Quotation

Quotations cannot be altered, but there are other ways of dealing with this problem.

1. Avoid the quotation altogether if it is not really necessary.

2. Paraphrase the quotation, giving the original author credit for the idea.

3. If the quotation is fairly short, recast it as an indirect quotation, substituting nonsexist words as necessary.

Problem	*Alternative*
Among the questions asked by the school representatives was the following: "Considering the ideal college graduate, what degree of knowledge would you prefer him to have in each of the curricular areas?"	Among the questions asked by the school representatives was one about what degree of knowledge the ideal college graduate should have in each of the curricular areas.

Sample Revised Passage

Substantial revisions or deletions are sometimes necessary when problems overlap or when stereotyped assumptions about men and women so pervade a passage that simple replacement of words is inadequate.

Problem	*Alternative*
Each student who entered the classroom to find himself at the mercy of an elitist, Vassar-trained Miss Fidditch could tell right away that the semester would be a trial. The trend in composition pedagogy toward student-centered essays and away from hours of drill on	The trend in composition pedagogy toward student-centered essays, represented by such writers as Ken Macrorie, Peter Elbow, and Janet Emig, has meant that some students are finally learning to write. Yet the movement away from hours of drill on grammatical correctness has brought with it a new problem: in the hands of the

grammatical correctness has meant, at least for him, that he can finally learn to write. But Macrorie, Elbow, and Janet Emig could drive the exasperated teacher of a cute and perky cheerleader type to embrace the impersonal truth of *whom* as direct object rather than fight his way against the undertow of a gush of personal experience. As Somerset Maugham remarked, "Good prose should resemble the conversation of a well-bred man," and both Miss Fidditch and the bearded guru who wants to "get inside your head" must realize it.

inexperienced teacher, student essays can remain little more than unedited piles of personal experiences and emotions.

Representation of Men and Women

Important as language is, striving for nonsexist usage is to little purpose if the underlying assumptions about men and women continue to restrict them to traditional roles. If women never enter an author's world, for example, it little avails a writer or editor to refer scrupulously to students as "they" and prehistoric people as "cave dwellers." Thus, teachers and other professionals must be alert to the possible sexist implications of the content as well as the language of educational materials.

It has been enheartening to note that in the last ten years, trade publishers, textbook publishers, and publishers of reference works have become acutely aware of sexist language, thus largely alleviating the problem of discriminatory reference. Still, vigilance must be exercised.

The following recommendations concerning educational materials are made to correct traditional omissions of women or perpetuations of stereotypes.

Booklists

1. Items for a booklist should be chosen to emphasize the equality of men and women and to show them in nontraditional as well as traditional roles. Many children's favorites and classics may contain sexist elements, but books that are valuable for other reasons should not be excluded. The annotations, however, should be written in nonsexist language.

2. Picture books should be chosen showing males and females actively participating in a variety of situations at home, work, and play.

3. Booklists should be organized by subject headings that do not assume stereotyped male and female interests.

Problems	*Alternatives*
Books for Boys	Arts and Crafts
Books for Girls	Sports
	Travel

Teaching Units

1. The topic and organization of teaching units should be carefully considered to avoid sexist implications. Literature by and about both women and men should be included wherever possible.

2. When materials are chosen that present stereotyped assumptions about men and women, they should be balanced by others that show nontraditional roles and assumptions. *Jemima Puddle-Duck* and *Peter Rabbit* read together, for instance, show foolishness is not a sex-linked characteristic. Vera Brittain's *A Testament of Youth* and Ernest Hemingway's *The Sun Also Rises* present the aftermath of World War I from provocative perspectives. Placing a book in the proper historical context and using discussion questions that reflect an awareness of the sexist elements are good strategies.

3. Activities suggested in teaching units should not be segregated by sex: boys can make costumes and girls can build sets.

Reference Books and Research Materials

Reference books can be implicitly sexist in their titles, organizations, content, and language. Editors of such books should follow the suggestions in this publication to ensure nonsexist language in bibliographies, indexes, style manuals, and teacher's guides. In research works, if both males and females were studied, references to individual subjects should not assume that they are all one sex.

Implementation of Guidelines

These guidelines for nonsexist language are suggestions for teachers, writers, and contributors to NCTE publications. For the editors of NCTE publications, however, they are a statement of editorial policy.

Traditionally, editors have set the style for their publications—deciding, for example, whether there should be a comma before the conjunction in a series or whether the first item in a list after a colon should begin with a capital letter. Style decisions have sometimes been made in response to public pressure. Writing *Negro* with a capital letter instead of a lowercase letter and, later, using *Black* instead of *Negro* were both style decisions of this sort for many publishing houses, newspapers, and magazines.

It is an editor's job to rewrite whenever necessary to eliminate awkward language, inconsistency, or inaccuracy. If a job title is inaccurately identified in an article as Director of Public Instruction but the title is actually Supervisor of Public Instruction, the editor changes the wording as a matter of course and without asking the author's approval. If the subject matter or tone of an article is totally inappropriate for the particular publication, it would also be the editor's prerogative to return the manuscript to the author. In the case of language inconsistent with the guidelines, it is the editor's duty to question the author's use of a particular term; on the other hand, the author has the right to insist on its use, but a footnote will be provided to reflect such insistence.

The choices suggested in these guidelines are intended as additions to the style sheets and manuals already in use.

References

Authors and editors who would like to see further suggestions for creating a graceful, nondiscriminatory writing style should refer to these publications. (Note that many of the publishers' guidelines are in the process of being revised.)

American Psychological Association Task Force on Issues of Sexual Bias in Graduate Education. "Guidelines for Nonsexist Use of Language." *American Psychologist* 30 (June 1975): 682–84.

Editorial and Art Content Criteria for Treatment of Minorities and Women. Lexington: Ginn and Company. (Available from the publisher, 191 Spring Street, Lexington, MA 02173.)

Fairness in Educational Materials: Exploring the Issues. Chicago: Science Research Associates, Inc. (Available from the publisher, 155 North Wacker Drive, Chicago, IL 60606.)

Guidelines for Bias-Free Publishing. New York: McGraw-Hill Book Company. (Available from the publisher's distribution center, Princeton Road, Hightstown, NJ 08520.)

Guidelines for Creating Positive Sexual and Racial Images in Educational Materials. New York: Macmillan Publishing Company, 1975. (Available in limited quantities from the publisher, 866 Third Avenue, New York, NY 10022.)

Guidelines for Developing Bias-Free Instructional Materials. Morristown: Silver Burdett Company, 1979. (Available from the publisher, 250 James Street, Morristown, NJ 07960.)

Guidelines for the Development of Elementary and Secondary Instructional Materials. New York: Holt, Rinehart and Winston School Department, 1975. (Available from the publisher, 383 Madison Avenue, New York, NY 10017.)

Miller, Casey, and Kate Swift. *The Handbook of Nonsexist Writing: For Writers, Editors and Speakers.* New York: Barnes and Noble Books, 1980. (Available from Harper and Row, 10 East 53rd Street, New York, NY 10022.)

Nilsen, Alleen Pace. "Editing for Sex." *Idaho English Journal* 6 (Spring 1983): 12+.

———. "Winning the Great *He/She* Battle." *College English* 46 (February 1984): 151.

Statement on Bias-Free Materials. New York: Association of American Publishers. (Available from AAP, One Park Avenue, New York, NY 10016.)

Note

Copies of *Guidelines for Nonsexist Use of Language in NCTE Publications* are available from NCTE, 1111 W. Kenyon Road, Urbana, IL 61801-1096. Ask for Stock No. 19719-012.

References

Bayer, A. (1970, August 7). A women's lib exposé of male villainy. *Life*, *69(6)*, 62A–62B.

de Beauvoir, S. (1953). *The second sex*. New York: Knopf.

DeWitt, K. (1995, June 10). Stand-by-your-man "Mrs." makes a comeback. *The Arizona Republic*, pp. 1.

Friedan, B. (1963). *The feminine mystique*. New York: Norton.

Gray, J. (1992). *Men are from Mars, Women are from Venus: A practical guide for improving communication and getting what you want in your relationships*. New York: HarperCollins.

Greenberg, P. (1996, October 29). Victory belongs to Dick Morris—for now. *The Arizona Republic*, p. B7.

Greer, G. (1971). *The female eunuch*. New York: McGraw-Hill.

Lakoff, G. (1987). *Women, fire and dangerous things: What categories reveal about the mind*. Chicago: University of Chicago Press.

Lakoff, R. (1974, July). You are what you say. *Ms*, 65–67.

Lakoff, R. (1975). *Language and woman's place*. New York: Harper & Row.

McAllester, S. (Ed.). (1971). *A case for equity: Women in English departments*. Urbana, IL: National Council of Teachers of English.

Miller, C., & Swift, K. (1992). In G. Goshgarian (Ed.), *Exploring language* (pp. 218–228). New York: HarperCollins.

Miller, C., & Swift, K. (1976). *Words and women: New language in new times*. Garden City, NY: Anchor Press.

Nilsen, A. P. (1984). Winning the great "he"/"she" battle. *College English* 46, 151–57.

Nilsen, A. P., Bosmajian, H., Gershuny, H. L., & Stanley, J. P. (1977). *Sexism and language.* Urbana, IL: National Council of Teachers of English.

Penelope, J. (1990). *Speaking freely: Unlearning the lies of the fathers' tongues.* New York: Pergamon Press.

Penfield, J. (1987). *Women and language in transition.* Albany, NY: SUNY Press.

Tannen, D. (1990). *You just don't understand: Women and men in conversation.* New York: Morrow.

CHAPTER FIFTEEN

"Students' Right to Their Own Language": A Retrospective

GENEVA SMITHERMAN
Michigan State University

We affirm the students' right to their own patterns and varieties of language—the dialects of their nurture or whatever dialects in which they find their own identity and style. Language scholars long ago denied that the myth of a standard American dialect has any validity. The claim that any one dialect is unacceptable amounts to an attempt of one social group to exert its dominance over another. Such a claim leads to false advice for speakers and writers, and immoral advice for humans. A nation proud of its diverse heritage and its cultural and racial variety will preserve its heritage of dialects. We affirm strongly that teachers must have the experiences and training that will enable them to respect diversity and uphold the right of students to their own language.

Passed by the Executive Committee of the Conference on College Composition and Communication (CCCC), November, 1972, and by the CCCC Membership, April, 1974

It has now been well over a generation since Kwame Ture (then Stokely Carmichael) issued his clarion call for "Black Power" and thus charted a new course for the civil rights movement in America.[1] But his cry, horrendous and frightening as it seemed to some in 1966, was not without precedent in the annals of the African American struggle. For just twelve years earlier, Richard Wright had entitled his book on the emerging independence movements in Africa *Black Power*. And surely Rosa Parks's historic

---

A nearly identical version of this essay was published in 1995 under the same title in *English Journal* 84(1), pp. 21–27.

refusal to give up her seat to Whites and move to the back of the bus on December 1, 1955, paved the way for Kwame Ture's Black Power—a bold call for new directions and strategies. These actions and events from the Black Experience symbolize the motive forces that led to the unleashing of Brown Power, Woman Power, Poor People's Power, Gay Power, and other human energy sources that fundamentally altered American power relations in our time.

The Historical Backdrop

As marching, fist raising, loud talking, and other forms of resistance marred the landscape of "America the beautiful," the power elites huddled to design reforms to acculturate the oppressed into the dominant ideology. The Unhip among researchers, scholars, and intellectuals assembled the database upon which these reforms were built, arguing, for instance, that even though the linguistic-cultural differences of those oppressed by race, class, or gender were *cognitively* equal to those of the mainstream, they were *socially* unequal. Early on, some scholars—like James Sledd in his 1969 *English Journal* article "Bi-Dialectalism: The Linguistics of White Supremacy," and me in my 1968 "Black Power Is Black Language" (delivered in April 1969 in Miami at my first CCCC Convention)—early on, such scholars tried to pull our coats (to enlighten) to the trickeration (deception) of the power brokers. They argued that it was purely academic to demonstrate, in Emersonian, armchair philosophizing style, the legitimacy of the oppressed's language and culture without concomitantly struggling for institutional legitimacy in the educational and public domains. If the patriarchally constituted social and economic structure would not accept nonmainstream speech varieties, then the argument for *difference* would simply become *deficiency* all over again.

Against this backdrop, enlightened academics saw their task clearly to struggle for such legitimacy. They were not romantic idealists; indeed, many of them had been baptized in the fire of social protest and street activism. No, not idealists, but those who know that without vision, people will perish. These progressive academics began working within their professional societies and organizations to bring about mainstream recognition and legitimacy to the culture, history, and language of those on the margins. And it was not only within NCTE and CCCC that this struggle was waged, but all across the alphabetic spectrum— the APA (American Psychological Association); the ASA (American Sociological Association); the MLA (Modern Language Association); the SCA (Speech Communication Association); the ABA (American Bar Association); the ASHA (American Speech and Hearing Association); and on and on across disciplines and throughout the Academy. Though the struggles were spearheaded by Blacks, it quickly became a rainbow coalition as Hispanics, women, Native Americans, and other marginalized groups sought redress for their ages-old grievances against an exploitative system.

Let us recall that the Cause was just if the methods awkward. The Enlightened were, after all, attempting to effectuate change *within the system*. And even those of us who were more revolutionarily inclined recognized the folly of doing nothing while waiting for the Revolution to come.

The Birth of "Students' Right"

In this sociohistorical climate in the fall of 1971, the officers of CCCC appointed a committee to draft a policy resolution on students' dialects, and thus the first Committee on Students' Right to Their Own Language was born. After months of intense scholarly work and political struggle, both within and outside our committee, in March 1972 we presented the CCCC Executive Committee (of which I was also a member at the time) with the position statement which has come to be known as the "Students' Right to Their Own Language." When I say "intense struggle," it is not dramatic hyperbole; for instance, we debated for hours the question of the student's right to *his* own language versus *his or her* own language: remember, this was over twenty years ago.

In November 1972, the CCCC Executive Committee passed the "Students' Right" resolution and began to pave the way to make this admittedly controversial resolution a matter of CCCC policy. They recognized that their membership, as well as other language arts professionals, would need to be educated about the current research on language variation, usage, and the history of American English. A committee was appointed to develop a background document that would elaborate on the assertions in the brief "Students' Right" statement before presenting the resolution to the full body of CCCC and eventually to the profession at large. The background document was presented to the CCCC Executive Committee at the Philadelphia NCTE Convention in November 1973. Subsequently, this document and the resolution itself were distributed to CCCC membership.

In April of 1974, at the CCCC business meeting in Anaheim, California, the "Students' Right to Their Own Language" became the official policy of CCCC. That fall, the complete background document was published as a full issue of CCCC's journal, *College Composition and Communication*. The "Students' Right" resolution appears on the inside cover of that issue. The document seeks to inform by presenting a set of fifteen issues, in the form of questions, about language, dialect, and teaching learning—e.g., "Does dialect affect the ability to write?"; "Why do some dialects have more prestige than others?" Included also is a bibliography of 129 entries keyed to these fifteen questions (CCC, 1974).

NCTE's Response to "Students' Right"

Although CCCC is politically autonomous, structurally it is an institutional arm of NCTE, sharing with NCTE some resources, headquarters, and, of course, concern for language education. Further, many CCCC members, myself included, are members and workers of both organizations. In 1971, after the formation of what was to become the Committee on Students' Right to Their Own Language, CCCC leadership and its members began working within NCTE to promote the concept of the students' right to their own language. For the next three years, there was a concerted effort by CCCC to persuade NCTE to endorse the CCCC position statement. However, this did not occur. Instead, at its 1974 Annual Convention, NCTE passed a weaker version of the CCCC's "Students' Right to Their Own Language." Although many of us on the Students' Right Committee and within CCCC were profoundly disappointed, we consoled ourselves by the thought that the action taken by NCTE was at least not a *negative* vote on the issue.

There are two crucial differences between the CCCC and the NCTE actions regarding "Students' Right to Their Own Language." First, the NCTE resolution distinguishes between spoken and written language in relationship to students' dialects, and although it "accept(s) the linguistic premise that all these dialects are equally efficient as systems of communication," the resolution goes on to "affirm" that students should learn the "conventions of what has been called written edited American English" (NCTE, 1974). This was an issue that the CCCC Students' Right Committee struggled with and deliberately decided *not* to focus on. We recognized that spelling, punctuation, usage, and other surface structure conventions of Edited American English (EAE) are generally what's given all the play (attention) in composition classrooms anyway. Based on the groundbreaking linguistic research of scholars such as Chomsky (e.g., 1968), Labov (e.g., 1970, 1972), Halliday (e.g., 1973) Hymes (e.g., 1964, 1972), Dillard (e.g., 1972), Shuy (e.g., 1965, 1967), and Fishman (e.g., 1970), the CCCC background publication contends that:

> dialect . . . plays little if any part in determining whether a child will ultimately acquire the ability to write EAE. . . . Since the issue is not the capacity of the dialect itself, the teacher can concentrate on building up the students' confidence in their ability to write. . . . [T]he essential functions of writing [are] expressing oneself, communicating information and attitudes, and discovering meaning through both logic and metaphor . . . [thus] we view variety of dialects as an advantage. . . . [O]ne may choose roles which imply certain dialects, but the decision is a social one, for the dialect itself does not limit the information which can be carried, and the attitudes may be most clearly conveyed in the dialect the writer finds most congenial. . . . [Finally,] the most serious difficulty facing "non-standard" dialect speakers in developing writing ability derives from their exaggerated concern for the *least* serious aspects of writing. If we can convince our students that spelling, punctuation, and usage are less important than content, we have removed a major obstacle in their developing the ability to write. (1974, p. 8)

The second crucial difference between NCTE's and CCCC's treatments of the "Students' Right" issue is that CCCC committed tremendous time and energy resources to the illumination of this language issue. For several years after the passage of the position statement by the 1972 CCCC Executive Committee, CCCC committees worked to produce two documents (although one was never published) to provide guidance to teachers on the meaning and implications of the "Students' Right" position and the impact of this policy on classroom practice.

Although NCTE did not come on board with the full vigor we in CCCC would have liked, it did agree in its version of the "Students' Right" resolution to make available to other professional organizations the suggestions and recommendations in the CCCC background document and to

> promote classroom practices to expose students to the variety of dialects that occur in our multi-regional, multi-ethnic, and multi-cultural society, so that they too will understand the nature of American English and come to respect all its dialects. (NCTE, 1974)

Implementation of "Students' Right"

After the NCTE action, CCCC moved into the next phase of the "Students' Right" history. To be sure, there was high interest and enthusiasm, but unfortunately there was also lingering confusion—you know, "Well, what they want me to do?" Although the CCCC background document was informative in terms of theory, it did not go far enough in praxis. CCCC leadership acknowledged that there was a need for more explicit teaching materials, sample lesson plans, and a more specific pedagogy. The Executive Committee thus appointed the Selection and Editorial Committee for Activities Supporting Students' Right to Their Own Language, on which I also served.

This committee was charged with assembling a publication of practical classroom assignments, activities, lectures, and teaching units that would show and tell how to apply the philosophy of the "Students' Right" resolution to the day-to-day experience of teaching and learning. Many of the people who served on this committee, as on the other Students' Right Committee, are well-known and active members of the profession. We spent nearly four years compiling and editing some excellent material, solicited from practitioners at all levels of education, only to be informed that CCCC had "reluctantly decided" not to publish the collection.

What had happened since the passage of the original "Students' Right" resolution some years earlier was that the nation was moving to a more conservative climate on the social, political, and educational fronts. It was a move which would be solidified in 1980 by the election of President Ronald Reagan. Thus the mood of CCCC, as the mood of America, had shifted from change and promise to stagnation and dreams deferred.

Product and Process of "Students' Right"

We have overviewed the process; now let us look at the product in relationship to this process.

Even though earlier I generously labeled our group "progressive," we were not all of like mind about the "Students' Right" resolution, nor its implications. And we certainly were not of identical persuasion on the issue of America's linguistic ills and solutions to them. Hey, some of us even had reservations about the use of little four-letter words—not dem big, bad foe letter ones, with initial fricatives and sibilants; just the little ti-notchy ones like *damn* and *hell*. (Apropos of this, I do hereby confess to being the first to introduce "cussing" into committee deliberations, to the distinct relief of my old comrade, Ross Winterowd, of the University of Southern California.) Yet despite our diverse ideologies and political perspectives, we shared a spirit of collective enlightenment on the language question.

The "Students' Right" background document is a compromise publication, born of the contradictions among radicals, moderates, and conservatives. It is, moreover, the consequence of the talented editorial hand of Richard (Jix) Lloyd-Jones from the University of Iowa and of the skillful diplomacy of late linguist Melvin Butler of Southern University, our committee chair, whose tragic, untimely death prevented him from witnessing the fruits of his labor. For some of us, then as now, the document is seen as equivocating; it doesn't go far enough. For others, then as now, it is perceived as too permissive.

Yet, short of totalitarianism and fascism on the one hand, or armed revolutionary struggle on the other, compromise is what comes from working *within* the system. And so those of us who embrace the dialectical vision of history applaud the recently renewed momentum and interest in the "Students' Right to Their Own Language," for without struggle, there is no progress.

As should be obvious to all writing teachers worth their training, the *Students' Right* document is the product of multiple writing styles. After deciding to use the admittedly wack (corny) twenty-question format of the once-popular television quiz show, we divvied up the work and the writing. Although we critiqued each other's writing, and despite the admirably awesome editing job done by Melvin and later Jix, still it must be conceded that the document is stylistically uneven. Yet the final product is preferable to what any *one* individual might have written because it reflects a *collective* response to the language question: "What should the schools do about the language habits of students who come from a wide variety of social, economic, and cultural backgrounds?" (CCC, 1974, p. 1).

African Americans weren't the only "submerged minorities" (a term we wrestled with in committee deliberations), forcing the question, as the "Students' Right" framed it, "Should the schools try to uphold language variety, or to modify it, or to eradicate it?" Yet a good deal of the background document (i.e., examples, illustrations, bibliographic references, etc.) focuses on *Black* speech. This is logical given not only the large numbers of African Americans among the oppressed, but also given that Blacks were the first to force the moral and constitutional questions of equality in this country. Further, of all underclass groups in the United States, Blacks are pioneers in social protest and have waged the longest politically principled struggle against exploitation.

Finally—and this is an ironic footnote in American life— whenever Blacks have struggled and won social gains for themselves, they have made possible gains for other groups—e.g.,

Hispanics, Asians, gays, etc., even some White folks! For instance, the nineteenth-century emancipation of African slaves in this country paved the way for the first Women's Movement, during which, in fact, Black champions for the abolition of slavery, Frederick Douglass and Sojourner Truth, for example, fought vigorously for women's rights. In similar fashion, then, *Black* students' right to *their* own language has made possible *all* students' right to their own language.

The Need to Recognize Students' Language and Culture

Let me remind you that those who do not learn from the past are doomed to repeat it. In spite of recently reported gains in Black student writing, chronicled by the NAEP, and higher scores on the SAT, the rate of functional illiteracy and dropouts among America's underclass is moving faster than the Concorde. A genuine recognition of such students' culture and language is desperately needed if we as a profession are to play some part in stemming this national trend. I write "genuine" because, in spite of the controversy surrounding policies like the "Students' Right to Their Own Language," the bicultural, bilingual model has *never* really been tried. Lip service is about all most teachers gave it, even at the height of the social upheaval described earlier. You see, the game plan has always been linguistic and cultural absorption of the Other into the dominant culture and indoctrination of the outsiders into the existing value system (e.g., Sledd, 1972) to remake those on the margins in the image of the patriarch, to reshape the outsiders into talking, acting, thinking, and (to the extent possible) looking like the insiders (e.g., Smitherman, 1973). In bilingual education and among multilingual scholars and activists, this issue is framed as one of language *shift* versus language *maintenance* (see Fishman 1966, 1983): that is, the philosophy of using the native language as a vehicle to teach and eventually *shift* native speakers *away from their home language* versus a social and pedagogical model that teaches the target language—in this country, English—while providing support for *maintaining the home language*—Spanish, Polish, Black English, etc. All along, despite a policy like the "Students' Right," the system has just been perping—engaging in fraudulent action.

I am a veteran of the language wars, dating to my undergraduate years when I was victimized by a biased speech test given to all those who wanted to qualify for a teaching certificate. I flunked the test and had to take speech correction, not because of any actual speech impediment, such as aphasia or stuttering, but because I was a speaker of Black English. Such misguided policies have now been eradicated as a result of scientific enlightenment about language and the renewed commitment to cultural pluralism that is the essence of the American experiment.

A few years after my bout with speech therapy, I published, in the pages of *English Journal*, my first experimental attempt at writing the "dialect of my nurture": "English Teacher, Why You Be Doing the Thangs You Don't Do?" (Smitherman, 1972). Encouraged by former *EJ* editor Stephen Tchudi (then Judy), I went on to produce a regular *EJ* column, "Soul N Style," written in a mixture of Black English Vernacular and the Language of Wider Communication (i.e., Edited American English), and for which I won a national award (thanks to Steve Tchudi, who believed in me—Yo, Steve, much props!). In the 1977 edition of *Talkin and Testifyin: The Language of Black America*, I called for a national language policy, the details of which I had yet to work out. A decade later, I had come to realize that such a policy was needed, not just for African Americans and other groups on the margins, but for the entire country, and that the experience of African Americans could well be the basis for what I called a tripartite language policy (Smitherman, 1987). Like I said, I been on the battlefield for days.

CCCC's "National Language Policy"

Over the years since 1971, CCCC has evolved its linguistic and social consciousness beyond the issue of students' right to their own dialect to encompass the students' right to multiple ways of speaking. In 1987 it established the Language Policy Committee to study the current English-Only movement and to develop a position for CCCC on English Only's call for a constitutional amendment to make English the sole language of this country. That committee, like its predecessor the Students' Right Committee, formulated a CCCC position that has become organizational policy. In March 1988, CCCC adopted the National Language Policy, which is as follows:

> There is a need for a National Language Policy, the purpose of which is to prepare everyone in the United States for full participation in a multicultural nation. Such a policy recognizes and reflects the historical reality that, even though English has become the language of wider communication, we are a multi-lingual society. All people in a democratic society have the right to equal protection of the laws, to employment, to social services, and to participation in the democratic process. No one should be denied these or any other civil rights because of linguistic and cultural differences. Legal protection, education, and social services must be provided in English as well as other languages in order to enable everyone in the United States to take full advantage of these rights. This language policy affirms that civil rights should not be denied to people because of linguistic differences. It enables everyone to participate in the life of the nation by ensuring continued respect both for English, the common language, and for the many other languages that have contributed to our rich cultural and linguistic heritage. This policy has three inseparable parts:
>
> 1. to provide resources to enable native and non-native speakers to achieve oral and literate competence in English, the language of wider communication.
>
> 2. to support programs that assert the legitimacy of native languages and dialects and ensure that proficiency in the mother tongue will not be lost; and
>
> 3. to foster the teaching of languages other than English so that native speakers of English can rediscover the language of their heritage or learn a second language.

The formulation of such a national language policy would mean that on *all* levels of education, every student would be required to develop competence in at least three languages. One of these would be, of course, the Language of Wider Communication, which everyone would learn. The second would be the student's mother tongue—e.g., Spanish, Polish, Black English,

Italian, Arabic, Chinese, Appalachian English. The legitimacy of the home language would be reinforced, and students' ability to function in that language would be part of their expanded linguistic repertoire by the end of twelve years of schooling. Third, every student would have command of at least one totally foreign language. That language would vary, depending on the options and social conditions in local communities and schools.

"Students' Right" and a New Paradigm Shift

In retrospect, then, the "Students' Right to Their Own Language" served its historical time and paved the way for this next evolutionary stage. We're now in the period of a new paradigm shift, from a provincial, more narrowly conceived focus to a broader internationalist perspective. We thus are being forced to address the issue of multiple linguistic voices, not only here, but in the global family. NCTE and CCCC, having grappled with these issues through the "Students' Right" era is, I think, well positioned for a leadership role in formulating a national language policy for this nation. Not just a policy for the narrow confines of, say, composition classrooms, which was our more modest goal in developing the CCCC "Students' Right" resolution, but a language policy that would impact *all* levels of education in *all* school subjects and in *all* social and institutional domains.

This is what is needed to carry us into the new millennium. I thus herein issue a call to all language arts educators and the entire NCTE membership to sign onto the CCCC National Language Policy. We—and your students—await your response.

Note

1. Kwame Ture, then Stokely Carmichael, first used the Black Power slogan in a speech in June 1966 on a protest march in Greenville, Mississippi. The march, designed to go across the state of Mississippi, had been initiated by James Meredith, the first Black to be admitted to the University of Mississippi, who had been ambushed and shot early on during the march. Carmichael and other civil rights leaders had come to Mississippi to continue Meredith's march. The concept of empowerment, as well as the

accompanying rhetorical strategy, had been carefully worked out by the leadership of the Student Non-Violence Coordinating Committee (SNCC), which was waiting for the opportune moment to introduce the slogan of Black Power into the discourse of the civil rights movement. A few days before Stokely's speech, SNCC worker Willie Ricks had begun using the slogan in local meetings to rally the people. And it was actually Ricks who convinced SNCC leadership—and Carmichael—that this was the historical moment to drop Black Power. In retrospect, Kwame Ture confessed that Stokely Carmichael "did not expect that 'enthusiastic response' from his audience of sharecroppers, farm workers, and other everyday Black people in Mississippi."("The Time Has Come," 1990).

References

Chomsky, N. (1968). *Language and mind.* New York: Harcourt, Brace & World.

Conference on College Composition and Communication. (1974). Students' right to their own language [Special issue]. *College Composition and Communication 25*(3), 1–32.

Conference on College Composition and Communication. (1988). National language policy. Urbana, IL: National Council of Teachers of English.

Dillard, J. L. (1972). *Black English: Its history and usage in the United States.* New York: Vintage Books.

Fishman, J. A. (1966). *Language loyalty in the United States: The maintenance and perpetuation of non-English mother tongues by American ethnic and religious groups.* The Hague, Neth.: Mouton.

Fishman, J. (1970). *Sociolinguistics: A brief introduction.* Rowley, MA: Newbury House.

Fishman, J. (1983). Bilingual education, language planning, and English. *English World-Wide. 1*(1), 11–24.

Halliday, M. A. K. (1973). *Explorations in the functions of language.* London: Edward Arnold.

Hymes, D. (Ed.). (1964). *Language in culture and society: A reader in linguistics and anthropology.* New York: Harper & Row.

Hymes, D. (1972). Introduction. In C. Cazden, V. John, & D. Hymes (Eds.), *Functions of language in the classroom* (pp. xi–lvii). New York: Teachers College Press.

Labov, W. (1970). *The study of nonstandard English.* Urbana, IL: National Council of Teachers of English.

Labov, W. (1972). *Language in the inner city: Studies in the Black English vernacular.* Philadelphia: University of Pennsylvania Press.

National Council of Teachers of English. (1974). *NCTE resolution #74.2.* Urbana, IL: National Council of Teachers of English.

Shuy, R. (1965). *Social dialects and language learning: Proceedings of the Bloomington, Indiana, conference, 1964.* Urbana, IL: National Council of Teachers of English.

Shuy, R. (1967). *Discovering American dialects.* Urbana, IL: National Council of Teachers of English.

Sledd, J. (1969). Bi-dialectalism: The linguistics of white supremacy. *English Journal 58*(9), 1307–15.

Sledd, J. (1972). Doublespeak: Dialectology in the service of Big Brother. *College English 33*, 439–56.

Smitherman, G. (1972). English teacher, why you be doing the thangs you don't do? *English Journal 61*(1), 59–65.

Smitherman, G. (1973). "God don't never change": Black English from a Black perspective. *College English 34*, 828–33.

Smitherman, G. (1977). *Talkin and testifyin: The language of Black America.* Boston: Houghton Mifflin.

Smitherman-Donaldson, G. (1987). Opinion: Toward a national public policy on language." *College English 49*(1), 29–36.

"The Time Has Come, 1964–66." (1990). *Eyes on the Prize II: America at the Racial Crossroads (1965–1985).* (1990). PBS video series.

CHAPTER SIXTEEN

In a Contact Zone: Incongruities in the Assessment of Complex Performances of English Teaching Designed for the National Board for Professional Teaching Standards

ANTHONY R. PETROSKY
University of Pittsburgh

GINETTE DELANDSHERE
Indiana University

In this chapter, we take a perspective that places teaching, its meaning and representations, at the center of teacher assessment. We discuss the difficulty of working from that perspective by describing the assessment problems that emerged in the context of the Early Adolescence English Language Arts Assessment Development Lab (ADL) conducted by the University of Pittsburgh and the Connecticut State Department of Education. The ADL was set up to develop a performance assessment system to be used for certifying English language arts teachers by the National Board for Professional Teaching Standards (NBPTS, 1989, 1993). Here we take this assessment development work as a site to raise questions about the nature of current measurement practices for complex performances—in this case, performances of teaching that include an extraordinary range of teachers' materials and reflections, representing multiple aspects of their English teaching.

To provide a context for this discussion, we first describe the assessment tasks we designed for the NBPTS. Drawn from our previous work (Delandshere & Petrosky, 1998), the specific assessment issues we address concern (1) the relationship of complex teaching performance to numerical procedures used to assess them, (2) the incongruities between the epistemological assumptions underlying traditional measurement practices and those underlying complex teaching performances, and (3) the possibilities of alternative forms of assessment for complex teaching performances. Our arguments to address these issues are interrelated, calling into question the appropriateness and usefulness of traditional measurement practices such as numerical ratings of performances for the assessment of teaching through portfolios that include complex tasks requiring the enactment and critique of teaching and of teaching materials.

Finally, we propose an alternative form of assessment by which representations of teaching could be described, analyzed, and evaluated. We conclude by opening up a discussion on the relationships of progressive assessment practices and professional development.

Assessment Tasks

The discussion in this chapter references only one of the tasks we developed for the NBPTS portfolio assessment—the Post-Reading Interpretive Discussion Exercise (PRIDE). To understand the arguments we develop here, however, it is helpful to understand the scope and nature of this assessment portfolio. There were three main assessment tasks included in what we referred to as the School Site Portfolio: (1) PRIDE, (2) the Planning and Teaching Exercise (PTE), and (3) the Student Learning Exercise (SLE). For all three tasks, teachers were asked to prepare and submit a range of teaching materials including examples of their students' written work, their teaching plans, videotapes of their teaching in some instances, and written commentaries on these materials.

For PRIDE, the task on which we focus in this chapter, teachers are asked to submit a twenty-minute videotape of their classroom work with a group of students engaged in an interpretive discussion of a selection of literature, a three- to ten-page written commentary addressing various aspects of the interpretive discussion, and other relevant instructional artifacts used in the discussion of the literary selection. For PTE, teachers are asked to document their plans for teaching over a three-week period that illustrate an integrated approach to English language arts. To do this, teachers prepare a daily chronicle of the activities that take place in the classroom during the three weeks, a twenty-minute videotape of their teaching during that time, and reflective commentaries on their work and the work of their students related to this curriculum unit. In SLE, teachers are asked to collect selected pieces of student writing from three different students for a period of three months as well as instructional artifacts related to the students' writing. Teachers also write a commentary about each student, analyzing the student's development on different aspects of writing and how their instruction has influenced that development.

For all three tasks included in the portfolio, we developed sets of directions that could help teachers provide windows into their teaching by suggesting ways to present moments from their teaching that would be visible and understandable to others. None of these tasks is a traditional test exercise. They are all instances of actual teaching, planning, and learning presented according to specifications to make them accessible to others. While we were experimenting with these assessment tasks, teachers were limited to six months to prepare their complete portfolio for submission to NBPTS for judging. In addition to preparing the portfolio, teachers also were asked to complete a knowledge examination and assessment center exercises (Petrosky, 1994a, 1994b; Delandshere & Petrosky, 1993) that asked them to critique a videotape of beginning teaching and to evaluate a class set of student essays.

NBPTS accepted the assessment tasks we developed but asked for modifications to the scoring system to make it more efficient and less time consuming. We never did develop a scoring system satisfactory to NBPTS, and although its development continued with another contractor, our initial work provided us with a rich site—a contact zone, in fact—where, in their interaction, philosophical and methodological issues of measurement and assessment, as distinct yet overlapping practices, created interesting dilemmas in our attempts to understand and assess complex teaching performances. And while the development of an assessment can be regarded as a technical venture, we experienced this development also in its ideological and methodological tensions. This experience gave us an opportunity to examine and question key measurement assumptions and to begin reconceiving assessment in much broader terms.

The Relationship of Complex Teaching Performances and Numerical Procedures

We developed assessment tasks as opportunities for teachers to represent actual teaching moments from their classrooms and other activities that engaged them in the work of their profession. These tasks were grounded in an ideology that values knowledge that is created by teachers in response to particular situations and issues, and that is made visible in the enactments of their teaching and in the reflective critiques they engage in personally or with others. This visibility of teaching and thinking about teaching was important to us because it meant that it could be critiqued from an ideological perspective that valued the dialogic—the articulation of points of view or interpretations in continual interchange. We imagined that teachers could learn from what others saw, interpreted, and valued in their teaching and in their thinking about their teaching. In this sense, we conceived of the board assessment as a piece of a larger professional development effort that NBPTS was creating through regional, state, and professional organization groups. As we describe later, the assessment tasks enabled this visibility, but the measurement methods we used did not. In fact, they actually concealed the visibility we desired to create.

Initially, we worked from assumptions that support the measurement notions of score reliability and validity (e.g., Crocker & Algina, 1986; Thorndike & Hagen, 1961) because we were pressed to provide empirical evidence of these in the context of the assessment system we were developing. At the same time, we were aware of the need to develop an assessment system consistent with the ideology of English teaching and learning represented in the professional standards developed by the NBPTS English/Language Arts Standards Committee (NBPTS, 1993) and in which we grounded our assessment tasks. The statistical notions of random sampling, error and true scores, and consistency, for example, in which measurement is grounded, might be regarded as technical matters, but they are also ideological in the sense that they privilege certain methods of assessment—methods which in our case were not consistent with the ideology of teaching and learning from which we were working. And it is precisely this site—the intersection between assessment methods and the substantive or conceptual framework of English language arts teaching, and the incompatibilities and contradictions between them—that constitutes the essence of our arguments here.

Because the assessment tasks ask teachers for detailed documentation of and commentaries on their work, the responses teachers produced were lengthy and diverse (e.g., videotape, written commentary, text under discussion, instructional artifacts). The reader or assessor of these performances must watch, read, and reflect on all of these materials. To do so, we initially developed rating schemes to guide the assessors in taking notes on performances, to cluster those notes as evidence around particular dimensions, and then to use Decision Guides to rate the teachers' performances according to the dimensions of teaching that the task captured. We developed these dimensions from three sources: the NBPTS English/Language Arts Standards, the research literature on English language arts teaching, and preliminary field tests with the portfolio tasks (Koziol, 1994). The dimensions—which we came to think of as lenses through which teaching performances could be interpreted and assessed—were: (A) Learner-Centeredness, (B) Cultural Awareness, (C) Content Knowledge, (D) Integrated Curriculum, (E) Coherent Pedagogy, and (F) Professional Roles and Concerns (for a more detailed account of the dimensions, refer to Delandshere & Petrosky, 1993; Koziol, 1994).

The Decision Guides[1] provided a performance description for each rating point for each dimension on a four-point scale (i.e., (4) highly accomplished to (1) unaccomplished). We continually changed the rating descriptors because no matter what words we used (i.e., *expert* and *novice, accomplished* and *unaccomplished*, and so on), the language seemed offensive to someone. Each set of indicators representing a pattern of behaviors attempted to address the teacher's knowledge of the activity being assessed, the teacher's enactment of that knowledge during the activity, and the teacher's reflection on the activity and its impact on student learning. We estimated that it would take an assessor forty-five minutes to one hour to read and rate a single teacher's performance on PRIDE. This would also require the assessor to have extensive practice and experience in reading, interpreting, and evaluating the performances. And given the fact that most assessors had little if any experience observing and assessing teaching, we designed (although never implemented) assessor practice institutes and procedures that closely resembled intensive professional development seminars rather than the traditional two- or three-day calibration exercises usually associated with training in numerical rating procedures.

The main purpose in developing procedures to obtain numerical ratings of performances along multiple dimensions was to be able to estimate measurement indices such as reliability coefficients (Delandshere & Petrosky, 1993, 1994). The assignment of numerical ratings is also efficient and is possible by simply recognizing features of the performance that fall consistently within the same categories of ratings without much interpretation or justification for the rating. In other words, a few moments were selected in the teaching performance as sufficient evidence to support a particular rating but without consideration for the whole performance or for counterevidence, thereby possibly masking important aspects of teaching. Because ratings are only partial representations of the performances that allow their classification in a priori categories, we found such methods and procedures contradictory or inconsistent with the ideology of the assessment of English language arts (ELA) teaching and the assumptions about teaching and learning we were working from in this development.

Incongruities between Epistemological Assumptions Underlying Measurement and Interpretations

For most of this century, making judgments about educational achievement or the status of peoples' knowledge has been mediated through measurement—the assignment of numerical ratings to test responses. These numerical ratings are generally thought to represent the quality of properties being measured (Stevens, 1951; Narens & Duncan, 1986). The ability to adequately consider audience when writing a persuasive essay, for example, might be represented by a three on a four-point scale, and a four might then represent the ability to expertly consider audience. The scores are used in this way to make value judgments about the quality of an aspect of the complete performance.

An alternative to the measurement practice of assigning numerical ratings to performances would be to formulate written judgments—which we called interpretive summaries—based on descriptions and interpretations of the performances along the critical dimensions we had identified. Such an alternative may not be necessary in situations where a one-to-one correspondence between the number of points assigned and the number of correct responses is assumed (as is the case in many achievement tests). Complex teaching performances, however, are context dependent and do not easily accommodate the notion of correctness; consequently, they defy such one-to-one correspondences. In other words, every action taken or statement made by the teachers during these complex teaching performances cannot simply be assigned a point, and the number of these actions or statements is certainly not the most important characteristic of the performance. For example, more or less teacher participation in a literature discussion does not necessarily result in a more interpretive discussion by the students. The focus here is on interpretation rather than on the counting or measuring of aspects of participation.

For PRIDE, for example, we found that context made all the difference in the roles teachers took as discussion leaders. We observed that the teacher roles in discussions had to be interpreted in relation to the nature of the discussions, even though we began by considering teachers' roles as salient indicators of the quality of interpretive discussions. For instance, teachers who initiated discussions with interpretive questions and then sat back, letting students' interpretations lead the discussion, had discussions that were as fruitful as those of teachers who initiated discussions with brief lectures and then participated in the discussions along with their students. In other words, there was no single set of teacher behaviors that would most likely lead to a discussion during which students developed interpretive understandings. Discussions depend on a mix of actions and context—the students, their experience with discussions, the teacher, the teacher's manner and goals, the text under discussion, and so on—that have a tremendous interactive effect on the nature of discussions.

Therefore the notion of a "correct" pattern of actions is challenged because of the range of possible courses of teacher actions which cannot be specified a priori but which need to be interpreted in context. The difficulty in anticipating teachers' possible courses of actions also makes it difficult to describe numerical ratings in terms of corresponding teacher behaviors. This dilemma is compounded by the fact that similar behaviors by different teachers, or by the same teachers in different situations, might have to be interpreted differently depending on the nature of the discussions in which they engage the students.

For example, the Decision Guides we used for PRIDE focused assessors on three dimensions of a teacher's performance. First, in order for teachers to receive an "accomplished" rating (i.e., a rating of 4) on the Content Knowledge dimension, they had to demonstrate knowledge of how meaning is created in the transaction between readers and texts. On the Coherent Pedagogy dimension, they had to use their discussion to allow students to develop a repertoire of strategies for interpreting literature with a community of learners. And for the Learner-Centeredness dimension, they had to anticipate and accommodate the ways students learn to interpret literature through discussions. Enacting teaching consistently with these understandings would earn a teacher a rating of four on each of these three dimensions.

The teaching performances we observed, however, were not stable on these dimensions. Often, teachers would demonstrate that they knew meaning is created in transactions between readers and texts, and then proceed to begin the discussion with a lecture or summary review before turning to the work of analytic or thematic analyses from questions posed by students or prompted incidentally in process. At other times, teachers prompted discussions with interpretive questions but prodded students for correct answers. And other teachers who said they knew meaning resides in the transaction between readers and texts then went on to conduct discussions in order to cover a curriculum rather than in response to students' needs and abilities.

The point we want to make here is that even though the enactments of teaching seem straightforward—a teacher knows about the creation of meaning with texts, uses that knowledge to structure a discussion, and takes students' needs and abilities into account—we observed many variations that resulted in successful or unsuccessful discussions. The interpretations in context, along with the many variations in performance, made it impossible to represent them in any usable way in Decision Guides keyed to numerical scales. Even if it had been possible to devise these Decision Guides, they would simply allow assessors to identify and code predetermined indicators similarly across all individual performances. We needed in this case interpretative procedures that allowed the assessors to consider the task as a whole and to make judgments relative to the contextual factors of each individual performance.

In response to these problems with numerical ratings and as an alternative, we devised a procedure for assessors to make visible the salient characteristics—the dimensions—of the performances and their uses of these dimensions to describe, analyze, and make interpretive judgments of the performances. To this end, we created what we called interpretive summaries.[2] That is, assessors write interpretive summaries that are both descriptive records and interpretations of the salient characteristics of the performances along each relevant dimension. We see these summaries as a compromise between a numerical representation of performances and open-ended, unstructured interpretations that would allow a teaching performance to be assessed in its own right rather than through preconceived notions.

Assessors were taught to write these multipage summaries on the dimensional aspects of a teaching' performance based on structured notes they took while reading the performance using Decision Guides with numerical rating scales designed specifically for each task. As we mentioned elsewhere, these

> written summaries of evidence, based on individual performances, appeared to provide a more faithful and useful representation of

these performances. (By "faithful," we mean the consistency between the philosophical framework of the assessment and the way in which the performances were evaluated, and by "useful," we mean that they would lend themselves to the instructional purposes of the assessment and concretely exemplify quality performances.) (Delandshere & Petrosky, 1998, p. 15)

Pressured to continue with a system of numerical ratings, we attempted to make them coexist with this alternative interpretive assessment process opened to interpretation and to making evidence visible through interpretive summaries or warrants. In this contact zone, we place the assessors in the impossible position of having to construct a summary and interpretations of a teaching performance using unique evidence from the performance while at the same time recognizing the "level" of performance in comparison to categories of aspects of performances defined a priori. We found that the two approaches could not coexist, because when numerical ratings are possible, they define the way in which the performances are assessed, and the interpretive summaries become justifications for the ratings rather than the basis for them, or the explanations and interpretations of the whole performance. In this contact zone there are philosophical and technical incompatibilities that we would like to explore further. To do so, we begin with two fundamental questions that have guided our assessment work, and continue the discussion by questioning the meaning of two main measurement concepts—domain sampling and measurement consistency or reliability—for our work.

Fundamental Questions

In observing the assessors struggle to reconcile traditional measurement practices with an interpretive assessment approach, we asked two fundamental yet simple questions: "Why do we assign numerical ratings when assessing complex performances? And what is the meaning and usefulness of such ratings given the nature of the performances and the multiplicity of assessment purposes?" (Delandshere & Petrosky, 1998, p. 14).

With regard to the first question, we believe that assigning numerical ratings is the result of historical practice, when sorting large numbers of people into categories of achievement was regarded as the main purpose of assessment, and when measurement was regarded as the most objective and efficient method for doing so. It is also a result of historically situated theories of learning and intelligence that are mostly and simply understood as the acquisition of information (Mislevy, 1993; Spearman, 1904, 1927) at a time when the type of information or knowledge worth acquiring was much less controversial than it is today. A more extreme view of educational measurement sees it as lacking substantive theories (Goldstein, 1994). The outcome of these perspectives on assessment was such that all items on a test were assumed to be important and worth knowing, and to be equivalent and representative of what one needed to know (Loevinger, 1957; Messick, 1989). Consequently, the test scores were assumed to represent the amount of knowledge individuals possessed, and on the basis of these scores, they could be classified in categories of performance. The meaningfulness of such test scores rests on the assumptions made in constructing the test, assumptions under which each correct response to an item is assigned a point and each successive point represents an increment in knowledge.

The performance tasks that we designed were not conceived based on an incremental view of knowledge, and therefore quantification of the responses to the tasks is highly problematic. This is why we became concerned about the meaning and usefulness of ratings given the tasks we were designing and the differences in the assumptions we held. We worked from theories of English teaching and knowing that varied greatly from the early learning theories for which test theories were developed. As we have already seen, teaching is highly context dependent. In the PRIDE example, the text under discussion mattered, as did the students, their questions, their familiarity with discussion, and the classroom work that surrounded the discussion. Therefore the same teacher performance could be interpreted and assessed quite differently depending on the mix of these different contextual factors. In other words, a course of action taken by a teacher does not have an absolute meaning definable independently of the context, and therefore the course of action cannot be assigned a number of points or a rating in a predetermined manner. Performances on PRIDE fluctuated greatly across teachers, but would also likely change for one teacher across multiple performances with different situations, students, and texts. This inconsistency is incompatible with the fundamental measurement assumption of stability, as we will examine later.

Another problem with numerical ratings results from the way they necessarily reduce, or atomize, complex patterns of performance into simple ratings. Ratings do not constitute very valuable or informative feedback for teachers. We reasoned that if this kind of assessment was going to have long-term effects on teaching practices, then it needed to provide teachers with fairly detailed feedback on their performances. When we tried to back-build feedback to teachers from the ratings by using descriptive, generic language from the Decision Guides, the resulting feedback did not appear to be particularly useful to the individual teacher either. The feedback was cryptic and abstract because the Decision Guides for the ratings were abstract. Cryptic and generic feedback might not be a problem if the purpose is simply to make a certification decision. But what, we asked, would teachers learn or understand about their performances from such feedback? How would they change their practice? It was not very useful for a teacher to know, for example, that she received a rating of three on the Learner-Centeredness dimension of PRIDE because she "responded to *general* students' abilities as readers and discussers mainly to help students learn to interpret literature or manage their own discussion." In addition, when such numerical ratings are aggregated across tasks to form total scores on the complete assessment or subscores on the assessment components, their meanings are completely lost. Aggregated ratings, then, are disassociated from the individual performance characteristics, and they in fact begin to be considered as test scores or real numbers which can be added, averaged, and so on with no intrinsic meaning other than their numerical value.

Since we began designing this assessment with the assumption that it would be part of professional development for teachers, we had a difficult time resigning ourselves to the thought that numerical ratings were only useful for sorting teachers into pass/fail categories, that they provided little information on teachers' performances that could be used for professional development purposes. The distance between the ratings and the meaning of the teaching performance poses another ideological problem that illustrates the incongruities in this contact zone, where numerical ratings are used to represent complex teaching knowledge. What would a score of three mean, for example, if it represented a teacher's performance on all three of the portfolio tasks? What would it mean if it represented the teacher's performance on the whole assessment? Aggregating and therefore uncoupling ratings from the tasks they represent mask the performances in a way that makes them no longer identifiable or visible. The description, interpretation, and evaluation of the performances are all subsumed under a numerical representation assumed to have the same meaning across all performances and all teachers. We thought that interpretive summaries held far more promise for providing both descriptive and evaluative information on teachers' performances and for making the assessors' explanations and judgment of the performance visible to the teachers and to other readers of these summaries.

Critical Tasks and Domain Sampling

The nature of the performances that we considered for this assessment and the way we created them led us to examine further the notions of domain sampling and generalizability. As we have said elsewhere,

> Domain, universe of generalization, and sampling are central concepts in measurement theory. Items are sampled from domain, responses are sampled from the examinee, and inferential statistical models, which rest on sampling assumption, are used to generalize to a larger universe of similar responses. (Delandshere & Petrosky, 1998, p. 18).

The logic of inference rests on the following assumptions: (1) there are within individuals stable traits that can be measured from their responses to test items, (2) score fluctuations between repeated testing of an individual are the result of measurement error, and (3) there is a universe of items or tasks which are equivalent and can be sampled to represent the construct domain or universe, yielding scores from which we can infer back to the domain.

The first and second assumptions are interrelated and postulate (1) the existence of individual characteristics or traits which can be measured and inferred from test scores, and (2) that behaviors exhibited on tests are stable. In other words, the claim is that there are generic individual traits or knowledge that manifest themselves consistently and generalize across items, tests, occasions, contexts, and so on (Feldt & Brennan, 1989). In tasks such as PRIDE, however, the interaction between *any teacher, his or her interpretation* of the task, and the context is what constitutes the teaching performance. Therefore the performance will change depending on the teacher's interpretation of the task and the context; the performance does not manifest itself consistently or generically across contexts. Consistency of performance on tasks such as PRIDE may exist at a superficial level only—in the way, for instance, that a teacher takes notes or encourages turn taking—but the meaning of the entire performance is context dependent. The nature of the discussion changes with different groups of students, different student responses, different texts, and different teachers' reactions to the students and their responses. This is so, we think, because the task is not assessing a stable personal trait. Therefore fluctuations in the ratings of a particular teaching performance on different occasions across multiple testings would be the result of changes in the context. Yet, as the second assumption states, any change in performances or interaction between the individual, the tasks, and the context is considered measurement error (Feldt & Brennan, 1989; Shavelson & Webb, 1991).

This incompatibility between assumptions points to the difficulty of considering these complex teaching performances as "individual traits" for which "true scores"—meaning consistent scores free of measurement error—can be obtained. This notion of certainty and stability of measurement might have been regarded as necessary and possible when the main purpose was to sort and rank people, but when we consider assessment as a way to understand teaching and learning, notions of certainty and stability not only get in the way of understanding, but they are also fundamentally incompatible with how we conceive of teaching and learning as a process of inquiry.

The third assumption relates to the possibility of designing equivalent tasks to constitute a domain from which representative tasks could be sampled. PRIDE is a good example of the difficulties we had when we tried to imagine these kinds of performance tasks as traditional items that represent and sample a domain of items which define an individual ability or trait (Popham, 1984). We might be tempted, as we were, to change the mode of student response in PRIDE by designing another equivalent task, so that students write their responses rather than speak them in a discussion. But if we do this, we no longer have the same critical task, and the focus would be on students' written response to literature rather than on how their roles in discussions shape or build their interpretations. As a result, we would be hard-pressed to say that the two tasks, with different modes of students' responses, are equivalent, or that they equally represent the same domain. In order to construct equivalent tasks, we would have to design another task that includes a class discussion of a literary selection. This does not seem possible, because critical moments of teaching—such as conducting a discussion, responding to students' writing, or conducting a writing workshop—are unique, and we do not have equivalent tasks or activities to represent them.

In brief, we came to see a task such as PRIDE as a critical task in the English profession—that is, a task that captures a particular theory of teaching interpretation of literature through discussion. Working from this theoretical framework, we constructed the task purposefully rather than selecting it randomly from a group of possible tasks. The fact that PRIDE captures the entirety of the theory rather than fragments of it (just as items on a math test are all fragments of what is assumed to constitute mathematics knowledge) makes it an assessment occasion or a task quite different from those that test theory considers items. The theoretical and purposeful (as opposed to random) nature of the task makes generalizing from the teaching performances on these kinds of tasks an interesting issue. Clearly, it is difficult to generalize from an individual performance to other or to a class of similar performances. But the understandings that we could have developed from assessing these teaching performances in light of the theoretical perspectives from which we worked could have been beneficial to both the participating teachers and to the continuous development of English teaching as a field. This is also more consistent with a conception of assessment as a professional development activity rather than as a system of sanctions and rewards.

Reliability and Assessor Training

One of the reasons we continued using a system of numerical ratings was the request for reliability estimates as defined by measurement theory. Although there are different types of reliability, inter-rater agreement seemed to be of most concern. Inter-rater agreement is the degree to which different raters give the same performance the same ratings because they can be trained to similarly identify and rate behaviors. This type of reliability is easiest to achieve when observing simple behaviors and where the ratings consist of recording the presence or absence of behaviors. If, for instance, we are rating a motor development task in which children are being rated for their ability to grasp and drink from a cup, we might rate a successful drink as a four and an unsuccessful drink—no grasp, no drink—as a one. In this task, the correspondence between the behavior and the rating is fairly clear, and there is almost a one-to-one correspondence between the presence of the behaviors and the higher ratings.

When, on the other hand, the one-to-one correspondence between the numerical rating and the behaviors being assessed is not clear, it is much more difficult to teach assessors to rate and to obtain inter-rater agreement. To imagine the problems faced by teachers evaluating PRIDE, consider the breadth and depth of materials they have to review and assess, the fact that they must have a common understanding of the Decision Guides, and the fact that they must have a common understanding of accomplished teaching represented in the performance. Few of the teacher-assessors who worked with us had any experience observing or critiquing teaching or teaching materials, and they were by no means atypical. Observing and critiquing colleagues' teaching is not yet a part of the culture of English teachers and neither is self-observation through videotaping or self-reflective critique.

Consequently, it did not seem to us that the teacher-assessors we worked with had what we might call substantial shared understandings of teaching and learning English.

Based on traditional measurement practices, we were told it should be possible to train prospective assessors in three or four days by "calibrating" them to the rating scale—the Decision Guides in our case—with sample or marker performances. These sample or marker performances are preassessed and included in the training because they are assumed to represent the various marker points on a rating scale. A large part of the assessors training is to teach them to see the performances and the dimensions on which they are rating them in identical ways. If assessors understand the performances or dimensions differently, the common thinking is that they are biased. If the bias cannot be eliminated, then the assessors are eliminated from the pool of potential assessors.

We tried to train assessors over three to five days using the traditional calibration methods, with varying success. Mostly, it was a frustrating experience for everyone involved for a number of reasons. First, and most important, the rating of a performance such as PRIDE is an interpretive act rather than a recognition of behaviors that match actions elucidated on a Decision Guide. Assessors, in other words, have to carefully read the performance and take into consideration all the materials before them, including twenty minutes of videotape. They then have to analyze the quality of the interpretive discussion by weighing the teacher's participation, the students' participation and responses, and the material under discussion. The assessors have to interpret the quality of the discussion's interpretive work, given both the descriptions provided in the Decision Guide and their understandings of interpretation in a literary discussion with students similar to those on the tape. Also, assessors have to be able to adjust their interpretations for changes in the contextual factors at play in any given task.

Measurement theory and practice do not recognize the assignment of ratings as acts of interpretation. Measurement works within a framework of recognitions and identifications, presence and absence. The aim is to make rating criteria as clear and simple as possible in order to avoid any ambiguities. Performances are broken down into identifiable components with behaviors that can be counted and consistently recognized across multiple testing. Performances on tasks such as PRIDE challenge this kind of thinking because they are so context dependent, so richly variable in terms of what might constitute success, and so open to interpretation, since as teachers we have little common understanding of what constitutes an interpretive literature discussion. As pointed out earlier, only the most superficial aspect of these performances can be readily identified, recognized, and rated.

Assessor training typically begins with an orientation to the assessment and its goals. Assessors are then trained in groups to read and rate one particular task. No assessor, then, ever sees a teacher's complete performance on the assessment, and individual assessors' ratings are aggregated in various ways to produce a score or scores for the complete assessment. During training, assessors are given sample or marker performances for each rating point to calibrate them and to teach them to analyze the performances as defined by the Decision Guides. They are constantly calibrated against preassessed performances, and in order to qualify as assessors, they have to pass a calibration test in which they rate preassessed performances.

When assessing teaching performances, the only framework available to assessors is their own teaching experience, or an abstraction of it, on which they fall back when viewing and critiquing the teaching of others. Under these circumstances, Decision Guides and marker performances have strange and often unpredictable effects on potential assessors. Assessors become defensive of their own teaching because suddenly they are being asked to make value judgments about examples of teaching that may be similar to theirs. So interpretations and ratings of those examples vary widely as defensiveness becomes entrenched. One way to overcome the assessors' defensiveness is to allow them opportunities to explain their own teaching and how their views inform their assessments of others' teaching performances. When this happens, as we argued that it should, we are no longer in the realm of traditional calibration training but in the realm of assessment as professional development education. This of course cannot be accomplished on a three- to five-day training model.

We believe it would require several weeks of daily work for

teachers to begin to develop the kinds of understanding and interpretation necessary to undertake a useful and meaningful assessment of teaching performances. Such learning activities would have to begin with experiences viewing and critiquing teaching, including the assessors' own teaching. The objective here would be the improvement of one's teaching, but also the development of our understanding of English teachers as a field of study. We could no longer focus on the assignment of numerical ratings, because they had been revealed as incompatible with our conceptual framework as well as with the purposes of assessment that we envisioned. Now we would like to consider alternative forms of assessing performances that break with the constraints of traditional measurement theory.

Alternative Forms of Assessing Complex Performances

To begin, we need to clarify that we cannot conceive of a teacher certification system that is not also concerned with ongoing professional development and the improvement of teaching practice in general (Petrosky & Bishop, 1995). Certification in itself does little to encourage development and change in the profession. What will happen once teachers are certified? What happens to those who are not? Our prime concerns are the impact of the assessment and the consequences for teaching and learning. In other words, what can teachers learn by participating in such an assessment either as teachers or as assessors? As we have already mentioned, one of the critical issues is the kinds of responses or feedback teachers receive on their performances and on the procedures that are put in place to encourage teachers' continuing engagement in the study of their teaching.

As we turn now to a discussion of alternative ways to make judgments about teaching performances, we work from two main ideas. First, we see assessment as the process by which members of the profession—teachers—can recognize and exemplify accomplished teaching. And second, we conceive of assessment as an integral part of teaching and of the continuing professional development of teachers. Therefore the assessment should be designed more like a sophisticated professional development

system—similar to the National Writing Project, for example—
in which teachers compose and receive detailed and particular
feedback on their performances that can be used in the study and
development of their teaching and other professional development activities. Such activities could be organized to encourage
the difficult work of critiquing teaching and teaching materials,
including self-critique, so that this kind of reflective work could
become a part of the culture of English teaching. Consequently,
the kinds of alternative assessment we would like to imagine
should be able to provide information both for making judgments about accomplished teaching and for providing feedback
to teachers that could be used in ongoing professional development. We now review some work that seems more promising
and more consistent with our conception of assessment.

Adjudication

One alternative strategy to numerical ratings of performances
would be similar to a process proposed by the Stanford Teacher
Assessment Project (Athanases, 1990), a two-phase assessment
process in which adjudication is used in the second phase for
decision making. At the first phase, individual assessors read teachers' performances on specific tasks and prepare written interpretive reports for each case. So, for example, if the assessment is
composed of three tasks, then each task is assessed by a different
assessor, who prepares a brief or warrant—a written case report—
on the teacher's performance on the task. At the second phase,
another assessor (one not participating in the assessment of individual tasks) reviews all performances for a teacher—through
the written reports of the first-phase assessors and, if necessary,
through a review of the actual performances—and prepares a
written recommendation for certification. This recommendation
is presented to a panel of assessors composed of the first-phase
assessors. The adjudication, then, takes places between the assessor
presenting the recommendation and the panel of assessors.

Once a decision is reached, the second-phase assessor writes
a case report for the teacher in which the reasons for the decision
are explicitly presented with reference to the teaching performances and to the reasoning of the panel in its use of the avail-

able evidence. In such a system, an appeals procedure could be established whereby a teacher could write a response taking exception to the recommendation. This response could prompt reconsideration and further elucidation of the committee's original decision.

Such a system attempts to consider multiple points of view by having multiple assessors participate in the reading and assessment of the performances. It is also concerned with dialogue and negotiation of shared understandings among the assessors through the adjudication process, which we see as a critical professional development activity and indispensable to further developing English teaching as a field of study. In addition, this system includes written interpretive documents supporting the certification decision that could be used in professional development activities, and such materials would constitute considerable and credible feedback to the teacher.

Multiple Readings and Interpretations

Another assessment alternative might be based on hermeneutics principles similar to those Moss (1996) and Moss, Schutz, and Collins (1998) have proposed. They argue, as we have, that the evaluation of complex performances of teaching is an interpretive act, grounded in ideology. Hermeneutics is a research tradition that proposes ways to consider information from multiple sources of evidence and to attend to the researchers' biases and preconceptions in order to formulate interpretive judgments (Gadamer, 1989). We could draw from this research tradition for the assessment of complex teaching performances. In this case, the multiple sources of evidence would be both the performance and the readings and interpretations of the performance by multiple assessors. Here also multiple assessors' interpretations of the same performance and their biases—which are recognized as unavoidable—are repeatedly tested and revised against evidence gathered from the multiple sources in an iterative process. In other words, the assessors do not read from fixed, predetermined criteria, but instead the meanings of the performances and the principles by which they are evaluated are co-determined within the context of these performances. In this process of analysis and interpretation, the intent is not to eliminate the assessors' preconceptions or prejudices but to test them critically as part of the assessment, and to bring them to an awareness level. The participant-researchers are engaged in a transaction with the performance and with each other to develop understandings, interpretations, and judgments of the performance. Drawing from a model of paired assessors (working together on the same performance) that we had proposed for the NBPTS, Moss et al. (1998) also used assessor pairs to analyze the working of hermeneutics principles in the assessment of similar teaching performances. Instead of reviewing single assessment tasks, however, assessors review a teacher's performances on all the assessment tasks. Under this system, assessors also write an interpretive summary of the performance and could provide a certification decision based on supporting evidence. The written summary, which includes specific evidence of performances, can be reviewed by others, used as feedback to the teacher, or used as part of an appeals process, as well as for other professional development activities.

Ideally, multiple assessors should be engaged in the reading, interpretation, and judgment of a performance in order to ensure that individual assessors' biases and preconceptions are clearly attended to and tested against the evidence and other possible interpretations of the performances. Clearly, this system requires equal participation of all assessors in the discussion of the performance and would require a great deal of education, experience, and practice of interpretive work, which constitutes extensive professional development activities as well as continuing development for the profession.

Dynamic and Principled Assessment

In a radical attempt to include teachers more actively in the assessment of their teaching, Delandshere (1996) proposes a dynamic and principled assessment system in which teachers decide how they want to represent their teaching and participate in defining the principles according to which it will be assessed. The argument here is that predefined and structured assessment tasks force teachers to fit their teaching to someone else's ideas of what teaching should look like and take away their responsibility to define what is important in their teaching and the learning of their students. The proposal is to make assessment an integral part of teaching, a tool of inquiry into teaching as a process of continuous learning. Teachers would ask their own assessment questions and gather evidence of teaching and student learning to address these questions. The assessment of their performance, as documented by them, would be in the conversation they engage in with a team of assessors and in the critical responses and feedback they receive from them. In other words, the teachers take an active part in the assessment conversation. Consistent with the hermeneutics principles proposed earlier, the assessment conversations would be occasions to negotiate the assessment principles and test the different interpretations of the performance against existing evidence. As in the previous alternatives we have proposed, case summaries would be written based on these assessment conversations and would serve as feedback to the teachers and possibly as the basis for discussion of teaching in professional development activities.

In order to implement such an assessment system, a set of "constitutive principles" for the assessment would need to be established to guide the preparation of the assessment materials, the assessment procedures, and the use of the assessment materials and decisions. We imagine these principles as more akin to principles of inquiry than to specifications for the content of the assessment. Teachers would participate in defining these principles because each teaching performance presented would be an occasion to test and revise the principles. Since we imagine that this would be an ongoing process, and a process in which other teachers participate as assessors, it is simultaneously a form of assessment and professional development.

Implications for Professional Development

Regardless of the assessment alternatives, the question of the education and selection of assessors is a critical one. It seems to us that observing, analyzing, and making judgments about teaching should be a major part of teachers' professional development. Participating in an assessment of teaching would begin to develop these assessors' skills because it helps teachers analyze their own teaching. We consider the assessment of teaching a form of advanced—progressive, if you will—professional development marking the distinction between what is traditionally called "assessor training" and professional development. Such a distinction is necessary only if the assessment is separate and external to the practice of teaching. In the alternatives we propose, the assessment of teaching is a part of teaching and of learning about teaching.

As already noted, however, teachers have little, if any, experience analyzing and critiquing teaching and teaching materials. None of these activities is yet a part of what might be called the culture of teaching English, although they certainly do exist as a part of the professional work of particular teachers in particular situations in different places in the country. So, first, teachers would need to spend a considerable amount of time observing and critiquing teaching and teaching materials as a part of their education to assess teaching performances. Second, teachers would need to do the difficult, time-consuming work of engaging in discussions in which they become accustomed to thinking about the assumptions from which they work—the assumptions about teaching and learning that define their knowledge and actions as well as their reflection on their own practice. Every act of teaching, like every assessment of teaching, proceeds from assumptions about teaching and learning. And a part of the assessment of teaching entails the interpretation of those assumptions, so that decisions can be based on teachers' knowledge and its representations in their actions and activities rather than on superficial, or mechanical, aspects of teaching.

Third, the perspectives and theories used by the assessors as lenses through which they interpret the performances need to be clarified. Various ways to prepare written cases—such as interpretive summaries or case reports or warrants—could be developed and tried out, and a review and analysis of cases would document and make the assessors' perspectives explicit to others. Prospective assessors also need to view and read a wealth of teaching performances so that they can develop and test the theories of teaching and learning from which they work, and get a sense of how the enactment of teaching can vary greatly.

Defining the principles by which judgments about teaching are made is by far the most difficult aspect of the assessment. The designers of different systems have struggled with trying to establish criteria, rubrics, and so on. The establishment of criteria presupposes that the field is prepared to agree on notions of accomplished teaching for various aspects of English instruction—such as discussions of literature and writing instruction. The problem with criteria is that they are list-like and often address different aspects of the performance separately. Such lists also invite the assessors to break down the performance in similar ways and to verify that different criteria are being met, diverting attention from the entire performance and its meaning. We need to find a way to articulate an assessment framework that preserves the performance in its entirety, and possibly to work from a theoretical framework in which the relationships and connections between the different concepts, ideas, and aspects of performance are explicitly articulated. Such theoretical frameworks could be exemplified with cases of teaching that are consistent or inconsistent with the framework. The assessment work would then consist of analyzing the ways in which the teaching performances are consistent and inconsistent with the theories, allowing simultaneous evaluation of both the performance and the theories of teaching from which assessors are working. This would make it possible for theory and practice to inform one another. Theories are tools for practice, hence they should be practically demonstrable, while practice ought to be theoretically defensible. If the theories from which we work are articulated explicitly, they become public so that participation in the discussion, the theorizing, and the assessment is possible.

Notes

1. Here is an example of a Decision Guide that we developed to rate teachers' performances for PRIDE on the Content Knowledge dimension. Similar guides were developed for other dimensions (e.g., Coherent Pedagogy, Learner-Centeredness). We attempted to account for numerous pat-

terns in performances by making it possible for assessors to rate a single teacher's patterns of performance differently on each of three dimensions in order to capture as much variation as possible in the performance. The guides, however, were still limited by their inability to define the range of performances for assessors, so that assessors more often than not had to infer a rating that the guides did not define.

PRIDE   Decision Guide   Dimension C: Content Knowledge

What is the candidate's understanding of reading and interpretation, and of discussion as a means for interpreting literature?

4	3	2	1
C says or implies the following in the Commentary:	C says or implies the following in the Commentary:	C says or implies the following in the Commentary:	C says or implies the following in the Commentary:
• meaning is created in the transaction between readers and texts.	• texts can have multiple interpretations that readers defend through references to the text.	• meaning resides in the text and the task of readers is to identify and label it.	• the task of readers is to gather bits of information in order to comprehend the text.
• readers' personal experiences and backgrounds are central to interpreting literature.	• readers need to call upon their personal knowledge and experience in order to become engaged while reading a text (e.g., often through pre-reading activities).	• text-based questions motivate and guide Ss' reading.	• "correct" interpretations need to be communicated to Ss.
• discussion is a vehicle for creating meaning as well as a communicative skill to be learned by both Ss and teachers.	• discussion is a vehicle for communicating and defending ideas.	•discussion is primarily a means for teachers to guide Ss to acceptable answers.	• discussion is a means for teachers to find out what bits of information Ss know about the text.

2. Following is an example of a fourth-generation interpretive summary developed by Linda Jordan, an ADL research associate, for the teacher assessment program used by the Connecticut State Department of Education. Petrosky was a reviewer for that Connecticut project. It is included here as an example both of what we had worked toward and of what seems to us to be a sophisticated interpretive summary—an interpretive summary, in short, that we would have liked to have had the time and

resources to develop as a part of our NBPTS work.

Unfortunately, this summary is not written for the PRIDE exercise that is used as the example throughout this chapter. It is written for a teacher's performances on the Student Learning Exercise that was, like PRIDE, one of the tasks in the School Site Portfolio. That task asked teachers to submit portfolios of three different students' writing. The task requested that each student represent, from the teacher's point of view, writers of different abilities.

The task was evaluated on the same three dimensions: Content Knowledge, Learner-Centeredness, and Coherent Pedagogy. For the Content Knowledge dimension, the evaluation focused on the teacher's pattern of knowledge, which included her understanding of (1) what writing is, (2) what writing is useful for, and (3) how writers go about the work of writing. For the Learner-Centeredness dimension, the evaluation focused on the teacher's pattern of attentiveness to students in terms of her understanding of (1) the needs and abilities of the students, and (2) how she accommodated those needs. The Coherent Pedagogy dimension evaluation focused on a pattern of performance that included (1) the type of writing tasks the teacher posed for students, and (2) the ways the teacher approached and evaluated the students' work.

Even though this interpretive summary is not for PRIDE, you can see here the kind of interpretation of a teacher's performance grounded in evidence that we intended with the summaries.

Teacher XXXX
Interpretive Summary

Your response to the Student Learning Exercise was evaluated along three dimensions: Dimension A—Learner-Centeredness; Dimension C—Content Knowledge; and Dimension E—Coherent Pedagogy.

C. Content Knowledge: To determine the level of your performance on this aspect of your teaching, we analyzed your understanding of what writing is, what it is useful for, and how writers go about the "work" of writing. In particular, we consider the work your students do to generate texts, revise them, and address issues of correctness and convention.

Descriptive Summary

Writing in your classes is primarily an opportunity for students to practice analytical skills, usually in response to literature, or to practice working in particular genres like poetry. The content of the student writing, the nature of your comments, and your analyses as presented in the Commentaries demonstrate that your concern is focused primarily on the form of student writing rather than on ideas that students express in

---

their writing. You indicate, for example, that "one of the major objectives" of your ninth grade class is "studying and practicing different forms and styles of writing after the initial survey of content." As this statement indicates, in this class students first survey literary content, then practice form. You state that Student B is able to write in response to literature when the "theme is extracted for her and the assignment is based on the theme." Here, it appears that by "extracting the theme for her," you sacrifice the opportunity for Student B to use her writing to develop her own understandings and ideas about the themes of the text she is reading. And, although this task does not directly address issues of reading and interpretation, there is considerable indication here that you routinely take responsibility for identifying possible themes of literary works for your students, which will limit their opportunities to learn how to use writing as a way of thinking through issues posed by texts that they read. See, for instance, your description of order #6 on the Student Writing Caption Sheet: "The class determined *through my questioning* that an overarching theme of many of the works we read is being trapped..." [emphasis added].

The Commentary for Student A, a high school junior, indicates more concern for using writing as a way to develop thinking. You attend to this student's ability to make general statements based on what she has read. However, this concern appears to be prompted by district curriculum requirements for the development of "formal analytic abilities" and "the writing of formal analytic essays" deemed appropriate for the level of high school study, rather than an understanding of writing as a way for students at all levels to develop thinking or to communicate ideas.

Neither the analyses presented in your Commentaries nor the comments you make on papers demonstrates that reflection on writing as a process is a central part of your writing instruction. You state that you ask students to do "process reflections" so that they "can better understand how they write as well as they understand what they write." This indicates that you are aware of the importance of what you call the "metacognitive component" of teaching writing, but you provide no examples of students doing such reflection and no indications of how they might learn to do so through your comments or conferencing. Such reflection appears to be secondary to concerns of mastering district curriculum objectives.

You see "writing process" as being both specific to different genres and individual writers. However, you provide only one example of revision in your student folder (the original and revision of Student C's character sketch), one in which you see "not much difference between the first and second drafts." Although you state that it is important for students to master certain conventions of using written language, you make no reference to editing as a stage of writing that allows students to recognize and correct errors and/or patterns of errors in their papers.

Evaluation and Recommendations

We assigned your performance a 2 on Dimension C because although you are aware of writing as a process and the importance of students developing metacognitive understandings about writing, this content knowledge about the teaching of writing is subordinated to a concern with following district curriculum objectives that treat writing as a rigid linear developmental process, with students moving from plot summary to interpretive work and analysis. We recommend that you refocus your analysis of student writing and learning around what you know about writing as an individual process of revision and reflection. You will need to find ways to address district curriculum requirements within the context of a writing pedagogy designed to help students construct meaning through revision and reflection.

A. Learner-Centeredness: To determine the level of your performance on this aspect of your teaching, we analyzed how you understand or anticipate the needs and abilities of your students. We also analyzed how you go about accommodating those needs.

Descriptive Summary

Your analysis of student writing and your reported writing instruction indicate that you use student papers and information gained through conferences to generate hypotheses about what students know about forms of writing and their own writing. For example, you state that Student A "has incorporated direct quotes from the text into her analysis where she believes that a paraphrase or summary does not do justice to the author's words." Another example of such a hypothesis is your speculation that Student B "feels as if it is not really 'her place' to assess or look critically at a book so she turned the assignment into a summary instead."

However, it appears that at times you allow your concerns about following an established curriculum to determine what students need to know and do; there is no indication that you tailor instruction based on these hypotheses about individual needs and abilities. Students appear to move through already-established assignments, rather than having opportunities to explore and address issues raised by their own writing.

You have different expectations based on perceived abilities of students, who are tracked into "below average" and "above average" and "honors" classes.

Evaluation and Recommendations

We assign your performance a score of 3 on Dimension A because your primary approach to analyzing students' needs and abilities is to generate hypotheses about what student can do through reading their work and talking with them in conferences. We recommend that you continue this approach and extend it to metacognitive issues, to discover and make use of the underlying understandings that students have about conventions of written language and about writing as a process of composing. You might also consider how to tailor your instruction and your expectations based not on tracking but on your own careful and professional observations of students as writers.

E. Coherent Pedagogy: To determine the level of your performance on this aspect of your teaching, we analyzed the writing tasks you pose for students and how you approach and evaluate their work.

Descriptive Summary

The writing tasks you pose for students are connected through the literature curriculum, often in terms of regular assignments like the dialectical journals or the "Probst Prompts." These tasks were arranged so that students generally write in response to reading, either in the same genre or in forms designed to encourage analysis, such as the analytic essay or the dialectical journal. You indicate that "One of the jobs of the teacher is to create assignments that are similar to those given in college English courses." However, you do not indicate what your own understanding of "college assignments" is, and what you will expect your own students to do in response to them.

You generally approach students' work in terms of the form mandated by the curriculum, within the context of the individual assignment. Neither your comments on student papers nor your analyses as represented in your Commentaries indicate that you attend to the content or ideas represented in student papers. There are some indications that you have begun to approach students' work historically, with reference to past problems or writing strategies.

When you make direct comments on student papers, you primarily praise students without making visible to them what they have done successfully. For example, you write "Good analysis" or "Wonderful job" without showing students what, exactly, in their papers constitutes "good analysis." When you address problems with error in written comments, your tendency is to correct the errors or to direct students in a general way to fix them. For example, you tell Student A to "Make a complete sentence" rather than helping the Student to learn to recognize for herself patterns of sentence boundary errors.

Evaluation and Recommendations

We assigned your performance a score of 3 on Dimension E because the writing tasks you pose for students provide opportunities for students to work on significant discourse level problems, such as integrating their texts with the words and ideas of others. However, these tasks are connected primarily through the literature curriculum, rather than being purposefully sequenced to help students develop writing strategies. We recommend that you develop ways of sequencing your literature-based assignments to purposefully move students to more sophisticated levels of writing. If your curriculum requires you to create assignments "similar to those given in college English courses," it will be important for you to consider carefully the nature and quality of the models for "college assignments" that you use, as well as the understandings about writing and reading that they are grounded in. There is, of course, a wide range of such assignments; you might usefully examine a variety of college writing textbooks in order to make informed judgments about what constitutes the kind of "college writing" that will help your students address the kind of complex intellectual problems posed in good college writing and literature programs (Coles and Vopat have written an anthology collecting college assignments called *What Makes Writing Good*.) You might also consider reading about how experienced writing teachers comment on student papers.

References

Athanases, S. Z. (1990). *Assessing the teaching of literacy in the elementary grades: Project overview* (Teacher Assessment Project Tech. Rep. No. L1). Palo Alto, CA: Stanford University.

Crocker, L., & Algina, J. (1986). *Introduction to classical and modern test theory.* New York: Hott, Rinehart, and Winston.

Delandshere, G. (1996). From static and prescribed to dynamic and principled assessment of teaching. *Elementary School Journal, 97*(2), 105–20.

Delandshere, G., & Petrosky, A. (1993). *Early Adolescence English Language Arts Assessment Development Laboratory.* Preliminary Report. University of Pittsburgh.

Delandshere, G., and Petrosky, A. (1994). Capturing teachers' knowledge: Performance assessment a) and post-structuralist epistemology, b) from a post-structuralist epistemology, c) and post-structuralism, d) none of the above. *Educational Researcher, 23*(5), 11–18.

Delandshere, G., & Petrosky, A. (1998). Assessment of complex performances: Limitations of key measurement assumptions. *Educational Researcher, 27*(2), 14–24.

Feldt, L. S., & Brennan, R. L. (1989). Reliability. In R. L. Linn (Ed.), *Educational measurement* (3rd ed.). New York: American Council on Education/Macmillan.

Gadamer, H. G. (1989). *Truth and method.* J. Weinsheimer & D. G. Marshall (Trans.). New York: Crossroad.

Koziol, S. M. (1994). *Validation of the early adolescence English language arts assessment dimensions* (Assessment Development Laboratory Tech. Rep. 5). Pittsburgh, PA: University of Pittsburgh.

Loevinger, J. (1957). Objective tests as instruments of psychological theory. *Psychological Reports, 3*(Supp. 9), 635–94.

Messick, S. (1989). Validity. In R. L. Linn (Ed.), *Educational measurement* (3rd ed.). New York: American Council on Education/Macmillan.

Mislevy, R. J. (1993). Foundations of a new test theory. In N. Frederiksen, R. J. Mislevy, & I. I. Bejar (Eds.), *Test theory for a new generation of tests.* Hillsdale, NJ: Lawrence Erlbaum.

Moss, P. A. (1996). Enlarging the dialogue in educational measurement: Voices from interpretive research traditions. *Educational Researcher, 25*(1), 20–28.

Moss, P. A., Schutz, A. M., & Collins, K. M. (1998). An integrative approach to portfolio evaluation for teacher licensure. *Journal of Personnel Evaluation in Education, 12*(2), 139–61.

Narens, L., & Duncan L. R. (1986). Measurement: The theory of numerical assignments. *Psychological Bulletin*, 99(2), 166–80.

National Board for Professional Teaching Standards (NBPTS). (1989). Toward high and rigorous standards for the teaching profession. Washington, DC: Author.

National Board for Professional Teaching Standards (NBPTS). (1993). Early adolescence/English language arts standards. Detroit, MI: Author.

Petrosky, A. (1994a). Producing and assessing knowledge: Beginning to understand teachers' knowledge through the work of four theorists. In T. Shanahan (Ed.), *Teachers thinking, teachers knowing* (pp. 23–38). Urbana, IL: National Council of Teachers of English.

Petrosky, A. (1994b). Schizophrenia, the National Board for Professional Teaching Standards' policies, and me. *English Journal*, 83(7), 33–42.

Petrosky, A., & Bishop, E. (1995). A practical guide to teacher assessments. *Voices from the Middle*, 2(4), 30–32.

Popham, W. J. (1984). Specifying the domain of content or behaviors. In R. A. Berk (Ed.), *A guide to criterion-referenced test construction*. Baltimore, MD: Johns Hopkins University Press.

Shavelson, R. J., & Webb, N. M. (1991). *Generalizability theory: A primer*. Newbury Park, CA: Sage.

Spearman, C. (1904). General intelligence objectively determined and measured. *American Journal of Psychology*, 15, 201–93.

Spearman, C. (1927). *The abilities of man: Their nature and measurement*. New York: Macmillan

Stevens, S. S. (1951). Mathematics, measurement, and psychophysics. In S. S. Stevens (Ed.), *Handbook of experimental psychology*. New York: Wiley.

Thorndike, R. L., & Hagen, E. (1961). *Measurement and evaluation in psychology and education* (2nd ed.). New York: Wiley.

CHAPTER SEVENTEEN

The International Problems of Shifting from One Literacy to Another

MILES A. MYERS

Institute for Research on Teaching and Learning,
Berkeley, California

The content of education, which is subject to great historical variation . . . expresses . . . both consciously and unconsciously, certain basic elements in the culture, what is thought of "as education" being in fact a particular selection, a particular set of emphases and omissions.
RAYMOND WILLIAMS, *The Long Revolution*

When I was invited to write this chapter, I was asked to reflect on the participation of the National Council of Teachers of English (NCTE) in the English Language Arts Standards Project and, among other things, to consider why I imagined the Standards Project appeared progressive and whether I still support the project. First of all, I have been around long enough to realize that some of the ideas I thought were "progressive" have turned out to be regressive, such as the public housing policies of the late 1960s and the open classroom policies of the same period. Both policies did serious damage to people and communities. They turned out not to be progressive. We do not yet know the fate of the standards movement.

Now let me summarize briefly why I supported (and continue to support) the standards movement. First, an "adequate" curriculum in the K–12 schools has become (or is becoming) a national civil right. I discovered this for the first time in 1991 when, in connection with a court case, I was asked whether NCTE published a book on what students should know and be able to do in English/language arts at each grade level. Thus began my education in a new way to define equity—not by access (*Brown v. Topeka* in Kansas), not by dollar gap (*Serrano v. Priest* in California), but by an adequate curriculum in each required subject area. In other words, if one is denied an adequate curriculum, one is being denied the opportunity to enter the mainstream of jobs, citizenship, and personal growth (see more details below and Myers, 1996).

Is the standards movement an attack on the public schools, an effort to destroy public education? One so-called progressive was quoted in the *Los Angeles Times* as saying so. Imagine a doctor in a public hospital saying, "The call for standards in health care is an attempt to destroy publicly owned hospitals." Just substitute "K–12 education" for "health care" and "public schools" or "public school teachers" for "public hospital" and you have the claim which has been pronounced from journals, meetings, and other forums throughout our profession—often in the name of progressivism. More than one study has shown what this sentence communicates to the public: that the hospitals or schools are afraid of standards. NCTE's officers communicated the reverse—not only were teachers not afraid of standards, but they welcomed the opportunity to work on them.

NCTE officers' responses were influenced by what was happening in other parts of the world, especially conversations between NCTE leaders and International Federation of Teachers of English (IFTE) leaders from other countries. At the 1995 IFTE conference in New York City, leaders from professional organizations of English teachers from Scotland, Canada, New Zealand, England, Wales, Australia, and the United States met in a week-long discussion focused on the worldwide standards movement in English education, beginning with a review of what had happened since the last IFTE conference in Aukland, New Zealand, in 1990. It soon became apparent that there was a remarkable similarity in the origins, problems, and forms of standards development in each country. These similarities are the focus of this chapter.

Similar Origins—Timing and Political Parties

Efforts to establish various national curriculum content standards started in 1985 in England, Canada, and Australia; in 1989 in the United States; and in 1991 in New Zealand. Many date the standards movement in the United States from the 1989 Governor's Conference, during which President George Bush and the fifty governors issued a statement of six broad goals for U.S. schools which by 1991 had been turned into the policy document *America 2000: An Education Strategy* (U.S. Department of Education, 1991). This document called for the development of standards in five core subject areas, one being English. Throughout 1990 there was a struggle over whether the subject area should be called English, reading, or language arts. NCTE pushed for English/language arts, thereby protecting the traditions of both its university/secondary members (English) and its elementary members (language arts). The legislative processes settled on English. By 1992 the U.S. Department of Education had funded the English Language Arts Standards Project managed by NCTE, the International Reading Association (IRA), and the Center for the Study of Reading at the University of Illinois, Urbana, and by 1993 President Bill Clinton was pushing H.R.804 through Congress in an effort to create a twenty-member National Education Standards and Improvement Council (NESIC) to oversee the federal government's standards effort, which now included geography, history, mathematics, art, civics, science, and foreign language.

In England and the United States, the standards movement had three overlapping projects: devising (1) a content framework for standards; (2) a description of standards-based curriculum materials; and (3) standards-based assessments showing examples of student performance. To meet the challenges of these various definitions of standards, each often promulgated by a different agency, NCTE decided to organize its Standards Project as a three-stage effort. In the first stage, NCTE joined with IRA to describe "content standards" which cut across all grades. These standards were not grade specific, nor were they intended to be test specifications. The focus in this first stage was on content priorities and the changing content of English/language arts. The second stage concentrated on standards-based curriculum materials at three grade levels—elementary, middle, and high school. The third stage focused on assessments selected and/or developed by teachers that showed student performances at three score levels (emergent, early, and fluent in K–3, and high, middle, and low in grades 4–5, middle school, and high school). In this third stage, the National New Standards Project (University of Pittsburgh and University of Rochester) funded NCTE to develop alternative ways of expressing student achievement. Later, the standards prepared by NCTE and IRA were applied to NCTE's accreditation standards for student teaching programs at university schools of education.

In England, the first English standards report was the Kingman Report (1988) and the second was the Cox Report (1991), both from the National Curriculum English Working Group (English for ages 5–16). In 1987, the first assessment plan was introduced by the Task Group on Assessment and Testing. A revised English standards document was introduced in 1992 by the National Curriculum Council, and a revised assessment plan was introduced in 1993. In England, unlike the United States, there were separate National Task Forces for standards and assessment. In the United States, there was often considerable confusion over the differences between these two tasks

Between 1970 and 1990 in many countries in the IFTE group, liberals became more market oriented on economic and job issues, and conservatives became more regulatory on cultural issues. In the United States, this meant that Bush and Clinton had similar education agendas, both giving a high priority to education standards. In England, the Conservatives and Liberals also shared similar positions, the standards movement in England starting with Labor Prime Minister James Callaghan and carried forward by Conservative Margaret Thatcher. Callaghan in 1976 opened the great debate on education by criticizing the English tradition of letting local schools control the curriculum (Cox, 1995, p. ii). Ten years later, resisting local control of education became a Conservative position. For example, in November 1986, Secretary of State for Education Kenneth Baker called for mandated book lists in English (Goodson & Medway, 1990, p. 72).

By 1987, Conservative British Prime Minister Margaret Thatcher was calling for a national focus on the quality of education and Secretary Baker was appointing the Kingman Committee to:

> (1) recommend a model of the English language, whether spoken or written, which would: (a) serve as the basis for how teachers are trained to understand how the English language works; (b) inform professional discussion of all aspects of English teaching; (2) recommend principles which should guide teachers; and (3) recommend what, in general terms, pupils need to know. (Goodson & Medway, 1990, pp. 72–73)

In March 1988, the Kingman Report called for the development of new curriculum content standards in English, and within the same year, England's Parliament passed the Education Reform Act giving the national education minister the power (1) to prescribe the English curriculum which all schools would be required to teach up to age sixteen; (2) to establish national testing in English at grades 7, 11, and 14; and (3) to appoint a working party to develop the national English curriculum. By June 1988, Brian Cox was heading up the National Curriculum English Working Group, which was charged with preparing a national document describing the English curriculum.

Later, the Task Group on Assessment and Testing proposed, first, a combination of external national exams and teacher assessments and, second, a moderation process which was to be used to negotiate differences between local scoring of assessments and national and regional scoring (Black, 1993). The external exams were called Standard Assessment Tasks (SATs) and were designed to resemble carefully constructed classroom work.

In Canada, where the standards movement was largely restricted to individual provinces, Ontario seems to have taken the first step toward standards in January 1987, when the Ontario government announced that a minimum of five compulsory English credits would be required for secondary school graduation in Ontario, and that new curriculum guides and examinations would be developed to outline the requirements for those five credits. A month later, the Ontario government issued a new *English Curriculum Guideline* describing mandatory examinations across the province during the 1987–88 school year ("Ontario Sets," 1987).

In Australia, as was the case in the United States, efforts to define curriculum content began with a variety of activities in local areas, leading to collective demands by states and territories. State education ministers, using the platform of the Australian Education Council (AEC), called in 1986 for "a national collaborative effort in curriculum development in Australia" and two years later for "a statement of national goals" and for "a national approach to monitoring education" (AEC, 1986). By 1989 the state, territory, and commonwealth ministers of education in Australia had endorsed ten common national goals for schooling in Australia (AEC, 1989) and appointed Garth Boomer chair of the Australian Cooperative Assessment Program (ACAP), which included two representatives from New Zealand and the directors of curriculum from each Australian state. AEC contracted with ACAP to use the national goals to develop the profiles of Australian standards for English. Both the profiles, published in 1994 as *English—A Curriculum Profile for Australian Schools,* and the national statement for English, also published by the Australian Education Council in 1994, became Australia's English standards. Although Boomer's leadership helped involve Australia's English professionals in the project, throughout the project many English-teaching professionals remained skeptical.

The Australian standards effort was organized around eight English-performance levels that showed "progression in student learning" during the compulsory years of schooling (years 1–10) (Australian Education Council, 1994, p. 5) and around four strands of knowledge—Text, Contextual Understanding, Linguistic Structures and Features, and Strategies. Text refers mainly to ideas and information, and Contextual Understanding refers to rhetorical relationships and point of view. Linguistic Structures includes sentence structure, and Strategies refers primarily to cognitive matters. Later, these four were reduced to two—Text and Language. At the end, the Australians put Strategies, Linguistic Structures, and Contextual Understanding under Language (Australian Education Council, 1994).

In 1991 in New Zealand, the minister of education requested that a new curriculum for English teaching be developed for New Zealand, and four years later the Ministry had issued *The New Zealand Curriculum Framework* (1994), which specified seven essential skills in English: communication, information, problem-solving, self-management, and social, physical, and study skills. There was a great deal of interaction between New Zealand and Australian English teachers, but the documents from the two countries are different.

Similar Origins—Reasons

Why did a standards movement, broadly conceived, take place in all of these countries? First, legislators in each nation began several years ago to emphasize the importance of "human capital" over monetary capital and natural resources (e.g., land, minerals). As a result of this emphasis, all of these countries adopted policies in which the literacy of the labor force was identified as a primary asset requiring government "investment." In all of these nations, English teaching professionals, often for the first time in recent memory, were asked to communicate to the general public the goals and overall direction of the profession in its work in tax-supported public schools.

A second reason for the standards movement was that equity issues had surfaced in all of these countries. In New Zealand, for example, the 1840 Treaty of Waitangi guaranteed that the Maori culture, including Maori literature and language, would be a major force in the culture of New Zealand. But increasing Maori protests in the late 1980s about the failure of the schools to provide equal opportunity led in the 1990s to a reexamination of equity in the public school curriculum. Similarly, in England the Labor Party led the drive for standards as a way to protect the working class from the inequalities of job opportunities in an economy which was reducing the workforce, and in the United States, equity leaders were looking for a new approach to guaranteeing the equal educational opportunity anchored in the U.S. Bill of Rights. Under the U.S. Constitution, equity had been defined in U.S. education law as equal access (*Brown v. Topeka*, 1954) and as an equal dollar gap (*Serrano v. Priest*, 1970s). In access cases, expert witnesses included regional demographers and experts on school boundaries who described the schedules for bus lines and explained why students could or could not attend particular schools; and in dollar gap cases, the experts were school accountants and tax experts showing how dollars were distributed to different schools and programs.

But the new equity cases in the United States were beginning to argue that students should have equal access to the literacy they need to become functioning citizens. That is, because the U.S. Constitution guarantees equal opportunity, the U.S. Constitution requires that education provide the foundation for equal opportunity in the workforce or the civic life of the country. If education provides an inadequate foundation, then the child or student has been denied an equal opportunity.

But how is adequacy defined? In court cases in Alabama and Kentucky, experts in the content of the English curriculum defined *adequacy* as adequacy in English/language arts. These experts, of course, needed professional documents to which they could point as a source for their estimates of what was required for adequacy. In new equity cases, the Standards document of IRA and NCTE appeared to be able to help provide a foundation for descriptions of curriculum adequacy in English/language arts (Myers, 1996).

In 1994, NCTE sponsored a conference on the topic of the new definition of equity, featuring Judge Eugene Reese, who had ruled that the entire school system of Alabama was unconstitutional because Alabama schools did not provide a curriculum making it possible for Alabama students to enter the twenty-first century. In Judge Reese's case, professors of education were asked to visit Alabama schools and to testify in court about what they found. One witness testified that one classroom had only one text, an out-of-date geography book. Another said some classrooms had no books. The issue was not economics (too little money to buy books) but the absence of adequate information available to teach an adequate level of knowledge about a subject. The pattern of testimony in the Alabama case suggested that writing entire pieces, writing to different audiences (not doing one true/false test after another all day), and reading entire texts (not simply doing one drill sheet after another on sound blends and syllables) could become part of the U.S. constitutional guarantee of opportunity to learn if one could establish that writing to different audiences and reading or writing entire texts were a necessary foundation for civic and work life.

The third purpose of the English Standards Project in the United States was to slow down the privatization of education and to stop the accompanying elimination of tax-supported schooling or public schools. Other countries had a slightly different view of what "public schools" means, but in the United States the standards movement was intended to respond to the claim that the public schools were incapable of defining a clear mission or implementing a solid, rigorous curriculum intended for all students. In fact, some commentators suggested that public school teacher resistance to standards was evidence that public schools should be privatized through tax-supported vouchers.

A final goal of the standards movement in the United States was to secure staff development funds for K–12 teachers. In the United States, national standards had to be translated into state and local standards and curriculum documents. The NCTE/IRA Standards document became one of the cultural artifacts legitimizing public financial support of thousands of local conversations in which K–12 teachers worked together to identify the core of English/ language arts. In the beginning, most of the costs of these meetings of classroom teachers were paid for by the federal government; later, foundations added their support, and still later local sources provided support. In the 1996–97 school year, the federal government provided $300 million for local standards conversations, and these dollars were apparently matched two to one by other sources. The expectation is that as much or more was spent for released time for teachers in 1997–98 and 1998–99.

There was, however, some professional opposition to the participation of English teachers in the standards movement. Some of the NCTE members who opposed the standards effort in the United States feared that standards would inevitably exclude many students. Others based their opposition on a fear of hegemony, charging that standards contributed to the myth of nationhood that necessarily and inevitably undermined the more humane notion of a global culture (see Bauman, 1990). Some argued that subject matter groups were forums and should never take an action requiring a position on curriculum questions. NCTE printed articles expressing this opposition in its journals and *The Council Chronicle*.

Similar Problems—The Tensions among Local Government, State Government, Federal Government, and National Efforts

In addition to standards being taken up in different countries at about the same time and for similar reasons, different countries had to face similar tensions between local and national efforts. Some groups wanted to keep standards development at the local level, others wanted standards developed by the federal or central government of the nation, still others wanted state governments to lead, and still others wanted standards developed by national, nongovernmental bodies. Sometimes the standards effort was divided into parts—content standards at one level and assessment specifications at another. Often the size of the country helped shape the decision.

Through the development of central government curriculum and testing, the central government in England took a step toward direct control of content subjects in schools, despite a long tradition in which local schools had controlled curriculum. In the United States, where the federal government had played a minimal statutory role in education, the federalization of education had been restricted to a few special programs—the vocational programs initiated during World War I; some national science, mathematics, and special education programs initiated after World War II; and the Title I legislation for disadvantaged students initiated in the 1960s. In 1990 federal government spending accounted for only about 6 percent of the total cost of elementary and secondary education in the United States, and low spending meant few controls.

In the U.S. standards debate, proposals were advanced to expand substantially the federal government's investment in and control over education. For example, Richard Klein, who in the *New York Times* attacked NCTE's Standards for being vague, called for the United States to adopt the expensive French system in which every lesson every day is mandated in every school by the central government (Klein, 1996). President Clinton, who in his 1997 State of the Union proposed a national test of fourth-grade students in reading, insisted that "national" did not mean "federal." He also called "local control" the "fig leaf of education" because "local control" is used, he said, to hide the great differences in curriculum content across the country. These differences are, according to many, differences of opportunity. Many of those opposed to national testing find it difficult to argue that education is not a civil right and that civil rights are not national business. For many observers, opposition to national testing was simply a modern form of conservative opposition to civil rights for all. Don't test, and no one will ever know!

Groups in several countries tried to protect the authority of local education agencies by defining standards not as mandates but as consensus goals. England called its content standards "attainment targets," "programmes of study," and sometimes "the curriculum content." Some Canadian provinces called their standards "reference sets" (Atkin, 1994, p. 68). U.S. English teachers sometimes called their standards "a flag" or "a banner," as in "standard bearer." New Zealand called its standards a "syllabus," and in Australia, Boomer called the standards "influences by consensus." Said Boomer,

> It is important to note that none of these "framework" statements and profiles will actually be 'frames' in that they will not be binding on any [education] system. Each system will continue to have jurisdiction over its own curriculum. . . . They will, therefore, have to be of sufficient generality to allow for local variation and realization if they are to be national influences by consensus. (Boomer, 1992)

NCTE made the same claim in its standards work, establishing a nationwide network of Standards Task Force groups at the local and state level.

The argument over which level of government should do what was sometimes confused by the different use of the term "standards," which sometimes referred to "curriculum content," sometimes to teaching standards, and at other times to "assessments."

Many groups in the United States called their assessment standards "benchmarks," but in England the term "exemplification" was used more often for assessment standards. Many NCTE groups supported an exemplification rather than a specification approach to assessment benchmarks. The judgment process of exemplification called for rubrics, exemplars, commentaries, and extensive staff development to prepare teachers for the judgment process. Specification often emphasized checklists or machine-scored tests. Many assessment projects had to struggle with the shift from pre-standard era normative testing to mastery levels. Normative testing determined grade level mastery by the mid-point on a bell-shaped distribution in which all students cannot get to the top. In standards mastery, levels were standards based, and therefore all students could achieve at a level above the standards. This raises the question of the relationship between tests and standards. In England, for example, when students did relatively well on the first national tests, the Conservatives complained that the standards were too low. When high standards created failures, schools and teachers got blamed.

The tension between national and state agencies over who has authority over local schools has also been a worldwide problem. In the United States, there was an attempt with Goals 2000—the Department of Education project to establish goals and standards for achievement in U.S. schools—to establish through a federal testing program a tight fit between federal curriculum standards, as designated by the National Education Standards and Improvement Council, and local tests, as mandated by Title I and other devices. The plan did not work. Governors of states protested that education standards and assessments were a state prerogative. At the 1996 summit of governors, the governor of Virginia threatened to walk out if the summit group did not make clear that education was a local prerogative. The governors rejected federal oversight, but they joined the business community to get foundation funds for a national—not federal—oversight agency, now called Achieve. In the United States, there were also very active standards efforts funded by such states as California, Nevada, Michigan, Georgia, Colorado, Kansas, Delaware, Virginia, Massachusetts, and elsewhere. As this book nears publication, the federal oversight and testing role has shifted to the

National Assessment of Educational Progress (NAEP), where NAGBY (the National Assessment Governing Board) has applied a set of achievement standards to NAEP scores. A commission of the National Academy of Science has questioned whether NAGBY's achievement standards can be applied to NAEP scores. In addition, NAGBY has received federal funding to develop a fourth-grade reading test which would be used nationally, be standards-based, and be "voluntary" for each individual. Recent political events—for instance, the national election—suggest that this test may never see the light of day.

Similar state protests against federal standards occurred in Australia, where states warned that the national government was intruding too far into local areas of education decision making. When the Australian AEC met in July 1993 to consider the final report on standards, the AEC voted to refer "these matters back to the states and territories . . . to determine if the initiatives should be proceeded with" (AEC, 1993). Still, as a result of the national effort, most Australian states began a major review and reform of the curriculum:

> Victoria and the Australian Capital Territory aligned existing curriculum frameworks to the national statements by revision. Important curriculum reviews . . . were concluded . . . in the Northern Territory in 1992, and soon afterwards in Queensland in 1994. South Australia conducted a curriculum review in 1990. . . . Tasmania was the only state which failed to initiate a major curriculum reform. (Watt, 1997, p. 23)

In general, the proposed tight fit between federal or national mandates and local actions has not been the trend in education worldwide.

Similar Problems—Subject Groups and Government

At the New York City IFTE conference, many participants described how unprepared English teacher organizations were for new roles in government projects and for the attacks and opposition from agencies and groups which hoped to put forward (and often did put forward) their own view of the essentials of K–12

English/language arts. Many government efforts began as government-appointed committees, but, as a result of pressure from government for one kind of curriculum or another, subject matter groups often had to step in with their own efforts to get what they wanted. Of course, there were those who were fearful that subject matter groups could not work with government or even act as a representative to government, and as a result the role of subject matter organizations in the national standards movement varied a great deal from one country to another.

Only in the United States (and possibly New Zealand) did the subject matter groups—music, math, science, and English in particular—attempt to lead the development of standards, although subject matter leaders such as Garth Boomer (Australia) did lead the standards effort in some countries. Michael Watt has reported that professional organizations of English teachers were left out of the standards work in Australia (personal communication, 1997). In the United States, the National Council of Teachers of Social Studies (NCSS) was left out of the leadership of federal standards development in civics, geography, and history—all taught by social studies teachers. NCSS did, however, develop its own social studies framework.

In England, Australia, New Zealand, and the United States, subject matter organizations of teachers of English/language arts experienced serious tensions between the organizations of English teachers and the government, whether liberal or conservative, over the substance and process of standards development for English/language arts. In New Zealand in 1986, the leaders of the New Zealand Association for the Teaching of English (NZATE) began working with a government curriculum committee to develop an English syllabus for the oldest secondary students, and in 1989, after five drafts had been prepared, the New Zealand government contracted with the president of the NZATE to produce a sixth draft.

At the 1990 IFTE conference in Auckland, participants in New Zealand's standards development process described a series of conflicts between the English-teaching community and the New Zealand Ministry of Education in the preparation of a standards document. By October 1990, the president of NZATE was no longer invited to government meetings on New Zealand standards. In fact, a change in government led new government officials to call for starting over.

These general problems were present from the beginning of the U.S. standards movement, leading eventually to the termination of government funding of the IRA/NCTE Standards Project in March 1994. At the first meeting of the English Standards Advisory Board, the federal oversight person for the project told the Advisory Board that the standards effort could not consider Opportunity to Learn as part of the Standards document. Needless to say, Janet Emig, chair of the Advisory Board, and other members of the board responded that the Standards document would discuss opportunity to learn standards.

Another dispute between the federal government and IRA and NCTE was over the process by which standards were to be written. The government wanted a small group to meet and to write the standards. The reason: the small-group process costs less money and is less likely to stir up political controversy in its deliberations. But the English Language Arts Standards Project was *not* designed as a small-group activity. Instead, IRA and NCTE decided to develop their present Standards document through a national conversation organized around national and affiliate meetings and local task forces focusing on standards. Thousands of English/language arts teachers participated. This approach obviously produced its own set of problems, including the problem of finding a common language that the profession could endorse. But this approach did generate a national discussion organized around national, state, and regional committees. Today, that discussion continues primarily in school districts and at school sites. One of the central issues in the U.S. standards effort has been the level of specificity at each level of governance. The fact that NCTE/IRA Standards are the only national standards and that they are stated as *general principles* has pushed the debates about English specifics to state-district arguments.

Most subject matter groups experienced some public attacks by those attempting to mobilize a political constituency for action on particular issues. For example, in most countries the conservative press attempted to attack English teachers as being antistandards. In England, *The Mail* (London), headlining "Class War Returns to Britain's Schools," charged that the National

Association for the Teaching of English (NATE) had drawn up a political agenda "to challenge how the government plans to improve standards in our 26,000 schools" ("Class War," 1993, p. 5). *The Mail* said it had uncovered "a startling dossier revealing how the Left is seeking to dominate state school English teaching." This charge appeared to be intended to mobilize the Right against government workers, who were assumed to be left-wingers, and against the standards adopted by government.

The Mail did not report that NATE had prepared and supported an earlier draft of England's standards statement and that NATE was objecting to the decision of the Thatcher government to throw out all of the previous work that English teachers had completed on curriculum standards between 1987 and 1993. By 1992 the government's National Curriculum Council "regarded the teaching profession an enemy to be resisted" (Cox, 1995, p. 63).

In the meantime, government officials who had been hostile to the Cox Report were beginning to turn their hostility toward the Task Group on Assessment and Testing (TGAT). TGAT had proposed that the national assessment be composed of external tasks (Standard Assessment Tasks) and teacher assessment of student work. Through an audit process of group moderation by area teachers, the scores at the local level would be brought into alignment with area norms and results on SATs. The government, through its review councils, modified the TGAT report. For one thing, the government rejected the combined use of SATs and teacher assessment to get a score. The government wanted only the SAT score, thereby seriously reducing the influence of teacher judgment.

In early 1993, some of the major teachers' unions in England voted to boycott all national curriculum assessments given during the summer of 1993. Ultimately, the boycott had an impact, and, according to Atkin (1994), the assessment plan had collapsed. In fact, by September 1993, a report was issued calling for a reduction of testing, and the government apparently agreed.

After withdrawing funding for the NCTE/IRA Standards and proposing in the federal register to contract with a new group to write the U.S. standards document in English, the U.S. Department of Education identified at least two groups willing to write standards in English. NCTE asked its affiliates across the country to write to the Department of Education to comment on why only NCTE/IRA should write the standards for English. Quoting from these letters, *Education Week* reported that teachers across the country told the federal government that it had made a mistake in terminating the NCTE/IRA funding, and that English teachers across the country would not cooperate with a new project. Within a month, the Department of Education announced it would *not* fund another English standards project. The English effort was being left in the hands of NCTE and IRA, which formed several leadership teams to complete the project. John Mayher led one of these later teams for NCTE.

In the United States, tensions between the government and the academic Left of the English profession were particularly hostile and primarily centered on the difference between teaching the basic skills to get a job and teaching a critique of the social system in order to force social change. For some, these tensions have been an argument over "what is basic?" For many parents, of course, learning the conventional genres and spelling is the direct road to employment, and for them, employment means money, and money means power. The professional academic Left in the United States often had a different view. Kathleen McCormick describes how this social class conflict emerged at the 1990 Pittsburgh conference on literacy sponsored by the Modern Language Association:

> One of the questions that the conference organizers had suggested we raise in our discussion groups involved the conflict between notions of literacy as "empowerment" and literacy as means to greater worker productivity. We quickly discovered that those terms did not seem dichotomous for people involved in community and workplace literacy initiatives, though they did for academic theorists, and they seemed so to me. Indeed the question did not even make sense to those working outside the academy where, for example, helping a single mother become sufficiently skilled to get off welfare would both empower the woman and make her a more productive worker. There seems to be a general sense among the academic left that personal empowerment can only come by working against the system. (McCormick, 1994, p. 95)

Some of these differences obviously represent deep social class differences. Basil Bernstein (1990), for example, has described the relationship in British schools between a social class attitude and a form of pedagogical practice, noting that one form of teaching practice (or literacy) is promoted by "professional agents of symbolic control," and that another form of teaching practice (or literacy) is promoted by "members of the middle class whose work had a direct relation to the production, distributions, and circulation of capital" (1990, p. 85). These kinds of problems were never discussed at the IFTE conference, but they seemed to lurk just under the table. They surfaced now and then when participants from the same country found themselves disagreeing about why the public was dissatisfied or why government seemed to be attacking teachers. In any case, the topic deserves more examination (see Myers, 1996, pp. 195, 217–18).

Similar Problems—Tensions about Curriculum

Within the standards discussions in all countries there have been numerous models of what English/language arts content should be. In England, the Cox Report identified five purposes for English: (1) a personal growth model, (2) a cross-curricular model (English across the curriculum), (3) an adult-needs or workplace model, (4) a cultural heritage deliver-the-tradition model, and (5) a cultural analysis model focusing on developing critiques of various cultural situations and worldviews. Cox (1991, pp. 21–22) claimed that his standards report encompassed all of these models. But some of England's teachers charged that the Cox Report had ignored the cultural analysis model of English. In the United States, the NCTE/IRA Standards document emphasized four purposes: (1) obtaining (reading, viewing) and communicating (writing, speaking, listening, representing) information, (2) literary response and evaluation, (3) learning and reflection (metacognitive strategies), and (4) problem solving (methods of inquiry). These purposes were generally placed within three contexts: (1) workplaces, (2) personal growth, and (3) academic studies. But E. D. Hirsch (1996) and others charged that the NCTE/IRA Standards did not sufficiently emphasize cultural traditions.

When one examines the standards documents from various

countries, one finds substantial agreement on the framework for the content of English/language arts, although there were some variations. The U.S. standards added viewing and representing to the list of language arts, introduced the notion of nonprint "texts," gave new importance to speaking and listening, added new texts for classroom reading, added new audiences for writing, gave new importance to metacognition—to knowing how to learn, learning how to learn—and acknowledged the importance of personal response and the shaping of one's personal experiences. Cox's U.K. standards emphasized speaking and listening, reading, and writing, but did not mention viewing and representing.

The U.S. standards emphasized the importance of Standard English, but not as much as the standards from England. Cox devoted a chapter or more to the teaching of Standard English, even asserting that "teachers should explain how standard English has come to have a wide social and geographic currency" (Cox, 1991, p. 201).

Personal growth models inspired considerable debate in all countries. The personal growth model, based primarily on the work of James Britton and others, says that in English classes students learn to use language in order to shape and structure their experiences, either their response to reading or their response to life's events. By bringing structure to experience, students learn to struggle with key moral questions. The emphasis on the self and the personal in the United States was closely tied to the Dartmouth Conference, at which James Britton, drawing on the U.K. work of the Institute of Education at the University of London, put forth a personal response agenda for the curriculum content of English/language arts. Britton contrasted his agenda to that of Kitzhaber, who, drawing on the work of The Institutes of the National Defense Education Act (NDEA) in the United States in the 1960s, proposed in his keynote address at Dartmouth an agenda organized around a tripod of conceptual knowledge—language, literature, and composition (Dixon, 1967; Britton, 1970).

During the 1970s, according to participants at the IFTE conference, the personal growth model was dominant in Britain, Canada, Australia, and New Zealand (it was popular in the United States, but not dominant), but by the late 1980s the personal growth model had begun to decline in Britain and, later, in Australia. The decline resulted from two kinds of attack—the charge from the conservative Right that the personal growth model ignored workplace skills and charges from the liberal Left that the personal growth model ignored the political and historical context of language. Other critics in England charged that some students were being immersed in "personal growth" and "real literature" without knowing some of the basics about how to start reading—without, so the claim goes, receiving any visible, explicit teaching in sound-letter(s) relationships (Times Education Supplement, p. 52).

This last has been a very familiar charge in the United States, where the debate has recently become phonics versus whole language. Many in the United States believe in and are accustomed to a stand-alone approach in teaching in which all class time is devoted to practice, observation, drill, and the explicit teaching of small "bits" of information. These people find the absence of drill sheets and explicit instruction in prefabricated, universal knowledge somewhat confusing, if not a conscious exclusion of some students from knowledge. One U.S. student complained, "I didn't feel she was teaching us anything. She wanted us to correct each other's papers and we were there to learn from her. She didn't teach anything, absolutely nothing" (Delpit, 1995, p. 31). Many others have come to understand and appreciate approaches to English curriculum that are primarily literary and narrative and that depend on an immersion pedagogy. The challenge may be how to produce stand-alone skills from immersion (Myers, 1996).

In Australia, public-professional disputes broke out over whether to emphasize personal or public writing, creativity or the basics of genre. Some thought genre study was a compromise between progressives and conservatives. Cope and Kalantzis, who reported that in Australia, "'back to basics' people have shouted in protest at the way teaching has changed with the rise of progressivism" (1993, p. 5), proposed genre-based teaching as a compromise, replacing both "back-to-basics" and "progressivism." Those supporting a progressive Britton-curriculum of expressive writing and literature at the center of the English curriculum protested the Cope and Kalantzis emphasis on genre. For example,

Sawyer and Watson (1987) called genres "mind-forged manacles" and Dixon (1987) agreed. Both charged that "direct reading," "explicit drilling in form," and genre teaching ("teacher-presents-model-student-follows-model") were reopening the question of whether "conscious knowledge of structure makes for more effective performance in writing." They argued that this question had been put to rest by research showing that explicit teaching of the structure of grammar did not improve writing (Sawyer & Watson, 1987, pp. 48–49).

Many teachers and theorists emphasizing emancipatory pedagogies in the United States, the United Kingdom, Australia, and New Zealand have shared the view that expressionism and critical theory or cultural studies provide the organizing principles for an English/language arts curriculum committed to social justice (see, for example, essays in Berlin & Vivion, 1992). Genre study, emancipationists have argued, undermines a critical approach. At NCTE's Heidelberg Conference in 1996, however, Kress repeated his arguments for the explicit teaching of genre: "Genres are social constructs" which, like all the codes of power, should be taught explicitly. Genre study, says Kress, is a necessary foundation for critique and emancipation. Students should not have to challenge culture by inventing genre for themselves: "It seems to me entirely inappropriate to ask those least able to carry that burden" (Kress, 1987, p. 44).

In the end, the standards of the Australian government put language and text at the center of the English/language arts, moving literature and personal experience out of the center and more or less dodging the question of whether genre should be the central focus. To avoid arguments about whether to emphasize process or content, the Australians also, as noted earlier, put strategies, linguistic structures, and contextual understanding under the larger category of Language. Language, in other words, includes both Content and Process. Thus, by making Text and Language the large headings, the Australian standards kept genre near the center of the standards document. In the United States, the arguments were over whether to emphasize process or product. Genre was hardly mentioned.

Conclusion

During the 1990 (Aukland) and 1995 (New York City) IFTE conferences, I got the impression that the standards movement was IFTE-wide, if not worldwide, and my follow-up reading on the question, using many of the materials and citations distributed at IFTE, confirmed that first impression. Yes, there were important differences, but the larger picture was one of similar origins, reasons, and tensions. One important difference was the role played by the subject matter groups in the different countries. Many subject matter groups participated to some degree or other, but some backed off from participation to avoid any conflict with government policy. A few groups were pushed out. In the United States, all subject groups had a group on the Left opposed to any participation in the standards effort, and a group on the Right supporting vouchers and indifferent to or opposed to the standards effort. With the exception of the boycott in England, no subject matter groups in any country coordinated efforts with any teacher unions or with any organized parent groups, or attempted any direct action to influence standards policy. (I still think a state lawsuit should be undertaken, and I outlined how this might be done in a speech before the leadership council of the California Association of Teachers of English in August 1999.) The NCTE/IRA Standards document set a new sales record in NCTE and in IRA. By the middle of 2000, the standards effort was still underway in the United States, and most of the activities were at the state, district, and school site levels.

References

Atkin, J. M. (1994). Developing world-class education standards: Some conceptual and political dilemmas. In N. Cobb (Ed.), *The future of education: Perspectives on national standards in America* (pp. 61–84). New York: College Entrance Examination Board.

Australian Education Council. (1986). *Australia Education Council report*. Canberra: Author.

Australian Education Council. (1989). *Australia Education Council report.* Canberra: Author.

Australian Education Council. (1993). *Australia Education Council report.* Canberra: Author.

Australian Education Council. (1994). *English—A curriculum profile for Australian schools.* Carlton, Victoria: Curriculum Corporation.

Bauman, Z. (1990). Modernity and ambivalence. In M. Featherstone (Ed.), *Global culture: Nationalism, globalization, and modernity.* London: Sage.

Berlin, J., & Vivion, M. (1992). *Cultural studies in the English classroom.* Portsmouth, NH: Boynton/Cook.

Bernstein, B. (1990). *The structuring of pedagogic discourse: Vol. 4. Class, codes, and control.* London: Routledge.

Black, P. (1993). Performance assessment and accountability: The experience in England and Wales. Address at meeting of the American Educational Research Association, Atlanta, April 1993.

Boomer, G. (1992). The advent of standards in Australian education. *Curriculum Perspectives* (Journal of the Australian Curriculum Studies Association), April.

Britton, J. (1970). *Language and learning.* Harmondsworth, U.K.: Penguin.

"Class War Returns to Britain's Schools." (1993, January 3). *The Mail,* p. 5.

Cope, B., & Kalantzis, M. (1993). *The powers of literacy: A genre approach to teaching writing.* Pittsburgh, PA: University of Pittsburgh Press.

Cox, B. (1991). *Cox on Cox: An English curriculum for the 1990s.* London: Hodder & Stoughton.

Cox, B. (1995). *Cox on the battle for the English curriculum.* London: Hodder & Stoughton.

Delpit, L. (1995) *Other people's children: Cultural conflict in the classroom.* New York: New Press.

Dixon, J. (1967). *Growth through English.* Oxford: Oxford UP for NATE.

Dixon, J. (1987). The question of genre. In I. Reid (Ed.), *The place of genre in learning: Current debates* (pp. 9–21). Geelong, Australia: Centre for Studies in Literary Education, Deakin University.

Goodson, I., & Medway, P. (1990). *Bringing English to order: The history and politics of a school subject.* New York: Falmer Press.

Hirsch, E. D. (1996). *The schools we need and why we don't have them.* New York: Doubleday.

Kingman, J. (1988). *The Kingman report.* Report of the Committee of Inquiry into the Teaching of English Language. London: HMSO.

Klein, R. (1996, March 18). Text and subtext. *New York Times*, Op. ed. page.

Kress, G. (1987). Genre in a social theory of language: A reply to John Dixon. In I. Reid (Ed.), *The place of genre in learning: Current debates* (pp. 44–159). Geelong, Australia: Centre for Studies in Literary Education, Deakin University.

McCormick, K. (1994). *The culture of reading and the teaching of English.* Manchester, UK: Manchester University Press.

Moon, B., Murphy, P., & Raynor, J. (Eds.). (1989). *Policies for the Curriculum.* London: Hodder & Stoughton/Open University.

Myers, M. (1996). *Changing our minds: Negotiating English and literacy.* Urbana, IL. National Council of Teachers of English.

New Zealand Ministry of Education. (1994). *English in the New Zealand curriculum.* Wellington, NZ: Learning Media.

"Ontario Sets a Standard for English Exams." (1987, February 28). *Toronto Star,* pp. A1, A12.

Sawyer, W., & Watson, K. (1987). Questions of genre. In I. Reid (Ed.), *The place of genre in learning: Current debates* (pp. 46–57). Geelong, Australia: Centre for Studies in Literary Education, Deakin University.

Times Education Supplement. (1995, November 10). *The [London] Times.*

U.S. Department of Education. (1991). *America 2000: An education strategy.* Washington, DC: Government Printing Office.

Watt, M. G. (1997, July 10–13). National curriculum collaboration: The state of reform in the states and territories. Paper presented at the conference of the Australian Curriculum Studies Association, University of Sidney, New South Wales, Australia.

Williams, R. (1961). *The long revolution*. London: Chatto & Windus.

INDEX

EDITORS

Curt Dudley-Marling is professor of education and director of the Donovan Urban Scholars Program at Boston College. He is a former co-editor of *Language Arts,* co-author with Lynn Rhodes of *Readers and Writers with a Difference: A Holistic Approach to Teaching Struggling Readers and Writers* (1996), and author of *Living with Uncertainty: The Messy Reality of Classroom Practice* (1997) and *A Family Affair: When School Troubles Come Home* (2000).

Carole Edelsky is professor of curriculum and instruction at Arizona State University. She is one of the founders of PEAK (Public Education for Arizona's Kids), a community organization that advocates on behalf of public education, and is currently working on local and national efforts to stop high-stakes testing. Edelsky was the recipient of NCTE's Elementary Section's Oustanding Educator in Language Arts Award in 2000.

CONTRIBUTORS

Martha R. Arrieta, a native of Mesa, Arizona, taught for five years in a first-grade dual language classroom. She is a 1992 graduate of Arizona State University with a master's degree in early childhood education.

Sheridan Blau teaches in the Department of English and the Graduate School of Education at the University of California Santa Barbara, where he directs the South Coast Writing Project and the Literature Institute for Teachers. He has served as a member of the Assessment Development Panel for National Board Certification in English Language Arts for the National Board for Professional Teaching Standards and as a senior advisor to the Test Development Committee for California's statewide testing program in reading and writing. He is a past president of NCTE and has published widely on topics ranging from Milton and Herbert, to the teaching of composition and literature, to the politics of educational reform.

Jane S. Carpenter graduated from Boston University, taught elementary reading in the Virgin Islands, and subsequently has been an elementary resource teacher in the Calexico Unified School District, Calexico, California, for twenty-five years. She has also been teaching at San Diego State University as a part-time lecturer in language arts methodology classes. Carpenter has long had an interest in how second language learners acquire literacy skills in a second language.

Elena R. Castro taught bilingual elementary students for twenty years. Currently, she is the coordinator of elementary curriculum for Calexico Unified School District in Calexico, California. She is also part-time faculty at San Diego State University Imperial Valley Campus in the teacher education department.

Barbara Comber is associate professor for the Centre for Studies in Literacy, Policy and Learning Cultures at the University of South Australia. Her interests include teachers' work, social justice, critical literacies, public education, and school-based collaborative research. She has edited two books exploring critical literacy and critical inquiry and is currently involved in two ethnographic longitudinal studies that investigate elementary school children's literacy development.

Phil Cormack is director of the Centre for Studies in Literacy, Policy and Learning Cultures at the University of South Australia. His research and teaching combine an interest in literacy and the education of adolescents. He has directed research projects in student alienation, authentic assessment, and classroom discourse, all related to the middle years of school. His current work involves research on the history of adolescence, schooling, and literacy; literacy and assessment; and the experience of students at risk of not completing secondary school.

Caryl Gottlieb Crowell has been a bilingual teacher for twenty-five years. She holds a B.A. in Spanish, an M.Ed. in bilingual education, and an education specialist's degree in reading. She feels that teachers have much to offer in the way of knowledge and insights concerning learning and teaching and has contributed to the field of education through many articles and chapters in edited volumes and as co-author with Kathryn Whitmore of *Inventing a Classroom: Life in a Bilingual, Whole Language Learning Community* (1994).

Ginette Delandshere is associate professor in the School of Education, Indiana University, Bloomington. Her areas of interest are the study of inquiry, teaching, and learning, including educational measurement and assessment and related policy analysis.

Don Dippo is associate dean of education at York University in Toronto, Canada. His research interests include the social and political organization of knowledge, teaching as an occupation, and teacher education.

James Paul Gee is the Tashia Morgridge Professor of Reading in the Department of Curriculum and Instruction at the University of Wisconsin at Madison. He is the author of *Social Linguistics and Literacies: Ideology in Discourses* (1990), *The Social Mind: Language, Ideology, and Social Practice* (1992), *The New Work Order: Behind the Language of the New Capitalism* (1996), and *An Introduction to Discourse Analysis: Theory and Method* (1999).

Barbara Gerard is currently a consultant for the Office of Multicultural Education of the New York City Board of Education, where she was previously assistant director. She is adjunct associate professor at Hunter College and Long Island and Nova Southeastern Universities. Gerard has distinguished herself in the fields of multicultural and bilingual education, professional development, and cross-cultural/ global relations and has been at the forefront of issues relating to the arts, culture, and women.

Nanci Goldman teaches ESL and special education and is a curriculum consultant. Formerly co-coordinator of Inner City Programs for the Toronto Board of Education, Goldman works as director of Horizons, an innovative program that partners Upper Canada College and Toronto public schools. She is co-author of *Integrated Programs for Adolescents*.

Brenda Harrell obtained bachelor degrees in education and Spanish from Grand Canyon University and a master's in bilingual education from Arizona State University. She has taught third-grade dual language classes at Valley View Elementary in Phoenix, Arizona, since 1994.

Miles A. Myers, English teacher and department chair at Oakland High School, Oakland, California, for a dozen years in the 1960s and 1970s, is the former administrative director of the National Writing Project and former executive director of the National Council of Teachers of English. He is currently co-director of the Institute for Research on Teaching and Learning in Berkeley, California.

Alleen Pace Nilsen wrote her doctoral thesis on the subject of sexism and language. Shortly afterward she became a member of the National Council of Teachers of English's Women's Committee, where she helped to develop the *NCTE Guidelines for Nonsexist Use of Language in NCTE Publications*. In 1977 she edited and co-authored *Sexism and Language*, and between 1980 and 1987 she was co-editor of the *English Journal*. She has been on the faculty of Arizona State University since 1975 where she works with pre- and inservice English teachers.

Jennifer O'Brien has taught for nearly thirty-five years, during which time she has worked as a primary and secondary teacher-librarian, classroom teacher, curriculum writer, teacher-researcher, and teacher educator. Her current interests include writing about critical literacy in classrooms and documenting the careers of experienced literacy teachers.

Bob Peterson is a twenty-year veteran teacher in the Milwaukee public schools, where he teaches fifth grade in the bilingual La Escuela Fratney. Peterson is a founding editor of *Rethinking Schools* and a founder of the National Coalition of Education Activists. He regularly presents workshops and speaks at educational conferences.

Anthony R. Petrosky is director of teacher education at the University of Pittsburgh. His first collection of poetry, *Jurgis Petraskas* (1983), received the Walt Whitman Award from Philip Levine for the Academy of American Poets and a Notable Book Award from the American Library Association. His second collection of poetry, *Red and Yellow Boat*, was published in 1994. With David Bartholomae, Petrosky is co-author and co-editor of four books: *Facts, Artifacts, and Counterfacts: Theory and Method for a Reading and Writing Course* (1986), *The Teaching of Writing* (1986), *Ways of Reading: An Anthology for Writers* (1987), and *Reading the Lives of Others* (1995). He has taught as a visiting professor in Shanghai, China; Sofia, Bulgaria; and Kwangju, South Korea, where he was a Senior Fulbright Scholar for two years.

Irma Rivera-Figueroa has been an educator for twenty-two years, sixteen as a bilingual teacher (K–3) and six as a dual language program director. She has a master's degree in early childhood education from Arizona State University and is currently enrolled in Northern Arizona University's Administrative Certification Endorsement program.

Carolyn J. Rogers is an educator in southwestern United States. She has been involved in education for the past fifteen years as a teacher, a consultant, a curriculum supervisor, and an administrator.

Joyce Rogers has been an elementary and secondary school ESL educator in Toronto, Canada, since 1966. Her professional experiences range from classroom teaching; to program consulting with ESL, classroom, and subject area teachers; to coordinating boardwide curriculum development and program implementation. She has enjoyed the never-ending challenge of helping students succeed no matter what part of the world they come from.

Frank Serafini has been an elementary school teacher for eleven years working in inner-city schools in the Phoenix metropolitan area in intermediate multi-age classrooms. Currently a doctoral candidate in curriculum and instruction for reading education, Serafini's interests include classroom-based assessment, children's literature, teacher research, and reflective teaching practice. His dissertation focuses on the National Board of Professional Teaching Standards. He has taught university classes at Arizona State University and Northern Arizona University for eight years.

Patrick Shannon, a professor of education at Penn State University, is a former preschool and primary grade teacher. His most recent book is *iSHOP, You Shop: Raising Questions about Reading Commodities* (2001).

Juan Sierra has a variety of teaching experiences in urban, migrant, and multilingual classrooms. Although he has taught for fifteen years in kindergarten through eighth grade, he prefers first graders because of the authenticity of their writing. He is currently principal of a large elementary school in urban Phoenix.

Brian A. Smith holds degrees in education (M.Ed.) and journalism (B.A.) and has worked in secondary schools as a teacher of English in Canada, Africa, and Australia. He is former national director of youth services for both Australian and Canadian National Red Cross Societies and was head of communications for the Toronto Board of Education for fifteen years. Smith is currently teaching English in a private secondary school in Toronto.

Geneva Smitherman is professor of English at Michigan State University and director of MSU's African American Language and Literacy Program. Her research and teaching interests include sociolinguistics, Ebonics, language policy and planning, language attitudes, dialects, and literacy. She has published numerous articles and books including *Talkin That Talk: Language, Culture, and Education in African America* (2000) and *Black Talk: Words and Phrases from the Hood to the Amen Corner* (2000).

John W. Wann is in his eleventh year as Valley View School principal; he is also an endorsed bilingual teacher. Valley View's dual language program graduated its first core class to high school last spring; more than half of the school's population is now in the dual language program. Wann's work includes struggling against current antibilingual sentiments (Ron Unz initiatives) and nurturing community school concepts in gardening, an onsite animal habitat technology, and neighborhood in-home libraries.

John Willinsky is Pacific Press Professor of literacy and technology at the University of British Columbia and author of, most recently, *If Only We Knew: Increasing the Public Value of Social Science Research* (2000).

Robert C. Wortman taught kindergarten and K–1 multi-age classrooms and was principal of Borton Primary Magnet School, a court-ordered desegregation school with a bilingual strand, for thirteen years. He is currently director of Title I and K–3 programs in Tucson Unified School District. He also teaches in the Department of Language,

Reading, and Culture at the University of Arizona. He was named 1994 National Distinguished Principal for the state of Arizona by the National Association for Elementary School Principals and has authored *Administrators: Supporting School Change* (1995) and co-authored (with Myna Matlin) *Leadership in Whole Language: The Principal's Role* (1995).

This book was typeset in Sabon by Electronic Imaging.
The typeface used on the cover is Myriad.
Cover calligraphy by Barbara Yale-Read.
The book was printed on 50-lb. White Lynx Opaque by Versa Press.